Specializing the Courts

THE CHICAGO SERIES IN LAW AND SOCIETY
Edited by John M. Conley and Lynn Mather

Also in the series:

Additional series titles follow index

Specializing the Courts

LAWRENCE BAUM

The University of Chicago Press
Chicago and London

Lawrence Baum is professor of political science at Ohio State University. His most recent book *Judges and Their Audiences* won the 2007 Pritchett Award for best book on law and courts.

The University of Chicago Press, Chicago 60637
The University of Chicago Press, Ltd., London
© 2011 by The University of Chicago
All rights reserved. Published 2011
Printed in the United States of America

19 18 17 16 15 14 13 12 11   1 2 3 4 5

ISBN-13: 978-0-226-03954-1 (cloth)
ISBN-13: 978-0-226-03955-8 (paper)

ISBN-10: 0-226-03954-4 (cloth)
ISBN-10: 0-226-03955-2 (paper)

Library of Congress Cataloging-in-Publication Data

Baum, Lawrence.
    Specializing the courts / Lawrence Baum.
        p. cm.
    Includes bibliographical references and index.
    ISBN-13: 978-0-226-03954-1 (cloth : alk. paper)
    ISBN-13: 978-0-226-03955-8 (pbk. : alk. paper)
    ISBN-10: 0-226-03954-4 (cloth : alk. paper)
    ISBN-10: 0-226-03955-2 (pbk. : alk. paper)   1. Judges—United States.
2. Courts—United States.   I. Title.
    KF8775.B386 2011
    347.73'14—dc22
                                                    2010019714

To Martin Shapiro

CONTENTS

TABLES

Most people who study and observe the courts think of judges as generalists. That conception is understandable, because the judges who receive the most attention *are* generalists. To take the most prominent example, the Supreme Court's agenda includes an array of issues that range from antitrust to free speech.

Alongside these generalists, however, stand a large number of judges who hear narrower sets of cases. In the federal courts, specialized courts decide cases in fields such as taxes, international trade, and bankruptcy. The states have their own specialized courts, both those that appear on organization charts and those that are created within courts. The extent of specialization is quite substantial in criminal law, where a great many judges on state trial courts hear only criminal cases and many are full-time or part-time specialists in narrow subsets of criminal cases.

Because they do important things, some specialized courts and judges have been frequent subjects of inquiries by students of the courts. Indeed, social scientists and legal scholars have done very impressive research on specialized courts. However, judicial specialization as a general phenomenon has received only limited attention. This book focuses on that general phenomenon, addressing three issues about it.

First, what is the landscape of judicial specialization in the United States? By surveying that landscape, I show that the courts are considerably more specialized than most students and observers of the courts realize. Moreover, since the late nineteenth century there has been an uneven but marked growth in the extent of specialization in the federal and state court systems.

Second, how and why have the courts become as specialized as they are? Many judges and other people believe that the quality of being generalists is part of the essence of courts. For that reason, it is striking that so much specialization exists in the courts. Surveying the historical evidence, I show that this development has come about through a long series of specific decisions, decisions based on the belief that judicial specialization would bring desirable results in a particular context. The growth of judicial specialization has been the inadvertent result of those specific decisions rather than a matter of conscious design.

Finally, what are the effects of judicial specialization? The existence of so much specialization in the courts is interesting in itself, but specialization can also affect the outputs that courts produce. The effects of specialization are complex, and they are contingent on the conditions under which a particular court operates. However, they have been highly consequential in fields such as patent law and criminal law.

Because it examines all three of these issues, the book is broad in its scope. It is also broad in the sense that it considers a large and diverse set of courts. The disadvantage of discussing so many types of courts is that none are considered in as much depth as they merit. Certainly, no expert on any court that I examine will find my discussion of that court entirely satisfactory. But this breadth is necessary to provide a full sense of judicial specialization in the United States.

Readers will not necessarily share my fascination with the subject of judicial specialization, but I hope to show that the world of specialized courts includes some tribunals that any aficionado of the judiciary should want to know about: the Weed Court in Chicago, the Philadelphia court that operated in a stadium during football games, and the court that the State Department set up in Berlin to hear a single case—and then fired its judge when he tried to hear a second case.

More important, of course, is what can be learned by examining the subject of judicial specialization. Attention to specialized courts broadens our understanding of issues such as the forces that shape judicial behavior and the structure of courts. It also informs the study of theoretical issues relating to the causes and effects of structural attributes of government. Finally, it helps in thinking about the specialization that pervades most of government and society. I hope that this book contributes to knowledge on these subjects and that it encourages other people to consider the benefits to be gained from the study of judicial specialization.

ACKNOWLEDGMENTS

I have been thinking and writing about specialized courts for a long time. Over the years, a great many people have assisted me with the thinking and research that culminated in this book.

A large number of students have helped with research that is incorporated in the book. I am pleased to acknowledge the assistance of Eileen Braman, James Brent, Jeff Budziak, Kathryn Exline, Marcus Holmes, John Kilwein, Karen Laderman, Leonard Williams, Margie Williams, and Dana Wittmer. I apologize to any students whose work in decades past has escaped my memory.

Several professional colleagues have offered ideas about issues that I consider and helpful comments on drafts for the book. These colleagues include Steve Burbank, Chuck Cameron, David Jacobs, David Levi, Quan Li, Wendy Martinek, Dana Patton, Marie Provine, Mike Solimine, and Randy Schweller. I benefited a good deal from suggestions by participants in a seminar at the University of Kentucky. I especially appreciate the insights and encouragement I received from Jim Brudney, Roy Flemming, Mitu Gulati, Chuck Myers, and Isaac Unah.

Paul Light, Jonathan Lurie, Freda Solomon, and Tom Walker shared with me what they learned from their own research into specific specialized courts. I owe special thanks to Candace McCoy for offering her distinctive and perceptive thoughts about problem-solving courts. The anonymous reviewers for the Press provided very good ideas for revision of the book.

Three scholars gave me crucial help in strengthening the book. Alex Wendt improved my understanding and presentation of theoretical perspectives on institutions. As he has done twice before, Dave Klein made insightful comments that resulted in fundamental improvements in the book. And

Lynn Mather's careful readings and perceptive comments on drafts were enormously helpful.

It has been a pleasure to work with the University of Chicago Press. I appreciate the considerable assistance of Rodney Powell, Maia Rigas, and Elissa Park, and I am grateful for John Tryneski's shepherding of the project and his enthusiasm for it.

My most fundamental debt is to Martin Shapiro. His 1968 book, *The Supreme Court and Administrative Agencies*, first alerted me to the issues raised by judicial specialization. His case study on patent policy and law in that book gave me the idea for a dissertation that included an analysis of one specialized court, and in turn that analysis gave me greater appreciation of the significance of judicial specialization. He also provided valuable help in my first attempt to formulate my ideas about this issue for publication. It is highly unlikely that this book would exist without him.

Because the sweep of the book is so broad, it could hardly be free of all errors. Thus there is special importance to the usual statement that the many people who helped me are not responsible for those errors. Individually and collectively, they made the book a good deal better than it could have been without their assistance.

ONE

A First Look at Judicial Specialization

Specialization is a hallmark of modern society. Heralded by Emile Durkheim (1893/1933) and Adam Smith (1776/1963), the division of labor is fundamental to economic production and an array of other activities. For example, not only do specialists in law dominate legal practice in the United States, but most individual lawyers specialize in subsets of legal problems (Ariens 1994; Heinz et al. 2005, chap. 2).

Most of government follows that pattern. Administrative agencies typically have narrow responsibilities, and most people who work in those agencies are even more specialized in their functions. Legislators also specialize a good deal. In the United States, members of Congress vote on a wide range of issues, but they do most of their work as policy makers within specialized committees and subcommittees. Over the past century, state legislatures have moved toward a similar reliance on specialized units. Chief executives diverge from this pattern to a degree: they have broad jurisdiction and typically divide their attention among many issue areas. But specialization is the general rule in the executive and legislative branches.

The phenomenon of specialization in government and society receives relatively little attention, because it is taken for granted. By and large, people assume that specialization is both inevitable and desirable, a source of benefits to the organizations in which it occurs and to the people whom those organizations serve.

The judicial branch is an exception. The dominant image of judges in the United States is one in which they specialize in judging but not in any particular subject matter. In that important sense, we think of judges as generalists. For some people this attribute is essential to courts. "To the extent that they specialize," Martin Shapiro (1968, 53) wrote, courts "lose the one quality that clearly distinguishes them from administrative lawmakers."

Further, courts' lack of specialization is often cited as a virtue, especially by judges themselves (Higginbotham 1980, 268; Posner 1983; Wood 1997; see Cheng 2008, 521n2). Federal judge Deanell Tacha expressed a view that is widely shared among judges and others:

> I like the fact that federal judges are generalists. I often say that judges may be the last generalists left in professional life, and I have resisted mightily any suggestion that the federal courts become specialized in any particular area.[1]

As advocates of generalist judges see it, the widely perceived advantages of specialization are accompanied by drawbacks. Specialization leads people to take a narrow perspective that limits and biases their understanding of the matters they address. Further, specialization makes judges more susceptible to external control or "capture." By avoiding those drawbacks, the judiciary benefits the society it serves.

When Judge Tacha referred to judges as "the last generalists," she alluded to another theme that helps to explain the appeal of the generalist model. Diane Wood, another federal judge, referred to "generalist judges in a specialized world" (Wood 1997, 1755). For judges who are generalists, their lack of specialization distinguishes them from most other people with high standing and achievements. The implicit message is that, through their ability to address a wide range of legal issues, judges have avoided the specialization that people in other pursuits adopt as a matter of necessity. In this respect, judges stand apart from—and, arguably, above—members of other professions. For judges and those who identify with them, this is an attractive idea.

This strong belief in the value of a generalist judiciary stands in sharp contrast with the belief in the benefits of specialization that permeates society as a whole. Most of the time, the two beliefs simply coexist. But tension can arise between them when people propose to bring specialization to the courts, so that decision makers have to choose between them.

Questions to Address

In this book, I raise and analyze three questions that relate to this tension: to what extent has the judiciary moved away from the generalist ideal to-

---

1. Howard Bashman, "20 Questions for Chief Judge Deanell Reece Tacha of the U.S. Court of Appeals for the Tenth Circuit," How Appealing blog (http://howappealing.law.com/20q/), posted January 5, 2004.

ward specialization, what difference does it make whether judges are generalists or specialists, and what forces bring about judicial specialization? At the outset, I should provide a preview of each question and of the answers that I ultimately offer.

The Extent of Specialization

Judge Tacha and Judge Wood each serve on a federal court of appeals, a generalist court. The other courts in the United States on which most political scientists and legal scholars focus their attention—the Supreme Court, federal district courts, and state supreme courts—are also generalists. These courts feature some elements of specialization, but judges on all these courts spread their attention and effort across a wide range of cases.

When we move beyond the courts on which scholars focus, however, the picture changes. The federal court system includes several courts with narrow jurisdiction, such as the Tax Court and the Court of Appeals for the Armed Forces. In the aggregate, those courts do much of the work of the federal judiciary.

Specialized courts are common in the states as well. Organization charts of state court systems suggest that specialization is substantial but relatively limited. Those charts are misleading, because there is a great deal of specialization within courts at the trial level. At that level, individual judges are often assigned temporarily or permanently to hear certain types of cases, and many specialized units have been created within courts that have broad jurisdiction. In its organization chart, the Illinois court system is a model of simplicity, with a single trial court—the Circuit Court—that hears cases of all types. In reality, however, administrative rules and practices in the Cook County Circuit Court in Chicago have created an array of specialized courtrooms.[2]

The extent of specialization in the American judiciary should not be exaggerated. Compared with the other branches of government and the world outside government, the judiciary remains a bastion of generalists. Yet the degree of specialization in the courts is noteworthy. So is the uneven but marked trend toward greater specialization. Altogether, judicial specialization is more widespread than most students and observers of the courts recognize. And it is sufficient in extent to constitute an important feature of the judiciary, one that merits the attention of people who seek to understand the courts.

2. I discuss the specialization of courts in Chicago at the beginning of chapter 4.

The Consequences of Specialization

The people who see specialization as a desirable quality in general and those who favor generalist courts both believe that specialization can make considerable difference. Surely they are right. The extent to which people specialize within organizations is a dimension or attribute of organizational structure, and like other structural attributes it can shape what those organizations do. The outputs of courts whose judges are generalists and those whose members are specialists potentially differ in at least two important ways.

The first involves what I call the "neutral virtues" of specialization, perceived benefits that underlie its dominance elsewhere in government and society. In the judiciary these virtues are quality of decisions, efficiency, and uniformity in the law. It is reasonable to posit that judicial specialization enhances these virtues, but the empirical evidence of this enhancement is remarkably slim. Advocates of specialization assume that the courts they propose will provide benefits such as greater efficiency and that existing specialized courts have indeed produced those benefits. But there is little careful analysis of the performance of specialized courts, so it remains uncertain to what extent specialization actually does enhance the neutral virtues.

The second way that specialization might affect court outputs involves nonneutral effects on the substance of judicial policy: specialization of courts could change the ideological content of their policies (on a liberal-conservative dimension) or their support for competing interests in a field (such as tort plaintiffs and defendants). This second kind of effect is of particular interest. If specialization causes courts to adopt different policies from those they would adopt otherwise, that result implicates important theoretical and normative questions about specialization as an attribute of courts.

It seems unlikely that specialization affects what courts do in a straightforward and uniform way. Rather, those effects—and especially the nonneutral effects—could be expected to vary with the circumstances of a particular court. Indeed, the evidence presented in the book shows that the impact of specialization is highly contingent on those circumstances.

Under certain circumstances, specialization does have considerable effect on the substance of judicial policy. Sometimes it changes the environment in which judges work, creating influences that lead them to favor certain interests. At other times it leads to the selection of judges who lean to one side in the competition between interests in their court. And in some instances specialization is bundled with other provisions that work together to move a court in a particular direction. These effects are not entirely predictable, because they depend largely on the idiosyncratic conditions under which specialization is adopted and carried out.

The Causes of Specialization

If judicial specialization is consequential, then its growth merits explanation. Why has specialization proceeded so far despite the strength of the generalist ideal for judges?

Of the three questions that this book addresses, I give this one the most detailed attention. In part, the reasons are practical. The causes of specialization are not as easily summarized as its extent, and we know considerably more about the causes of specialization than about its consequences.

More important, much can be learned from studying the sources of judicial specialization. This inquiry informs our understanding of the forces that shape the structural attributes of courts. It also speaks to broader issues about government institutions and public policy making, issues on which scholars have offered differing perspectives. Those perspectives are useful in understanding judicial specialization, and the ways that specialization has come about help in assessing the validity of differing perspectives.

The book's key finding about the causes of specialization is that the movement toward greater judicial specialization has been a product of inadvertence rather than design. Although some advocates argue for wholesale specialization of the judiciary, in practice specialized courts are created to serve specific purposes. Some of those purposes are connected with the potential effects of judicial specialization on the neutral virtues and on the substance of policy. Judges' self-interest, broadly defined, has also helped to bring about specialization.

Of these motivations for judicial specialization, an interest in shaping the substance of judicial policy has been the most powerful. Yet advocates and policy makers who act on that motivation do not always engage in careful analysis of the linkages between specialization and policy. Rather, they usually make choices on the basis of what I call folk theories, commonsense notions that do not fully accord with reality. In part for this reason, specialized courts often behave in ways that diverge from the hopes of the people who created them.

There is another side to the question of causes. Arguably, the movement toward greater specialization in the judiciary is no more noteworthy than the considerable degree to which judges remain generalists. In light of the high levels of specialization elsewhere in government and society, why has specialization not proceeded even further in the courts?

More than anything else, the continued existence of so many generalist courts reflects the power of the belief that courts *ought* to be generalists. That belief is reinforced by the long history of generalist courts in the United States; in a form of path dependence, this history has created an expectation that the dominance of generalist courts will continue. As I emphasize, however, the extent of specialization in the courts and the growth in specialization make it a significant phenomenon.

Legal scholars and social scientists have written a good deal about judicial specialization, scholarship that is summarized in the appendix of this chapter. But research on this subject has been narrow. No study has considered all three of the questions that I have described. Moreover, these questions are usually considered for specific courts or sets of courts. If judicial specialization is a significant phenomenon, it merits a more comprehensive analysis. This book is intended to provide that analysis.

The remainder of this chapter addresses the book's first question, the extent of judicial specialization in the United States. Chapter 2 frames the questions of causes and consequences in theoretical terms. Chapters 3 through 6 discuss four broad areas of judicial policy. These chapters provide a more detailed picture of the extent of specialization, but they are aimed primarily at probing its causes and consequences. Chapter 7 pulls together evidence from the preceding four chapters to reach conclusions about those causes and consequences in light of the frameworks presented in chapter 2.

Extent: The Landscape of Judicial Specialization

I have not yet defined judicial specialization. This omission might suggest that specialization is easy to define or at least that we always know it when we see it. In reality, neither proposition is accurate.

An organization such as a court system can specialize along any of several lines (Simon 1947, 28–35). What I mean by judicial specialization is one form of functional specialization—by fields or areas of legal policy. Fields are usually understood in terms of the attributes of cases, such as bankruptcy or taxes. But fields can also refer to the attributes of litigants, such as people who are homeless or addicted to illegal drugs.

Judicial specialization is best conceived in terms of the relationship between individual judges[3] and fields of legal policy. When people refer

---

3. It is common for cases to be heard and decided in courts by officials other than judges, such as referees. I use the term "judge" to refer to all these decision makers.

Table 1.1 Examples of federal courts with high and low concentration on the two dimensions of specialization

	Concentration of judges	
Concentration of cases	Low	High
Low	District courts	Bankruptcy courts
High	Foreign Intelligence Surveillance Court	Court of Appeals for Veterans Claims

to judicial specialization, they usually mean that certain judges hear only a narrow set of cases. Based on this usage, we can define judicial specialization as the extent to which individual judges concentrate on a limited range of cases. But there is also a second dimension of judicial specialization, the extent to which cases in a particular field at one level of the court system are concentrated among a limited number of judges (Baum 1977, 826–27; Revesz 1990, 1121–30; Nard and Duffy 2007, 1642). These two dimensions can be labeled concentration of judges (or judge concentration) and concentration of cases (or case concentration). To help in discussing these dimensions, table 1.1 provides examples of federal courts with different combinations of high and low specialization on these two dimensions.

Concentration of judges is both familiar and straightforward. Judges range from those who hear very broad ranges of cases to those whose work focuses on very specific types of cases. As table 1.1 suggests, most courts that are considered generalists, such as the federal district courts and the U.S. Supreme Court, are low in judge concentration. In contrast, most courts that we think of as specialists, such as the bankruptcy courts and the Court of Appeals for Veterans Claims, are high in judge concentration.

Still, there is considerable variation among specialized courts in concentration of judges. Tax Court judges hear cases in only one specific area of law. In contrast, the Pennsylvania Commonwealth Court hears a broad set of public law cases, and the Court of Appeals for the Federal Circuit has what one federal judge called a "hodge-podge" jurisdiction (Wood 1997, 1765). Further, a specialized court may take up only a small portion of its judges' time. This is true of some specialized units within state trial courts, such as homeless courts, in which a judge might sit only one day a week or even one day a month. It is also true of federal "borrowed-judge" courts in which judges on the district courts or courts of appeals serve part-time. The Foreign Intelligence Surveillance Court is an example.

Concentration of cases is less familiar as a concept, and it is not what we usually think of as specialization. For those reasons, it requires some exploration. Whether a judge hears a wide or narrow range of cases, why is it important if that judge (or the court on which the judge serves) holds a monopoly over a field of legal policy in a particular jurisdiction?

Two examples from table 1.1 illustrate that importance. Judges on the Foreign Intelligence Surveillance Court are borrowed from the federal district courts, and warrants for electronic surveillance constitute only one part of their work. In contrast, the Court of Appeals for Veterans Claims is the full-time occupation of its judges. What the two courts have in common is that a small number of judges hear all the cases in a field at one level.

Judges who hold such a monopoly have enormous impact on the state of the law in their field of work. In turn, the power of a single court and set of judges to shape the law can affect their decisions. One reason is that the court becomes a focus of attention for the interest groups that care about the law in the field of the court's work. More subtly, judges' awareness of their importance in a field can shape their perceptions of their role and ultimately their choices.

Even the level of judge concentration can be a matter of debate in certain situations. But case concentration is even more ambiguous, because its extent depends in part on the unit of analysis. In most states, for instance, tort cases are widely dispersed among judges. But in a county with only a single judge, that judge has a monopoly over tort (and other) cases.

The best solution to this ambiguity is to compare the actual level of case concentration in a field of legal policy with the level that is inevitable, given the basic structure of the court system. If one judge hears all the tort cases in a county because there is no other judge in that county, that result is unavoidable; if the state legislature consolidates all tort cases in a single trial court, that is a different matter. Thus, my interest is in decisions that produce case concentration beyond the unavoidable level.

Like judge concentration, case concentration varies considerably. Some types of federal and state cases are heard by a wide array of judges, a high proportion of all the judges who serve at one level in a jurisdiction. For instance, ordinary contract and criminal cases are divided among large numbers of trial judges.[4] Even among courts that are labeled as specialists,

---

4. The reference to criminal cases is a reminder that of the cases that go to trial, in some fields of law a high proportion are decided by juries rather than judges (although judges mete out sentences in most criminal cases that are resolved by juries and review the validity of jury verdicts in civil cases). In the book, I leave aside the portion of court decision making that is done by juries rather than judges.

some have low to moderate case concentration. There are more than three hundred bankruptcy judges, so cases in that field are dispersed widely. In contrast, most specialized courts concentrate cases in a field among a relatively small number of judges.

Bankruptcy courts illustrate the imperfect correlation between the two dimensions of specialization: a court or an individual judge can be high on one dimension and low on the other. Still, there is a positive correlation. On the whole, courts with relatively high judge concentration have relatively high case concentration as well.

The discussion so far should make it clear that the usual distinction between generalist courts and specialized courts is somewhat artificial. Judge concentration and case concentration are conceptually distinct, and each is a continuum rather than a dichotomy. For both reasons, courts are not always easy to classify as generalists or specialists. Still, most courts either stand near the generalist end of both continua or stand near the specialist end on at least one continuum. Moreover, the correlation between the two dimensions heightens the differences between those two sets of courts. Even though the term "specialized court" is imprecise, I will use that term to refer to courts that are highly specialized in terms of judge concentration, case concentration, or both.

In examining judicial specialization thus far, I have discussed only courts within the judicial branch. The federal and state executive branches include a good many courts and judges that are specialized along one or both dimensions, such as the federal immigration courts and the administrative law judges who decide disability cases within the Social Security Administration. A few administrative agencies can be considered the equivalent of specialized courts, because their only responsibility is to adjudicate cases (Revesz 1990, 1134–36).

For the most part, I leave administrative adjudicators aside. Beyond the need to keep the book's scope manageable, I made this exclusion for two reasons. One is that subject-matter specialization is generally taken for granted in the executive branch, so the question of how to explain departures from the generalist ideal for courts is not directly relevant to administrative tribunals.[5] The other reason is that the consequences of judicial specialization are more difficult to probe for administrative tribunals, because their location in the executive branch reduces their comparability with generalist

---

5. It is true, however, that in some states administrative law judges serve in multiple agencies and hear a wide range of cases (Coan 1975, 88; Kittrell 1996, 42; M. Dickerson 1999, 121–22).

courts. The frequent criticisms of immigration judges by the federal courts of appeals suggest that the two take different approaches to certain aspects of immigration law. But these differences may reflect other attributes of adjudication in immigration law rather than degrees of specialization.[6]

The book does consider two types of administrative bodies that adjudicate cases. The first is bodies that were originally created as administrative tribunals but that later moved into the judicial branch. These bodies are examined in order to understand the origins of specialized courts. Second, because of the strong expectation that criminal cases will go to courts, I give attention to some tribunals in the executive branch that serve as alternatives to the courts in adjudicating criminal or quasi-criminal cases.

With that background, I turn to the landscape of specialization in the federal and state court systems.

Federal Courts

The federal district courts, courts of appeals, and Supreme Court clearly qualify as generalists on the dimension of judge concentration. The range of cases that come to them is broad, and that range has become increasingly broad over time with expansions in the scope of federal jurisdiction and litigation. As late as the 1950s, a federal judge recalled, the district court for Oregon was "sort of a specialized court" because it concentrated most of its efforts on a limited range of cases (Stein 2006, 113). Such a characterization would be unlikely now.

On the other dimension, the district courts and courts of appeals generally have very low case concentration.[7] For the most part, cases in particular categories are heard by twelve courts at the appellate level and ninety-four at the trial level, and thus by large numbers of judges. (Here and throughout the book, I treat the Court of Appeals for the Federal Circuit—often called simply the Federal Circuit—as separate from the other courts of appeals.)

The generalist courts do exhibit some specialization in three respects.

---

6. Examples of criticisms include *Floroiu v. Gonzales* (2007) and *Shahinaj v. Gonzales* (2007). See Liptak (2005) and MacLean (2006a). The effects of specialization and accountability on executive-branch judges are discussed in Guthrie, Rachlinski, and Wistrich (2009). Legomsky (2007) and Baum (2010) discuss specialization in relation to the work of immigration judges.

7. The Supreme Court features high case concentration in an absolute sense: a single court with nine justices has a monopoly over each field of federal law at the highest level of the federal court system. But in the hierarchical court system of the United States, that degree of concentration (and its equivalent in state supreme courts) is inevitable.

First, rules of venue and geographical patterns in litigation sometimes produce a highly uneven distribution of cases in a particular field across federal districts or circuits. The court of appeals for the District of Columbia Circuit has exclusive jurisdiction over some types of administrative appeals, and it is a venue for some other types alongside the circuit that is a litigant's residence or place of business.[8] As a result, administrative appeals are twice as plentiful on the docket of the D.C. Circuit as a proportion of all cases as they are in the other circuits. But they still constitute only about one-third of all cases in the D.C. Circuit, and they cover a wide subject matter (Administrative Office of the U.S. Courts 2010, 94).

Even in the absence of special rules of venue, particular types of cases can be heavily concentrated on the dockets of some courts. In 2008, more than half of the marine contract cases terminated in the courts of appeals were in the Second Circuit; more than half of the district court terminations in that field were in the Southern District of New York. The same was true of Federal Labor Standards Act cases in the Eleventh Circuit.[9]

Even more striking is the concentration of cases from the Board of Immigration Appeals. In 2008, when the concentration was especially strong, 45 percent of the petitions to review BIA decisions that were filed in the courts of appeals came to the Ninth Circuit and an additional 28 percent to the Second Circuit. These cases were so plentiful that they constituted a large part of the caseloads of those two circuits: in 2008, the proportions were 34 percent in the Ninth Circuit and 41 percent in the Second Circuit (Administrative Office of the U.S. Courts 2010, 94–99; see Committee on Federal Courts 2005).

The second form of specialization in the district courts and courts of appeals involves the assignment of judges to cases. Several practices can create situations in which certain judges hear disproportionate numbers of cases in a particular field. Most district courts have rules under which "related" cases can be assigned to the same judge. Some districts allow non-random assignment of cases to judges, and as a result some types of cases may go

8. These jurisdictional rules are catalogued in U.S. Code 28 §§ 1291, 1294 (Historical and Revision Notes) (2006). The district court for the District of Columbia is also an exclusive or optional venue for some types of administrative appeals. The Environmental Law Institute has summarized relevant venue provisions in the environmental field at http://www.endangeredlaws.org/pdf/dc_cir_jurisdiction_11_03.pdf.

9. These results are based on analysis of Federal Court Cases: Integrated Database, 2008, supplied by the Federal Judicial Center to the Inter-university Consortium for Political and Social Research, available at http://www.icpsr.umich.edu/icpsrweb/ICPSR/studies/25002.

primarily to a subset of judges.[10] District judges who administer decrees may thereby gain temporary monopolies or near-monopolies over specific policy issues, such as the setting of rates for the use of copyrighted music.[11] Assignments of cases by the Judicial Panel on Multidistrict Litigation, forum-shopping by litigants, and selective participation by senior judges also can lead to degrees of judge concentration and case concentration. These various mechanisms, singly or in combination, create situations such as the one in which senior district judge Jack Weinstein of the Eastern District of New York has heard a substantial number of mass tort cases (Weinstein 2009).[12]

One anomaly resulted from financial holdings by most of the judges on the Court of Appeals for the Fifth Circuit, which required their regular recusal from cases involving certain types of energy regulation. In 1972, the remaining judges were designated as an "oil and gas panel" to hear those cases. Over time, the panel included as few as three judges. Because high proportions of cases in the energy field went to the Fifth Circuit, those judges had considerable impact on judicial policy in the field (Pierce 1992; *Hall v. Federal Energy Regulatory Commission* 1983).

Occasionally controversies have arisen over allegations of bias by chief judges or others in the assignment of cases to panels or individual judges. The best known controversy was the battle over civil rights assignments in the Fifth Circuit during the early 1960s (*Armstrong v. Board of Education* 1963; Atkins and Zavoina 1974; Bass 1981, 233–47). The regional character of civil rights issues in the 1950s and early 1960s brought most cases involving those issues to the Fourth and Fifth Circuits. In the Fourth Circuit, there were only three judges. In the Fifth Circuit, with even more desegregation business, conservatives complained that Chief Judge Elbert Tuttle assigned

---

10. Statutory provisions allow nonrandom assignment of cases on the courts of appeals (28 U.S. Code § 46). The parallel provision for the district courts (28 U.S. Code § 137) is less explicit, but the argument that the statute requires random assignment of cases to district judges has been rejected in cases such as *In re: Atamian* (3rd Cir. 2007). Non-random assignment may raise issues of due process, especially in criminal cases, if the assignment process seems to work against some litigants. That issue was considered in the context of prosecutors' steering of cases to particular judges in *United States v. Pearson* (10th Cir. 2000). The assignment of cases involving certain criminal offenses to judges who are expected to take "tough" stances in those cases, discussed in chapter 4, also raises due process questions.

11. Under consent decrees involving the American Society of Composers, Authors, and Publishers (ASCAP) and Broadcast Music, Inc. (BMI), a "Rate Court" was set up in the district court for the Southern District of New York to adjudicate disputes over licensing rates. However, it appears that very few disputes ever got to the judge who presided over the rate court (Rifkind 1985, 17–18; see Fujitani 1984).

12. These mechanisms can also produce concentrations of cases in one district or circuit in a particular time period.

civil rights cases in a way that ensured pro-civil rights panels. The Fifth Circuit resolved that controversy by adopting rules that brought about random assignment, and other circuits have similar rules (Cheng 2008, 523n17).

The third form of specialization involves opinion writing in the appellate courts. Studies of the Supreme Court (Brenner 1984; Brenner and Spaeth 1986) and the courts of appeals (Atkins 1974; J. Howard 1981, 250–55) have found some evidence of opinion specialization. One clear example was Justice Harry Blackmun's frequent writing of the Supreme Court's opinions in tax cases (Brudney and Ditslear 2009, 1270–71). A thorough study of the courts of appeals showed considerable specialization (Cheng 2008). To the extent that opinion writers have disproportionate impact on court doctrine, opinion specialization produces a degree of case concentration.

In the aggregate, these instances of specialization are significant. Still, the district courts, the courts of appeals, and the Supreme Court are fundamentally generalist courts. In contrast, there are other federal courts that clearly qualify as specialists along one or both dimensions. Table 1.2 describes the current specialized courts in the federal judicial system.[13]

The table distinguishes between what I call "freestanding" courts and what I have described as borrowed-judge courts. Freestanding courts have their own permanent judges. In contrast, borrowed-judge courts are staffed by judges who are delegated from their home district court or court of appeals.

Among the freestanding courts, the table also makes the standard distinction between Article I and Article III courts. The defining characteristics of Article III courts that Article I courts lack are life tenure and a guarantee against reduction in judges' salaries.[14] The differences between these two types of courts in judges' security of tenure have led some commentators to posit that judges on Article III courts act more independently of the other branches, whether they are generalists or specialists (see Hendrickson 2003, 2006).

Table 1.3 depicts levels of specialization along both dimensions for the courts shown in table 1.2. In some instances, a court arguably could be placed in a different cell of the table. Such ambiguities aside, the table underlines the variation in degrees of specialization that exists even among specialized courts.

Nearly all the specialized federal courts feature high concentration of cases, in that they hold monopolies over the types of cases they hear at a

13. The table includes only courts in the judicial branch. Federal military tribunals are discussed in chapter 3.

14. On the distinction between Article I and Article III courts and its implications, see *Ex parte Bakelite Corporation* (1929) and Fallon (1988).

Table 1.2 Current specialized courts in the federal judiciary

Court type	Attributes
Freestanding courts:	
Trial:	
Court of Federal Claims (Article I)	• Jurisdiction: Monetary claims against the federal government. Appeals go to Court of Appeals for the Federal Circuit. • Judges: Sixteen judges nominated by the president and confirmed by the Senate, holding fifteen-year terms. • History: Court of Claims created in 1855. Two-level structure for the Court of Claims established in 1925. Trial level became Claims Court in 1982. (Appellate level merged into Court of Appeals for the Federal Circuit.) Claims Court became Court of Federal Claims in 1992.
Court of International Trade (Article III)	• Jurisdiction: Cases involving international trade issues, primarily lawsuits against the federal government. Appeals go to Court of Appeals for the Federal Circuit. • Judges: Nine judges nominated by the president and confirmed by the Senate, holding life terms. No more than five judges can be from the same political party. • History: Board of General Appraisers created in 1890. Became Customs Court in 1926 and Court of International Trade in 1980.
Tax Court (Article I)	• Jurisdiction: Tax cases brought against the federal government, primarily to challenge tax assessments before payment. Appeals go to courts of appeals. • Judges: Nineteen judges nominated by the president and confirmed by the Senate, holding fifteen-year terms, plus special trial judges appointed by the chief judge. • History: Board of Tax Appeals created in 1924. Became Tax Court in 1942 and United States Tax Court in 1969.
Court of Appeals for Veterans Claims (Article I)	• Jurisdiction: Challenges to administrative denials of benefits to military veterans. Appeals go to Court of Appeals for the Federal Circuit. • Judges: Three to seven judges nominated by the president and confirmed by the Senate, holding fifteen-year terms. No more than the smallest whole number above half of the total number of judges (e.g., four of seven) may be members of the same political party. • History: Court of Veterans Appeals created in 1988. Became Court of Appeals for Veterans Claims in 1999.
Appellate:	
Court of Appeals for the Federal Circuit (Article III)	• Jurisdiction: Appeals from Court of Federal Claims, Court of International Trade, Court of Appeals for Veterans Claims; administrative appeals involving government employees and contracts, patents and trademarks, and international trade; appeals from district courts in patent cases and claims against the federal government. • Judges: Twelve judges nominated by the president and confirmed by the Senate, holding life terms; other. • History: Created in 1982 through merger of Court of Customs and Patent Appeals and appellate level of Court

Table 1.2 (*continued*)

Court type	Attributes
Court of Appeals for the Armed Forces (Article I)	of Claims, with jurisdiction that had been held by those courts and additional jurisdiction. Other fields added to its jurisdiction later. • Jurisdiction: Appeals in military justice cases. • Judges: Five judges nominated by the president and confirmed by the Senate, holding fifteen-year terms. Judges must be civilians, no more than three from one political party. • History: Court of Military Appeals created in 1950. Became Court of Appeals for the Armed Forces in 1994.
Borrowed-judge courts:	
Trial:	
Foreign Intelligence Surveillance Court	• Jurisdiction: Applications for warrants for electronic surveillance of foreign intelligence information. Appeals from denials of warrants go to Foreign Intelligence Surveillance Court of Review. • Judges: Eleven district court judges designated by the chief justice, serving up to seven years. At least three of the judges must reside within twenty miles of Washington, D.C. • History: Created in 1978.
Removal Court	• Jurisdiction: Applications for removal of aliens from the U.S. as terrorists. Appeals go to court of appeals for the District of Columbia circuit. • Judges: Five district court judges designated by the chief justice, holding terms of five years. The judges must be from five different federal circuits. • History: Created in 1996. The court has not been convened.
Appellate:	
Foreign Intelligence Surveillance Court of Review	• Jurisdiction: Appeals from denials of warrants by the Foreign Intelligence Surveillance Court. • Judges: Three judges from the district judges or courts of appeals, serving up to seven years. • History: Created in 1978.
Subordinate courts:	
Bankruptcy	• Jurisdiction: Bankruptcy cases. • Judges: Varying numbers of judges (316 in 2010), appointed by the court of appeals of their circuit for fourteen-year terms. • History: Position of bankruptcy referee within district courts created in 1898. Referees' administrative responsibilities reduced in 1938. Referees designated as judges in 1973. Appeals go to district courts or bankruptcy appellate panels.

Sources: Web site of Federal Judicial Center (http://www.fjc.gov/public/home.nsf/hisc); Web sites of individual courts; United States Code.

Table 1.3 Specialized federal courts, classified by concentration of cases and judges

Concentration of cases	Concentration of judges		
	Low	Moderate	High
Low			Bankruptcy courts
Moderately high		Court of Federal Claims	Tax Court
High	Foreign Intelligence Surveillance Courts; Removal Court	Court of Appeals for the Federal Circuit	Court of International Trade; Court of Appeals for Veterans Claims; Court of Appeals for the Armed Forces

Note: Placement of the courts in cells is necessarily arbitrary, and some courts might be placed in different cells.

particular court level. The Tax Court does not have a full monopoly. It hears the great majority of disputes between taxpayers and the Internal Revenue Service (IRS), but the district courts and the Court of Federal Claims also hear some tax cases. The Tax Court hears challenges to IRS decisions before the tax is paid; the other courts hear challenges by taxpayers to recover taxes they have already paid. The Court of Federal Claims has a monopoly over some types of cases, but it shares jurisdiction with other tribunals over some other case types. As noted earlier, the bankruptcy courts are a special case because there are so many bankruptcy judges.

On the dimension of judge concentration, there is basically a dichotomy between the freestanding courts and borrowed-judge courts. The Court of Appeals for the Federal Circuit is an intermediate case, reflecting jurisdiction that is unusually broad for a specialized court. The Court of Federal Claims has somewhat narrower jurisdiction than the Federal Circuit. Still, it is best considered an intermediate case as well, because the types of claims against the federal government that it hears range widely.

In addition to the existing courts, several specialized federal courts were created and later abolished. Table 1.4 lists a sampling of those courts. Most of these courts were intended to be temporary, and two courts had "Emergency" and "Temporary Emergency" in their titles. (Despite those titles, the former court lasted for nineteen years, and the latter for twenty-two years.) In contrast, the Commerce Court, intended to be permanent, was eliminated after only three years (Dix 1964). Several decades later, unhappiness with the performance of federal special prosecutors led to elimination of that position. As a consequence, the Special Division of the court of appeals for the D.C. Circuit, which appointed special prosecutors, was also abolished.

The importance of specialized courts as a component of the federal judiciary can be gauged in multiple ways. The bankruptcy courts decide far more cases than the district courts, and the Tax Court decides thousands of cases each year. But other specialized courts hear relatively small numbers of cases. On the other hand, the areas of judicial policy that specialized courts address are consequential. Taxes, patents, trade, and bankruptcy are each important to the economy, and bankruptcy law affects the lives of large numbers of people. Specialized courts have substantial effects on public policy in those fields. The Foreign Intelligence Surveillance Court operated quietly for many years, but the controversy over bypassing of the court by the George W. Bush administration underlined the importance of its work (see Schmitt and Curtius 2005). Thus, a significant portion of the work of federal courts is done by specialized bodies.

Table 1.4 **Some specialized federal courts of the past**

Specialized courts	Description
Court of Private Land Claims (1891–1904)	Trial court with its own judges; heard cases involving Spanish and Mexican land titles in the Southwest.
Court for China (1906–43)	Trial court with its own judge; heard criminal and civil cases in which U.S. citizens were defendants.
Commerce Court (1910–13)	Appellate court with its own judges. (Borrowed judges were to be substituted later, but court's abolition came first.) Heard appeals from decisions of the Interstate Commerce Commission.
Emergency Court of Appeals (1942–61)	Appellate court with borrowed judges; heard appeals from administrative decisions in price control cases.
Temporary Emergency Court of Appeals (1971–92)	Appellate court with borrowed judges; heard cases involving wage and price controls and, later, energy regulation.
Special Court, Regional Rail Reorganization Act of 1973 (1974–97)	Trial court with borrowed judges; heard cases arising from reorganization of freight lines in the East and Midwest.
Special Division, U.S. Court of Appeals for the District of Columbia Circuit (1978–99)	Court with borrowed judges; appointed independent counsels to investigate allegations of criminal conduct by executive-branch officials; made other decisions involving investigations by independent counsel.

Sources: Web site of Federal Judicial Center (http://www.fjc.gov/public/home.nsf/hisc); United States Code; secondary sources. The Court of Private Land Claims is discussed in Bradfute (1975) and the Special Division at the beginning of chapter 2. The other courts are discussed in chapters 3–6.

Specialized federal courts have come and gone over time, but the overall level of specialization has gradually grown since the late nineteenth century. The biggest single step was the establishment of the Federal Circuit in 1982. The creation of that court and later expansions of its jurisdiction changed the intermediate level of the federal court system from one with little case concentration to one in which cases in several fields are heard by a single court. At the trial level as well, far more judicial work is done by specialized judges and courts than was true before 1890.

State Court Systems

Patterns of specialization in the state court systems are far more difficult to describe than federal court specialization. The most obvious reason is that court systems vary widely across states. Even more important are the differences between the structures described in organization charts and the realities of the courts. Organization charts depict a good many specialized courts in the states (see Strickland et al. 2008), as summarized in table 1.5. But at the trial level, formal and informal practices produce far more specialization than those organization charts indicate.

The great majority of appellate courts in the states are officially generalists, but a degree of judge concentration exists in some of these courts. For example, at certain times death penalty cases have constituted a large share of the agendas of some state supreme courts (see Stempel 1995, 81). The Arizona Court of Appeals has used special panels to decide workers' compensation and tax cases (Berch 1990, 188). Similar practices may have arisen informally in other states, and substantial opinion specialization may exist in some courts.

A few state appellate courts are officially specialized. Alabama, Oklahoma, and Texas have courts that hear only criminal appeals. In Oklahoma and Texas, these courts serve as the equivalent of supreme courts for criminal cases. The Commonwealth Court of Pennsylvania is an intermediate appellate court that specializes in cases with government litigants and appeals from administrative agencies (see Craig 1995).

Specialization on organization charts is more common at the trial level. At that level, half the states have courts whose jurisdiction is limited to some set of criminal cases—typically, misdemeanors. About one-third have separate probate courts, whose jurisdiction varies widely. Other types of specialized courts are less common, but several exist in multiple states: family courts, juvenile courts, tax courts, workers' compensation courts, traffic courts, water courts, and chancery courts.

Table 1.5 Formal specialization in state court systems, 2006

State court systems	No. of states with particular type of court
Appellate:	
Criminal	4
Cases involving government	1
Tax	1
Trial:	
Criminal and quasi-criminal:	
Criminal	25
Traffic	2
Juvenile	7
Family and family-related:	
Probate	16
Family	9
Probate and family	1
Economic issues:	
Chancery	3
Claims (against government)	3
Tax	4
Workers' compensation	3
Small claims	1
Property and resources:	
Housing	1
Environmental	1
Water	2
Land	1

Source: Data are from Strickland et al. (2008).
Notes: Courts are listed only if they are put in separate boxes in the organization charts in the source used (see above), except that the Tennessee court with separate sets of judges for chancery and probate cases is put in both categories. Trial and appellate courts with jurisdiction over all civil cases are not listed, and the common practice of giving some trial courts jurisdiction over cases with relatively high stakes and others jurisdiction over cases with lower stakes is not treated as a form of specialization. However, courts with moderately broad specializations are included. Among these are probate courts and the Pennsylvania Commonwealth Court, an intermediate appellate court that specializes in cases involving government. Some specialized trial courts exist only in certain counties within a state. Some courts listed as trial courts have appellate jurisdiction as well.

Some of the totals in table 1.5 underline the difference between organization charts and reality. We know that juvenile courts, small claims courts, and traffic courts are far more widespread than the table indicates. Units within courts, some established by legislation and some by courts themselves (either officially or unofficially) produce considerably more specialization than organization charts show.

This specialization takes different forms. In some courts, judges serve officially and permanently in specialized courtrooms. In Ohio, for instance, some judicial positions in the county-level Courts of Common Pleas are designated for the hearing of probate, juvenile, or domestic relations cases. "Parajudges" or "quasi-judges" with titles such as magistrates and referees may also hold positions in which they hear specific sets of cases (National Center for State Courts 1976; McFarland 2004). It is common for parajudges to hear traffic cases, for instance (Goerdt 1992, 15). To take another example, some states use hearing officers to handle cases involving child support (Prugh 2007, 77).

Also common are assignments of judges within courts to full-time specializations in particular fields, assignments that may be for definite or indefinite periods. Criminal cases, for example, are often heard by a subset of a court's judges at any given time. Courts frequently assign judges to more specific specializations, such as domestic relations, drug court, mental health court, juvenile court, or business court. Depending on the numbers of cases in a field, the judge's assignment can be full-time or part-time. Part-time arrangements are the equivalent of borrowed-judge courts in the federal judiciary, in that one judge in a court may hear all the cases in a particular field but also hear a range of other cases.

Sometimes judges receive special temporary assignments to deal with a particular type of case, most often when there is a troublesome backlog. "Rocket dockets" have been used recently to deal with foreclosure cases in a Florida city (Corkery 2009) and debt collection cases in Baltimore (Schulte and Drew 2008). Another example of temporary assignment illustrates the enormous variety in the forms that specialization takes in state trial courts. In the 1990s, two Florida cities established "spring break courts" that operated each spring for a few years (D. Baker 1997; *Sarasota Herald-Tribune* 1998). Visiting young people who had been arrested for misdemeanor offenses such as underage drinking were allowed to undertake a short period of community service to avoid formal prosecution (Key West) or as a substitute for fines (Panama City Beach).

As a consequence of formal and informal specialization in its several versions, there is a great deal of judge concentration and case concentration in state courts. The level of specialization on either dimension cannot be estimated with any precision, but there is relevant information on judge concentration from a 1977 survey of judges in general jurisdiction trial courts (Ryan et al. 1980, 23).[15] At the time of the survey, 16 percent of the judges of those courts were serving in specialized courtrooms, primarily criminal.

---

15. General jurisdiction courts hear broad ranges of cases. Despite their title, in most states they hear only civil and criminal cases with relatively large stakes.

(Another 23 percent were hearing only civil cases, but that category is too broad to be considered a specialization.) Because a great deal of specialization occurs outside of general jurisdiction courts,[16] the overall concentration of state trial judges in 1977 was at a fairly high level. As I will discuss, that level almost surely is higher today.

The variable associated most closely with the degree of actual specialization in state courts surely is the population of the area that a court serves, because opportunities for specialization increase with the numbers of cases and judges. There is no systematic relationship between the population of a state and the number of specialized courts on a state's organization chart.[17] But that number is a crude indicator of actual specialization, and the most meaningful level is the county or other unit of trial-court jurisdiction rather than the state. Within states, metropolitan counties certainly have the most specialization of judges. In Ohio, for instance, the counties in the most populous quartile have a mean of 2.4 divisions with their own permanent judges in juvenile, probate, domestic relations, or some combination of those fields. In contrast, the counties in the least populous quartile have a mean of 0.8.[18]

Beyond population, variation in specialization appears to be largely idiosyncratic. The general jurisdiction courts in Chicago, for instance, have a long-standing propensity to establish specialized courtrooms that seems to distinguish them from some other large cities (see Willrich 2003). A state chief judge who sees value to specialized courts can help spur the growth of specialization in the court system, as a former chief judge of New York did (Kaye 2004).

The successes achieved by the court unification movement in the twentieth century (Berkson and Carbon 1978; Baar 1993) may give the impression that state courts have become less specialized over the last century. But the unification movement attacked the fragmentation of court systems into many distinct types of courts, not specialization as such (see Hurst 1950, chap. 5). Although court unification eliminated some courts with narrow subject-matter jurisdiction, proponents of unification supported specialization within courts (Pound 1912–13; *Journal of the American Judicature Society*

16. It appears that judges in formally specialized divisions of general jurisdiction courts were not included in the survey (Ryan et al. 1980, 268).

17. This finding is based on analysis of the organization charts in Strickland et al. (2008).

18. By a specialization, I mean that one or more judges specialize in a particular field or combination of fields. These data were calculated from the listing of courts at the Web site of the Ohio Supreme Court (http://www.supremecourt.ohio.gov/JudSystem/trialCourts/default.asp).

1918; Haines 1933, 3–4). Further, the Progressive movement that fostered court unification also favored court units to deal with specific issues such as juvenile crime (see Willrich 2003). And because court unification in a state reduced the number of separate courts, it facilitated increases in judge and case concentration through specialized units within courts.

Two developments in recent years have further enhanced specialization at the trial level. One is the creation of new court divisions to hear certain types of cases involving businesses as parties (Bach and Applebaum 2004). Several states now have business or commercial courts throughout the state or in particular localities. A variant is courts to hear cases involving techno-logical issues, typically with businesses as parties.

The other development is the burgeoning of what are usually called "problem-solving" courts within trial courts (Symposium 2002; Winick and Wexler 2003). The great majority of these courts hear criminal cases that in-volve a particular type of offense or defendant. The most common form of problem-solving court is the drug court (Nolan 2001). Several other types of courts have been given the problem-solving label. Among them are men-tal health courts, homeless courts, drunk driving courts, community courts, and domestic violence courts. Like business courts, problem-solving courts vary along both dimensions of specialization.

Altogether, today's state trial courts are more specialized in practice than their federal counterparts in judge and case concentration. The growth in judicial specialization has also been more pronounced in the states. That difference between the federal and state systems requires explanation.

Cross-National Comparison

It would be useful to compare the landscape of judicial specialization in the United States systematically with the landscape in other nations. Such comparisons, however, are difficult to make. One reason is the difference between formal and actual specialization. A second reason is that the bal-ance between courts and administrative tribunals differs across countries. In social security or labor law, a specialized court in one nation may be the equivalent of an administrative body in another (Skoler and Weixel 1981; Blankenburg and Rogowski 1984). Because the United States uses executive-branch tribunals so much, it appears to be more of a bastion of generalist judges than it actually is.

Still, with some caution, comparisons can be made between the United States and other countries. I focus on the common-law countries that are most similar to the United States, primarily Canada, Great Britain, and Australia, and on the civil law countries of Western Europe, especially France and Germany.[19]

Among the common law countries, the United States seems fairly typical in the level of judicial specialization. Canada and Australia are similar to the United States in combining a court structure that is basically generalist with a variety of specialized courts and court units. Like states in the United States, Australian states and Canadian provinces vary in the degree of specialization at the trial level. Specialization is more prominent in the court system in Great Britain.[20] The High Court of Justice, the trial court with jurisdiction over civil cases that have relatively high stakes, has divisions and other units to hear particular types of cases. The Court of Appeal, the primary first-level appellate court, is divided into civil and criminal divisions. At the trial level, the movement to create problem-solving courts in the United States has had its counterpart in other common law countries, largely due to American influence, though the extent of this development differs among countries (Nolan 2009).

On the whole, the judicial systems of civil law countries in Western Europe feature greater specialization than those of the common law countries (Glendon, Gordon, and Carozza 1999, 66–71; Shapiro 1981, 150). There is usually a separate system of administrative courts, which sometimes lie in the executive branch rather than the judiciary. Constitutional courts, distinct from the regular high courts, are common. Germany stands out for its level of specialization: "subject matter specialization is the foundation of the judicial structure" (V. Williams 1996, 600). Alongside the ordinary courts in Germany are separate hierarchies of courts, spanning the state and federal systems, for labor, public and administrative law, taxes, and social insurance. Within the ordinary courts there is additional subject-matter specialization at the trial and appellate levels.

The higher level of specialization in civil law countries is related to the relatively low status of judges and the lack of a sharp distinction between the judiciary and the bureaucracy (Merryman 1969, 117–18; Shapiro 1981, 150–54; Provine 1996, 177–80, 201, 204). Entry into the judiciary usually

---

19. The entries in Kritzer (2002) provide basic information on the structure of the various court systems, along with more detailed information on specialized courts in some nations. Especially useful sources on particular countries include Crawford and Opeskin (2004) and French (2000) on Australia; Hausegger, Hennigar, and Riddell (2009, chap. 2) on Canada; Abraham (1998, 282–98) and J. Bell (1988, 1758–64) on France; Meador (1981), Clark (1988, 1808–14), and Blankenburg (1996, 259–65) on Germany; and Spencer (1989), Slapper and Kelly (2001) and Ward and Akhtar (2008) on Great Britain.

20. There are some differences in structure within Great Britain; here, I describe the system in England.

comes at an early career stage, and judges move up through a civil service–like system. In this respect, the career judiciary of civil law countries differs fundamentally from the "recognition judiciary" of common law countries (Georgakopoulos 2000).[21] Moreover, people tend to view judges as part of the civil service corps rather than as significant public officials. Under the circumstances, it is natural for the judiciary to be given some of the specialization that is characteristic of the bureaucracy.

Even in Germany, however, the courts are less specialized by subject matter than the bureaucracy. In most other countries, that difference in specialization between the two branches is considerably greater. The United States is not unique in either the lack of specialization in its judiciary, compared to other sectors of government and society, or the considerable degree of specialization that does exist.

Plan of the Book

Earlier in the chapter, I outlined the coverage of the remaining chapters in the book. Here, I describe that coverage in greater detail.

Chapter 2 introduces the issues of the causes and consequences of judicial specialization. The first part of the chapter analyzes the potential effects of high levels of specialization along its two dimensions on the neutral virtues of quality, efficiency, and uniformity and on the substance of judicial policy. This analysis includes a framework for examination of the relationship between specialization and substantive policy. The second part of the chapter analyzes the motivations and processes that might bring about judicial specialization. Working from theoretical perspectives that scholars have presented, it develops alternative expectations about how and why specialization has grown.

The four chapters that follow examine specialized courts in four broad areas of judicial activity, areas that together include the preponderance of specialized courts.[22] For each court and set of courts, these chapters discuss

21. One similarity, however, is that judges in both civil law and common law systems typically come to the courts as generalists rather than receiving special prior training to match their judicial responsibilities (see Magalhães, Guarnieri, and Kaminis 2006, 142).

22. The most significant omissions are probate courts and family courts, except for domestic relations courts of the past that heard primarily criminal cases. Most cases in probate courts involve the estates of people who have died, but probate courts hear other kinds of cases such as guardianships and commitments to mental institutions. A degree of specialization in debt collection cases exists in many small claims courts; they are discussed only briefly in the book, primarily because they were not intended to be specialists.

how and why specialization came about as well as the performance and policies of specialized courts.

Chapter 3 discusses federal courts that deal with issues relating to foreign policy and national security. These courts fall into several categories. One category includes courts involved in military justice, including the tribunals and commissions that the George W. Bush administration created to adjudicate the status and guilt of Guantánamo detainees. Among the other categories are extraterritorial courts outside the United States and the courts that rule on warrants for electronic surveillance for national security purposes.

Chapter 4 examines specialization in criminal law in the states, with a primary focus on courts that hear specific subsets of criminal cases. These courts have taken multiple forms. Most numerous are the "socialized" courts of the early twentieth century and problem-solving courts of the current era, and the chapter gives attention to the movements that led to creation of these two sets of courts.

Chapters 5 and 6 turn to courts that deal with economic issues, found at both the federal and state levels. Chapter 5 examines federal courts that address disputes between government and private parties. Some courts in this category hear cases involving government revenue or expenditures. Others review government regulation of the economy. A different category of courts, discussed in chapter 6, deals with economic issues that occur primarily between private parties. This disparate set of courts includes the Federal Circuit in its patent jurisdiction, the Delaware courts in the field of corporate governance, federal bankruptcy courts, and state business courts.

The final chapter returns to the issues of explanation discussed in chapter 2, applying the empirical material in chapters 3–6 to the questions of causes and consequences. In that chapter I present my conclusions about how specialization has come about and about its impact on court policies.

Appendix: The Scholarship on Judicial Specialization

There is no scholarly field or subfield devoted to specialized courts. However, a good deal of scholarship exists on judicial specialization. This work has been done by scholars in several academic disciplines, and it takes a wide range of approaches.

Legal scholars have produced the largest body of research and writing on specialized courts. Their work deals primarily with specific specialized courts in the federal judiciary. Analyses of a court's rulings and doctrinal outputs are common. Courts whose work falls in a field with large numbers of specialized lawyers receive the most attention, so the Tax Court and the work of the Federal Circuit in patent law have been very extensively discussed in both general and field-specific journals (e.g., Maule 1999; Allison and Lemley 2000). Much of this work is normative, evaluating existing specialized courts and assessing proposals to create new forms of specialization (e.g., Landau and Biederman 1999; Pegram 2000).

These normative concerns have led to consideration of the potential benefits and drawbacks of judicial specialization in general or, more often, in the federal judiciary. Work that takes this approach, either as its primary focus or one of several concerns, includes Nathanson (1971), Currie and Goodman (1975), Jordan (1981), Meador (1983), Dreyfuss (1990), Revesz (1990), Bruff (1991), T. Baker (1994), Stempel (1995), Kondo (2002), and Damle (2005). A few scholar-judges have contributed to this scholarship (Posner 1983; Wood 1997). Stephen Legomsky's (1990) book examines judicial specialization from a cross-national perspective, evaluating specialization in general and one possible model of specialization. Some scholarship, including two important early works (Rightmire 1918–19; Frankfurter and Landis 1928, chap. 4), surveys actual specialized courts in the federal judiciary with less of a normative focus.

Several book-length studies examine single federal courts or related sets of courts. Sociologist Carroll Seron (1978) wrote about evolution of the federal bankruptcy courts. Legal scholar Lynn LoPucki (2005) analyzed the performance of bankruptcy courts in cases involving large companies. Another legal scholar, Harold Dubroff (1979), collected a series of articles on the Tax Court into a book. More recently, political scientist Robert Howard (2009) has published a book on the roles and behavior of the Tax Court and other federal courts in tax cases (see also R. Howard 2005, 2007). Historian Jonathan Lurie (1992, 1998) wrote a two-volume history of the Court of Appeals for the Armed Forces. Political scientist Louis Fisher wrote a book about military tribunals in general (2005) and one about a tribunal that tried would-be Nazi saboteurs during World War II (2003). Political scientist Isaac Unah (1998) analyzed the behavior of the Court of International Trade and the Federal Circuit in the field of international trade (see also Unah 1997, 2001; Hansen, Johnson, and Unah 1995).

In contrast with the federal courts, very little scholarship has considered judicial specialization as a general phenomenon at the state level (see Hurst 1950, chap. 8). The preponderance of research on state specialized courts has been concerned with specific types of courts. However, in recent years much has been written about the broader category of problem-solving courts. This work includes a book by Greg Berman and John Feinblatt (with

Sarah Glazer 2005) and a number of articles (e.g., Dorf and Fagan 2003; McCoy 2003; Casey and Rottman 2005).

Scholarly and quasi-scholarly writing on problem-solving courts is heavily tinged with advocacy, especially by their proponents. The same is true of the scholarship on specific types of problem-solving courts, but there is a body of work that is primarily empirical rather than normative. Subjects of this scholarship include community courts (Fagan and Malkin 2003), mental health courts (Griffin, Steadman, and Petrila 2002), and domestic violence courts (Mirchandani 2005). The largest concentration of research by far is on drug courts in their various forms (Hoffman 2000; Nolan 2001; Goldkamp 2003; Butts and Roman 2004a).

There is also a body of research on the socialized courts that were created in the early twentieth century. Juvenile courts have been the subject of considerable work, primarily by historians and sociologists (Lou 1927; Ryerson 1978; Polsky 1989; Getis 2000; Tanenhaus 2004). A few scholars have studied women's courts (Solomon 1987; Cook 1993; Quinn 2006). A book by historian Michael Willrich (2003) provides a rich account of a cluster of Chicago courts in that era.

On the whole, other specialized state courts have received less scholarly attention. The primary exception is the Delaware Court of Chancery, because of its important role in shaping corporate law. Aside from research on its legal doctrines, there have been several broader studies of the court (Quillen and Hanrahan 1993; Dreyfuss 1995; D. Sullivan and Conlon 1997). Other business-oriented courts have been the subjects of some research (Bach and Applebaum 2004). There are scattered studies of other types of specialized courts, such as the Pennsylvania Commonwealth Court (Craig 1995).

Studies of judicial specialization often discuss the origins of particular courts or types of courts, so they provide considerable raw material for the inquiry in this book. Scholars occasionally write about the forces that have brought about broader developments, most often the invention and diffusion of problem-solving courts (see also Frankfurter and Landis 1928, 146–48). But to this point, no study has considered the sources and growth of specialization as general phenomena.

TWO

Perspectives on Causes
and Consequences

In the late nineteenth century, social reform groups began to argue for a fundamental change in the procedures for juvenile defendants in criminal courts.[1] In their view, juveniles should be sent to a separate court that would emphasize treatment rather than punishment. The result was the juvenile court. First established in Chicago in 1899, juvenile courts rapidly spread to other places. By 1918, nearly every state had adopted legislation authorizing juvenile courts.

In practice, juvenile courts did not revolutionize juvenile justice as much as their proponents had hoped. One reason is that many of the judges who presided over juvenile courts did not share the treatment orientation that underlay the creation of these courts. Even so, juvenile courts evoked considerable criticism. Some people criticized them on the ground that they deprived defendants of basic procedural rights while still subjecting them to serious sanctions. In contrast, others criticized them as unduly lenient toward people who committed serious crimes. These criticisms have led to major changes in juvenile courts, but in their various forms they remain ubiquitous.

A century after the juvenile court was invented, the mayor of Providence had a more specific concern. As he saw it, laws involving the illegal possession and use of guns were not being enforced adequately. The mayor successfully lobbied the Rhode Island legislature to establish a gun court in Providence. The city funded the court, and the mayor said that the judge

1. In this chapter I refer briefly to courts that are discussed in greater detail in chapters 3–6. Sources will be cited only for specific facts; more extensive citations of sources about those courts are provided in those later discussions. The Special Division of the federal court of appeals for the District of Columbia is not discussed in later chapters, so full citations are provided in this chapter.

initially assigned to the court was "the first judge I ever bought" (Daly 1995). That judge was chosen because of his reputation for taking a hard line in criminal cases. Among other things, according to one report, he had sentenced a repeat murderer to death despite the inconvenient fact that Rhode Island did not allow for the death penalty (Walker 1994, 6). Anecdotal evidence indicates that the mayor got the tough sentencing he sought.

In the aftermath of the Watergate episode, Congress in 1978 established a system of special prosecutors for cases in which a high official in the president's administration was suspected of a crime.[2] Not trusting the Justice Department to appoint special prosecutors, Congress gave that power to a three-judge Special Division of the federal court of appeals for the District of Columbia, to be composed of judges from the courts of appeals as a whole. There was a long tradition of designating the chief justice to appoint judges to serve part-time on specialized courts and special panels (Ruger 2004, 358–67), and Congress followed that tradition in the special prosecutor legislation. Congress reinstituted the system of special prosecutors (now called independent counsel) in 1994 after a two-year hiatus, and once again it gave the chief justice appointment power.

Members of the Democratic majority in Congress in 1994 apparently did not notice that under Chief Justices Warren Burger and William Rehnquist, the Special Division nearly always had had a two-to-one majority of judges appointed by Republican presidents and a Republican presiding judge (Ruger 2004, 393–94; Barrett 2000, 44–46). Rehnquist's appointments under the 1994 law followed that pattern. The first act of the new Special Division, taken over the strong opposition of its Democratic member, was to designate a highly respected but strongly Republican lawyer named Kenneth Starr to investigate possible criminal violations by President Bill Clinton (Toobin 1999, 72–73; K. Gormley 2010, 143–54; *In the Matter of a Charge of Judicial Misconduct or Disability* 1994). Starr carried out his role with zeal, and his expanded investigation ultimately brought about Clinton's impeachment. In the view of unhappy Democrats, including Clinton himself (P. Wilson 2004), there was a direct line from the appointment power of the chief justice to the impeachment.

The three episodes I have described all involve specialized courts in the field of criminal justice, but they differ in some important respects. In two instances, the courts were created in order to change the substance of

---

2. The statute was the Ethics in Government Act (1978). Statutes mentioned in the text or footnotes are listed by name, with accompanying information, in the book's references under Legislative, Statutory, and Regulatory Materials.

judicial policy. In the third, Congress established a special court panel as a convenient device without considering its potential impact. The effort to change judicial policy through a gun court seems to have served its purposes, but the similar effort with juvenile courts has had more mixed effects. And even though few members of Congress could have had that result in mind, their use of the Special Division to appoint special prosecutors may have brought about a president's impeachment.

In the remainder of this book I focus on the questions of causes and consequences that these episodes raise. Why do policy makers act to create specialized courts, and what are the effects of judicial specialization? In this chapter I offer some theoretical perspectives to guide the inquiries into those questions. The appendix to the chapter lays out the research strategy that I used to identify and analyze evidence on causes and consequences.

Consequences: The Impact of Judicial Specialization

Temporally, of course, the causes of judicial specialization come prior to its effects. But I begin with the effects of specialization because expectations about those effects help to motivate the establishment of specialized courts.

The significance of judicial specialization rests primarily on its effects— the difference it makes for a court's outputs if that court has high levels of judge concentration or case concentration. There is good reason to posit that the two dimensions of specialization have powerful effects on court outputs. As I noted in chapter 1, these potential effects can be summarized in terms of Martin Shapiro's (1968, 53) suggestion that specialization makes courts more like administrative agencies.

Before developing this idea, I should offer two important caveats. The first is that generalist courts and administrative agencies are not as different in their characteristics as they appear to be on the surface. Shapiro (1968, chap. 2) himself made this point about federal courts and administrative agencies, identifying shared traits such as incremental decision making. And Michael Lipsky (1980) has argued persuasively that urban trial courts in state court systems share important attributes with other "street-level bureaucracies" that reside in the executive branch, such as welfare and police departments. The second caveat is that even specialized courts differ from administrative agencies in some basic traits. Among other things, courts are typically small organizations in which there is little hierarchy among judges.

For these reasons, the idea that specialization makes courts more like agencies should not be overstated. At the same time, the ways that specialized courts might differ from their generalist counterparts can be understood largely in terms of this idea.

First, specialization might improve judicial outputs by providing the same broad advantages that are identified with bureaucratic specialization, what I have called the neutral virtues of specialization. The propositions that specialists can do more than generalists and that they can do their work better seem self-evident to most people. These propositions were articulated at least as far back as Adam Smith's *The Wealth of Nations* (1776/1963, 7–8), and they are routinely repeated (e.g., Simon 1947, 10, 20). The organization of the bureaucracy reflects general acceptance of those propositions.

Second, specialization may affect the substance of judicial policy through mechanisms that are characteristic of administrative agencies. As noted in chapter 1, by substance I mean the place of judicial policy on a spectrum that is defined by ideology or by the interests of competing sides in a field, as distinguished from the quality of outputs. Even if specialization had no systematic effects on the substance of policy, it would affect policy in a field simply by changing the mix of judges who hear cases in that field. But there are also good reasons to posit that specialization does have systematic effects.

The neutral virtues and the substance of judicial policy are not fully independent of each other. In particular, changes in the quality of decisions could affect their substance as well. Still, the distinction between the two kinds of effects is quite useful for analytic purposes.

The Neutral Virtues

In analyses of judicial specialization, people frequently cite neutral virtues as likely products of specialization (Currie and Goodman 1975, 63–68; Dreyfuss 1990, 377–78; Jordan 1981, 747–48; Meador 1983, 481; Legomsky 1990, 7–16; Bruff 1991, 330–31; Damle 2005, 1275–79). Along with the efficiency and quality that are ascribed to specialization in general, supporters of judicial specialization proposals point to uniformity as a third neutral virtue. Moving from low to high case concentration reduces the number of judges who decide cases in a field of legal policy, sometimes changing from a situation in which large numbers of generalist courts occupy a field to one in which a single specialized court does so. Such a change would seem very likely to reduce inconsistency in the law (see Kondo 2002, 47–49).

In contrast with uniformity, efficiency is potentially fostered by high judge concentration. Like people in other positions, judges who regularly handle a single class of cases are expected to dispose of their work in less time than their counterparts on generalist courts who see that class of cases less frequently. A second, ancillary gain in efficiency is often expected: generalist courts can work through their caseloads more quickly if they are no longer responsible for the cases that go to a specialized court or if they never receive those cases in the first place.

The third neutral virtue, what I call quality, is usually described as expertise. This is especially true in discussions of judicial specialization (but see Legomsky 1986, 1388). However, expertise is not parallel with efficiency. Enhanced efficiency is an outcome, but expertise is a trait that might affect outcomes. For instance, any gains in efficiency from concentration of judges result in part from the expertise that judges develop (Unah 1998, 94). When commentators speak of judicial expertise as something more than a source of efficiency, what they really mean is that expert judges will produce higher-quality decisions than nonexperts.

Of course, quality could have multiple meanings. The most useful way to define that term is in relation to what judges are trying to accomplish. If judges seek to interpret the law well, expertise helps them choose the best interpretation. If they seek to make good policy, expertise helps them identify the case outcomes and legal doctrines that constitute good policy as they define it.

High judge concentration is widely assumed to produce greater expertise and thus higher-quality policy outputs in the same way that it seems to do in other organizations (Currie and Goodman 1975, 67–68; Dreyfuss 1990, 380; Bruff 1991, 330). Further, specialization can lead to the selection of judges who are already expert in a court's field, through both self-selection and the use of expertise as a criterion for choosing judges (Dreyfuss 1990, 378).

Some commentators have identified ways in which specialization along one or both dimensions might actually detract from the neutral virtues (Currie and Goodman 1975, 68–74; Jordan 1981, 748; Posner 1983, 783–88; Dreyfuss 1990, 379–82; Revesz 1990, 1155–65; Damle 2005, 1281–86; Morley 2008, 381–91). Gains in efficiency could be countered by the need to litigate jurisdictional boundaries between generalist and specialized courts and the inconvenience to litigants of bringing cases to a geographically centralized court. Concentration of judges could reduce efficiency if it means that some judges are assigned exclusively to a category of cases that does not fully occupy their time in certain periods (see Posner 1996, 259–62). Some proposals for specialized courts, such as the Court of Military Appeals, have been questioned on that ground (U.S. Senate 1949, 53).

Commentators also have pointed to potential adverse effects on quality. The uniformity gained from concentrating cases in a single court could

Table 2.1 Linkages between judicial specialization and the substance of judicial policy

Mechanism by which effect occurs	Stage at which effect arises	
	Selection of judges	Experiences of judges
Immersion in subject matter	Assertiveness (J); insularity (J); professional bias (J)	Assertiveness (J); insularity (J); stereotyping (J)
Influence of interested groups	Bias toward interests (C, J)	Bias toward interests (C, J)

Note: "C" and "J" refer to the dimension of specialization that potentially produces this effect. J, concentration of judges; C, concentration of cases.

have a corresponding cost, the absence of diverse decisions on an issue that ultimately produce better policy (see Nard and Duffy 2007). If high concentration of judges brings the benefits of expertise, it may also detract from judges' knowledge about developments in other fields of law that could inform their judgment. In addition, specialized courts might be less attractive to prospective judges than their generalist counterparts, so that the average level of ability on these courts (and thus the quality of their decisions) would be lower. These perceived adverse effects of specialization help to account for the belief in the desirability of a generalist judiciary.

The extent to which these potential advantages and disadvantages of judicial specialization actually occur can be difficult to ascertain, and quality is especially difficult to measure. With a few exceptions (e.g., Nash and Pardo 2008), scholars and participants in debates over judicial specialization have not sought to measure its benefits and drawbacks rigorously. When they reach conclusions about the performance of existing specialized courts, they generally rely on assumptions about that performance or on anecdotal evidence.

The Substance of Policy

The potential effects of specialization on the substance of judicial policy require more extensive discussion, since those effects are more complicated and more consequential. Table 2.1 summarizes the most likely effects. As the table shows, those effects operate through two mechanisms, immersion of judges in a relatively narrow subject matter and enhancing the influence of groups that care about case outcomes and legal doctrine, what I will call interested groups. These effects may come into play at two stages: the selection of judges and the experiences of judges as their courts operate.

The table indicates that high concentration of judges can affect the substance of policy in more ways than high case concentration, because a judge's immersion in a particular field might shape the judge's thinking in several respects. However, both dimensions of specialization may enhance the influence of interested groups, perhaps the most powerful mechanism by which specialization can affect judicial policy. Concentration of cases seems likely to enhance this influence more than concentration of judges.

The table implicitly highlights the linkages between judicial specialization and the attributes of administrative agencies. Each of the potential effects of specialization on the substance of policy captures a trait that is associated more closely with the bureaucracy than with the judiciary.[3] These linkages will be developed more fully in the discussion that follows.

Immersion in a Subject Matter

Judges who specialize in a narrow range of policy become immersed in the subject matter of the cases on which they focus. Concentration of judges and cases also encourages the selection of judges who were already immersed in a court's field, because their presumed expertise is seen as a qualification for the position. Immersion from either source can affect the substance of the policies that judges adopt.

Some effects are directly connected with expertise and with judges' own perceptions of their expertise. Specialized judges who are expert in the subject matter of their court's work at the time they take their positions or who develop that expertise through constant work in one field tend to feel greater confidence in their judgment than their generalist counterparts. Because of this confidence, they are likely to be more assertive than generalists in their policy making. One possibility is that they will be more willing to overturn administrative decisions (Currie and Goodman 1975, 71; Bruff 1991, 332; Hansen, Johnson, and Unah 1995; Unah 1998, chaps. 7–8). Another is that they will be more inclined to make sweeping decisions that change policy substantially.[4]

In his classic book on bureaucracy, Anthony Downs (1967, 103–7) pointed to another effect of immersion in a field: insularity. People come to see the decisions they make from the perspective of the field in which they work and give little weight to other perspectives. That tendency is reflected

3. Assertiveness is arguably an exception, in that generalist judges are often assertive (usually labeled as activist) in their policy making. But judicial activism is easy to exaggerate, and the boldness of administrative agencies is probably underestimated because it is seldom well publicized.

4. These effects are not limited to specialized courts, because judges on generalist courts are often expert in one or more fields of policy that are within their courts' jurisdiction. However, for judges who hear a wide range of cases, these effects are less pervasive.

in the much-cited Miles' Law: "where you stand depends on where you sit" (Miles 1978). Specialization creates the potential for such insularity in the judiciary (Jordan 1981, 748; Damle 2005, 1281–83).

One possible manifestation of insularity concerns the authority of higher officials. Within organizations, highly specialized subordinates tend to accord less authority to their superiors than do generalists, because they see themselves as more knowledgeable than the generalists above them (Wilson 1989, 91–101). Specialized judges might respond in this way to higher courts that are generalists.

Another potential effect of immersion in a subject matter is professional bias. At any given time, the set of people who work in a particular field such as patents or bankruptcy is likely to have a narrower range of opinion about the issues in their field than does the general public or political and social elites as a whole. That relative consensus reflects similarities in interests and values among people in the field, forged in part by their interactions. People who are appointed to a specialized court because of their prior work in the court's field may bring a professional bias with them, and other judges may develop that bias through their service on the court. One possible effect is that judges change their positions on issues in a field in response to swings in professional opinion (see Posner 1983, 781). On the whole, however, the more likely effect of professional bias is that judges strongly adhere to certain positions.

Whether or not they were specialists prior to their judicial service, judges who are immersed in a particular type of case may develop stereotypes about cases. Criminal law provides a familiar example, one that is especially clear because of the skew in the outcomes of cases. A judge who constantly hears criminal cases gains the impression that the overwhelming majority of defendants are guilty. The judge then brings that impression to each criminal case.[5] One virtue sometimes ascribed to juries is that their amateur status leaves jurors free of that stereotype, so they are more likely to treat the presumption of innocence as real. What happens to judges in criminal law can occur in other fields where cases share salient attributes. The higher the level of judge concentration, the more likely it is that the judge will develop stereotypes about cases in a field.

---

5. Certainly this stereotype can develop even among nonspecialized judges who hear a substantial number of criminal cases. This effect of judge concentration is stronger when a class of cases that ordinarily would constitute only a small portion of a judge's work becomes the exclusive subject of the judge's work.

Influence of Interested Groups

In every field of litigation, of course, there are sets of litigants and lawyers on the two sides. Other sets of people do not participate directly in litigation but care about the outcomes of cases and the content of legal doctrine, either because they have a stake in the field or simply because they have strong policy preferences about it. To refer to all these people I use the bulky term "interested groups," because that term is somewhat broader than what we usually mean by interest groups. For convenience, however, I sometimes refer to interested groups simply as interests. People in these groups would like to exert influence that advances their goals in the courts. Each dimension of specialization increases both the incentives of interests to seek this influence and their opportunities to attain it.

The impact of specialization on the influence of interested groups begins with the selection of judges. Groups may seek and attain influence over the selection of judges for generalist courts such as the federal courts of appeals (L. Bell 2002; Scherer 2005). However, both dimensions of specialization enhance the potential for influence over choices of judges, in two ways.

First, high case concentration encourages interests to participate in the selection of judges. If a single court decides every case that affects an interest at a particular court level, the representatives of that interest have very good reason to seek influence in the selection process. One example is groups with an interest in patent law, which can focus on the Court of Appeals for the Federal Circuit at the intermediate appellate level. Those interests have much less reason to lobby over the selection of judges to the dozens of district courts that hear patent cases at the trial level.[6] If a particular type of case is heard by only a single judge, as was true of the Providence Gun Court, those who care about the court's outputs will have a very strong interest in helping to choose that judge.

High judge concentration increases the chances that efforts to influence the selection of judges will bear fruit (Revesz 1990, 1147–53; Komesar 1994, 145; but see Stempel 1995, 97–105). If a court hears only tax cases, then groups that care about tax policy need not compete with their counterparts

6. Although the state and federal supreme courts do not feature high case concentration by my definition, the fact that they hold a monopoly over cases at their level of the system helps to explain why interest groups give so much attention to the selection of supreme court justices. One example is groups with a stake in tort law at the state level (Goldberg et al. 2005; Sample, Jones, and Weiss 2007). Of course, the power of supreme courts to shape policy in the judiciary as a whole also makes it attractive to seek influence over the selection of their judges.

in other fields when they try to influence the selection of the court's judges.[7] Judge concentration also enhances their legitimacy as participants in the selection process: who knows more than tax lawyers do about the qualifications of prospective judges to decide tax cases (Currie and Goodman 1975, 70–71; Dreyfuss 1990, 379–80; Bruff 1991, 331–32)?

Both dimensions of specialization also increase the potential influence of interested groups over sitting judges. As it does in the selection process, high case concentration strengthens the incentive to seek influence over judges' choices. In addition, interested groups are more capable of influencing judges who hear only a narrow set of cases (Dreyfuss 1990, 380; Bruff 1991, 332). Specialized judges interact more frequently with the lawyers who represent a particular interest. Thus the specialized bar in a field, such as those that exist in patents and international trade, has a better opportunity to shape judges' attitudes toward the issues they confront in a field. Moreover, to the extent that judges benefit from the cooperation of lawyers and litigants or care about their approval, specialized judges are dependent on a relatively narrow set of court participants.

The constellations of interests on the two sides in a field of policy are sometimes more or less equal in strength. If so, the influence of the two sides over the selection of judges and over sitting judges may largely cancel out. In contrast, in some fields one side holds a permanent advantage, often because it is more concentrated and thus better organized than its competitor. This difference is reflected in Marc Galanter's (1974) distinction between "one-shotters" and "repeat players." In fields such as debt collection, where one-shotters and repeat players contend with each other, repeat players are likely to be in a much better position to exert direct or indirect influence over a court. And where influence is highly unequal, a court might be captured by one side just as some administrative agencies are (see Dal Bó 2006).

Government is a special case (Kritzer 2003). Governments tend to do very well in litigation because of several advantages. One advantage is a strong version of repeat player status. In many fields of litigation, a single government appears in every case that a court hears. In some fields, such as criminal law, the government's opponents are primarily one-shotters or relatively weak for other reasons. Another advantage is the power of government to set substantive and procedural rules under which courts work and,

---

7. Howard Gillman (2006, 141) has pointed out another effect: for those who seek to shape court policy in general, specialization makes it easier to do so through the selection of judges. "It is comparatively more difficult to find decision makers who will be reliable on a wide range of issues than it is to find appointees who will act reliably over a narrowly defined set of policies" (see Posner 1996, 254).

for many courts, to choose judges. Where judicial specialization increases the incentives and opportunities to influence what courts do, governments are in an especially good position to benefit as a result.[8]

Organizational Missions

The influence of interested groups and some effects of immersion in a subject matter may be understood in terms of organizational missions. The concept of mission can be defined in different ways (Bendor 1985, 254–55; J. Wilson 1989, 95). As I use the term, it refers to goal consensus (see Downs 1967, chap. 18): an organization has a mission to the extent that its decision makers agree on a central goal for the organization.

The content of organizational goals differs widely, and in government one key dimension on which goals vary is the extent to which an organizational mission implicates the substance of policy. Administrative agencies often begin life with a policy-oriented mission (Wilson 1989, 95–101; Macey 1992). Such a mission can also develop after an agency is created. Missions to advance certain policies sometimes fade or even disappear altogether, but they often continue for considerable time.

Missions of any type are less common in generalist courts than in administrative agencies. One reason is that judges are not subject to organizational processes of socialization and control to the same degree as members of many other types of organizations, including administrative agencies (e.g., Kaufman 1960; Derthick 1979, 27–32; W. Gormley and Balla 2004, 42–44). Missions that do develop in generalist courts tend to concern process-related issues such as coping with heavy caseloads (Heumann 1978; Wold 1978). Missions that concern the substance of policy are less common because judges divide their attention among multiple fields and because they usually disagree about the issues in a particular field. Generalist courts sometimes take on policy-oriented missions, a product of consensus among judges about issues that are highly salient to them (see Shapiro 1968, 55–56). But those missions are unusual.

Policy-oriented missions are more likely to develop in courts with a high level of specialization along either dimension. Both judge and case concentration facilitate the selection of judges on the basis of their agreement with the goals that the court was created to further. For their part, prospective

---

8. In the federal courts, one special attraction of specialized courts to executive-branch officials might be that they need not have Article III status. The absence of life tenure provides a source of potential influence over sitting judges and an opportunity to replace judges whose patterns of decisions are unfavorable to the government.

members of a court find the court more attractive if they agree with those goals. For both reasons, when a specialized unit is created within a court, the judges deputized to staff that court are usually enthusiastic about the purposes the unit is to serve. This was true of the judges who first staffed juvenile courts and problem-solving courts such as drug courts and mental health courts. High case concentration also facilitates monitoring of court policies for consistency with the intent of those who sought to institutionalize a particular mission, because it is easier to keep track of policy in a single court than in a multiplicity of courts.

The potential for a court to pursue a policy-oriented mission underlines the significance of judicial specialization. High concentration of judges or cases can change judges' perspectives, the environment in which they operate, and ultimately the policies they make.

The Contingent Effects of Specialization

The effects of structural attributes of government organizations on the substance of their policies are not necessarily straightforward. As one scholar said, "Institutional effects may be complex and contingent, making institutional design a risky endeavor for political actors seeking to craft institutions that will favor their policy goals" (Mullin 2008, 137). Certainly that is true of judicial specialization. The effects of specialization may be contingent on variables such as the specific form that specialization takes in a particular court, the other attributes of a court, and the conditions under which the court does its work.

These contingencies are illustrated by courts that review the decisions of administrative agencies, such as the federal Tax Court and Court of Appeals for Veterans Claims. It is plausible that these courts will review administrative decisions aggressively, because specialized judges gain the confidence to take assertive positions and because the private interests that contest government actions in those courts wield considerable influence. It is also plausible that these courts will tend to uphold administrative decisions, because appointments are typically made by the executive branch and because the federal government is a repeat player that appears in every case. Whether one or the other of these outcomes occurs is very difficult to predict without other information about these courts.

The long-term effects of judicial specialization are especially difficult to predict. Appointments to specialized courts by presidents or chief judges reflect a set of considerations that are not easy to anticipate at a court's inception. The relative strength of interests that compete to shape a court's policies, sometimes uncertain in the short run, can change a good deal over time. One effect is that initial missions can atrophy. If the Court of Claims was given an implicit mission in the mid-nineteenth century, we would hardly expect that mission to govern its policy making more than a century later.

There are some situations in which the effects of specialization are relatively straightforward and predictable, at least in the short run. The most likely situation is when the prospective membership of the specialized body is known at the time the body is created, as was true when two courts were merged to create the Court of Appeals for the Federal Circuit. And sometimes the interests on the two sides of a court's cases differ so much in their strength that the overall outcome of conflicts between them is nearly certain. To the extent that small claims courts have become specialists in debt collection actions by businesses against individuals, businesses have an inherent advantage.[9] But these instances are exceptions to the rule.

Causes: The Sources of Judicial Specialization

This book's inquiry into causes addresses a macrolevel question, why specialization in the American judiciary has reached its current level. In the final chapter, I will return to the other side of that question, why specialization has not progressed even further. However, the answers to those questions must be built from microlevel inquiries into actions that affected the level of judicial specialization, especially decisions to create specialized courts or enhance their jurisdiction. In this section I present a set of theoretical perspectives and develop their implications for these microlevel and macrolevel inquiries. I then examine the goals that might underlie decisions about judicial specialization.

These decisions are made primarily in two places. The first is legislatures, which establish the general structure of courts through statutes. The second is individual courts, which determine how cases are allocated among their judges. Decision makers in the executive branch play a part in legislation about judicial specialization, often initiating proposals for specialized courts. They have also acted on their own to create some specialized courts, primarily military tribunals.

9. However, even here the pattern of outcomes may be uncertain—and the evolution of some small claims courts into debt collection courts certainly was not predicted by those who created these courts (see Moulton 1969). A close analysis of the scholarship on small claims courts, during an era when they were receiving considerable attention, is in Yngvesson and Hennessey (1975).

Policy makers who make choices about judicial specialization can be influenced by a variety of interested groups. Groups that have a direct stake in cases are the most obvious seekers of influence. People with broader interests in the functioning of the courts also may participate in decisions. Those people may be in the courts (such as administrators of court systems who favor problem-solving courts) or outside them (such as the good-government groups that advocated juvenile courts). And when legislators make choices about specialization, judges might play a significant role in shaping those decisions.

In the book's microlevel inquiries into specific decisions about judicial specialization, I am concerned with two issues that relate to motives. The first is the identities and relative importance of the goals that underlie decisions about judicial specialization. In particular, when a specialized court was created, why did advocates seek its creation, and why did legislators or judges establish it?

I call the second issue purposiveness, for want of a better term. What I mean by purposiveness is the strength of the connection between the goals of participants in the policy process and their use of judicial specialization as a means to further those goals. More directly, the question is the extent to which choices about specialization in a given field of legal policy are made consciously and carefully.

A third issue, related to the second, involves one connection between the micro- and macrolevels. Public policies often diffuse, in the sense that prior adoptions of a policy encourage future adoptions, and that has been true of judicial specialization. The issue I will consider, to be described later in this section, is the mechanisms by which diffusion of specialized courts occurs.

The findings about specific decisions can be aggregated to identify the mix of goals that has been responsible for the movement toward greater specialization in the courts. That aggregation will provide a basis for addressing a fourth issue, the most fundamental question about the movement toward specialization: to what extent has it been deliberate rather than an inadvertent byproduct of choices made for other reasons?

Theoretical Perspectives

One potential source of theoretical perspectives with which to frame these issues is scholarship on the bases for specialization in government. Little of this research concerns the bureaucracy, because scholars generally take specialization of administrative agencies and their officials as a given (but see Macey 1992). In contrast, several scholars have examined the movement toward legislative specialization through the development of standing committees to screen and consider legislation (e.g., Jameson 1894; Gamm and Shepsle 1989). There are also studies of the use of special districts to carry out specific functions that otherwise would be undertaken by general-purpose local governments (Bollens 1957; Burns 1994; Mullin 2008). The most extensive research on choices about specialization concerns the courts, research that I summarized in the appendix to chapter 1.

These bodies of research provide insights on the reasons for specialization, and the scholarship on court specialization is an important source of data on specific decisions about specialized courts. However, broader theoretical perspectives on institutions and on public policy making offer the most useful frameworks for thinking about how and why judicial specialization comes about. I begin with economic and sociological perspectives on choices about institutions and then turn to a conception of public policy making developed by political scientist John Kingdon, one that I call the process stream perspective.

By some definitions, specialization as an attribute of courts can be characterized as an institution (see Ikenberry 1988, 226). But whether or not that label is appropriate, theoretical work on choices about institutions is quite relevant to judicial specialization.[10]

One perspective is economic in orientation (McCubbins 1985; McCubbins, Noll, and Weingast 1987; Moe 1989, 2005; Bawn 1995; Alt and Alesina 1996; Shipan 1997; Koremenos, Lipson, and Snidal 2001; D. Lewis 2003). From this perspective, sometimes labeled rational-choice institutionalism, people design institutions consciously as means to advance their instrumental goals. Interest groups seek institutions that favor the policies they prefer. Government decision makers adopt institutions that serve their own purposes—most often the policies they prefer, either for their own sake or to advance goals such as power and reelection. In other words, the attributes of institutions are means to other ends rather than ends in themselves.

A second perspective can be derived from clusters of theory that include historical institutionalism as well as formulations from sociology and constructivism in international relations (March and Olsen 1984, 1989; Brigham 1987; Thelen and Steinmo 1992; Goldstein 1993; Finnemore 1996; Meyer et al. 1997; Wendt 2001; Pierson and Skocpol 2002; Hay 2006; Offe 2006; Sanders 2006). Perhaps the best term for the perspective that these clusters offer is sociological, though that term fits some work better than others.

---

10. Surveys of the formulations in this work are found in Goodin (1996) and Hall and Taylor (1996).

This perspective differs from rational-choice institutionalism in several respects. The first difference concerns the relationship between patterns of preferences and power and the state of institutions. From an economic perspective, the attributes of institutions are fairly direct reflections of the preferences of individuals and groups who have the power to determine the form of institutions at any given time. For scholars with a sociological perspective, in contrast, the relationship is not so straightforward.

One reason is that from this perspective, choices about institutions are not entirely conscious and purposive; indeed, the term design overstates the intentionality of these choices. Two other reasons can be understood in terms of path dependence, a recurring concept in the sociological scholarship.[11] Of the various aspects of path dependence that scholars have discussed, the most relevant is what Scott Page (2006, 88) calls self-reinforcement: "making a choice or taking an action puts in place a set of forces or complementary institutions that encourage that choice to be sustained."

To the extent that path dependence exists, institutions do not necessarily change when the conditions that supported them have weakened. One reason is the practical difficulties involved in changing institutions, difficulties that create a degree of inertia. The standard advantages of the status quo in the policy process apply to proposals for change in institutions.

Another, less obvious reason is that existing institutions shape preferences and expectations and thereby reduce the chances that people will seek change in institutional arrangements (see Keohane 1988, 382). "It is not just that institutional arrangements may make a reversal of course *difficult*. Individual and organizational adaptations to previous arrangements may also make reversal *unattractive*" (Pierson 2000, 491; emphasis in original). Thus, as scholars with a sociological perspective see it, the causal relationship between preferences and institutions runs in both directions.

A second difference between the two perspectives on institutions concerns the motivations that shape choices about institutions. Rational-choice institutionalists emphasize instrumental goals, especially achieving public policy that is viewed as desirable. In the sociological perspective, decisions about institutions are often intended to make those institutions consistent

---

11. A related concept, often used by international scholars, is the "stickiness" of institutions (e.g., Krasner 1976, 341–43; Garrett and Lange 1995, 633; Ikenberry 1998–99, 51–53). Thelen (2004, 25–28) underlines the imprecision that exists in the use of both this term and path dependence.

with important values rather than to advance instrumental goals.[12] In other words, the attributes of institutions may be ends in themselves.

In addition to these two perspectives that relate directly to institutions, one well-known depiction of the policy-making process provides the basis for a third way of thinking about choices concerning judicial specialization. Drawing from the "garbage can" model of organizational choice (M. Cohen, March, and Olsen 1972; March and Olsen 1976), John Kingdon (1984, 2003) argued that the policy-making process does not follow a sequence in which problems are identified and then possible solutions to those problems are developed.[13] Rather, problems and prospective policies travel simultaneously in separate streams. Under favorable political conditions a policy is attached to a problem as a potential solution, and adoption of that policy is given serious consideration. Kingdon (1984, 21) offered a way of thinking about the conditions under which at least serious consideration is possible:

> The separate streams of problems, policies, and politics come together at certain critical times. Solutions become joined to problems, and both of them are joined to favorable political forces. This coupling is most likely when policy windows—opportunities for pushing pet proposals or conceptions of problems—are open. . . . Policy entrepreneurs, people who are willing to invest their resources in pushing their pet proposals or problems, are responsible . . . for coupling solutions to problems and for coupling both problems and solutions to politics.

As applied to choices about structural attributes of government bodies, what I call the process stream perspective (Kingdon did not give it a name)

---

12. One complication in distinguishing between instrumental goals and values is that instrumental goals may be shaped powerfully by values (see Wendt 1999, 113–35). However, the distinction between institutions as means to other ends and as ends in themselves is clear.

Even if values are not instrumental, they may be chosen and applied in ways that are consistent with rational-choice conceptions of behavior (Chong 2000; Finnemore and Sikkink 1998). In this respect, the economic and sociological perspectives are not as far apart as they initially seem.

13. Kingdon was concerned primarily with agenda setting, including the specification of alternative policies, but his formulation can be applied to the policy process as a whole. In extending and adapting that formulation to the analysis of judicial specialization, I am developing implications with which Kingdon would not necessarily agree. For critiques of his formulation and of the garbage can model from which it draws, see, respectively, Mucciaroni (1992) and Bendor, Moe, and Shotts (2001). For an application to institutional change in trial courts, see Flemming (1998).

Table 2.2 Implications of alternative theoretical perspectives for issues concerning the movement toward judicial specialization

| Level | Issue | Theoretical perspectives | | |
		Economic	Sociological	Process stream
Micro-	Goals underlying specific decisions	Instrumental, primarily as means to advance preferred policies	Both instrumental and based on values about institutions	Variable, often mixed
	Purposiveness of specific decisions	High	Variable	Often low, with idiosyncratic elements
Micro- to macro-	Diffusion mechanisms: learning vs. emulation	Learning	Largely emulation	Primarily emulation
Macro-	Deliberate or inadvertent movement toward specialization	Inadvertent, reflecting instrumental choices in individual decisions	Possibly deliberate, based on widely shared values	Inadvertent, reflecting different motives for different decisions

points to a complicated and somewhat unsystematic process. Like the sociological perspective, this perspective predicts an imperfect match between current patterns of preferences and power and the state of institutions. But Kingdon gives more emphasis to the uncertainties of government decision making. One important feature of his argument is that people can perceive and present a particular policy option as a solution to multiple problems rather than a single one. Structural attributes are especially malleable in this sense, because they can easily be linked to a variety of goals (see Schickler 2001).

These three perspectives lead to different expectations about the four issues that I have raised concerning the process of judicial specialization, expectations that are summarized in table 2.2. I have noted some of those differences already, but they merit more systematic discussion.

The first issue is the goals that motivate specific decisions about specialization. The three perspectives are relevant to specific goals, which I consider in the next subsection of this chapter. They also have implications for broad patterns in the goal orientations that underlie decisions about judicial specialization. The economic perspective leads to an expectation that policy makers will choose specialization when it serves their instrumental purposes. In contrast, the sociological perspective suggests that to some degree these choices reflect attitudes about judicial specialization in itself. The process stream perspective does not address that distinction directly, but it points to the likelihood of variation across decisions and the possibility that a multiplicity of motives will come into play in any specific decision.

The second microlevel issue is purposiveness. The economic perspective suggests that choices about judicial specialization result from careful calculations about the fit between specialization and the goals that people seek to advance. These are, after all, rational choices. Successful advocates of specialized courts may not always get what they want from the courts they create, but they do as well as they can in light of uncertainty about the effects of structural attributes.

In contrast, the sociological perspective suggests that the state of judicial specialization does not reflect full and regular consideration of alternatives. New institutional arrangements may be adopted primarily because of their positive connotations. Existing arrangements may be maintained even when changes would seem to serve policy makers' goals. For instance, specialized courts may continue to exist although they no longer serve the purposes for which they were created. To a degree, the survival of juvenile courts might be interpreted in that way.

The process stream perspective also suggests that judicial specialization is not highly purposive. More specifically, it points to the importance of idiosyncrasy in the decisions that determine degrees of specialization. Whether a proposal for a specialization in a particular field is seriously considered and ultimately adopted often depends on a complex combination of circumstances.

The third issue concerns the diffusion of specialized courts.[14] Like any other policy, the idea of using a specialized court to deal with a particular type of case such as juvenile criminal cases can diffuse geographically across states and localities. The idea of judicial specialization can also diffuse from one field of legal policy to another, as has occurred with problem-solving courts.

Diffusion can occur through several mechanisms (Simmons, Dobbin, and Garrett 2006, 789–801; Shipan and Volden 2008, 841–44). The most interesting issue is the relative importance of two mechanisms, learning and emulation. In learning, evidence from other localities or settings that a

---

14. On diffusion of innovations in general, see Rogers (2003). Diffusion of public policies is widely studied in political science (e.g., J. Walker 1969; Berry and Berry 1990; Glick and Hays 1991; Shipan and Volden 2006; see Graham, Shipan, and Volden 2008).

policy would be successful leads to its adoption. In emulation, the existence of a policy in other localities or settings encourages its adoption in itself, without regard to its prospects for success.

The economic perspective emphasizes learning (see Weyland 2006, 35). Advocates are expected to support specialization and policy makers to adopt it when they have evidence that it would serve their goals. If a specialized court in a field of policy has advanced those goals in locations where it already exists, there will be an impetus to establish a similar court in other places.

In contrast, the sociological perspective suggests that emulation plays a significant role in diffusion of specialized courts. This is because the widespread use of specialized courts in other localities or other fields of policy can attach a positive value to specialization in general or in specific fields of policy (see Meyer et al. 1997). Thus, juvenile courts could spread widely without strong evidence that they were effective, because their establishment in some places suggested in itself that they were a desirable innovation.

The process stream perspective also allows a substantial role for emulation. But from this perspective, emulation may be less systematic than the sociological perspective suggests. Once adopted in some jurisdictions or policy areas, judicial specialization remains a potential solution to new problems that policy entrepreneurs might identify. Moreover, its adoption elsewhere gives it greater visibility and legitimacy, making it easier to adopt again without much thought.[15] By 1978 the idea of creating special-purpose courts that borrowed federal judges from their regular courts was well established, and so was the idea of having the chief justice appoint those judges. So why not employ that device once again to choose special prosecutors?

The final, macrolevel issue is the extent to which the overall movement toward specialization has been deliberate rather than inadvertent. From the sociological perspective, this movement may be deliberate. If values shape choices about institutions, then policy makers take into account the perceived desirability of judicial specialization as such. Thus, the growth of specialized courts may reflect a widely shared judgment that specialization is a positive quality. Similarly, limits to that growth may reflect a strong belief in the value of judging by generalists.

In contrast, the economic perspective depicts institutional design as a process in which the form of institutions is not an end in itself. Specialized courts are created to serve specific goals or sets of goals in specific situations.

---

15. Another approach that points to similar patterns is Weyland's (2006, 45–53) analysis of the part that cognitive heuristics may play in the diffusion of public policies.

If these choices cumulate to make the courts more specialized, that result is an inadvertent byproduct of those choices rather than an outcome that was chosen deliberately. The process stream perspective leads to a similar conclusion, adding the suggestion that a diverse combination of motives could lead to growth in judicial specialization.

The differing possibilities suggested by these three perspectives provide both guidance for the book's inquiry into the causes of judicial specialization and ways to interpret findings about those causes. At the same time, the findings from that inquiry will suggest something about the value of these perspectives for understanding of a phenomenon such as judicial specialization.

The Goals That Motivate Choices about Specialization

The first issue concerning the sources of judicial specialization is the identity of the goals that motivate choices about specialization. Having discussed this issue in broad terms, I now turn to specific goals. Two categories of possible goals relate to the potential effects of judicial specialization: an interest in the substance of judicial policy and an interest in the neutral virtues of specialization. A third category relates to elements of policy makers' self-interest that are distinct from those potential effects. As I will discuss, this type of self-interest is considerably more important for judges than it is for officials in the other branches.

The two types of effects on court outputs that judicial specialization might have were discussed in the first section of the chapter. In this section, my concern is different: how those potential effects function as an incentive for people to put forward and adopt specialization proposals. To the extent that specialization produces the intended results, the goals that underlie its adoption coincide with its effects. However, a specialized court may not achieve the effects that motivated its adoption. By the same token, specialization may affect judicial policy in ways that were not anticipated.

The Substance of Policy

In their analyses of legislation about structural attributes of government, scholars who take an economic perspective emphasize interest in the substance of public policy. Scholars give considerable attention to efforts by members of Congress to shape bureaucratic policy through choices about the prospective implementation of statutes (McCubbins, Noll, and Weingast 1989; Moe and Wilson 1994; Zegart 1999; D. Lewis 2003). Indeed, among rational-choice institutionalists there is widespread acceptance of the "structure and process hypothesis, according to which Congress exerts ex ante influence over subsequent agency decisions by imposing on the agency a particular organizational structure and decision-making process" (Spence 1999, 414).

Research on legislative efforts to shape judicial policy provides some support for the structure and process hypothesis.[16] Because there are quite plausible linkages between specialization and the substance of judicial policy, policy makers in the other branches of government might well use specialized courts to shape judicial policy. Indeed, this has been the case, as juvenile courts and the Providence Gun Court indicate. The question is how often policy makers take this path. Two realities may limit the use of this type of mechanism to shape judicial policy, but neither is as serious a problem as it might seem.

The first reality is the difficulty of predicting the effects of a structural attribute on the substance of policy (Shipan 1997, chaps. 2–3). That difficulty certainly applies to judicial specialization, whose effects may be contingent on complex circumstances. Advocates might hesitate to press for a specialized court as a means to advance certain policies when it is unclear whether the court they propose will actually have its intended purpose.

The seriousness of this problem is reduced by people's tendency to exaggerate how well they can predict the impact of a prospective policy. Participants in the policy process develop expectations based on common-sense beliefs—what might be called folk theories about the impact of prospective policies.[17] In the case of judicial specialization, these folk theories sometimes relate to differences in the support that generalist and specialized courts would give to competing interests in a particular field of policy. Some nineteenth-century members of Congress, for instance, concluded that a single court of claims in Washington, D.C., would be more sympathetic to the government's interests than district courts around the country. Whether or not that conclusion was valid, those who reached it treated it as a matter of common sense rather than digging more deeply.

The second reality is the widespread allegiance to judicial neutrality as a value. Neutrality is inherent to most people's conceptions of what courts

16. See Landes and Posner (1975); G. Anderson, Shughart, and Tollison (1989); and Schwartz, Spiller, and Urbiztondo (1994). Charles Shipan (1997) has done more extensive analysis of legislative efforts to shape judicial policy through institutional design.

17. I borrow the idea of folk theories from Geary (2005) and Hutto (2008), though my use of the term differs somewhat from theirs. The concept of folk theorems in game theory (Morrow 1994, 268–79) is more distant from my meaning.

should be (see Tyler 1988). As a result, efforts to manipulate court structures and processes to achieve certain policy ends have a tinge of illegitimacy. This tinge helps to explain the repeated failures of bills to remove the Supreme Court's jurisdiction over some issues on which the Court has made unpopular decisions (Curry 2005, chaps. 6–7; L. Bell and Scott 2006). Even changes in structure and process that seem technical, such as splitting a large judicial circuit, arouse opposition if they are perceived as efforts to influence court policies (Barrow and Walker 1988). The same would be expected of proposals for judicial specialization.

Advocates of specialized courts can reduce this problem by framing their proposals publicly in terms of the neutral virtues of specialization rather than their policy goals. Efficiency, quality, and uniformity may provide persuasive rationales for specialized courts, rationales that divert attention from advocates' interest in the substance of policy. Thus, supporters of a specialized court for patent appeals emphasized the need for uniformity of decisions even though many really wanted to change the standards for determining whether patents were valid.

I have argued that governments as litigants are in an especially good position to benefit from judicial specialization. If so, government officials have an especially strong incentive to support specialization as a means to advance their interests in court. And because government itself sets the structure of the courts, public officials who seek the benefits of judicial specialization for their governments are in a better position to get what they want than are advocates for private interest groups. Congress frequently limits court jurisdiction to protect the government's interests (Chutkow 2008), and it might employ judicial specialization for the same purpose.

Public policy makers are not always sympathetic to government interests that conflict with the interests of private-sector groups. For instance, members of Congress often support taxpayers rather than the Internal Revenue Service. Still, it is noteworthy that most specialized courts deal with government litigation. This fact suggests the possibility that governments frequently employ specialization to benefit their own interests.

The Neutral Virtues

The neutral virtues can be used to legitimize proposals for specialization, but they can also motivate such proposals. Considerations of efficiency and quality have been the primary reasons for the movement toward greater specialization in work organizations. Within government, that is true of the bureaucracy (Carpenter 1998, 163–64), and it is at least largely true of legislatures (Francis and Riddlesperger, 1982; Hamm and Hedlund 1994, 672–87; S. Smith 1994, 645; Cooper 1970, 47–58, 105; see Krehbiel 1991, chap. 4).

In most settings, there are no countervailing values for decision makers to balance against the neutral virtues. In the courts, in contrast, the association of specialization with efficiency, quality, and uniformity is countered by the positive connotations of a generalist judiciary. Those connotations result in part from the belief that a *lack* of specialization enhances the quality of judicial work in important ways. Thus, the idea of judicial specialization evokes a conflict between two sets of values. As a result, arguments for specialized courts on the basis of neutral virtues are frequently met with counterarguments about the benefits of a generalist judiciary.

The extent of this conflict varies by level of court. Commentators and judges evoke the value of generalist judges most often for the federal courts. In contrast, the resemblance between busy state trial courts and bureaucratic agencies detracts from the perceived relevance of the generalist model. This is probably one reason why judicial specialization is most common at the state trial level.

Despite the positive connotations of generalist courts, the neutral virtues can be a powerful source of interest in the creation of specialized courts. For one thing, representatives of the two sides in a field of legal policy sometimes perceive that they will benefit from the neutral virtues, for any of several reasons. High-quality judging makes it easier for lawyers to try cases and arguably makes outcomes more predictable. People also tend to believe that if specialized judges make legally correct decisions more often than nonspecialists, the correct decisions will tend to favor their own side (see, e.g., Landau and Biederman 1999). Further, a court's efficiency in getting to cases and reaching decisions leads to quicker resolution of disputes. This virtue is especially appealing to people who perceive that their interests suffer from delay. That was true of the federal government in customs litigation a century ago, and the prosecution may benefit from shorter processing times in criminal cases (see T. Schneider and Davis 1995, 26–29). The third neutral virtue, uniformity in interpretation of the law, clarifies legal rules and thus facilitates planning.[18]

The neutral virtues also appeal to people who do not have a direct stake in the substance of judicial policy but who care about the state of the courts.

18. Certainly a set of litigants sometimes benefits from inefficiency, low-quality judging, and conflicting legal rules, and a perception of those benefits might spur opposition to judicial specialization.

There are "friends of the courts" in law schools and in organizations such as the National Center for State Courts. These people look for ways to help courts do their work and to improve the quality of that work. They also accord a high value to efficiency and to expertise as a source of efficiency and quality.

Friends of the courts likely favor the generalist ideal as well. But they may find the neutral virtues of specialization appealing when they perceive that the generalist courts are not doing their jobs as well as they might in a particular field, so that a serious problem exists. The same is true of policy makers who make decisions about specialization. Both groups can reconcile the competing values by treating a proposed specialized court as a small and necessary exception to the general rule of maintaining a generalist judiciary.

The neutral virtues are an instrumental consideration, but they may be appealing because of the positive values associated with them. The sociological perspective suggests that these values might help to spur the movement toward judicial specialization. By the same token, this perspective suggests that the positive connotations of generalist courts would work against specialization.

Judges' Self-Interest

Although the concept of self-interest is a slippery one, legislators who make choices about judicial specialization sometimes act on self-interest as we usually think of it. For instance, they may take their interest in reelection into account when they decide whether to support a specialized court proposal. For legislators, however, self-interest is generally captured by the two considerations that I have already discussed. Efforts to shape the substance of judicial policy may appeal to interest groups that are important to a legislator or to groups of constituents. To the extent that judicial inefficiency or the quality of outputs is perceived as a problem, legislators may take credit for efforts to address that problem. The same is true of executive-branch officials who propose specialized courts, because anticipated benefits to them such as enhanced success for their agencies stem primarily from the potential effects of specialization on judicial policy.

Judges are different, in that their self-interest goes well beyond the substance of judicial policy and the neutral virtues. Judges certainly care about the substance of policy, sometimes even acting as entrepreneurs on behalf of particular policies (McIntosh and Cates 1997). They may also give considerable weight to the neutral virtues, because those virtues directly affect their work. But judges have other goals that are specific to their positions as judges, goals that relate to their job satisfaction (see Posner 2008, chap. 2). Among other things, judges benefit from job security, they want their jobs to be easier rather than more difficult, and they seek self-esteem and the esteem of other people. These motivations have several implications for judicial specialization.

First, judges may gain satisfaction from being a generalist or, alternatively, from working in a specialized court. As I have suggested, the positive qualities ascribed to generalist judges can make it important to judges that they remain generalists. Under certain circumstances, however, judges may find it satisfying to specialize. For instance, they might enjoy judging in a high-prestige field such as corporate law or tax law. Problem-solving courts can provide their own satisfactions to judges. Some judges conclude that they could do more good in a unit such as a drug court than they could by processing criminal cases in the standard ways. In addition, judges can gain acclaim by serving in a court that people perceive as innovative. The prospect of those satisfactions may lead judges to support the creation of problem-solving courts, and judges sometimes receive praise for initiating such courts.

Second, judges prefer to devote their efforts to cases that they find interesting and important and to rid themselves of cases that lack these qualities. This preference is reflected in the common practice of delegating work in minor or "easy" cases to central staffs in appellate courts or to parajudges in trial courts. The same preference may lead generalist judges to support proposals that assign less desirable cases to specialized judges (Scalia 1987; Taylor 1987). That has been an important consideration in the development of the bankruptcy courts.

Third, judges on specialized courts usually have a stake in continuation of those courts. Of course, this will be true when their job security depends on that continuation. Thus, specialist judges may favor expansion of their jurisdiction when such an expansion strengthens the rationale for maintaining their court. But judges typically prefer the status quo even when their jobs are secure, especially when they have developed an affinity for the field in which their court works.

Finally, specialization might increase budgetary resources for the courts, a matter of considerable concern to judges in periods of scarcity. If a particular type of specialized court appeals to policy makers in the other branches, they may be willing to provide money to the courts that they would not have allocated otherwise. Judges who sense what will appeal to legislators and executive-branch officials can propose changes in court structure with an eye to garnering resources. To take one example, federal funding of some problem-solving courts such as drug courts and mental health courts has made them more attractive within the judiciary.

Summing Up and Looking Ahead

In the first section of the chapter, I examined the possible consequences of specialization for court outputs. There are good reasons to posit that differing degrees of specialization affect both the substance of the policies that courts produce and the neutral virtues. The effects of specialization on substantive policy are especially important. But as I have suggested, those effects are likely to be complicated and contingent on particular circumstances.

In the second section, I framed the causes of judicial specialization in terms of several issues concerning motivations and decision processes. Different theoretical perspectives lead to different expectations about these issues, and each issue is open. To take one example, there is an array of goals that plausibly could motivate the movement toward judicial specialization, goals whose relative importance is uncertain. And on the broadest issue to consider, it is far from obvious to what extent the growth in judicial specialization has been deliberate rather than inadvertent.

In the four chapters that follow, I examine evidence on the causes and consequences of judicial specialization in four broad areas of policy. I pull that evidence together in chapter 7 to reach conclusions about why courts in the United States have become more specialized and how specialization has affected the outputs that courts produce.

Appendix: Research Strategy

Before beginning the analyses of specific courts and types of courts in chapter 3, I should discuss my use of evidence about the causes and consequences of specialization in particular fields of judicial policy. As a form of qualitative research, the aggregation and weighing of evidence from diverse sources involves interpretation just as quantitative analysis does (Kritzer 1996). That interpretive process should be made explicit (see Schickler 2001, 18–23).

For the book's inquiry into the *consequences* of judicial specialization, I drew primarily from existing studies of the behavior and policies of specialized courts. Scholars and (less often) practitioners have done quantitative and qualitative research on this subject. Some of that scholarship was described in the appendix to chapter 1. For some courts and sets of courts, this research is extensive. For others, it is nearly nonexistent.

The research that does exist varies in its relevance to my inquiry. Legal scholars have done considerable research on specialized federal courts, but most of that research focuses on specific doctrinal issues rather than broad patterns of policy and behavior. Some research on federal and state courts does consider broad patterns. The scholarship on juvenile courts differs considerably from research on the Court of Appeals for the Federal Circuit, but both bodies of research provide considerable information about the path of policy in those courts. For some courts, a single scholar has done extensive scholarship and thereby developed a good picture of a court's work. The book on the Court of Appeals for the Armed Forces by Jonathan Lurie (1998) is a good example.

Taken together, this body of research provides solid evidence about some specific specialized courts and sets of similar courts. But it is another step to ascertain the impact of specialization on what courts do. This step requires comparison of specialized courts with generalist counterparts, and systematic comparisons are uncommon.

One reason is that there is often no basis for direct comparison. For instance, no generalist court has heard cases that are equivalent to those that go to the Foreign Intelligence Surveillance Court or the Court of Appeals for Veterans Claims, since both of those courts were given new jurisdiction. Because the Court of Appeals for the Armed Forces was also assigned jurisdiction that had never been held by generalist courts, even Lurie's rich study is limited in what it can tell us about the impact of specialization on military appeals.

In other instances, comparison is possible because jurisdiction was transferred from generalist to specialized courts or because courts of the two types hear similar cases. However, comparison is often complicated by differences between courts. The Tax Court and the federal district courts deal with comparable issues involving federal taxation, but differences in their jurisdiction mean that simple comparison of decisional tendencies can be misleading.

Good comparative evidence does exist on some specialized courts. Perhaps the best example is the transfer of jurisdiction over patent appeals from the federal courts of appeals to the Federal Circuit. An extensive body of evidence makes clear how judicial policy changed as a result of that transfer. But patent law is very much an exception to the rule. In the absence of systematic comparative evidence, meaningful judgments are still possible in some instances. In particular, the behavior of some specialized courts is sufficiently distinctive to allow inferences about the impact of specialization. This is true of some problem-solving courts, for instance.

Altogether, the relevant evidence on the impact of specialization is substantial but partial. I could not make firm judgments about many of the courts that are discussed in the next four chapters. As a result, the book's conclusions about the effects of judicial specialization in chapter 7 are tentative in some respects. However, we know enough about enough courts to allow meaningful conclusions about the effects of enhanced specialization in the courts. In turn, those conclusions provide a good basis for some judgments about the desirability of judicial specialization.

The book's inquiry into the *causes* of judicial specialization benefited from a broader and deeper evidentiary base. This evidence provides a good basis for judgments about the reasons why most types of specialized courts were created. I gathered evidence from an array of primary and secondary sources. For federal courts, the most important primary sources were congressional documents, mostly committee hearings and reports. For state courts, advocacy statements and accounts by people who initiated and supported judicial specialization were most useful. Proponents of problem-solving courts have been especially prolific writers of arguments in favor of those courts and descriptions of how they come about.

The information from primary sources is much more voluminous and illuminating for some courts than for others. Among federal courts, for instance, congressional documents tell us a great deal about the creation and evolution of the bankruptcy courts and very little about establishment of the Temporary Emergency Court of Appeals. But for the preponderance of specialized courts, there is significant evidence in primary sources about the motives and processes that led to their creation.

The volume of relevant evidence from secondary sources, like that for primary sources, varies considerably across courts. For some courts there are one or more rich studies. Paul Light's (1992) story of the creation of the Court of Veterans Appeals is an example. Social scientists have written a great deal about the origins of juvenile courts. Law review articles often provide useful accounts, especially on federal courts and on decisions about specialization in the current era.

In my effort to assess primary and secondary evidence about the causes of specialization, three issues arose. The first is a specific one concerning the interpretation of statements about motives in primary sources. People typically have an imperfect understanding of their own motives, and their presentation of those motives is often biased (see Nisbett and Ross 1980, 202–26). In the case of judicial specialization, the most serious potential bias is exaggeration of the importance of the neutral virtues. Policy makers and advocates would prefer to say that they advocate or oppose a proposal for a specialized court because of their concern for virtues such as efficiency than to say that they want to obtain certain judicial policies or to enhance their own status.

This is a significant problem, but in practice it turned out to be less serious than I had expected. One reason is that primary sources often provide the perspectives of many participants in decisions about specialization, including both proponents and opponents of specialization proposals. The multiplicity of participants helps to limit the effects of both inaccurate self-perceptions and bias. Opponents of proposals frequently attribute certain motives to proponents. Those attributions themselves are biased, but they help to correct for the ways that proposals are presented by their supporters.

The other reason is that supporters of judicial specialization are often willing to acknowledge that they are acting on the basis of policy considerations. They do so primarily because they perceive broad support for the policy goals that they hope specialization will advance. This is especially true of criminal law and matters of foreign policy and internal security.

The second issue is what to do when the relevant evidence is relatively limited. There were a few types of specialized state courts, primarily types that exist in a limited number of states, for which primary and secondary sources on the specialization process (and on the impact of specialization) are nonexistent or very skimpy. Those courts are simply not discussed in the book.

Even among the courts that I do discuss, the evidence on some is not extensive. Sometimes this was because the provision that established a specialized federal court or added to its jurisdiction was one part, and far from the most visible part, of broader legislation. But for the courts that I consider, there was always meaningful evidence about the goals that underlay creation of a court. And in the frequent instances in which a new court was modeled on an existing court, the motives behind the earlier decision are relevant to the later decision.

The third issue is how to determine the extent to which choices about specialization were purposive. The volume of evidence in primary sources on the reasons for those choices is one important clue: in general, there is a correlation between how much was said about these reasons during and after a decision and how well thought out the decision was. This clue can be misleading, but the differences in the volume of evidence across decisions were quite substantial. As a result, they provided a good basis for the judgment that some decisions about judicial specialization were highly deliberate and others relatively casual. Participants in decisions to create specialized courts often described how they had come to that choice, and their statements are frequently illuminating on the issue of purposiveness.

The substantial quantity and high quality of evidence about the causes of judicial specialization for many courts and court types facilitated the building of general conclusions about causes. They provide a good basis for judgments on all the issues I have raised about how and why the courts have become more specialized.

THREE

Foreign Policy and Internal Security

Of the functions that the federal government performs, perhaps the most fundamental are conducting foreign policy (including military policy) and maintaining internal security. For that reason, presidents and members of Congress feel the strongest allegiance to the interests of the federal government in these fields. For the same reason, any interests that oppose the efforts of government in these fields are usually at a disadvantage.

Because of those conditions, efforts to prevent courts from acting against government interests can be expected to have greater legitimacy than they have in other fields. Thus, this is a good arena in which to look for the use of judicial specialization to strengthen the government's position in litigation. It is also a good arena in which to examine the consequences of judicial specialization. When policy makers employ specialization to improve outcomes for government, their incentives to make that endeavor successful are especially strong in foreign policy and internal security.

One step that Congress and the president could have taken at some point was to create a specialized court with a monopoly over cases in one of these two fields. There might be a National Security Court to hear all civil and criminal cases about internal security or a Foreign Affairs Court to hear cases involving relations between the United States and other nations. But there is no evidence that presidents or members of Congress have seriously considered such courts.[1]

There seem to be two primary reasons for that fact. The first is that shunting all foreign policy or internal security cases to a special court would have

---

1. There has been serious interest in creating a special court for trials of suspected terrorists, and the title most often given to the proposed court is the National Security Court. (This proposal is discussed in chap. 7.) But such a court would have relatively narrow jurisdiction.

a strong tinge of illegitimacy. That action would be seen as a radical departure from the ideal of generalist courts in the federal judiciary, and it would appear to be a blatant means to favor the government's interests.

The second reason is that generalist federal courts usually uphold the policies of the other branches on foreign policy and internal security when those policies are challenged. They have been especially supportive of presidential prerogatives in foreign policy (Glennon 1990; Koh 1990; Silverstein 1997; see Franck 1992; K. King and Meernik 1999). The courts' support for presidential interests has aroused only limited opposition from Congress, which itself tends to acquiesce to the executive on major foreign policy issues. The courts' stance reflects judicial sympathy for national interests in these fields, and that sympathy may be reinforced by judges' perceptions of pressure against interfering with the government's aims. In any event, federal judges have given the executive and legislative branches only limited cause for complaint with their foreign policy decisions.[2]

Although wholesale judicial specialization has been absent from these fields, Congress and the executive branch have established many specialized courts (some of them tribunals in the executive branch) with narrower responsibilities. Some of these courts have had jurisdiction over important issues in foreign policy and internal security.

These courts vary considerably in their characteristics. Several have taken unusual forms. Indeed, commentators have labeled two of them as the "strangest" federal court, and at least two other courts could contend for that title.

These courts fit into five categories. The first is overseas courts, bodies created to adjudicate cases outside the United States and its territories. The second is the system of military courts to decide criminal and quasi-criminal cases that are brought against military personnel. The third is military tribunals to decide cases involving nonmilitary personnel. Fourth, the Foreign

2. Certainly there are exceptions to this generalization. One noteworthy example in the foreign policy field was the Supreme Court's steel seizure decision of 1952 (*Youngstown Sheet & Tube Co. v. Sawyer*). Another is the series of decisions on the rights of suspected terrorists that culminated in *Boumediene v. Bush* (2008). But it appears that there have been no serious and sustained conflicts between federal courts and the executive branch over foreign policy, and in general judges have sought to avoid such conflicts.

Overall, judges probably have been more willing to countermand the other branches in internal security than in foreign policy. But here too, the courts have tended to acquiesce to the other branches. The Supreme Court's record in freedom of speech cases after World War I, such as *Schenck v. United States* (1919), is one example. And on the whole, the Court took a cautious path in addressing challenges to internal security policies during the cold war period (Casper 1972, 43–84).

Intelligence Surveillance Courts were established in 1978 to review applications for warrants for electronic surveillance in national security matters. Finally, the Removal Court was created in 1996 to hear government requests to "remove" "alien terrorists" from the United States.

In this chapter, I examine courts in each of these categories. One omission is the courts that were created to deal with customs matters. International trade is an important field of foreign policy. But the origins of those courts have more to do with government revenue than with foreign policy, so I discuss them in chapter 5 as adjudicators of government economic interests.

Overseas Courts

When the United States has taken control of foreign lands through wars, it has set up courts and court systems along with other government bodies. This is an important choice, though perhaps an inevitable one. More noteworthy are the courts of more limited jurisdiction that were established in places where the United States did not exercise sovereignty. These courts were specialized primarily by type of litigant and sometimes by type of case as well. They represented alternatives not to the generalist federal courts but to the courts of the countries in whose territories they resided.

The overseas courts resulted from the extension of influence by the United States and European powers into non-Western nations, primarily in Asia. As missionaries, traders, and other citizens of Western countries began to reside in countries such as China and Turkey, Western government officials perceived a need to protect their citizens from the laws and courts of the host nations. The result was a series of treaties from the 1780s on that gave American and European citizens degrees of insulation from the laws of the nations in which they resided. In turn, these treaties led to the creation of consular courts (Hinckley 1906; Raustiala 2006).

American consular courts typically had jurisdiction over disputes between Americans as well as civil and criminal cases in which Americans were defendants. These courts operated under the principle of "extraterritoriality" or "extrality," in that the body of law to be applied was that of the United States rather than the host country. Ambassadors, consuls, and their representatives sat as judges. The consular courts lasted for a long time. They were gradually shut down in the twentieth century, a process that was finally completed when the consular courts in Morocco and Tangier were terminated in the late 1950s (Scully 2001, 4–5).

The use of consular courts to protect the interests of Americans who were residing in other nations was straightforward. The impetus for creation of a nonconsular court in China, the United States Court for China, was more complicated and less obvious. For that reason, the Court for China merits closer examination.[3]

The Court for China was described by one scholar as "probably the strangest federal tribunal ever constituted by Congress" (Bederman 1988, 452). It had power to decide most civil lawsuits and criminal complaints brought against Americans in China.[4] Based in Shanghai, the court also heard cases in other cities. Within the category of American-defendant cases, the court had jurisdiction over cases with relatively large stakes. It also had power to hear appeals from the consular courts in cases with smaller stakes and to supervise the operation of those courts. It was more or less equivalent to a federal district court, and appeals from its decisions went to the Court of Appeals for the Ninth Circuit in San Francisco. Its single judge, however, was given a ten-year term rather than appointment for life.

Dissatisfaction with the consular courts had led to proposals for courts outside the consular system as early as the 1880s (Lobingier 1932, 431–33). There were several grounds for this dissatisfaction, and they were not entirely consistent with each other (Scully 2001, 93–110). Some people cited consuls' lack of legal training and lack of time to focus on judicial duties (U.S. Senate 1905). Others made allegations of corruption on the part of consular officials (Lee 2004, 937–40). A 1904 report on consular justice by a State Department official presented evidence of these problems, especially corruption. That report led President Theodore Roosevelt to propose a Court for China, which the administration "pushed through" Congress in 1906 (Scully 2001, 105).

The court's implicit mandate had several parts (Scully 2001, 109–10). If there was a dominant theme to these mandates, it was an effort to create a more stable legal order. On the criminal side, the court was intended to rein in American residents who engaged in lawless behavior. On the civil side, the key goal was to enhance American trade interests (G. Moore 1994, 76–79). A congressional report quoted a lawyer with experience in Shanghai who argued that American businesses found it difficult to develop working relationships with Chinese and other non-American enterprises because of lack of confidence in the consular courts. "Rather than assume the risk" of dealing with Americans, businesses "will engage in business with British

---

3. This discussion of the Court for China is based largely on Scully (2001).
4. The statute establishing the court can be found in *American Journal of International Law* (1907).

subjects. The British courts are the corner stone of British prestige in the Orient" (U.S. House of Representatives 1906, 2).

By serving these objectives, it was hoped, the new court would provide an example of high-quality justice for the Chinese, especially legal reformers. More important, it would serve American foreign policy interests more directly by showing that the institutions of the United States could protect the rights of Chinese citizens and others with whom Americans came in contact.

In light of its purposes, it is not surprising that the court originally was part of the Department of State. (In 1933 it was transferred to the Justice Department.) The State Department aptly referred to the court as "a part of the machinery for conducting the foreign relations of the United States." (Scully 2001, 184)

The court seems to have been successful in strengthening the American commercial position in China, primarily by creating greater legal certainty (G. Moore 1994, 100–101; Scully 2001, 146–48). On the criminal side of its work, however, the court did not fully live up to its promise (Scully 2001, chaps. 4–6; Lobingier 1932). A single judge presided over the court, and three judges served in that position between 1906 and 1924. The first and last of those judges (Lebbius Wilfley and Charles Lobingier) made strong efforts to control what they saw as inappropriate conduct by Americans in China. In doing so they were seeking to fulfill one of the court's missions, though Judge Wilfley may have given more emphasis to attacking vice and less to regulating commercial activity than Congress wanted.

Those efforts and other actions by the judges led to conflicts with some of the Americans in Shanghai, who used their political influence to undercut the positions of the first three judges.[5] Judge Wilfley weathered an impeachment inquiry in the House Judiciary Committee but resigned semivoluntarily after only two years in the position. Judge Lobingier, who gave more emphasis to commercial litigation, was denied reappointment under pressure from Americans in China. The judge in between, Rufus Thayer, took a more conciliatory stance toward local Americans. But he too aroused local opposition that ultimately drove him from office before his term had expired. The two judges who served between 1924 and the court's abolition

---

5. One rich analysis of the court's operation emphasizes the continuing tensions between the court and the government in Washington that resulted from the court's adaptation to local practices and conditions (Lee 2004). This interpretation suggests that the court was in a fundamentally weak position that its local opponents could exploit through complaints to Washington.

in 1943 played more passive roles, minimizing conflicts with local Americans and thereby avoiding the difficulties that had beset their predecessors.

The unusual conditions under which the Court for China operated limit the conclusions that can be drawn from its performance. The court's early judges sought to carry out what they perceived as mandates from the other branches, although their own preferences also came into play. It appears that they were largely successful in fulfilling their mandate in economic litigation, a mandate that was relatively clear. In criminal justice, however, their efforts were undermined by opposition from Americans in China and a lack of political support from Washington. As much as anything else, the work of the Court for China in criminal cases underlines the limits on what any court can accomplish under difficult circumstances.

If the Court for China is truly the strangest tribunal ever created by Congress, it is only because Congress was not responsible for the United States Court for Berlin.[6] That court was the remaining vestige of successive systems of courts established by American authorities in the sector of Germany that the United States occupied after World War II. The U.S. High Commissioner for Germany established the court in 1955, when the occupation of the U.S. sector of Germany ended but the United States retained a degree of control over a sector of Berlin.

The Court for Berlin was given jurisdiction concurrent with the German courts in Berlin over criminal cases "arising under any legislation in effect in the United States Sector of Berlin if the offense was committed within the area of Greater Berlin" (*United States v. Tiede* 1979, 238). Because of its source in the executive branch, the Court for Berlin could be classified as an Article II court. Defendants had the right of appeal, not to another court but to the U.S. Chief of Mission.

Established formally in 1955, the court never actually operated until 1978, when the State Department identified it as a useful way to deal with a thorny problem. Two East German citizens were charged with hijacking

---

6. This discussion of the U.S. Court for Berlin is based primarily on the book *Judgment in Berlin* by Judge Herbert Stern (1984), who presided over the only case tried in the court. Judge Stern's fascinating account has the unusual feature that the author refers to himself in the third person throughout the book. The court is also discussed in Bederman (1988, 475–88) and Lowenfeld (1985, 1000–1015). Lowenfeld's review of Judge Stern's book raises some questions about Stern's handling of the case.

Judge Stern's book was made into a 1988 movie with the same title. Stern was played by Martin Sheen, some years before Sheen ascended to the Oval Office on television. Having watched the movie as a matter of scholarly duty, I can attest that it is not a great work of cinematic art. Still, it may be the best movie ever made about a specialized federal court.

a Polish plane and ordering it to land in West Berlin. The case was thorny because the hijackers were viewed sympathetically in West Berlin but the U.S. government did not want to undercut its own efforts to punish airline hijackers and thereby deter hijackings. The West German government itself wanted to rid itself of the case and asked the U.S. government to take it. The U.S. reluctantly did so, putting the U.S. Court for Berlin in operation to try the defendants.

To preside over the case the State Department chose Judge Herbert Stern, a federal district judge in New Jersey. It quickly became clear to Judge Stern that the State Department viewed him as one of its employees, subject to its direction. Stern rebelled. Contrary to the wishes of the State Department, he ruled that the defendants were entitled to a jury trial (*United States v. Tiede* 1979). Ultimately, after the jury convicted the one remaining defendant on one of four counts, Stern sentenced him to time already served.

Near the end of this trial, some Berlin citizens brought a lawsuit to the court in an effort to prevent the building of U.S. Army housing in a public park. They argued that because of the unusual circumstances of the case, the court could hear a civil matter. The U.S. Ambassador to Germany directed Stern not to take the case. When Stern balked, he was fired and returned to his regular job as a district judge. The U.S. Court for Berlin shut down and was never reopened.

Another district judge might have behaved differently from Stern, but judicial rebellion was likely for two reasons. First, although the State Department could dismiss a judge from the Court for Berlin, it could not affect the judge's tenure on the federal bench. Second, a judge who was accustomed to independence could hardly be pleased with direction from the executive branch, direction that was highly inconsistent with the self-image of federal judges. Thus the outcome of the *Tiede* case points to some limits on the ability of the government to impose a mission on a court.

Military Justice

A separate system of justice for military personnel follows naturally from the separation between military and civilian life. Thus it is not remarkable that the U.S. military services have used courts-martial to prosecute service personnel for both the equivalents of civilian crimes and violations of military regulations. But some issues concerning military justice do not have obvious answers. One is the form of final review of judgments by courts-martial. Another is the extension of military jurisdiction beyond military personnel.

Review of Courts-Martial

For most of American history, review of verdicts by courts-martial remained within the military. Under procedures that evolved over time, legal officers and commanders participated in the review of verdicts (Walker and Nie-bank 1953, 229–30; Summerford 1973, 36–37). The Supreme Court held in *Dynes v. Hoover* (1858, 82–83) that, with limited exceptions, civilian courts had no role in the review of courts-martial.

Interest in giving civilian courts the power to review courts-martial grew primarily out of World War I and World War II, which brought unprecedented numbers of people into the military. Widespread dissatisfaction with the military justice system spurred limited changes in the system during and after World War I (Lurie 1992, 91–124). More fundamental change came after World War II, with the adoption of the Uniform Code of Military Justice in 1950 (Lurie 1992, chaps. 6–11). One feature of the Uniform Code was creation of the Court of Military Appeals (renamed the Court of Appeals for the Armed Forces in 1994), to serve as the highest court in the military justice system.

The Uniform Code, including the proposed court, was developed by the Morgan Committee (headed by a Harvard professor of law) that the Department of Defense established. The version of the court that Congress adopted differed in some respects from that in the Morgan Committee proposal, but most of its basic features remained the same (Summerford 1973, 40–63).

As enacted, the legislation created a court that was to be located administratively within the Defense Department but that would have civilian judges, three judges with fifteen-year terms. (The number of judges was increased to five in 1989.) The president had power to remove judges for cause prior to the expiration of their terms. The court's jurisdiction to hear appeals from decisions of military boards of review was discretionary except for a few narrow classes of cases. Its review of cases was limited to issues of law.

When Congress considered legislation on the Uniform Code of Military Justice, members and other interested parties gave the proposed court only limited attention. To the extent that the court did get attention, the issue of primary interest was whether to establish any kind of civilian review of military justice. In hearings and debates,[7] supporters of the court proposal

---

7. See U.S. House of Representatives (1949) and U.S. Senate (1949). The Library of Congress has compiled legislative history materials on the Uniform Code at http://www.loc.gov/rr/frd/Military_Law/UCMJ_1950.html. The legislative history is summarized in Willis (1972, 63–71).

argued for the value of civilian review as a way to improve the quality of military justice and to secure the rights of military personnel. Opponents expressed concern about potential interference with the command structure and the operation of the military.

Some witnesses at the congressional hearings and at least one member of Congress suggested that civilian review of military cases go to an existing federal court rather than a new specialized court.[8] A few military lawyers argued for use of the federal court of appeals for the District of Columbia (U.S. Senate 1949, 160–61, 264). One expressed concern that the proposed court would be "under the thumb of the Secretary of Defense" (U.S. House of Representatives 1949, 742).

There was no serious consideration of this alternative. The initial design for the Uniform Code structured the debate over judicial review by proposing a new court, and most participants in the debate seemed to assume that a specialized court was appropriate. The establishment of civilian review was a radical step in itself, in that it breached the long-standing and sharp distinction between the military and civilian courts. To entrust decisions over military justice to generalist federal judges would have been considerably more radical. It is noteworthy that the Supreme Court was not given jurisdiction to review decisions by the Court of Military Appeals (as distinct from hearing cases in separate habeas corpus actions) until 1983.[9] Further, the unique characteristics of military courts suggested the need for a court whose judges were, or would become, experts in the field (Lurie 1992, 242).

Almost as soon as the court was established, its judges sought to enhance the court's status. Some of their goals were symbolic, such as having the court's decisions included in the semiofficial Federal Reporter series. The judges have also sought the concrete benefit of Article III status with life terms (Lurie 1998, xii, 39–43, 185–88). These efforts have enjoyed only limited success. In 1967 Congress did make clear through legislation that the court had Article I status, an action "intended to counter contentions that the court is an instrumentality of the executive branch or that it is an administrative agency within the Department of Defense" (U.S. Senate 1967, 2). Congress also made formal what had been an informal parity

8. The discussion in this and the next paragraph is based in part on my discussion with Jonathan Lurie in March 2008.

9. There remains an unusual limit on that review: the Supreme Court cannot issue a writ of certiorari in a case that the Court of Appeals for the Armed Services chose not to accept under its own discretionary jurisdiction (10 U.S. Code § 867a, 2006). Recent efforts to eliminate this limit are discussed in Becker (2008).

between salaries of judges on the courts of appeals and those on the Court of Military Appeals. But the court's decisions are still not in the Federal Reporter, it remains administratively within the Defense Department, and its judges lack life terms.

Jonathan Lurie's (1998) history of the first three decades of the Court of Military Appeals shows that its record varied considerably over time and that judges differed in their approaches to military justice issues. However, it is clear that the court was not captured by the military. The court did a good deal to import the procedures and rights that existed in civilian courts into the military justice system (Summerford 1973, 136–37). Lurie (1998, 276) summarized its record: "To a greater extent than ever before the Court linked the Bill of Rights to military justice, sought to insulate the courts-martial from improper influence, and worked to insure the independence of the military justice, albeit with limited success" (see also Fidell 1997, 1215).[10] The limits on the court's success resulted from resistance by the military, including efforts to induce defendants to waive their right to appeal to the court (Lurie 1998, 63–64; *United States v. Ponds* 1952).

That resistance was part of the conflict that existed between the court and the military, including top-level military lawyers (see Willis 1972, 91–92). One manifestation of this friction was efforts by the military to limit the court's jurisdiction. The General Counsel of the Defense Department in the Carter administration actually proposed that the court be abolished (Lurie 1998, 257–59). Under this proposal, the intermediate military courts would become the final courts of appeal, except that cases raising constitutional questions would go to the Federal Court of Appeals for the Fourth Circuit. This proposal was basically a tactic in the general counsel's conflict with the chief judge of the court, and it had no chance of adoption. But the proposal underlined the depth of the disagreements that frequently arose between the court and the military.

The court's independence is noteworthy in light of the strong opposition that it faced from the military, although it received compensating support from the American Legion in at least one episode (Lurie 1998, 127–31). The absence of life terms may have had some constraining effects on the court's judges. However, several judges voluntarily left the court after only a few

---

10. The court's decisional tendencies since 1980 are less well documented than its early record, but Lurie (1998, 276) reports that "to some extent" the court "has retreated" from its relatively assertive stance because of the appointments of new judges.

years. One reason was that some judges found the court's work uninteresting (Lurie 1998, 219–20).[11]

It is difficult to estimate how generalist federal judges would have undertaken the same role if they had been substituted for the specialized court as overseers of military justice. They might have been even more assertive, because of their familiarity with the standards of civilian criminal justice. On the other hand, as only occasional reviewers of military cases, they might have been more willing to defer to the military justice system. What we do know is that the Court of Military Appeals demonstrated an independence that reformers favored and that some people in the military feared when the Uniform Code of Military Justice was enacted.

Extending Military Justice Beyond Military Personnel

The idea that civilians should be subject to military justice may seem strange. Yet there is a long history of American military tribunals and commissions that have tried civilians (L. Fisher 2005; Glazier 2005; Richards 2007; Sulmasy 2009, 30–66; Ex parte Quirin 1942, Brief for Respondent, 72–77).[12] Among them are the tribunals established by General Andrew Jackson in New Orleans (during the War of 1812) and Florida (during the Seminole War); the hundreds of military tribunals that operated during the Civil War and Reconstruction; the commission used to try the defendants who were charged with participating in the assassination of President Lincoln; and the provost courts that largely replaced civilian courts in Hawaii during the early part of World War II.

These tribunals arose under quite different circumstances, and the specific purposes for their establishment also differed. But their existence is explained primarily by a single motive. By and large, the civilian and military officials who established military tribunals for trials of civilians were concerned with the outcomes of cases, and they saw tribunals as a means

---

11. The judges have had varied backgrounds, with something of a trend over time toward experience with military justice. Not surprisingly, many have had good political connections in Congress or the executive branch. Biographical information was taken from Lurie (1998) and several other sources.

12. I leave aside the extensions of courts-martial to former military personnel and to families of military personnel, extensions that the Supreme Court ruled out in a series of decisions in the 1950s and early 1960s. See *United States ex rel. Toth v. Quarles* (1955), *Reid v. Covert* (1957), and *Kinsella v. Singleton* (1960).

to secure more desirable outcomes for the government as prosecutor than regular state or federal courts would produce.

In some instances this goal was expressed directly. The Civil War general who established martial law in St. Louis explained that the regular courts "can give us no assistance as they are very generally unreliable" (L. Fisher 2005, 47). Some people argued strongly that the commission created for the Lincoln assassination trial was inappropriate, but Secretary of War Edwin Stanton pushed for a commission to achieve the quick trial and execution of the defendants (Swanson and Weinberg 2001, 19). The Lincoln commission's procedures were unorthodox and unfavorable to the defendants. All the defendants were convicted, though not all were sentenced to death (Swanson and Weinberg 2001; J. Johnston 2001).

The use of military courts in Hawaii during World War II was part of the general military government established in that territory (Anthony 1955; Scheiber and Scheiber 1997). Under an order issued on December 7, 1941, cases involving offenses against federal or territorial law or military orders would go to provost courts (for cases with relatively small stakes) or to a military commission (for serious criminal cases). The civilian courts were closed. As the system evolved over the next several months, civilian courts were allowed to operate and hear some kinds of civil cases, with other cases remaining in the military courts. The military commission was seldom used, but the provost courts decided an estimated fifty-five thousand cases (Scheiber and Scheiber 1997, 516). The judges in provost courts were generally military officers, some of them nonlawyers.

The civilian courts in Hawaii certainly were available to try cases. The decision of military authorities to bypass them largely reflected an interest in the outcomes in cases. One of the officers who devised the military courts ascribed the army's decision to use them to the judgment that "civil judges could not be sufficiently severe under existing civil law, and they could not be given appropriate powers by us" (Scheiber and Scheiber 1997, 517; see 638). Once in operation, the provost courts adopted the pro-prosecution stance that the military authorities wanted, both in their procedures and in case outcomes. For one thing, sentences in the provost courts "almost invariably were stiffer than those prescribed by civil law on conviction for similar offenses" (Scheiber and Scheiber 1997, 516). The provost courts regularly convicted defendants for "failure to report to work" if they were absent or switched jobs without authorization—acts that were offenses under a military order—even for absences of a few hours (Scheiber and Scheiber 1997, 504–5).

The jurisdiction of the civilian courts was largely restored in March 1943.

However, the military courts retained the power to handle prosecutions for violation of military orders, which had a wide scope. (President Roosevelt ended martial law altogether in October 1944.) In a pair of cases that arose from prosecutions before and after March 1943, the Supreme Court ruled that the military's bypass of the civilian courts was illegal (*Duncan v. Kahanamoku* 1946). But like its ruling on the use of military commissions during the Civil War (*Ex parte Milligan* 1866), the ruling came after the war was over and thus had no effect on the practice in question.[13]

Another military court was convened during World War II to hear a single case (G. Cohen 2002; L. Fisher 2003, chaps. 3–4; Dobbs 2004, 204–70). In 1942, eight Germans were deposited by submarines and arrived on the East Coast with the assignment of committing sabotage. The eight were quickly apprehended. The FBI agents who questioned the suspects expected that the case against them would go to a civilian court, but the Roosevelt administration chose to convene a military commission instead.

That route offered several advantages. It might be difficult to secure convictions on the most serious charges in a civilian court. Among other things, the men had not committed any sabotage. Further, in a military commission a unanimous vote would not be required for the death penalty, and the proceedings could be quick and streamlined to favor the prosecution. They could also be secret. That attribute had special appeal because the president and other top officials did not want it known that the Germans had been quickly apprehended only because one of them had turned himself in. Disclosure of that fact would foster uncertainty about the government's ability to prevent and detect sabotage. It would also detract from the heroic image that J. Edgar Hoover sought for the FBI and for himself.

The commission proceeded as desired, convicting the eight men and sentencing them to death. (Only six were actually executed.) The colonel who was assigned to represent the defendants undertook that role with zeal, but the commission was clearly unsympathetic to his position. In the middle of the trial, the Supreme Court agreed to hear a challenge to the commission proceedings. It quickly ruled that the commission proceedings were acceptable,

---

13. However, during the war the federal district court in Hawaii issued several rulings against the provost courts or the imposition of martial law (Scheiber and Scheiber 1997, 606). In one episode, a general evaded service of a writ of habeas corpus issued by a federal district judge. When the judge held the general in contempt, the military government responded with an order forbidding the judge from any further action in the case and threatening the judge with a prison sentence of up to five years if he violated the order (McColloch 1949). The episode was reminiscent of Andrew Jackson's imprisonment of a New Orleans federal judge who had granted a writ of habeas corpus (Fisher 2005, 25–26).

although the Court's full opinion was not released until three months later, long after the executions had taken place (*Ex parte Quirin* 1942). Thus, the Roosevelt administration got what it wanted from the special commission it established.[14]

The effects of using military tribunals varied with the situation. In the Civil War, substituting military judges for judges and juries whose loyalty to the Union was limited undoubtedly made considerable difference to the outcomes of cases. In contrast, even civilian juries might have been inclined to convict the would-be German saboteurs during World War II, because they would have felt internal and external pressures similar to those that led to the Supreme Court's *Quirin* decision. Overall, the various military tribunals accomplished the goal of reducing the risk of outcomes in court that government officials wanted to avoid.

Guantánamo Detainees

The detention of suspected terrorists at the Guantánamo Bay Naval Station beginning in 2002 led to the creation of two types of special tribunals, Combatant Status Review Tribunals (CSRTs) to determine whether detainees should continue to be held and military commissions to try certain detainees for criminal offenses. Both tribunals had roots in past practices, but the special circumstances of the Guantánamo detentions make the choice of specialized tribunals noteworthy.

The CSRTs were established by the George W. Bush administration in response to the Supreme Court's decision in *Rasul v. Bush* (2004). In *Rasul*, the Court ruled that federal courts had the power to hear habeas corpus suits brought by prisoners at Guantánamo. The adverse decision apparently surprised officials in the administration, but they quickly developed a response. A week after the decision was handed down, the Defense Department established the CSRTs to review the detention of prisoners at Guantánamo. The CSRTs would replace a system of annual reviews for detainees, then awaiting its first cases, in which prisoners would have had very limited rights (Lewis and Sanger 2004). In some respects the CSRTs resembled "Article 5 Tribunals," referring to Article 5 of the Third Geneva Convention, which the military had used in other wars to determine the status of people captured

14. Another military tribunal was convened in 1945 to try two other would-be saboteurs from Germany (Fisher 2005, 127–29). Proceeding with little publicity and little Justice Department involvement (in contrast with the 1942 commission), the tribunal convicted the defendants and sentenced them to death. The death sentences were not carried out.

on the battlefield (see Ball 2007, 44–46).[15] In *Hamdi v. Rumsfeld* (2004), a case involving a U.S. citizen who was detained as an enemy combatant, the Court's plurality opinion had suggested that such tribunals might meet the Court's standards for an opportunity to contest detention.

Under the procedure announced by the Defense Department, tribunals would be composed of three military officers.[16] One of the officers would be a judge advocate—an officer who was a lawyer. A detainee would have a military officer as "personal representative," but not a lawyer. Detainees would be given unclassified information about the factual basis for their designation as enemy combatants. Detainees could call witnesses "if reasonably available." Standard rules of evidence would not apply; the tribunal could consider "any information it deems relevant and helpful," including hearsay evidence. The tribunal would decide a detainee's status by majority vote, using a preponderance of evidence standard.

For administration officials, the CSRTs were a way to limit the damage from the *Rasul* decision. They hoped that federal courts would find the CSRT procedure adequate and then turn away habeas corpus actions brought by Guantánamo detainees. Critics of the administration argued that the tribunal procedures were inadequate. One argued that "this counterfeit process was conceived to con the Supreme Court into believing the government was adhering to its June decision" (Hentoff 2004).

Whether or not such criticisms were justified, the Bush administration did devise the CSRT system to limit judicial intervention into Guantánamo. A specialized administrative tribunal provided greater control and reduced the likelihood of orders that detainees be freed. The high priority given to these goals was reflected in the speed with which the CSRT system was announced.

The operation of the tribunals in practice gave some credence to the criticisms that were brought against them at the outset (Denbeaux et al. 2006; Golden 2006). Because so much information was classified and potential defense witnesses were regularly deemed unavailable, detainees had only a limited ability to defend themselves. The great majority of decisions supported continued detention. On the occasions when a tribunal ruled against continued detention, in some instances a second hearing was held with the goal of getting a different ruling. In addition, executive-branch critics of

15. The rules for Article 5 Tribunals are found at Army Regulation 190–8, chap. 1–6 (http://www.army.mil/usapa/epubs/190_Series_Collection_1.html).

16. The rules for the CSRTs are in Paul Wolfowitz, "Memorandum for the Secretary of the Navy," July 7, 2004, at http://www.defense.gov/news/Jul2004/d20040707review.pdf.

tribunals that made rulings favorable to detainees were "allowed to provide further training" to members of the tribunals (Golden 2006, 20).

Stephen Abraham, an army officer who participated in the CSRT process, later attested to the weaknesses of the evidence on which the tribunals acted and the pressures on them to find that detainees were properly classified as enemy combatants (*Al Odah v. United States* 2007: Reply to Opposition to Petition for Hearing, i–viii; U.S. House of Representatives 2007). According to Abraham, when a panel on which he served ruled in favor of a detainee, it was told to reconsider the case; when the panel adhered to its judgment, the case was given to another panel that reached the opposite decision. Abraham was assigned to no more panels. He concluded from his experience that "the CSRT panels were an effort to lend a veneer of legitimacy to the detentions, to 'launder' decisions already made" (U.S. House of Representative 2007, 156).

In *In re Guantánamo Detainee Cases* (2005), Judge Joyce Hens Green of the federal district court for the District of Columbia held in a set of consolidated habeas corpus cases that the CSRT procedures did not meet the requirements of due process. The Detainee Treatment Act of 2005, enacted later in the year, prohibited the courts from hearing habeas corpus actions by Guantánamo detainees. The statute provided that court oversight of CSRT rulings against detainees could occur only in a limited review by the federal court of appeals for the D.C. Circuit.[17]

The Supreme Court ruled in *Hamdan v. Rumsfeld* (2006) that the prohibition on habeas corpus actions did not apply to pending actions. In the Military Commissions Act of 2006, Congress overrode that ruling by making the prohibition on habeas corpus actions retroactive. On the basis of the 2006 Act, the court of appeals for the D.C. Circuit vacated Judge Green's decision and dismissed the detainees' cases (*Boumediene v. Bush* 2007).

The Supreme Court reversed the D.C. Circuit in *Boumediene v. Bush* (2008), holding that the prohibition of habeas corpus actions in the Detainee Treatment Act was unconstitutional because the CSRTs were an inadequate substitute even with reviews in the D.C. Circuit. However, the Court

---

17. In *Bismullah v. Gates* (2007), a panel of the D.C. Circuit issued a mixed decision on procedural issues in the first set of appeals from CSRT rulings determining that detainees were enemy combatants. The court later denied the government's request for an en banc rehearing, with heated opinions on both sides, in *Bismullah v. Gates* (2008). In *Parhat v. Gates* (2008), a panel made the first decision on the merits in a review of a CSRT decision. The ideologically mixed panel overturned the CSRT decision, ruling that the government had not provided sufficient evidence to the CSRT in this case to allow the tribunal to make the judgment required by the statute.

explicitly allowed the CSRTs to continue operation and said that in the absence of undue delay, federal courts should not consider a detainee's habeas petition until after a CSRT had reviewed the detainee's case. In *Bismullah v. Gates* (2009), the D.C. Circuit held that the Supreme Court's decision in *Boumediene* effectively invalidated the D.C. Circuit's review of CSRT decisions, so review would be only in habeas proceedings in district courts. Two weeks later, at the beginning of his presidency, President Obama effectively terminated the CSRTs by establishing an administrative procedure to review the status of all detainees (*Federal Register* 2009).

The other type of special tribunal at Guantánamo, military commissions, was established in late 2001 (Golden 2004a; Gellman 2008, 162–68; Mayer 2008, 80–90). Bush administration officials anticipated bringing charges against Al Qaeda leaders and other suspected terrorists, and they sought to develop a structure for trials on those charges. An interagency group was set up to consider options, and the group identified several possible structures: criminal trials in regular federal courts, courts-martial, mixed civilian-military tribunals, and military commissions. Members of the group disagreed about the merits of the competing options. But the decision ultimately was made by a small group of people, primarily in the White House, who strongly favored the use of military commissions.

President Bush issued an order establishing commissions in November 2001. His order drew from President Roosevelt's order for a commission to try the would-be Nazi saboteurs (Glazier 2005, 6). Under the president's order, non-U.S. citizens suspected of certain offenses related to terrorism would be subject to trial in the commissions, consisting of three to seven members acting as a jury. The presiding officer would be a judge advocate. Rules of evidence were relaxed to allow admission of any evidence that would "have probative value to a reasonable person," "classified or classifiable" evidence could be kept secret, proceedings could be closed, a two-thirds majority would be sufficient for conviction, and no appeal to a regular court was allowed (*Federal Register* 2001).

White House Counsel Alberto Gonzales (2001) cited multiple advantages for the commissions over regular criminal trials:

> They spare American jurors, judges and courts the grave risks associated with terrorist trials. They allow the government to use classified information as evidence without compromising intelligence or military efforts. They can dispense justice swiftly, close to where our forces may be fighting, without years of pretrial proceedings or post-trial appeals. And they can consider the broadest range of relevant evidence to reach their verdicts.

Military commissions were also viewed as superior to courts-martial. As one Defense Department attorney later explained, the Uniform Code of Military Justice is "more solicitous of the rights of the accused than our civilian courts. Alternative processes are necessary to avoid the absurd result of adopting protections for terrorists that American civilians do not receive in civilian court" (Goldman 2006, 1).

Other accounts of the commission rules spelled out the kinds of evidence that commissions could consider but that other courts might not. Among this evidence was classified information that might be inadmissible in court, information gathered from suspects without limitations imposed by procedural rules and defense lawyers and, more specifically, evidence from confessions that were obtained through coercive interrogations (Golden 2004a; Swift 2007). In themselves, the language of the original presidential order and the rationales offered for the choice of commissions make it clear that this was a classic case of judicial specialization as a means to obtain more desirable outcomes in litigation. Strongly interested in securing convictions and in avoiding problems that might arise from regular criminal proceedings, administration officials saw military commissions as an attractive alternative.

It turned out to be very difficult to put the commissions in place at Guantánamo, where prospective defendants were held (Golden 2004b; Locy 2004; Blum 2005; Goldsmith 2007, 121–22). Considerable time was required to establish detailed rules for the commissions. There was uncertainty about which detainees to prosecute, and some Administration officials thought it might be better simply to hold suspects indefinitely than to try them and risk an acquittal. When cases were actually brought, military lawyers who were assigned to represent defendants played more aggressive roles than had been expected, and preliminary proceedings in the early cases exposed weaknesses in commission procedures. Perceptions that the commission process was fundamentally unfair were supported by the disclosure of messages from two prosecutors, one of whom wrote to the chief prosecutor that "you have repeatedly said to the office that the military panel will be handpicked and will not acquit these detainees" (N. Lewis 2005).

One of the early cases moving toward trial in a military commission, that of Salim Hamdan, was interrupted in 2004 by the decision of a federal district judge in the District of Columbia. This decision held that President Bush had lacked the power to set up the military commissions. The district court decision was reversed on appeal, but the Supreme Court ultimately ruled that the commissions had not been authorized by Congress and that their structure and procedures violated the Uniform Code of Military Justice and the Geneva Conventions (*Hamdan v. Rumsfeld* 2006).

In response to the Court's decision, the administration secured the enactment of provisions in the Military Commissions Act of 2006 that authorized commissions similar to those established in 2001. But problems continued. In June 2007, presiding judges on two commissions, Keith Allred and Peter Brownback, dismissed charges against Hamdan and Omar Khadr, respectively, on the ground that commissions could try only suspects who had been determined to be "unlawful enemy combatants" and that CSRTs had established only that Hamdan and Khadr were "enemy combatants" (*United States v. Hamdan* 2007; *United States v. Khadr* 2007a; Glaberson 2007a).

The Military Commissions Act authorized a Court of Military Commission Review to hear appeals from guilty findings by defendants and interlocutory appeals by the prosecution. The Court of Review would be composed of appellate military judges appointed by the Secretary of Defense. When the prosecutor appealed from the *Khadr* ruling, the Defense Department moved quickly to set up the Court of Review, appointing four civilians and twelve military officers.[18] A panel of three military judges reversed Judge Brownback's decision, holding that commissions themselves could determine whether a defendant was an unlawful enemy combatant (Glaberson 2007b; *United States v. Khadr* 2007b). The Court of Review has since ruled on preliminary issues in four other cases. It has denied defendants' requests for writs of mandamus in two cases, dismissed a prosecution motion on the ground that it had been made too late, and dismissed a prosecution appeal as moot after charges against the defendant were dropped.[19]

The first disposition of a case by a military commission was that of David Hicks, an Australian who accepted a plea bargain in 2007 under which he was sent to Australia to serve a nine-month jail sentence. In exchange for the short sentence Hicks agreed to several conditions, including a promise not to allege illegal treatment by the United States, a waiver of appeals and lawsuits, and a twelve-month gag order. The last provision would keep Hicks silent until after the Australian national elections, and the plea bargain

18. Some people raised questions about the impartiality of the civilian judges because of their prior activities and statements relating to the commission system (Bravin 2007). One of the four, Chief Justice Frank Williams of the Rhode Island Supreme Court, had indicated strong sympathy for the Bush administration's positions on the legal rights of suspected terrorists (Tucker 2008; F. Williams, Dulude, and Tracey 2007).

19. Information on the cases and the court's rulings is at http://www.defense.gov/news/courtofmilitarycommissionreview.html.

apparently resulted from the initiative of the Australian Prime Minister under pressure from the public (C. Rosenberg 2007; J. White 2007). An observer for the Law Council of Australia referred to the proceedings as "shambolic" (Lasry 2007, 3).

The first completed trial was that of Hamdan in 2008, presided over by Judge Allred. The trial began after a federal district judge in the District of Columbia ruled that challenges to the commission procedures could come only after a trial was completed (Shane and Glaberson 2008). Hamdan, who had been a driver for Osama bin Laden, was charged with conspiracy to commit terrorist acts and providing material support for terrorism. The commission jury convicted him of the material support charge but acquitted him on the conspiracy charge. The prosecution asked for a sentence of at least thirty years' imprisonment, but the jury sentenced him to sixty-six months, and Judge Allred gave him credit for the sixty-one months that he had already served.

A second trial was completed in 2008. After offering no defense, Ali Hamza al Bahlul was convicted of acting as a propagandist for Osama bin Laden and received a life sentence (Glaberson 2008). At the beginning of 2009, more than a dozen cases were in pretrial proceedings.

After ordering a suspension of commission proceedings, President Obama later decided to continue the commissions with modified procedural rules, choosing between commissions and the federal district courts on a case-by-case basis. A preliminary report by an administration task force indicated that among the criteria for this choice would be "evidentiary issues" and "the extent to which the forum would permit a full presentation of the accused's wrongful conduct." This language suggested that the administration would resort to military commissions when important evidence would be inadmissible in federal court (M. Davis 2009; Savage 2009b). However, the report and President Obama did indicate that evidentiary standards in commission proceedings would be tightened in some respects.[20] And later in the year, the administration decided to use a federal district court to try detainees who were accused of conspiring in the September 2001 terrorist attacks, despite strong disagreement from members of Congress and others who preferred military commissions for these cases (Savage 2009a).

In the proceedings that occurred during the Bush administration, judges varied considerably in their responses to cases. In rulings on motions, some

20. The preliminary report is available at http://www.justice.gov/opa/documents/preliminary-rpt-dptf-072009.pdf. President Obama's May 2009 remarks are available at http://www.whitehouse.gov/the-press-office/remarks-president-national-security-5-21-09.

judges seemed to give short shrift to defendants' claims, but others took them quite seriously (Wald 2009, xvii). The dismissals of charges by Judges Allred and Brownback were noteworthy, as were several pro-defendant rulings by Judge Stephen Henley in another case (*United States v. Jawad* 2008a, 2008b, 2008c, 2008d; see C. Rosenberg 2008b). The outcome of the Hamdan trial was noteworthy because the sentence handed down in that case contrasted with the more severe sentences given to some defendants convicted of terrorism-related offenses in federal district courts.

The formal character of the commission proceedings, which include "vigorous representation" (Wald 2009, xvi) by true defense attorneys, probably helps to explain the rulings by those three judges. Also relevant is the fact that all three had experience as military judges, an experience that likely affected their role perceptions.[21] It is true that they lacked the independence of federal judges. Indeed, Judge Brownback was replaced (and returned to retired status) during pretrial proceedings in the *Khadr* case after he threatened to suspend the case because some of the defendant's records at Guantánamo had not been provided to the defense (C. Rosenberg 2008a). But the backgrounds of these judges distinguished them from most military personnel who have served on tribunals over the past two centuries. And their expertise in military justice may have given them a confidence in their judgment that generalist federal judges would have lacked if they heard only a single military case.

The CSRTs adhered to their mission more fully. Beyond the attributes of the personnel who staffed them, this difference seems to have two sources. The first is the rules under which the CSRTs operated, which made it difficult for detainees to meet what was effectively a heavy burden of proof. The second is the environment in which the CSRT panelists worked, which put them under pressure to find that detention was appropriate. In both respects the difference with regular federal courts is clear, though even federal judges may feel pressure not to order a detainee's release. If district judges decide several habeas corpus cases brought by Guantánamo detainees, there will be a better basis for comparing those courts with the CSRT panels.

The Foreign Intelligence Surveillance Courts

In *Katz v. United States* (1967), the Supreme Court held that gathering of evidence through electronic surveillance was subject to the rules of the Fourth

---

21. Biographies of the three judges are posted at http://media.miamiherald.com/smedia/ 2008/04/02/10/judgesbios.source.prod_affiliate.56.pdf.

Amendment, including the requirement of a warrant. But the federal government continued to engage in electronic surveillance for national security purposes without obtaining warrants. In *United States v. United States District Court* (1972), the Supreme Court ruled that "domestic security surveillance" (as distinguished from surveillance of "foreign powers or their agents") required a warrant. Justice Powell's majority opinion suggested that Congress could adopt standards for determination of probable cause that differed from those for standard criminal cases. Powell also suggested that "in sensitive cases" the request for a warrant could go to a judge on a "specially designated court," such as the federal district court or court of appeals for the District of Columbia (*United States v. United States District Court* 1972, 323).

Half a dozen years later, Congress acted on the Court's suggestion. The Foreign Intelligence Surveillance Act of 1978 (FISA) required a warrant for surveillance whose target was a foreign power or an agent of a foreign power if the surveillance may capture communications of a "United States person" such as an American citizen or a noncitizen who was a permanent legal resident of the United States. The warrant application would go to one of seven district court judges from seven different circuits who had been detailed to the Foreign Intelligence Surveillance Court (often called the FISA court) by the chief justice for part-time service for a maximum of seven years. (The Patriot Act of 2001 expanded the number to eleven.)[22] If that judge denied the application, the government could appeal to the Foreign Intelligence Surveillance Court of Review, a set of three district court or court of appeals judges also detailed by the chief justice.

The FISA court is another contender for the "strangest" title: one commentator referred to it as "most certainly the strangest creation in the history of the federal Judiciary" (Bamford 1982, 368). In some respects the court operates in a standard way. Its judges follow the standard practice of considering warrant applications in private and ex parte, without anyone in court opposing the application. But the requirements for granting of warrants depart from the usual standard. The probable cause that the government needs to establish is only for the fact that the target of surveillance was a foreign power or an agent of a foreign power and that each of the places for

---

22. As of 2009, judges rotate through weeklong service on the court (Palazzolo 2009). According to one report, the George W. Bush administration obtained a set of orders it sought in 2007 (discussed later in this section) by waiting for a "friendly judge" to come on rotation (Bamford 2008, 291–92).

the surveillance was or would be used by a foreign power or its agent. This rule limits the judge to a narrow inquiry.

Warrant applications are also required to describe "minimization procedures" to limit the acquisition, retention, and dissemination of information gathered about U.S. persons to what is necessary for legitimate purposes. This provision was intended in part to prevent the use of FISA procedures for inappropriate law enforcement purposes. In practice, the minimization requirement is not difficult to meet (H. Schwartz 1981).

Congress anticipated that the court would operate under special security measures. The court met in a special secure room in the Department of Justice headquarters until 2009, when it moved into a secure area in a federal courthouse (Wilber 2009). Judges have to go through security clearances before they become members of the court (*Legal Times* 1997, 20).[23]

Congress considered judicial review of proposed domestic security surveillance for several years before enacting legislation. Some members opposed such review altogether as an inappropriate encroachment on the executive branch. But the Supreme Court's 1972 decision, a subsequent decision by the federal court of appeals for the District of Columbia (*Zweibon v. Mitchell* 1975), and disclosures about inappropriate surveillance by the executive virtually guaranteed that a warrant requirement would be established (see Cinquegrana 1989, 803–7).

Congress had to decide whether warrant requests would go before federal district judges at large, either in the country as a whole or in the District of Columbia, or to district judges chosen for that duty by the chief justice. That choice was considered explicitly by witnesses at hearings and by members of Congress. Those who expressed a view about the choice raised several issues. One consideration was the potential improvement in security if only a limited number of judges participated in these cases (U.S. Senate 1977, 10). Another was the expertise that specialization might bring (U.S. House of Representatives 1978, 148). Still another was the impact of specialization on the stances of judges toward government applications. Some people depicted the specialization of judges as a means to bring about closer and more expert scrutiny of the government's requests and practices (U.S. Senate 1977, 151–52; U.S. Congress 1978a). Others, however, thought that these judges would be too favorable to the government, in part because of their

23. Griffin Bell (1982, 105), Attorney General in 1978, reported that he persuaded Chief Justice Warren Burger to reject the CIA director's proposal that the court's judges undergo lie-detector examinations by the CIA and be investigated by the agency.

appointment by the chief justice (U.S. Congress 1978a, 9150; U.S. Senate 1976, 119).

The Administrative Office of the U.S. Courts suggested that if certain district judges were designated to rule on warrant applications, they should be made members of a special court, so that their power to hear cases from outside their districts would be clear (U.S. House 1978, 68, 73–74). The Senate passed a bill that included a specialized court to hear warrant applications, and a similar bill came to the House floor. The specialized court was eliminated in a House amendment by more than a two-to-one margin. That vote reflected an earlier House amendment that had narrowed the range of cases in which warrants were needed, but the short debate on the amendment indicated some suspicion of "special courts" (U.S. Congress 1978b, 28172–73). Northern Democrats were split evenly on the amendment. The overwhelming conservative support for it may have reflected negative views of the legislation as a whole more than negative views of the court proposal. The narrowing amendment was later eliminated, and the specialized trial and appellate courts were restored in conference.[24]

Because of the multiplicity of considerations involved, it is not certain why Congress created the FISA court rather than sending cases to the regular district courts. But that decision can be put in the context of the legislation as a whole. The statute placed a significant limit on executive-branch power, but some major provisions favored the executive. Most important was the narrow scope of judicial scrutiny into the basis for a warrant. Further, denial of a warrant could be appealed to the Court of Review[25] and then to the Supreme Court, with ex parte hearings at both stages. In contrast, there was no mechanism to appeal the issuance of a warrant. Finally, judges were required to write opinions only if they denied applications. Thus, the creation of a special court whose members would be selected by a conservative chief justice can be understood as part of a congressional effort to ensure that the restrictions on executive-branch prerogatives would not be too onerous (see Meason 1990, 1046–47).

Once established, the FISA court labored for many years in obscurity, an obscurity that resulted primarily from the secrecy of its proceedings and outcomes. The court's required annual reports did disclose that applications

---

24. The process that led to enactment of the legislation in 1978 is summarized in *Congressional Quarterly Almanac* (1978b).

25. To reduce confusion, I should note that I use the same abbreviated name for the Foreign Intelligence Surveillance Court of Review that I did for the Military Commission Court of Review.

for warrants were never rejected.[26] One result was that the Court of Review had never met. The number of applications submitted to the FISA court averaged around five hundred per year through the early 1990s, after which it grew somewhat and reached about one thousand in 2000.[27]

Commentators differed in their interpretations of this record (Cinquegrana 1989, 815). Some saw the court as essentially captured by the executive branch (Meason 1990, 1052). A law professor who had sat in on FISA court proceedings as an intern for the National Security Agency (NSA) said that "I was convinced that the judge . . . would have signed anything that we put in front of him" (Bamford 2006, 65). Others argued that the self-restraint of the executive branch accounted for its perfect success rate, in that it sent forward only strong applications (Maitland 1982).[28] Royce Lamberth, presiding judge of the FISA court, pointed out that the court required revision of some applications before approving them (*Legal Times* 1997, 18).[29] It is difficult to choose between these competing interpretations. As one member of Congress said of the government's record of success, "Either the act is working perfectly, or it really isn't working very well at all" (Kurkjian 1986).

Perhaps the record would have been appreciably different if cases had gone randomly to federal district judges rather than to members of a specialized court. In the view of some observers, appointment strategies by Chief Justices Burger and Rehnquist (McQuillan 1982, A28; Ruger 2007) or self-selection by district judges (Posner 2006, 101) populated the court with judges who were inclined in the government's favor. One commentator concluded that judges' frequent participation in these cases caused them to adopt a point of view favorable to the government—a form of capture (Meason 1990, 1052).

---

26. One application *was* rejected. But this rejection came at the request of the Reagan administration, which brought an application as a means to secure a ruling that the FISA court had no jurisdiction over physical searches (Cinquegrana 1989, 821–23). In 1994 Congress gave that jurisdiction to the FISA court.

27. Data from the annual reports are compiled at the Web site of the Electronic Privacy Information Center (http://epic.org/privacy/wiretap/stats/fisa_stats.html).

28. In a later era the New York City police commissioner complained that the Justice Department set too high a standard for its applications. Attorney General Michael Mukasey responded by defending that standard as a means to maintain the department's credibility (D. Johnston and Rashbaum 2008).

29. Behind the scenes, Lamberth chastised the Justice Department for making applications with what he saw as false or misleading information about the bases for the applications, and he prohibited one FBI official from further appearances in the court (Lichtblau 2008, 164–65). Still, no applications were rejected.

On the other hand, the narrow scope of the court's inquiry under the statute and the ex parte character of the proceedings would have affected the decisions of any judge. One commentator said the function of the FISA court is "at best a clerical and managerial one." The role of the court "has been limited to ensuring formalistic adherence to very narrow requirements that are not much more involved than making sure that the executive branch has dotted all its 'I's' and crossed all its 'T's'" (Meason 1990, 1057). Under this constraint, regular district judges probably would have ruled in favor of the government in at least the overwhelming majority of cases. After all, judges typically approve applications for ordinary search warrants at high rates, even though they have a wider scope of inquiry for these applications than do judges on the FISA court (Wittes 1996, 24).

Since 2002, the FISA court has become considerably more visible. This change stemmed primarily from the terrorist attacks in September 2001 (Kornblum 2003; N. Baker 2006, 162–65). Some Bush administration officials blamed the government's inability to prevent the attacks on limits on participation of law enforcement officials in investigations that involved surveillance, limitations that grew out of FISA. The administration sought and obtained amendments to FISA in the USA Patriot Act of 2001, including a change in language that allowed warrants under FISA if intelligence gathering was "a significant purpose" of surveillance rather than "the purpose." Attorney General John Ashcroft issued guidelines in March 2002 that eliminated the "wall" between intelligence and law enforcement. Another 2001 statute expanded the period when surveillance could take place without FISA court approval from twenty-four to seventy-two hours.

In a May 2002 decision, *In re All Matters Submitted to the Foreign Intelligence Surveillance Court*, the FISA court assessed the Ashcroft guidelines under the FISA statute. The court's decision and opinion became public several months later, after the Senate Judiciary Committee requested it. The opinion, joined by all the judges, was striking for its assertion of independence. The court held that the new guidelines were invalid under the minimization requirements of FISA, even with its 2001 amendment, and it rewrote some portions of the guidelines.

The government appealed the decision, putting the Court of Review into operation for the first time. Although the appeal was ex parte, the court allowed the American Civil Liberties Union and the National Association of Criminal Defense Lawyers to file amicus curiae briefs. In November 2002, under the title *In re: Sealed Case No. 02–001*, the Court of Review reversed the FISA court and upheld the Ashcroft guidelines. The court's opinion laid out an expansive reading of the government's powers under the original

FISA law and its 2001 amendment and gave a narrow reading to Fourth Amendment limitations on the government. It cited as a basis for the court's decision the threat of terrorism and the possibility that limits on law enforcement personnel had helped to prevent detection of plans for the 2001 terrorist attacks. The three judges on the Court of Review were all Reagan appointees, including one (Laurence Silberman of the D.C. Circuit) who was a leading conservative legal thinker. The Supreme Court refused to consider a petition to hear the case from the amici and two Arab-American groups, presumably on the ground that the Court lacked jurisdiction (Greenhouse 2003).

In 2005 the *New York Times* disclosed that a secret 2002 presidential order had allowed the NSA to monitor phone calls and electronic mail messages of people in the United States to recipients outside the country without obtaining warrants from the FISA court (Risen and Lichtblau 2005).[30] One commentator later speculated that the increasing frequency with which the court modified the terms of warrants it approved after 2000 helped to motivate the president's action (Bamford 2006, 66). More broadly, it appears that administration officials found the warrant procedure burdensome and preferred to avoid it (Leonnig and Linzer 2005b). David Addington, legal counsel to Vice President Cheney, reportedly said of the FISA court in 2004 that "we're one bomb away from getting rid of that obnoxious court" (Goldsmith 2007, 181).

The two presiding judges of the court during the 2002–5 period were informed of the NSA program during that time. Judge Lamberth and his successor as presiding judge, Judge Colleen Kollar-Kotelly, made efforts to limit the use of information from NSA wiretaps to obtain FISA warrants (Lichtblau 2008, 166–67, 171–73; Bamford 2008, 116–17). Other judges on the court were unaware of the NSA program. After its existence became public, Judge James Robertson resigned from the court (remaining a district judge), indicating privately that he was doing so because of the NSA program (Leonnig and Linzer 2005a; Lichtblau 2008, 216–17). Other judges on the FISA court also expressed resentment privately. According to one newspaper source, "What I've heard some of the judges say is they feel they've participated in a Potemkin court" (Leonnig and Linzer 2005a).

The administration agreed to provide a briefing for judges on the court, apparently in an effort to mollify them. In 2006 Senator Arlen Specter

---

30. In 2007 the Director of National Intelligence disclosed that this program was only one of several secret surveillance activities the administration had initiated (Eggen 2007; see Klaidman 2008 and Offices of Inspectors General 2009).

submitted a bill asking the FISA court to determine whether the NSA program was constitutionally acceptable, but the bill did not get far. Then, in January 2007, Attorney General Alberto Gonzales reported in a letter that a FISA court judge had issued orders authorizing the kind of surveillance that had been involved in the NSA program, subject to the court's approval, so the president would not need to reauthorize that program.[31] The content of the orders was uncertain (Lichtblau and Johnston 2007; P. Baker 2007; see Bamford 2008, 291–92).[32] According to one report, rulings later in 2007 by other FISA court judges gave a narrower interpretation to the administration's powers (Bamford 2008, 298; see Harris 2010, 334).

The administration ultimately sought legislation to broaden its surveillance powers and to provide immunity from lawsuits to the telecommunication companies that had cooperated with the NSA program. That effort resulted in part from a ruling by a FISA court judge, one that apparently ruled out warrantless surveillance of communications between two foreign points that were routed through the United States (Gr. Miller 2007). In 2007 the administration obtained a provision that expanded its surveillance powers for six months.

After considerable debate, Congress in 2008 amended the 1978 law in several respects.[33] It required FISA warrants for surveillance of U.S. citizens overseas, allowed surveillance without warrants under some new circumstances (including the situation in which the FISA court judge apparently had disallowed warrantless surveillance), and gave immunity to the telecommunications companies. The new law did say that electronic surveillance was allowable only if authorized by statute. But a future president might adopt President Bush's position that the president has inherent powers in this area that cannot be constrained by statute.

The record of the FISA court since 2001, like its earlier record, is difficult to interpret—in part because of the secrecy of some key decisions. But the

---

31. The letter is at http://www.talkingpointsmemo.com/docs/nsa-doj-surveillance/.

32. Chief Judge Kollar-Kotelly said she was willing to make the orders public, but the administration opposed that action. The court ultimately ruled against an American Civil Liberties Union motion to make the orders public (*In re Motion for Release of Court Records* 2007).

33. Foreign Intelligence Surveillance Act of 1978 Amendments Act (2008). In *In re: Directives [Redacted Text] Pursuant to Section 105B of the Foreign Intelligence Surveillance Act* (2008), the Court of Review upheld a FISA court decision that had rejected a telecommunication company's challenge to a government directive requiring it to assist in surveillance of certain customers without a warrant. The government's action was based on the temporary 2007 statute. The unnamed company had challenged the directive on Fourth Amendment grounds. The implications of the decision are discussed in Wilber and Smith (2009) and *Los Angeles Times* (2009).

court has played a somewhat more independent role than in the preceding period. One reason is the aggressiveness of the Bush administration.

As in the earlier period, it is quite uncertain whether judicial policy would have differed substantially if warrant requests had gone to federal judges at large rather than to a court dedicated to those cases. Judges who seldom heard warrant requests might have lacked familiarity with the issues and succession of cases and thus would have been hesitant to rule against the executive branch. Indeed, presiding judge Lamberth argued that because of their lack of experience in the area, district judges were inclined to reject challenges to "national security letters" that the FBI employed to demand that records about people be provided to it (Lichtblau 2008, 94–95). On the other hand, judges who came to specific cases without immersion in the FISA program might have been even more skeptical of the executive. In either case, judges' stance ultimately would have had only limited impact because of the Bush administration's bypass of the court and its capacity to obtain favorable legislation on issues involving terrorism.

The Removal Court

The final candidate for the "strangest" title is the Alien Terrorist Removal Court, usually called the Removal Court. This court is unusual in two respects. First, although it was intended to strengthen the government's hand in removing noncitizens who are suspected terrorists from the United States, it actually increased the role of the judiciary in oversight of efforts to remove noncitizens. Second, more than a decade after the court was authorized and its members appointed, it has never actually heard a case.

"Removal" is the official term for deportation. Removal proceedings occur primarily within the executive branch (Legomsky 2006, 371–85). The Department of Homeland Security (successor to the Immigration and Naturalization Service in this function) acts as a prosecutor at hearings before immigration judges, who are part of a Justice Department agency. Either side may appeal an immigration judge's decision to the Board of Immigration Appeals (BIA), also within the Justice Department. A person who contests removal on certain grounds can petition a federal court of appeals for review of an unfavorable BIA decision.

The Reagan administration argued that the immigration laws created a problem: when the Justice Department sought to remove noncitizens for terrorist activity, it could not use classified information as part of its case. That administration proposed that a court be established to consider these cases, with the power to order removal on the basis of classified information. A version of that proposal ultimately was enacted in 1996 as part of a broad bill that dealt with issues ranging from habeas corpus to plastic explosives.[34]

As enacted, the legislation established a court that followed the model of the FISA court in some respects. The chief justice would designate five district judges to sit on the court for five-year terms, and the chief could choose judges who already sat on the FISA court. When the attorney general possessed classified information that a noncitizen was an "alien terrorist," the attorney general could initiate a removal proceeding by filing an application with the removal court. A judge on the court would consider the application in a secret, ex parte proceeding. The judge was directed to grant the application if the judge found that the person was indeed an alien terrorist and that an ordinary removal proceeding with open evidence would pose a risk to national security. A judge who denied the application was required to put the reasons for denial in writing, and the government could appeal that ruling to the federal court of appeals for the District of Columbia in another secret, ex parte proceeding.

If the application was granted, the removal proceeding would go on a special track. The proceeding would take place in court rather than within the Justice Department.[35] The key difference with an ordinary removal hearing is that the subject of the hearing would be given only a nonclassified summary of the evidence brought forward in support of removal. Either side could appeal to the Court of Appeals for the District of Columbia.

Other provisions of the 1996 statute received considerably more attention in Congress. The inclusion of this provision in the statute reflected the advocacy of Senator Robert Smith of New Hampshire, growing concern about terrorism in the United States, and the frustration of Justice Department officials with difficulties in removing people whom they suspected of terrorism (Wittes 1996b; Valentine 2002). Supporters of this provision ascribed these difficulties to the existing procedures, and they argued that the provision struck a reasonable balance between national security needs and the rights of noncitizens who were threatened with removal (U.S. Senate 1996; U.S. House of Representatives 1996).

34. Antiterrorism and Effective Death Penalty Act of 1996. The provisions dealing with the new court are sections 501–507.

35. The legislation is not explicit about the court in which the proceeding would occur. Some commentators have assumed that cases would go to district courts, but other evidence indicates that they would remain in the Removal Court.

Chief Justice Rehnquist appointed members of the court in 1996. Advocates for the Removal Court proposal indicated that the court would have only limited business, but it is safe to say that nobody anticipated it would never be used. Explanations for this outcome differ (Shesgreen 2001). One explanation is that the government never found it necessary to go to the court, in part because other changes in legal rules made it easier to remove people through regular procedures and because the government frequently found grounds other than terrorism as bases for removal (Wittes 1997, 20; Gamboa 2001; Steinbock 2005, 73n324; Lunday and Rishikof 2008, 111n89). But some people have argued that the procedure was unattractive to government officials because of the requirement that a summary of the evidence for removal be given to the person who was the subject of a hearing, a requirement that was not in Senator Smith's original proposal (Valentine 2002).[36] Smith proposed in 2001 that the Justice Department be allowed to keep all evidence secret from suspected terrorists. His proposal was not enacted,[37] and the Removal Court has yet to hear its first case.

Discussion

The absence of specialized courts with broad jurisdiction over foreign policy or internal security is noteworthy, but there has been a good deal of judicial specialization in these fields. The military justice system below the top level might be regarded as inevitable. That system aside, Congress and officials in the executive branch have established an array of specialized tribunals in foreign policy and national security, and these tribunals have been given some important types of cases to decide.

The choice between generalists and specialists was given more extensive consideration in some instances than in others, but it was usually made quite consciously. Decisions to give jurisdiction to specialized courts have been motivated primarily by efforts to protect the perceived interests of the federal government. One interest sometimes is secrecy, as it was with the tribunal to try the would-be German saboteurs in 1942. Overall, however, the

36. Although all evidence ordinarily must be disclosed in proceedings in immigration court, the Immigration and Naturalization Service introduced evidence in some proceedings that was classified as secret and not disclosed to the defense (Committee on Immigration and Nationality Law 2004; Cockburn 2000).

37. However, Congress did adopt a provision requiring the attorney general to submit a report on why the Removal Court had not been used, as section 313 of the Intelligence Authorization Act for Fiscal Year 2002 (2001), and there was also an understanding that a Senate hearing would be held on the subject (Distaso 2001). I have not found any record of a report or hearing.

primary interest has been in obtaining case outcomes that federal officials favored. The government is typically in a strong position in criminal justice as investigator and prosecutor; officials sought to strengthen that position through certain forms of judicial specialization.

Each specialized court discussed in this chapter was proposed by the executive branch, and most were established unilaterally by the executive. When Congress acted on an executive-branch proposal, its members typically focused less on judicial specialization than on other aspects of the bills they considered. They gave more attention to basic provisions of the Uniform Code of Military Justice than to the Court of Military Appeals, and they focused on the advisability of giving any federal court power over electronic surveillance in national security cases rather than on the proposal for a specialized court. (The Court for China, established in stand-alone legislation, was an exception.) Enactment of broader legislation that created specialized courts typically reflected support for the purposes of the legislation as a whole rather than support for specialization as such.

Policy makers frequently have drawn from the examples of past and current courts when they created new ones. Military tribunals became established as an alternative to civilian courts early in the nation's history, and that option has been used several times in different circumstances. The past use of tribunals is sometimes used as a justification for new uses, and the 1942 commission to try would-be saboteurs provided a model for the military commissions that President Bush established for Guantánamo detainees (Glazier 2005, 6–7). Similarly, the Removal Court followed the design of the FISA court in important respects.

How successful has specialization been in serving the interests of the federal government as a litigant? That question is difficult to answer, because there is no specialized court in these fields that has a direct generalist counterpart. Still, the record provides some hints about the effects of specialization.

The clearest hint is that these effects vary with the backgrounds of the people who serve on specialized courts. At one end of the spectrum, the Court for Berlin and the surveillance courts have been staffed by judges who were borrowed from generalist courts. Such judges bring their judicial experience with them, and they also bring an expectation of judicial independence. That expectation may have been reflected in the negative reactions of judges on the FISA court to actions of the George W. Bush administration, and it certainly was reflected in Judge Stern's rebellion against the State Department in Berlin. At the other end of the spectrum, most members of military tribunals have been nonlawyers who were detailed to those tribunals as part of their military duties. Such judges could be expected to accept the pro-prosecution mission for which their court was created, and in general they have done so.

Other factors also affect the performance of specialized courts in this field. Some courts have operated under rules that channel their decisions in a particular direction, and that channeling can exert a powerful effect. The narrow scope of review that the FISA court was allowed to undertake probably guaranteed a very high rate of success for warrant applications, and the government might well have been equally successful if the regular district courts had ruled on those applications. Like some other military tribunals, the Combat Status Review Tribunals at Guantánamo were severely constrained by the rules that governed their operation. The rules under which the Guantánamo military commissions operated were not so skewed, leaving more room for an independent stance by officers who had experience as judges.

The relative neutrality of the rules under which the Court of Appeals for the Armed Forces operates helps to account for the court's record in its first three decades. The establishment of a court to deal specifically with criminal appeals from the military and the tendency to appoint judges with military experience (and putting the court administratively within the Defense Department) might be expected to foster capture of the court by the military and produce a strong orientation in favor of the government. But the court's judges were outside the military itself, and they reviewed cases under rules that were essentially the same as those that govern criminal appeals in civilian cases. In combination with the expertise that the judges developed through their specialization in military cases, these rules made possible the considerable assertiveness that the court displayed.

The courts that were considered in this chapter stand largely outside the legal mainstream in that they have dealt with unusual types of cases, often under unusual conditions. The chapters that follow examine courts within the mainstream, where the causes and effects of specialization might follow different patterns.

FOUR

Criminal Cases

Historian Michael Willrich (2003) described Progressive-Era Chicago as a "city of courts." Indeed, during and since that era, specialized courts have proliferated in Chicago under the umbrella of a trial court with broad jurisdiction. The largest portion of this proliferation has involved courts that hear criminal cases.

Chicago's specialization in criminal cases has taken two general forms. In the first, certain judges are assigned to hear only criminal cases, but within that category they decide a wide range of cases—such as a multiplicity of felonies or misdemeanors. For the period of time in which they have that assignment, they have a broad specialization in criminal law.

In the second form, narrower sets of criminal cases are assigned to specific judges as part or all of their work at a given time. A few of these courts, such as Chicago's pioneering juvenile court, have been defined by the attributes of the defendants who appear in them. But most of these courts have been defined by the types of offenses that come to them. At one time or another, Chicago has had (among others) a morals court, a court of domestic relations, a safety court, an auto theft court, a shoplifters court, a gun court, a gambling court, a racket court, a smokers court, a weed court, a perjury and vagrancy court, and two versions of a drug court.[1]

---

1. The morals court is noted in Willrich (2003, 172–207), the court of domestic relations in Willrich (2003, 128–71), the safety court in *Chicago Daily Tribune* (1939), the auto theft court in *Chicago Daily Tribune* (1932), the shoplifters court in Mullen (1973), the gun court in Fuller (1974), the gambling court in Possley (1986), the racket court in *Chicago Daily Tribune* (1928), the smokers court in Winter (1975), the weed court in Lepawsky (1932, 167), the perjury and vagrancy court in Moley (1929, 396), and the drug courts in Lindesmith (1965, 90–93) and Middleton (1992, 45).

Specialized criminal courts probably have been more common in Chicago than in most other large cities.[2] However, Chicago is hardly unique in assigning judges to broad or narrow ranges of criminal cases: in the state court systems, there is a great deal of specialization in and within criminal law. The extent of that specialization raises the question as to why it exists.

One possibility is that judicial specialization in criminal law results from government's interest in the outcomes of criminal cases. Like foreign policy and internal security, protection against crime is a basic function of government. Among both the general public (see Pastore and Maguire n.d., 140–41) and public policy makers, the strong majority view is that the courts should assist the other branches of government in carrying out this function. Moreover, governments as prosecutors are regular litigants in criminal cases. If public officials see specialization as a means to advance pro-prosecution policies, they have strong incentives to adopt it for that purpose.

On the other hand, judicial specialization may seem unnecessary to serve the government's interest. If the goal is to capture the trial courts, that object is largely achieved in the ordinary operation of those courts. Prosecutors are powerful figures in the courts, arguably more powerful than judges. They win the overwhelming majority of cases (although the preponderance of those wins come through guilty pleas), and their charging decisions and recommendations to judges give them considerable influence over sentences. What more do they need?

In reality, the relationship between the government's interest in the outcomes of criminal cases and the use of judicial specialization is complicated and variable. An interest in advancing the neutral virtue of efficiency has been the primary impetus for assigning judges to a broad range of criminal cases and for creating some of the courts that hear specific types of criminal cases. In contrast, for most courts that deal with specific types of offenses or defendants, the primary goal has been to address the problem of crime more effectively.

The specialized courts that have been created to fight crime more effectively can be categorized on the basis of two alternative orientations. Some of these courts have been given the mission of treating certain offenses more seriously, chiefly by imposing more rigorous sanctions. Other courts have had the mission of getting at the root causes of crime through treatment of

---

2. New York City is another city that has had a large number of specialized criminal courts. A 1937 article, for instance, referred to women's court, domestic relations court, homicide court, commercial frauds court, and adolescents' court, among others (Kross and Grossman 1937).

Table 4.1 Categories of specialized courts created to address crime more effectively

Historical category	Dominant orientation of courts toward defendants		
	Sanctions	Mixed	Treatment
Occasional efforts	Gun; Eagles (Philadelphia); Marine Navigation (NJ); Weed (Chicago)		
Socialized courts (Progressive Era)	Domestic relations	Women's	Juvenile
Problem-solving courts (current era)	Domestic violence; environmental	Community	Drug; mental health; homeless/veterans' treatment

Note: Courts listed in the table are those that are discussed in the text of the chapter 4; other courts are omitted. The domestic relations courts in this table should be distinguished from domestic relations courts of later eras, whose jurisdiction is mostly or entirely over civil matters; the drug courts in the table should be distinguished from the "old-style" drug courts of the 1980s.

offenders rather than simply imposing sanctions. A third set of courts has incorporated substantial elements of both those missions.

Much of the impetus for specialized courts in criminal law has come from two movements within and outside the courts. The first was a movement to create "socialized" courts that reached its height in the Progressive Era of the early twentieth century. The other is the current movement to create problem-solving courts. Those labels suggest that courts growing out of the two movements were oriented toward treatment rather than rigorous sanctions. Indeed, this is true of many of these courts. But other courts associated with the two movements have emphasized sanctions more than treatment.

Table 4.1 lists a large sampling of the courts with the mission of addressing crime more effectively; each of these courts is discussed in this chapter. The table classifies courts by their orientation and by the historical category in which they fit. Along with the clusters of courts in the Progressive and current eras, a third category that is not limited to a single era includes occasional efforts to attack specific offenses in a straightforward way through tougher sanctions.

Much judicial specialization in criminal law, and most of the specialization in cases involving specific types of offenders and offenses, occurs within courts. Thus, most of the "courts" that hear certain kinds of criminal cases are actually entities within larger courts. This status makes it easier to create or eliminate such courts; it also creates difficulties for efforts to identify and count them.

I begin the chapter's discussion of specialization in the field of criminal law with courts that were created primarily to enhance efficiency. I then turn to courts with the mission of fighting crime, examining the three historical categories in turn.

Promoting Efficiency

Broad specialization in criminal law is common in state court systems. Some of that specialization is established by law (Strickland et al. 2008). Texas, Oklahoma, and Alabama have appellate courts that hear only criminal cases. There are also many state trial courts that have jurisdiction only in criminal law, typically in misdemeanor cases. These courts are most often labeled municipal courts.

Considerably more numerous are trial courts that create specialization in criminal law officially or unofficially by assigning criminal and civil cases to different subsets of their judges at a given time. Because felony and misdemeanor cases often fall under the jurisdiction of different courts, the result is that some judges who specialize in criminal law hear only felony cases, and others decide only misdemeanor cases. The frequency with which civil and criminal cases are assigned to different judges increases with population size, and it is the dominant arrangement in large cities. In a 1977 survey of judges in state general jurisdiction courts, 40 percent of the judges were hearing only civil cases or only criminal cases at the time (Ryan et al. 1980, 23). If other trial courts were included, the proportion of civil and criminal specialists would have been higher.

The reasons for permanent or temporary assignments of judges to hear only criminal cases are not well documented, probably because the separation of criminal and civil cases is viewed as natural. Criminal cases have their own distinctive procedures. They also have their own sets of regular participants—prosecutors, defense attorneys, probation officers, and police officers. Thus, where the number of judges is sufficient for some to hear only criminal cases at a given time, there is often an expectation that separation of criminal and civil cases will enhance efficiency (Nardulli, Eisenstein, and Flemming 1988, 175).

Another consideration may come into play. Although preferences differ, many judges prefer civil to criminal cases, especially prosecutions for less serious offenses (Mather 1979, 14; Eisenstein and Jacob 1977, 112; Jacob 1997, 10–11). As a result, separating criminal and civil cases allows judges who have more seniority or influence with a presiding judge to avoid criminal cases.

The impact of this form of judge concentration is also uncertain. Because criminal cases are so common, even generalist judges devote a large portion of their effort to the criminal field. Thus, these generalists do not differ dramatically from judges who specialize temporarily or permanently in criminal law in the extent of their immersion in criminal law. But the differences that do exist may affect judges' perspectives. To take one example, judges who hear only criminal cases may be more susceptible to influence by attorneys and others who participate regularly in those cases.

Another possible effect results from external evaluation of judges' work. Permanent concentration of certain judges in criminal law means that evaluations are based solely on work in that field. For elected judges, electoral pressures to take pro-prosecution positions are thereby heightened.

This effect is illustrated by the Texas Court of Criminal Appeals. It appears that the court was established and achieved its current position as the state's highest court for criminal cases for a policy-neutral reason—an effort to reduce caseload burdens on the state supreme court (A. Solomon 2006, 436). But in the current era, candidates who depict themselves as hard-liners on criminal justice have a great advantage in winning election to the court.

There is some evidence that this incentive has affected court policy. In some recent periods, the court has taken positions so unfriendly to criminal defendants that it has been criticized by the news media and a conservative U.S. Supreme Court (M. Hall 2004; Hines 2004). This result may be idiosyncratic, in that the court apparently was more favorable to criminal defendants in an earlier period (see C. Miller, Cole, and Griffin 1995), and perhaps the court's leanings have been exaggerated. However, an analysis that matched cases in the Oklahoma and Texas Courts of Criminal Appeals with comparable cases in the supreme courts of other states found evidence that defendants fared less well in the specialized criminal courts even when the courts' partisan composition was taken into account (Christenson, Curry, and Miller 2009).

Beyond broad specialization in criminal cases, efficiency has been the key goal behind two forms of specialization in specific types of criminal cases. One form is the drug courts that grew out of the national "war on drugs" in the 1980s and its New York State version in the 1970s, which I will call old-style drug courts. Growth in the numbers of drug prosecutions put heavy pressure on many trial courts. Seeking to process a flood of cases, administrators in many urban courts established specialized courtrooms for drug offenses (Belenko, Fagan, and Dumanovsky 1994; B. Smith et al. 1994; Inciardi, McBride, and Rivers 1996, 66–68).

Old-style drug courts were characterized by efforts "to speed the disposition of drug cases" (Bureau of Justice Assistance 1993b, 3). The primary theory underlying these drug courts was that concentrating similar cases in certain courtrooms would allow more rapid case processing. Judges could develop routines to move cases efficiently, and they would develop expertise in drug cases that facilitated processing of cases. An important ancillary benefit was that other courtrooms no longer had to deal with large numbers of drug cases, so they could move more quickly through the remaining cases. In Chicago, where night drug courts were established, another advantage was more intensive use of courtrooms.

It is noteworthy that old-style drug courts were not mandated to enforce the drug laws more stringently. In the New York City borough of Queens, law enforcement leaders saw improved efficiency as a means to achieve quicker sentencing and thus improve the effectiveness of the law (Fried 1988). But this perceived benefit was secondary to protection of the courts themselves—not surprisingly, since the initiative for drug courts came primarily from within the courts.

These courts did not alter the formal procedures for the handling and disposition of cases. But the mechanics of case processing were changed in the interest of efficiency. Processing was usually routinized even more than in regular criminal courts, and special efforts were made to reduce postponements. In Chicago, the judges who were selected for the Night Drug Court all had pre-judicial backgrounds in criminal law, thus stocking the court with a high level of expertise that enhanced the drive for greater efficiency (Middleton 1992, 45). It appears that these drug courts were successful in achieving their goal of attacking backlogs of criminal cases, in part because of specialization in itself and in part because of the emphasis on speed that accompanied specialization.[3]

The impact of drug courts on defendants was mixed. The emphasis on speed put greater pressure on defendants to plead guilty, and enhanced efficiency reduced the need to dismiss cases. But at least in Chicago and New York, defendants were given more attractive offers in plea bargaining in order to facilitate the quick resolution of cases (Bureau of Justice Assistance 1993a; Belenko, Fagan, and Dumanovsky 1994). On the whole, defendants probably came out a little better (B. Smith et al. 1994, 46–47). This result

---

3. However, according to one account, the success of the Chicago Night Drug Court in achieving greater efficiency encouraged police officers to arrest more people for drug possession. The resulting growth in the number of drug prosecutions spilled over into the nondrug courtrooms, renewing the caseload pressures on them (Bogira 2005, 118–19).

was unintended (though perhaps predictable), but it did not conflict with the goal of easing caseload pressures on the courts.

A second form of specialization with similar aims involves the death penalty. Courts in Philadelphia, Milwaukee, and some California counties have assigned cases in which the prosecution seeks the death penalty to certain judges who are perceived as experts in the difficult procedural issues that arise in these cases (Keaton 1991). It appears that the motivation for this practice stemmed from the expectation that judicial expertise would improve the efficiency with which capital cases could be processed.

Nonetheless, the decision to concentrate capital cases before a few judges created the potential to shape the outcomes of these cases. Philadelphia began to assign death penalty cases to a select group of judges in the 1970s. According to one report (T. Rosenberg 1995, 23), "prosecutors have been able to knock lenient judges out of the program." One Philadelphia judge heard only death penalty cases for thirteen years, and some observers regarded him as highly favorable to the prosecution (Daughen 1995; *Philadelphia Inquirer* 1995). This outcome, however, is not inevitable. A California judge who educated judges on death penalty procedures and who presided over many cases himself as a specialist actually opposed capital punishment and was regarded as evenhanded (Keaton 1991; Chiang 1998).

Old-style drug courts and the assignment of death penalty cases to certain Philadelphia judges make it clear that judicial specialization can have significant effects on the substance of judicial policy even when it is undertaken for policy-neutral reasons. The forms of specialization that I discuss in the remainder of the chapter were adopted in the hope that they *would* affect policy.

Occasional Efforts to Attack Crime with Sanctions

According to a student of the Chicago courts, "after a vigorous campaign of the health department to prevent the spread of hay fever, a new weed court was established to punish those who failed to cut their ragweed, and to this court was assigned a retributive judge who was reputed to suffer from the disease himself" (Lepawsky 1932, 167). The reputed hay fever was real. A newspaper reported that the opening of weed court in 1930 was delayed because its judge "suffered an attack of hay fever and left on a vacation" (*Chicago Daily Tribune* 1930). Given the judge's malady, the court probably served its intended purpose.

The Chicago weed court exemplifies a common development. When political leaders seek more rigorous enforcement of the law against certain offenses, they sometimes establish a specialized court as a means to achieve that rigor. The theory that underlies this step seems to have two elements. First, the concentration of cases involving a particular offense in one courtroom signals judges and other courtroom participants that the offense should be taken seriously, and the signal is sometimes explicit. Second, judges can be assigned to the courtroom on the basis of a perceived inclination to enforce the law rigorously. The judge who was assigned to the weed court had a parallel in the first judge of the Chicago Speeders' Court, "who did not own an automobile and who was not owned by the owner of any automobile" (Harley 1917, 11).

Courts of this type have been scattered across the judicial landscape, often appearing and then disappearing within a short time. Most of the Chicago courts that I listed at the beginning of this chapter followed that pattern. They were created because local authorities sought more severe sanctions against specific offenses at a particular time.

Among the courts of this type that have been established in other cities, one example is "Eagles Court." That court was instituted in Philadelphia in 1997 to operate at Veterans Stadium during National Football League games. Reacting to an epidemic of unruly and violent behavior by fans, the municipal court established a branch in which fans charged with criminal misbehavior would be locked up and brought before a judge in the stadium for immediate trial and sentencing.[4] Seamus McCaffery, a self-styled tough judge on the municipal court bench, presided over Eagles Court.

The city council president accused the court of leniency in sentencing (*National Law Journal* 1997), but the court's existence increased the numbers of unruly fans who were subject to sanctions and certainly brought swifter sanctions. As a result, the court seemed to have its intended effect by helping to deter crime in the stadium. It turned out, however, that the best solution to the crime problem was to abandon the increasingly decrepit Veterans Stadium for a new venue in 2003. When crime in the stands declined precipitously in the new stadium, Eagles Court was disbanded (*Washington Post* 2003b). For his part, Judge McCaffery was elected to the Pennsylvania Supreme Court in 2007, after crediting his widespread name recognition to Eagles Court (Lounsberry 2007).

4. Some readers may recall that the late, unlamented Veterans Stadium was the venue at which fans booed the Easter Bunny and threw snowballs at Santa Claus (Weir 1993).

Another court at the scene of the crime was proposed by New York City mayor Edward Koch in 1985: courts in subway stations to handle crimes committed in the transit system. The proposal aroused considerable criticism, and it was not adopted (*Washington Post* 1985).

Another example was the Marine Navigation Court of New Jersey, initiated in 1955. The court was set up by the state Department of Conservation and Economic Development under a 1954 statute and staffed by an administrative official acting as a magistrate (Wright 1956; Lovejoy 1956). The court was established to bring about stronger enforcement of laws for the operation of power boats. A few years later the court was declared to be in violation of the state constitution because of its links with the executive branch (*State v. Osborn* 1960).

Alongside these singular courts stand a few types that have spread across multiple jurisdictions. One example is gun courts, established in several places since 1994. Gun courts hear cases involving illegal possession of guns, criminal use of guns, or both. The primary motive for their creation has been an effort to secure more rigorous enforcement of the law.

The first of these courts, serving two Rhode Island counties, was in Providence (McGrory 1994; Walker 1994).[5] As noted at the beginning of chapter 2, that court was established by state law, largely at the initiative of the Providence mayor, and the city of Providence funds the court. Its jurisdiction covers cases involving the illegal possession and use of guns. As in Eagles Court, the first judge was a tough-talking trial judge.[6] In 2003 gun courts as special Parts of a trial court were opened by court action in three New York City boroughs (F. Solomon 2005; Hynes 2005). These courts deal with felony prosecutions for illegal gun possession. Milwaukee and Baltimore also created gun courts, and a few cities established special gun courts for juvenile defendants.

Gun courts illustrate well the use of specialized courts to shape outcomes. The concentration of cases involving a particular offense in a single court division helps to set a mission for a court, and specialization allows cases to be funneled to a judge whose preferences are consistent with the mission. As a member of the Bronx district attorney's office said of the local gun court, "In the past, there was a possibility of judges interpreting the statute, but with all the cases in one [courtroom], everyone has to deal with the same judge" (Coleman 2006). Anecdotal evidence from Providence

5. Chicago established a gun court some years earlier, in an action that was separate from the small wave of gun courts created since the 1990s (Fuller 1974). Whatever may have been the original mission of the court, it was sometimes charged with undue leniency (Fuller 1974; *Chicago Tribune* 1982).

6. That judge, John Bourcier, had something else in common with Judge McCaffery of Eagles Court: elevation to the state supreme court. Because of that appointment Bourcier had a relatively brief tenure on the gun court, from 1994 to 1995.

and systematic evidence from Brooklyn indicate that sentence severity did increase substantially after the institution of gun courts (Matza 1995; F. Solomon 2005, 34–36).

The domestic relations courts of the early twentieth century and some recent courts that have been given the problem-solving label were created primarily to secure tougher enforcement of certain criminal laws. But these courts are best discussed later, in the context of the broader movements that encompassed them.

Traffic courts might fall into the category of courts that are created to attack violations of the law more vigorously, because safety considerations or an interest in maximizing revenue from fines could motivate their establishment.[7] On the other hand, special traffic divisions of trial courts might be established to improve efficiency or to relieve most judges (or all judges, if magistrates are substituted for them) of cases they dislike.

There has been only limited research on traffic courts, and it tells little about the reasons for creation of these courts or about patterns of case outcomes (G. Warren 1942; Goerdt 1992). It may be that when separate traffic courts are created, considerations of efficiency and judges' desire to avoid traffic cases outweigh an interest in shaping case outcomes. The use of traffic enforcement as a source of local revenue in small towns is legendary, but pursuit of that purpose does not require a specialized court. To take one example, a system in which justices of the peace receive a share of fines inclines them to find traffic defendants guilty even if traffic cases are only one part of their docket.

The mayors' courts of Ohio have been the subject of considerable controversy, because mayors who adjudicate traffic and other cases may have a strong incentive to impose fines in order to maintain the flow of municipal revenue. Despite two Supreme Court decisions (*Tumey v. Ohio* 1927; *Ward v. Village of Monroeville* 1972) and a federal court of appeals decision (*Depiero v. City of Macedonia* 1999; see Clines 1999) that raised serious due process questions about the functioning of mayors' courts, they have shown considerable staying power (Berens 1996; Woods 2006).

The *Tumey* case, a minor landmark in constitutional law, actually involved a "liquor court" over which a small-town mayor presided (see Douglass 1933, 13–31). The Ohio legislature had sought to strengthen the enforcement of prohibition laws through financial incentives. As described by the Supreme Court, "the system by which the fines to be collected were

---

7. Depending on the state and the offense, traffic cases may be either civil or criminal (see Economos and Steelman 1983, chap. 2).

to be divided between the State and the village was for the proper purpose of stimulating the activities of the village officers to such due enforcement" (*Tumey v. Ohio* 1927, 521). Despite its use of the term "proper," the Court concluded that the mayor's incentive to garner revenue for his village, combined with the local ordinance that gave a portion of fines directly to the mayor, violated the due process rights of defendants. There may be no better example of using financial incentives to achieve desired outcomes in criminal cases.

Socialized Courts in the Progressive Era

The Progressive movement that reached its peak in the early twentieth century encompassed a wide range of ideas (Rodgers 1982). Two of those ideas helped to bring about the creation and diffusion of what became known as socialized courts (Willrich 2003, xxxviii). The first was a belief in the application of scientific knowledge and professionalization to government, the second a commitment to bring the power and resources of government to bear on social problems.

One manifestation of the first idea was an effort to create courts that would achieve efficiency through the precepts of scientific management (Harrington 1982, 39–50). This approach was espoused by the early leaders of the American Judicature Society (Belknap 1992, 25–27). The primary founder of the society, Herbert Harley (1917), extolled the benefits of "business management for the courts." Harley praised the Municipal Court of Chicago as a unified court that operated efficiently through specialized units. Harley concluded that through his assignments of judges to those units, the chief judge made the best use of their abilities.

Socialized courts reflected a merger of the two Progressive ideas. The term "socialized" was used during and after the Progressive Era to refer to courts that use scientific methods to solve social problems that manifest themselves in court cases. In contrast with the formal, adversarial proceedings in traditional court, in socialized courts "the purpose of the hearing is to determine whether a serious problem exists . . . and to provide the means to meet the needs of the individuals involved" (Petersen and Matza 1963, 108). Referring to some of the socialized courts, legal historian Willard Hurst (1953, 5) cited "procedure and remedies" that were "focused on diagnosis, prevention, cure, education."

The impetus for these courts came from both within and outside the courts. Reformist groups lobbied for the creation of socialized courts, and judges themselves sometimes championed them. For judges, the appeal of these courts lay partly in their potential to provide solutions for social problems that came to court with litigants. As some judges saw it, the courts' traditional methods of adjudicating cases had demonstrated little success in addressing those problems. Thus, an alternative approach that had some promise of improving the situation was very attractive to them.

Socialized courts can operate on the civil side of the law, and the small claims courts that were established from 1913 on fit under this rubric to some degree (Harrington 1982, 54–58). For the most part, however, the courts that best reflected the ideas behind socialized courts dealt with criminal cases. The most popular of these courts by far were juvenile courts. Women's courts and domestic relations courts were also adopted in multiple localities.[8] As indicated in table 4.1, these courts differed considerably in the balance between sanctions and treatment in their responses to defendants. But the origins of each court reflected Progressive ideas, and each manifested a Progressive paternalism toward people who were perceived as needy (Rothman 1978).

Juvenile Courts

The creation of the first juvenile court in Chicago in 1899 and the diffusion of juvenile courts that followed have been analyzed in a large body of scholarship (Platt 1969; Hawes 1971, chaps. 10, 12; Mennel 1973, chap. 5; Ryerson 1978; Sutton 1985; Polsky 1989; Getis 2000; Tanenhaus 2004). Explanations for the invention and diffusion of juvenile courts differ, but certain themes related to Progressive ideas recur (see Sutton 1985, 128).

One theme concerns perceptions of juvenile offenders. In the eyes of those who favored juvenile courts, most offenses committed by young people resulted primarily from social circumstances, most fundamentally urban poverty. For that reason, they thought, juvenile offenders were more victims than wrongdoers. Thus, treating juveniles like their adult counterparts was unfair to them. It was also counterproductive, in that labeling juveniles as criminals and mixing them with adult criminals encouraged rather than discouraged future criminal activity.[9]

Another theme concerns the capabilities of courts. Proponents of juvenile

8. Also in this category was the Boys' Court of Chicago, in which defendants were young men who were too old for juvenile court (Willrich 2003, chap. 7).
9. There was, however, an element of the juvenile court movement with a more punitive orientation (McCoy 2003, 1515–16).

courts believed that well-informed treatment of juvenile offenders could be successful in preventing them from committing additional offenses and in improving their lives. The task was to create conditions under which scientific understanding was used to treat each offender appropriately.

The resulting prescription was a separate court for juveniles in which the central question in each case was not guilt or innocence but rather how an offender should best be treated. Because of this shift in emphasis, dependent and neglected juveniles could be brought to the same court as those suspected of crimes, and juveniles could be charged with offenses that were not criminal for adults. Probation, not yet a standard practice in the courts, was advocated as a way to help juvenile offenders take the right course under court supervision. The withdrawal of due process rights at the adjudication stage was justified on the ground that offenders were not actually charged with crimes, a rationale that appellate courts accepted in the preponderance of challenges that came to them.

A broad group of reformers worked to establish juvenile courts. In Chicago, where the first recognized juvenile court was created, women's groups took the initiative to secure the necessary state legislation. Some judges who sat in juvenile courts, especially Ben Lindsey of Denver, served as advocates for this innovation in other places (Schlossman 1977, 56). National and local reform groups worked together for legislation establishing juvenile courts (Sutton 1988, chap. 4). They enjoyed considerable success: by 1918, forty-seven states had authorized juvenile courts in at least part of the state through legislation, frequently copying statutes that already existed in other states (Ryerson 1978, 81; Sutton 1985, 128). Individual courts sometimes created juvenile courts in the absence of explicit statutory authority.

The rapid spread of juvenile courts across the country reflected several favorable conditions. Among them were the mobilization of an array of reformers on behalf of the idea, the dearth of organized opposition, and the perception that keeping juveniles out of incarceration would save money (Polsky 1989, 173; Feld 1999, 74). Most fundamental was the attractiveness of the idea of juvenile courts in the Progressive Era.

Although mandates for special procedures in juvenile justice became ubiquitous, specialization of judges in juvenile law did not go as far. A 1918 survey found that despite supportive state legislation, only 15 percent of relevant courts had specially organized juvenile courts within them. Moreover, only twenty-three judges in the country worked solely on juvenile cases (although some other judges gave a majority of their time to those cases) (Belden 1920, 30–37). In 1965 there were still relatively few judges who worked full-time on juvenile cases, and at most one-quarter of the judges who heard juvenile cases did so at least half-time (National Council of Juvenile Court Judges 1965, 16–17).[10]

Inevitably, the extent to which individual judges concentrate on juvenile cases is related to the population of the area in which a court sits. In the 1918 survey, all the large cities had specially organized juvenile courts, but such courts were quite uncommon in rural areas (Belden 1920, 29–30). In rural courts with few cases, specialization could go no further than hearing juvenile cases at special times (see Feld 1991, 172). Because judge and case concentration in juvenile justice is highest in large jurisdictions, the extent of specialization is considerably greater than a simple count of jurisdictions would suggest.

Overall, the institution of the juvenile court changed court procedures less than the rhetoric of its supporters suggested (S. Fox 1970). Many judges continued to treat juvenile defendants in traditional ways (Feld 1999, 69–74). This was understandable, because enactment of juvenile court legislation gave responsibility for juvenile cases to judges who were not necessarily committed to the primary mission of juvenile courts. "Aside from a few celebrities," one scholar notes, "juvenile court magistrates did not share the therapeutic orientation" (Polsky 1989, 176). Thus, for instance, the Milwaukee juvenile court took a punitive rather than treatment-oriented approach to children (Schlossman 1977, chap. 9). Further, legislatures generally provided no funding for additional personnel and other resources to carry out the therapeutic mission of juvenile courts. But one scholar concluded that even where these resources were available, juvenile courts "provided new bottles for old wine" (Mennel 1973, 144). Not surprisingly, in courts where judges devoted only part of their time to juvenile cases, their treatment of juvenile offenders was less likely to differ fundamentally from their treatment of adult defendants than in courts with full-time juvenile judges (Mennel 1973, 132–33; see Canon and Kolson 1971).

The treatment orientation declined further over time. By the 1960s, juvenile courts had become low-status institutions within the courts, and assignments to hear juvenile cases were often accepted with reluctance by judges who hoped to move on to more prestigious posts (Vinter 1967, 85;

---

10. Placement of jurisdiction over juvenile cases varies among and within states. Some places have separate juvenile courts or court divisions, some hear juvenile cases within family courts, and some have no special structure for juvenile cases. The states' jurisdictional arrangements are described on the Web site of the National Center for Juvenile Justice (http://70.89 .227.250:8080/stateprofiles/). The extent to which judges specialize in juvenile cases correlates with formal organization, but the correlation is imperfect.

see Jacob 1997, 11). Under the circumstances, it was unlikely that most juvenile judges sought to carry out the original mission of their court. In addition, growth in the numbers of cases in urban courts required rapid processing that ruled out the careful individualized treatment that designers of juvenile courts had had in mind (Lemert 1967, 94). If the juvenile court was an example of "the fusion of social control with greater humaneness," it also seemed to follow a common pattern in which humaneness wears away while social control remains (Ryerson 1978, 33).

Dissatisfaction with juvenile courts arose soon after they were first established, and it grew over time. The Supreme Court's decision in *In re Gault* (1967), which required that most due process rights be restored to juvenile defendants, reflected a perception that the special procedures of juvenile courts had turned out to be a bad bargain for juvenile defendants. As the Court had said a year earlier: "there may be grounds for concern that the child receives the worst of both worlds: that he gets neither the protections accorded to adults nor the solicitous care and regenerative treatment postulated for children" (*Kent v. United States* 1966, 556). The Court's mandates have had uneven effects on juvenile courts, thereby accentuating differences among them (Feld 1999, 112–13). The growing drive to try juveniles charged with serious crimes in adult court reflects a quite different perception, that the differences in sanctions between juvenile and adult courts allow serious offenders to escape with unduly lenient sentences (Feld 1999).

Yet juvenile courts continue to exist. Indeed, the consolidation of courts and growth in the numbers of judgeships probably have increased the concentration of judges on juvenile cases. To a considerable degree, the survival of juvenile courts reflects organizational inertia—or, put differently, institutional stickiness. More fundamentally, there seems to remain broad support for the idea that at least a portion of the juveniles who are charged with criminal offenses should be treated differently from their adult counterparts. Whatever may be the actual differences in treatment, the belief in their desirability helps to sustain juvenile courts.

Domestic Relations Courts

Family courts under several names are quite common in the states today (Babb 1998; Bozzomo and Scolieri 2004). The types of cases handled by these courts vary considerably, but family courts typically hear a range of cases involving family-related issues such as divorce. Some of these courts incorporate what had been separate juvenile courts. Some family courts hear certain kinds of adult criminal cases, but their dockets typically are dominated by civil cases.

Family courts were invented in the early twentieth century, and they spread widely in a fairly short time (Day 1928, 109–10). At that time too, they had various names and types of jurisdiction (R. Smith 1919, chap. 11; Lou 1927, 203–12; Flexner, Oppenheimer, and Lenroot 1929, 13–17, 65–67). One version of the family court, the first type to be created, was the domestic relations court that focused on criminal cases.[11] The first such court was in Buffalo. Similar domestic relations courts were created in New York City, Chicago, Boston, Kansas City, and Philadelphia (Waite 1921, 164; F. Johnson 1930).

The criminal jurisdiction of some domestic relations courts extended to a broad range of cases. The Chicago Court of Domestic Relations could adjudicate, among other things, the prohibition of cigarette sales to minors, laws against abortion, and (in its first year) violations of the child labor law and the maximum-hours law for women (Gemmill 1914, 115; Winchell 1921, 17–18). But most of the business of these courts was in nonsupport and desertion—in other words, offenses by husbands. In the first year of the Chicago court, 71 percent of the cases were for nonsupport of the family, and another 15 percent were for nonsupport of children outside of marriage (Baldwin 1912, 400; see Winchell 1921, 19).

Domestic relations courts grew out of the wing of the Progressive movement that fostered juvenile courts, and "the family-court movement has been in large part an outgrowth of the juvenile court" (Flexner, Oppenheimer, and Lenroot 1929, 49). The women's groups that helped to establish the juvenile court in Chicago worked with judges to create the city's domestic relations court as a branch of the municipal court (Willrich 2003, 133–36). Like the juvenile court, the domestic relations court was designed to use the power of the court to address a social problem through the application of "a new legal technique" (Flexner, Oppenheimer, and Lenroot 1929, 4; see C. Hoffman 1919–20). The wave of new legislation that made desertion and nonsupport criminal offenses provided courts with an opportunity to address those issues (Willrich 2003, 129, 147–48).

However, juvenile courts and domestic relations courts differed fundamentally in their founders' attitudes toward the people who were their pri-

11. This discussion of domestic relations court is based in part on the study by Willrich (2003, chap. 5), which examines the Chicago court closely and provides some information on domestic relations courts in general.

mary focus. In juvenile courts that followed their original mission, the child was seen primarily as a victim of circumstances whom the court should help. In the domestic relations court, in contrast, the husband was seen primarily as someone who had failed to do his duty. The court's task was to correct that failure. A domestic relations judge in New York City announced at a trial that "he was thoroughly in sympathy with the movement to stamp out the evil of family desertion, and that no deserter coming before him need expect mercy" (Igra 2007, 82).

Consistent with this mandate, the Chicago court initially took a punitive approach to men who were charged with nonsupport (Willrich 2003, chap. 5). "By reason of the great power conferred upon this court," wrote an early judge, "it is able to compel many drunken, lazy and shiftless men to contribute quite largely to the support of their families" (Gemmill 1914, 118). But the court's reach extended further. Some wives who brought criminal complaints against their husbands were ordered by the judge to go to the court's Psychopathic Laboratory for testing (Willrich 2003, 166).

The court's first judge presented himself as a general expert and reformer on domestic relations, announcing in court his views that spouses' mothers should not live with married couples, that husbands should get their own breakfasts, and that wives should receive regular salaries (*Chicago Daily Tribune* 1911b, 1911c, 1911d).[12] After a year the chief judge replaced him with another judge, citing the custom of regular rotation of judges but also emphasizing the "strain attendant" on a domestic relations judge. "Judge Goodnow has stood it for a year, but it was beginning to tell on him" (*Chicago Daily Tribune* 1912). His interventionist approach likely helped produce that strain.

The various domestic relations courts were created for multiple reasons, not all of which related to the concept of a socialized court (Winchell 1921, 15; *New York Times* 1909a, 1909b). Most noteworthy was the importance of financial considerations in New York City. One scholar has offered strong evidence that the New York court "was primarily a mechanism for relieving the public of the support of poor dependents" (Igra 2007, 83) rather than social reform.

---

12. An unsuccessful candidate for that position was a judge who was a confirmed bachelor. He argued that his status constituted a strong qualification for the position: "You see, the functions of the critic and of the professional are altogether different. . . . Now, I aspire to be a matrimonial critic, as it were, and I maintain that I am better qualified for that post because I am a mere student of matrimony, not a professional 'matrimonialist,' if there be such a word" (*Chicago Daily Tribune* 1911a).

The New York court seemed to follow its own mandate to focus on collection of support from wayward husbands.[13] Yet as in Chicago (Winchell
1921, 43), enforcement of support orders was often quite difficult. Even in
cases in which the New York court was assisted by a private organization,
few men paid their support obligations for even six months. "An astonish-
ing amount of effort and resources went into prosecuting men who almost
never resumed their breadwinning responsibilities" (Igra 2007, 97). In this
regard, the court's functioning was largely symbolic.

Women's Courts

Women's courts under various names were established within state trial
courts in most large cities, primarily in the second decade of the twentieth century. Like juvenile and domestic relations courts, they were largely a
product of the Progressive movement (F. Solomon 1987, 1). Their jurisdiction varied considerably (Worthington and Topping 1925). Some women's
courts heard all cases in which women were defendants. Others focused
on prostitution, and the Morals Branch of the Chicago Municipal Court
heard cases brought against both women and men. Along with prostitution, its jurisdiction included other offenses such as fornication, adultery,
and obscenity (Willrich 2002, 174, 188). The Los Angeles women's court
also adjudicated nonsupport cases against husbands (Cook 1993, 149). But
whatever their formal jurisdiction might be, nearly all these courts heard
primarily prostitution cases (F. Solomon 1987, 2).

Efficiency in handling cases was one motive for the creation of women's
courts, and one scholar argued that it was the primary motive (Cook 1993,
155). But these courts also reflected strong concerns about female defendants and about prostitution as an offense. In some respects, women's
courts grew out of the same impulses as juvenile courts, including a belief
in the ability of properly constituted courts to deal effectively with social
problems (Quinn 2006, 675). Female defendants were seen in part as victims rather than offenders, and the standard legal process was viewed as
aggravating their victimization.

However, there was also an interest in dealing "more wisely and hence
more effectively with the social evil," prostitution (Whitin 1914, 181). Social control over women's behavior was one strong theme in the creation of

---

13. The same was true of the family court in New York City, a later version of the domestic
relations court. A contemporary observer said that it was "largely a collection agency" (Moley
1932, 213n16).

these courts. That element of social control seemed to underlie the opposition of some feminists to creation of one of the New York City courts (*New York Times* 1910).[14]

Women's court judges sometimes were given that assignment on the basis of the perceived fit between their personal qualities and the court's task. In New York City, according to one contemporary account, "the selection of magistrates has been most carefully made and is indeed fortunate. The magistrates sitting in this court have a happy combination of judicial fairness, kindliness, and courage" (Worthington and Topping 1925, 310–11). In some courts women were chosen to serve as judges and in other court positions, and a few remained in women's courts for long periods (Cook 1993; Quinn 2006). At least in Chicago, however, most judges served for only short periods in what was considered to be an undesirable assignment, so that it was "a specialized court more in name than in fact" (Worthington and Topping 1925, 19).

Like juvenile courts, women's courts tended to adopt informal procedures (Cook 1986, 17; but see Worthington and Topping 1925, 308). In Chicago's Morals Court, defendants were required to waive their right to a jury trial to avoid transfer to another court branch (Willrich 2003, 186). Private interest groups concerned with prostitution or with the situations of female defendants participated in the operation of some courts (Cook 1993, 147; Moley 1932, 118–19, 132–35; Willrich 2003, 175, 177).

The multiple goals that the courts were intended to serve resulted in a mix of sympathetic treatment of defendants and onerous sanctions, making them an intermediate case between juvenile courts and domestic relations courts. Within a particular court, defendants were treated differently based on perceptions of them as victims or wrongdoers (F. Solomon 1987, 3). The mix between paternalism and punitiveness also varied among courts and over time. According to one study, punitive goals increasingly outweighed judges' interest in helping female defendants (F. Solomon 1987, 4–5). In this respect, the evolution of domestic relations courts was similar to that of juvenile courts.

A special problem arose in New York City. Official and unofficial reports in 1932 documented pervasive corruption in the magistrates' courts, corruption that extended to the women's court (Seabury 1932; Moley 1932). At the least, the judges of the women's courts seemed extraordinarily obtuse

---

14. There were women's courts in three boroughs in New York City. The one in Manhattan has been labeled the New York City Women's Court (F. Solomon 1987, 8). According to a later report, one of the New York courts (probably in Manhattan) was sometimes called the Court for Vagrant Women (Dwyer 2008).

in failing to recognize corrupt behavior on the part of participants such as police officers. And as the official report delicately put it, "It would, in my opinion, be impossible to reconcile the prevalence and the continuation of this system [of corruption] with competency and uprightness on the part of the presiding Magistrates" (Seabury 1932, 125). These reports were published seven years after the laudatory description of the women's court judges that I quoted three paragraphs earlier.

The women's courts of the Progressive Era gradually disappeared, though the New York court was not abolished until 1967 (Quinn 2006, 696). In a later period, a new women's court was established in Chicago (Lipetz 1984). In contrast with the earlier period, the court was created with no particular mission. Rather, it came about chiefly because most incarcerated female defendants were held at police headquarters rather than in the various police districts. Thus it was easier to hear their cases in a single courtroom. A combination of legal rules, practical considerations, and the attitudes of court personnel led to a pattern of lenient sentences for prostitution. It is not clear that specialization made a great deal of difference for the court, except that case concentration gave a single judge considerable power to determine the pattern of case outcomes. In any event, the origins of the court are a good example of judicial specialization by happenstance.

Problem-solving Courts of the Current Era

The premises that underlay the socialized courts of the Progressive Era seem quite distant today. Rehabilitation as a goal of the criminal justice system was largely discredited by the 1970s. That shift in thinking spurred a movement to limit the discretion of judges and parole boards over sentences, a movement that emphasized the need to respond to the offense rather than the offender. Further, both legislators and the general public tend to favor a straightforward tough-on-crime approach that conflicts with the more nuanced philosophy behind socialized courts.

Yet in the current era there has been a wave of new courts that reflect some of the same ideas as the socialized courts, entities that are most often called problem-solving courts (Berman and Feinblatt, with Glazer 2005; Kaye 2004; Dorf and Fagan 2003; Casey and Rottman 2005). The term "problem-solving" has been used in different ways, but its essence is a combination of two broad characteristics (see Nolan 2009, 10–11). The first is a focus on treatment of the problems of the individual defendant. That focus is captured in a term that is often applied to problem-solving courts, therapeutic jurisprudence (Winick and Wexler 2003; Carns, Hotchkin, and

Andrews 2002; McCoy 2003). The emphasis on treatment leads to closer monitoring of defendants and more extensive interactions with them than is typical of criminal courts.

The second is a relaxation of adversariness and an increase in cooperation among court participants. The prosecution, defense, judge, and other court participants are treated as sharing an interest in addressing the problems that caused a defendant to commit criminal offenses. As a result, they are asked to work together to achieve the best outcomes for defendants. These characteristics are reflected in the avoidance of formal adjudication.

In problem-solving courts, defendants are usually diverted from the standard court process before guilt or innocence is determined or encouraged to plead guilty in order to move into a problem-solving court.[15] Defendants who want to contest their guilt generally have to go elsewhere, to a traditional criminal court. Reacting to this trait of problem-solving courts, one scholar has argued that "it is not a court if you have to plead guilty to get there" (McCoy 2006, 964).

No court with the problem-solving level has become nearly as common as juvenile courts. Yet there are more than two thousand drug courts[16] and perhaps one thousand problem-solving courts of other types (Huddleston, Marlowe, and Casebolt 2008, 9, 19). How has the movement toward problem-solving justice achieved so much success in a seemingly unfavorable environment?

In his analysis of drug courts, James Nolan (2001, 178–84, 187) argued that there is a significant difference between the concept of rehabilitation and the therapeutic orientation of drug courts, an orientation that he identified as having general support in the current era. To a degree, then, advocates of drug court have been able to distance themselves from a discredited approach. Yet a therapeutic orientation seems at least as "soft" as rehabilitation and thus as vulnerable to attack by people who favor a tough approach to crime. There seem to be several reasons why the problem-solving movement has nonetheless enjoyed considerable success.

One reason is the selectivity of problem-solving courts. Most of the offenses that have been assigned to these courts are relatively minor. In addition, many of the offenders whose cases are heard in these courts, like juveniles in an earlier era, elicit sympathy from people in and out of the courts.

15. This movement away from adversariness creates dilemmas for defense attorneys who seek to represent their clients' interests (Quinn 2000; Meekins 2006).

16. When I use the term drug courts in this section, I refer solely to the courts established since 1989, as distinct from the old-style drug courts that were discussed earlier in the chapter.

A second reason is that advocates of problem-solving courts often depict them as hard-nosed in their dealings with defendants. Offenders must face up to their responsibilities, and those who fail to do so suffer punitive consequences (Nolan 2001, 62–66; see Hartley 2003, 235). The "tough-love" image of these courts makes them attractive to many people within both liberal and conservative campus. Thus, President Clinton supported drug courts enthusiastically, and congressional Republicans were willing to provide financial support for their creation.

Third, by no means do all courts with the problem-solving label actually emphasize treatment over sanctions. Domestic violence courts and environmental courts are primarily punitive in their approach to defendants, and to a lesser extent this is true of community courts. As a result, these courts are consistent with societal attitudes that emphasize punishment over rehabilitation, and they appeal to groups that think certain offenses do not get adequate attention from the criminal justice system.

Finally, the initiative for problem-solving courts generally comes from within the judiciary, and these courts are especially attractive to some judges. Many judges who hear criminal cases become frustrated with what they perceive as the courts' failure to prevent crime or to improve the lives of defendants who go through the courts. As a result, they welcome an alternative approach that seems promising. Indeed, judges and other court personnel gain considerable satisfaction from working in problem-solving courts (Chase and Hora 2000), and communication of this benefit helps in attracting other judges to create and preside over these courts. Some judges gain additional satisfaction from the notice and prestige they receive for their work in these courts (see Hora 2009, 134–35). These satisfactions are probably a major reason for the creation of problem-solving courts (Carns, Hotchkin, and Andrews 2002, 10n38).

A second attraction of problem-solving courts for judges is that they can enhance judges' power to shape case outcomes. "The judge goes from being a detached, neutral arbiter to the central figure in the team" (Chase and Hora 2000, 12; see Nolan 2009, 139–41). The shift may be even greater than that characterization suggests, because judges in ordinary criminal courts often have less power to determine outcomes than do prosecutors.[17]

---

17. Yet problem-solving judges are constrained by their interactions with other court participants, albeit in somewhat different ways from regular criminal courts. For instance, community court judges may participate in community advisory panels, whose decisions in turn shape judges' choices (Kundu 2005, 177). And a chief judge in Portland delegated the recruitment of problem-solving judges to a district attorney and public defender (Berman 2000, 81).

Thus problem-solving courts appeal to people on multiple grounds (McCoy 2003, 1517–18; Meekins 2006, 13–14). Considerations that range from job satisfaction to crime control to saving money have all helped to spur interest in the problem-solving model. As the process stream perspective suggests, the multiplicity of problems to which this model can be attached as a solution has facilitated its widespread adoption.

Like the Progressive Era courts, problem-solving courts have diffused widely. On one dimension, specific types of courts have spread from place to place. In addition to drug courts, mental health courts, drunk driving courts, and domestic violence courts have become common. More often than not, a single court is identified as the innovator, and personnel of other courts look to that court as an example. State and federal legislation and funding have encouraged the use of several types of problem-solving courts. Nongovernmental organizations promote drug courts and environmental courts, among others.

Simultaneously, the general idea of problem-solving courts has diffused from one type of criminal case to others. The problem-solving label has facilitated this dimension of diffusion, as entrepreneurs argue for the advantages of this approach to criminal cases and seek its adoption in new contexts (Winick and Wexler 2003; Berman and Feinblatt, with Glazer 2005). Sometimes this diffusion takes place within a single locality, when judges who favor the idea of problem-solving courts adopt the idea in multiple fields.

This broader diffusion of the problem-solving model has had its own organizational support. In New York State, a long-time chief judge of the state strongly encouraged the use of problem-solving courts and helped to create them (Kaye 2004; Eligon 2008). The New York court system also cosponsors the Center for Court Innovation, an organization that facilitates the creation of several types of problem-solving courts in New York and elsewhere. The California court system, working with the Center for Court Innovation, has sought to establish various types of problem-solving courts (Wolf 2005). The Ohio Supreme Court also has a program to encourage the creation of these courts.[18] At the federal level, the Bureau of Justice Assistance within the Justice Department promotes "problem-solving criminal justice" as a general approach.[19] Two national organizations, the National Center for State Courts (Casey, Rottman, and Bromage 2007) and the American Bar

18. Program materials are at http://www.sconet.state.oh.us/spec_dockets/default.asp.
19. The Bureau of Justice Assistance describes its Problem-Solving Criminal Justice Initiative at http://www.ojp.usdoj.gov/BJA/grant/cb_problem_solving.html.

Association (Garcia 2003), advocate the use of problem-solving courts. Like professional associations in other fields (Balla 2001), these groups play major roles in the diffusion process.

One indication of the success of these entrepreneurs is the wide array of courts that are labeled as problem solving, including some that do not seem to fit that label very well. As noted earlier, some courts with this label emphasize sanctions over treatment. One report even applies the label to gun courts (Huddleston, Marlowe, and Casebolt 2008, 19). In general, the courts that are defined by type of defendant fit the problem-solving model better than those that are defined by offense.

The level of enthusiasm for problem-solving courts among some of their proponents should be underlined. These courts are depicted as a sharp and welcome break from traditional ways of adjudicating criminal cases. For two directors of the Center for Court Innovation, they are "Good Courts" (Berman and Feinblatt, with Glazer 2005). One enthusiastic drug court judge predicted that "eventually, every court will be a problem-solving court" (Hora 2009, 136).

When it is put in place, the problem-solving model could have fundamental effects on the functioning of courts and their treatment of defendants. Cases might be given more time and consideration. Sanctions might change—sometimes in the direction of leniency, and sometimes in other ways. The adversarial model of adjudication, already worn away to a considerable degree in criminal courts, might be weakened further by an emphasis on outcomes that are reached by consensus. Yet the forces that operate to create the usual patterns of court operation and outcomes might be strong enough to withstand efforts at reform.

An examination of several types of problem-solving courts will provide evidence on this issue as well as how and why specific types of courts have come about.[20] I begin with courts that were created with a strong emphasis on treatment: drug courts, homeless and veterans' courts, and mental health courts. I then turn to the courts in which the theme of treatment is accompanied or overshadowed by an emphasis on sanctions: community courts, domestic violence courts, and environmental courts.

---

20. The problem-solving courts that will be discussed include most of those that have become at least fairly common as well as some less common courts. One omission is truancy courts, some of them based in schools, which are most common in Rhode Island (Weiner 1998; Tan 2000; Macris 2002). Another is youth or teen courts, a widespread structure in which young people participate in sentencing proceedings for other young people (M. Fisher 2002; J. Schneider 2008).

Drug Courts

Like juvenile courts in the Progressive Era, drug courts have been the proto-type for other courts with similar purposes. They are by far the most common of the problem-solving courts. At the beginning of 2010, according to one count, there were 2,459 drug courts.[21] Their existence and perceived success have also helped to generate a wide range of other courts (Terry 1999; Nolan 2001; Goldkamp 2003; A. Fox and Wolf 2004).

The current drug courts, like their old-style predecessors, grew out of rapid growth in the numbers of people whose drug use landed them in the criminal court system. Some were defendants in drug cases. Others were charged with crimes such as theft that resulted from their addiction to drugs. In Miami, people in the courts improvised the first new-style drug court in 1989. It appears that the founders' goals were to deal more effectively with drug addiction and other underlying problems that led to criminal behavior and thus to reduce caseload pressures that resulted from recidivism (Goldkamp 2003, 197–98; see Finn and Newlyn 1993). Defendants whose relatively minor offenses seemed to stem from addiction would be channeled into intensive treatment under the judge's active supervision. The judge was to provide support and encouragement, but offenders who failed to meet expectations were subject to removal from the program and more conventional sanctions.

The Miami innovation attracted favorable attention elsewhere, and some supporters of the drug court model proselytized on its behalf. The diffusion of this model was accelerated by personal connections. As governor of Arkansas, Bill Clinton visited the Miami drug court and learned about its operation from his brother-in-law Hugh Rodham, who worked as a public defender in the court. Janet Reno, whom Clinton appointed as attorney general, had played a major role in creating the court when she was state attorney in Dade County (Isikoff and Booth 1993). The Clinton administration advocated federal funding to support the establishment of new drug courts around the country, and a provision of a 1994 statute initiated that funding.[22] The availability of federal money has been a major, perhaps critical factor in the spread of drug courts around the country (McCoy 2003, 1526). The George W. Bush administration also expressed support for drug courts. The Obama administration thus far has been especially enthusiastic

---

21. This figure is from the Web site of the National Association of Drug Court Professionals at http://www.nadcp.org/learn/what-are-drug-courts/history.

22. The statute was the Violent Crime Control and Law Enforcement Act of 1994.

about drug courts, and they enjoy broad political support in Congress; one result has been increased federal funding for them (C. Johnson and Goldstein 2009; Maron 2009).

Courts began to set up drug courts specifically for juvenile defendants in the mid-1990s. The popularity of the drug court movement and the availability of federal funding led to the widespread adoption of juvenile drug courts (Butts and Roman 2004a; 2004b, 7; Roman, Butts, and Rebeck 2004, 49).[23] Of the drug courts counted in a 2007 survey, about one-quarter were for juveniles (Drug Court Clearinghouse 2007).

Drug courts differ in some major respects. One difference is between courts that defer prosecution for defendants in the drug court program and those in which defendants enter the program after adjudication of their cases, typically through a guilty plea. Each form is common, and some courts use both. Another difference is in categories of defendants who are ineligible for drug court, such as those charged with violent crimes (most courts exclude them) and those who have been treated for drug problems in the past (about half the courts exclude them) (Bhati, Roman, and Chalfin 2008, 30).

As noted earlier, enthusiasm for drug courts in the political arena reflects the intertwining of some elements that appeal to liberals and others that appeal to conservatives. Within the courts, support for drug courts reflects the benefits to judges and other personnel that accrue from problem-solving courts of all types. Enhanced satisfaction with work is a strong benefit for some drug court judges. As one judge said of the drug court, "It works. It makes sense. It's cost effective. And it makes you feel good" (Nolan 2001, 110). This satisfaction helps to account for the zeal with which some drug court judges approach their work and proselytize for the use of drug courts elsewhere.

Drug courts also enhance judges' roles. Judges are clearly the most important participants, and their interactions with defendants are at the center of the action in cases. One scholar referred to "the cult of personality" around drug court judges (Bean 2002, 236), and many judges enjoy the focus on them and their control of court proceedings. When a defendant in a Miami drug court case understandably looked at his public defender for assistance, the judge told the defendant, "Don't look at him; he's not gonna help you" (Finn and Newlyn 1993, 4).

---

23. A variant of the juvenile drug court is the tobacco courts that have been set up in Florida and Utah (Nii 1998; Navarro 1998; Langer, Warheit, and Alan 2000). These are not technically criminal courts, since possession of tobacco by a minor is a civil violation in those states.

Because drug courts have proliferated, and because judges often rotate through them, judicial participation in drug courts has been broad. By 2007, it was estimated that more than four thousand judges had served on drug courts (Ca. Cooper 2007). Despite widespread enthusiasm for drug courts, it seems highly unlikely that all those judges have been committed to the vision of drug-court proponents.

It is difficult to characterize the effect of drug courts on the outcomes of cases, in part because of variation among courts. One effect of the judge's centrality is that the functioning of a drug court can change considerably when a new judge arrives (M. Hoffman 2000, 1517; Satel 1998). In addition, comparison of defendants' fates in regular criminal courts and drug courts is complicated. On the surface, there seems to be a radical difference between an emphasis on punishment in regular courts and drug courts' emphasis on treatment. But the "coerced treatment" (Nolan 2001, 200) that occurs in drug courts is not necessarily less punitive than outcomes in ordinary courts, and defendants who fail to meet judges' expectations may end up in jail. One criminal justice scholar goes further, arguing that the differences in outcomes are more limited than they appear to be: "it is difficult to distinguish monitoring of drug court clients from intensive supervision probation" (McCoy 2003, 1528).

How well drug courts work in reducing drug problems is also an open, and disputed, question (Paik 2009, 575; see R. King and Pasquarella 2009). Some proponents of drug courts cite anecdotal and quantitative evidence that these courts achieve a high level of success in overcoming drug addiction (Berman and Feinblatt, with Glazer 2005, 155–58). Other commentators read the evidence less positively (Nolan 2001, 127–32). To a degree, this disagreement reflects the inevitable limitations of evaluation research (see National Institute of Justice 2006). One judicial skeptic concluded that "perhaps the most startling thing about the drug court phenomenon is that drug courts have so quickly become fixtures of our jurisprudence in the absence of satisfying empirical evidence that they actually work" (M. Hoffman 2000, 1479–80). But that is hardly unusual in the world of public policy, and the same comment could have been made about juvenile courts in an earlier era.

One difference with juvenile courts is that only a small proportion of offenders with drug problems participate in drug court programs.[24] Indeed, drug courts, like some other problem-solving courts, have been called

---

24. According to an estimate for 2005, only 4 percent of the "at-risk arrestee population" were enrolled in drug court programs (Bhati, Roman, and Chalfin 2008, 33).

"boutique courts" (McCoy 2003, 1528; W. Davis 2003, 34). No matter how successful they are, they can make only a small dent in the problem of drug addiction.

As of 2007, nearly three hundred drug courts accepted defendants in drunk-driving cases. There were also more than one hundred separate drunk-driving courts, sometimes called DWI (for driving while intoxicated) or DUI (for driving under the influence) courts (Huddleston, Marlowe, and Casebolt 2008, 9; see Mays, Ryan, and Bejarano 1997; Flango 2005). The philosophy underlying DWI courts is like that of drug courts, and the two are similar in important respects. However, the widespread perception of drunk driving as a serious offense and the activities of Mothers Against Drunk Driving create strong pressures against what might be perceived as undue leniency for defendants. These pressures seem to account for the fact that drunk-driving courts are more likely than drug courts to take defendants only after they have been convicted (National Drug Court Institute n.d.). DWI courts are designed for offenders who are identified as alcoholics. That focus reflects the analogy with people who are addicted to illegal drugs, and it may also reflect a perception that alcoholics are less blameworthy than other drunk drivers. That DWI courts have developed even while drunk driving is the subject of increased opprobrium underlines the appeal of the problem-solving model to judges and other people in trial courts.[25]

Mental Health Courts

Courts have long adjudicated cases involving the civil commitment of individuals to mental institutions. Mental health courts are different, in that they deal with criminal defendants who are identified as suffering from mental health problems. The people who create mental health courts have been inspired by the example of drug courts. And of the various problem-solving courts, mental health courts are perhaps the closest analogues to drug courts (Goldkamp and Irons-Guynn 2000; Watson et al. 2001; Griffin, Steadman, and Petrila 2002; Bernstein and Seltzer 2003).

In general, the motivations for creation of the two types of courts have been similar. Even more than people addicted to drugs, those who suffer from mental illness can be viewed as blameless for their condition and for the behavior that results from it (Bernstein and Seltzer 2003, 160). Further,

25. It is interesting that a study of a "drunk court" in an unnamed city in the 1960s identified it as a socialized court. The study's description of the court suggests that it had much in common with the later DWI courts that explicitly follow a problem-solving model (Wiseman 1979).

the high proportions of criminal defendants whose offenses seem to reflect mental illness, like the large influx of drug-addicted defendants, created pressures to find another way to response to these defendants. Advocates argued that both courts and communities would benefit if a treatment-oriented approach was more effective than conventional punishment in preventing future offenses. The early mental health courts in Fort Lauderdale (created in 1997) and Seattle (1999) were established after incidents that seemed to underline the failure of ordinary criminal courts to prevent crime by mentally ill people. The attractiveness of emphasizing treatment was reflected in the 2000 legislation that authorized federal money to support mental health courts.[26] The preamble to the statute cited the Fort Lauderdale and Seattle courts.

Like the Miami drug court, the Fort Lauderdale mental health court resulted from the initiative and commitment of local court personnel (Siegel 1999; Lerner-Wren 2000). A presiding judge was the key participant in creation of the Seattle court (Barker 1999). Mental health courts have also followed a pattern of diffusion similar to that of drug courts. The first prominent courts, especially the Fort Lauderdale court, provided models for other localities. The early mental health courts inspired support at the state and national levels. A 2008 publication counted more than 150 mental health courts (Thompson, Osher, and Tomasini-Joshi 2007, vii); according to a 2009 estimate, there were more than 200 (Waters, Strickland, and Gibson 2009, 34).

Mental health courts take various forms. "If you have seen one mental health court, you have seen one mental health court" (Council of State Governments Justice Center 2008, 7). As early as 2001, one commentary noted that the label of mental health court had been stretched so far that "the concept has come to have little meaning" (Steadman, Davidson, and Brown 2001, 458), and there appear to be some differences between the courts that were established early and those that came later (Redlich et al. 2005). What these courts have in common is their emphasis on treatment, which leads to a diversion of cases from the ordinary criminal track before or after adjudication of guilt. As in drug courts, in most mental health court programs offenders who fail to meet their responsibilities in treatment programs are subject to imprisonment.

The mental health courts that have been studied so far appear to follow the intended model well, treating defendants primarily as people who need treatment and drawing on available resources to obtain treatment for them

---

26. The statute was entitled America's Law Enforcement and Mental Health Project (2000).

(Goldkamp and Irons-Guynn 2000). One indication of this orientation is that actual use of the jail sanction seems to be rare (Griffin, Steadman, and Petrila 2002, 1288). Accounts of some courts emphasize the informal, empathetic style of their judges (Siegel 1999; Em. Schwartz 2008).

If it is fair to characterize most drug courts as boutique courts, the same certainly is true of mental health courts. These courts reach only a small proportion of the defendants whose criminal charges result from mental health problems (see Mattingly 2004). The San Francisco Behavioral Health Court, to take one example, has been reported to have no more than 150 participants per year (Waters, Strickland, and Gibson 2008, 48).

Like drug courts, then, mental health courts are inherently limited in their impact. Within that limitation, the success of mental health courts in achieving a positive effect on defendants is uncertain despite some relevant research (Lurigio and Snowden 2009, 207–10). In light of the wide variation among individual courts, it might turn out that some are considerably more effective than others.

Homeless and Veterans' Treatment Courts

Few groups are viewed as sympathetically as military veterans, and the development of homeless courts reflects their favorable image. A public defender in San Diego learned that homeless Vietnam veterans often accumulated misdemeanor citations for offenses such as riding on public transit without a valid ticket and that unpaid misdemeanor citations created practical problems for the veterans. As a result of the defender's initiative, a program was established in which the citations were resolved through plea bargains in exchange for participation in an agency program that was designed to help resolve the veterans' problems. The program was gradually expanded to include other segments of the homeless population. In 1999 a grant from the Bureau of Justice Assistance in the Justice Department enabled the San Diego homeless court to hold monthly sessions that alternated in location between two homeless shelters (Perry 2000; Kerry and Pennell 2001; Binder 2003; Cl. Cooper 2003).

Support and advocacy from the California court system and the American Bar Association Commission on Homelessness and Poverty helped to spread the idea of a homeless court to other cities.[27] One census identified thirty-seven homeless courts in 2007, two-thirds in California and all but

---

27. The American Bar Association's resolution supporting homeless courts is at http://www.abanet.org/crimjust/policy/am06108a.pdf.

one in the West (Huddleston, Marlowe, and Casebolt 2008, 19). Like the San Diego court, other homeless courts meet only occasionally, so they do not create high levels of judge concentration. Media coverage in San Diego and elsewhere has been highly favorable (T. Wilson 2001; LeDuff 2004; Powell 2004). Although other segments of the homeless population are not viewed as positively as veterans, efforts to help people in difficult straits to overcome those difficulties are widely viewed as appropriate.

The emphasis of these courts on resolving the legal problems of homeless people and helping them with nonlegal problems makes them somewhat distinctive even among problem-solving courts. That distinctiveness also underlines the attractiveness of the homeless court model for court personnel who initiate and participate in these courts. According to one report about San Diego, court personnel in its homeless court "find it a very rewarding and often a heart-warming experience" (Urry 2006, 14).

A Buffalo judge who already presided over a Drug Treatment Court and Mental Health Treatment Court established the first Veterans' Treatment Court in January 2008 (Michel 2008a, 2008b; Daneman 2008; Eckley 2008). Like the San Diego Homeless Court, the Veterans' Treatment Court was established with the mission of helping military veterans who became criminal defendants. The court's emphasis is on dealing with the mental health problems of veterans, and it provides an array of services to veterans who come to the court. The court is limited to defendants who are charged with misdemeanors and nonviolent felonies.

The Buffalo court received considerable publicity, and one result was the initiation of veterans' courts in other localities (Russell 2009). By March 2010, similar courts had been established in twenty-one other localities around the country.[28] Money and personnel from the Department of Veterans Affairs and other federal agencies have played a part in the creation of some courts (Marek 2008). At least three states have enacted legislation encouraging the creation of additional veterans' courts, and bills have been introduced in Congress to provide grants for these courts.[29]

The veterans' courts do not process large numbers of cases. Eight months after its establishment, the Buffalo court had included only forty-six defendants in its program (A. Levin 2008). Even so, these courts underline the strength of the impulse to provide special treatment for a class of criminal

28. This number is from the Web site of the National Drug Court Institute, at http://www.ndci.org/learn/veterans-treatment-court-clearinghouse.

29. This information is from the Web site of the National Association of Drug Court Professionals at http://www.nadcp.org/learn/veterans-treatment-court-clearinghouse/veterans-treatment-court-legislation.

defendants that attracts sympathy. Along with homeless courts, veterans' courts are the version of problem-solving courts that gives the greatest weight to helping offenders.

Community Courts

According to one count, there were three dozen community courts across the country in 2010.[30] Community courts are often defined in vague terms, and the courts that have been given that label differ a good deal (A. Thompson 2002; Rottman 2002; Lanni 2005). However, they have some traits in common. Most cover only one portion of a city. Their jurisdiction is limited to relatively minor criminal offenses and violations of ordinances, frequently with an emphasis on "nuisance" offenses such as loitering and public intoxication. Statements of purpose by proponents of community courts typically refer to attacking offenses that affect life in a community and to providing help for offenders. Most community courts require defendants to plead guilty to remain in the court (rather than being transferred to a regular criminal court) and to receive the treatment it offers.

The balance between punitive and treatment goals varies among courts, but the first goal is usually dominant. In community courts, according to one commentary, the judicial branch "is no longer an impartial arbiter of state power, but instead seeks to serve a victimized community that is in need of repair" (Fagan and Malkin 2003, 902). More than anything else, community courts are designed to secure stronger enforcement of laws against offenses that usually receive a low priority from police, prosecutors, and judges, in the interest of making an area more "livable."

Use of the criminal justice system to help clean up problems in part of a city is a long-standing practice. Judges often are enlisted in those efforts, asked to mete out more severe sanctions for certain offenses (see Caruso 2002). In effect, the community court movement seeks to institutionalize this kind of orientation by making it part of a court's fundamental mission.

The initiative for creation of community courts can arise from different segments of the community. In some instances the business community has been dominant, seeking a court that serves its needs. In other instances, non-business groups have played more important roles.

---

30. This count is from the Web site of the Center for Court Innovation, at http://www.court innovation.org/index.cfm?fuseaction=Document.viewDocument&documentID=669&document TopicID=17&documentTypeID=10. This source also describes some attributes of each court.

The first community court was the Midtown Community Court in Manhattan, a court that has served as a model for other community courts. The Midtown court was established in 1993 as a demonstration project with support from the City of New York, the state court system, and a non-profit group called the Fund for the City of New York (Sviridoff, Rottman, Ostrom, and Curtis 2000; Wolf 2001; Quinn 2006, 696–710).

The genesis of the court was linked to the growing interest in attacking "quality-of-life" offenses, such as prostitution, shoplifting, turnstile jumping in subway stations, and disorderly conduct. Thus, it reflected the "broken window" theory that drove criminal justice policy under Mayor Rudolph Giuliani, a theory under which attacking relatively minor crimes would have broader effects on criminal activity and community life (A. Thompson 2002, 85). But the court was not designed to be solely punitive. Rather, it was to emphasize restorative justice, which meant that offenders would be sentenced to community service. The court would also provide social services to offenders.

Within the Midtown area, one advocate for the court was a resident who was unhappy about ineffective enforcement of the prostitution laws. However, a stronger impetus came from business owners who were concerned with the petty criminal activity that discouraged people from coming to areas such as Times Square. Business organizations in Times Square provided a majority of the operating funds for the court in its early years. Critics saw the court as essentially a tool of the business community (Quinn 2006, 698–701, 711–13). Manhattan district attorney Robert Morgenthau said that "it bothers me that people who can put up money and have influence can get their own court" (Gordon 1994, 55).

At least in the first few years of its operation, the Midtown court fulfilled the expectations of its founders. The dominant outcome of cases was a sentence to community service. In comparison with the Downtown court in Manhattan, which heard similar cases in a traditional setting, community service was far more common and jail sentences and sentences to time already served were far less common in the Midtown court (Sviridoff et al. 2000, chap. 6; Weidner 2001, 137). This adherence to the court's mandate was facilitated by a high level of continuity in court personnel (Sviridoff et al. 2000, 101). However, the court's effect on the problems it was aimed at correcting is the subject of considerable disagreement (Berman and Feinblatt, with Glazer 2005, 61–66; Quinn 2006, 703–10, 715–24).

Other community courts in which the business community has played a central role include the Downtown Austin Community Court (Davenport 1999; Quin 2001), the Philadelphia Community Court (Durkin et al. 2009,

3–5), and the St. Louis Downtown Community Court (Walter 2002; Wittenauer 2003). The St. Louis court, established in 2002, is of particular interest. Like their counterparts in Midtown Manhattan, business groups in St. Louis sought stronger enforcement of laws against nuisance crimes in order to make downtown more attractive. The court's mission was reflected in the title of a newswire article about its creation: "New Court Aimed at Eradicating Pesky Behaviors Downtown" (Wittenauer 2003). The Downtown St. Louis Partnership provided the bulk of the funding for the court through an assessment on its members, mostly businesses.

Once in operation, the St. Louis court ran into controversy. In 2004 the court's judge was criticized for an order that allowed people who had been accused (but not yet convicted) of nuisance crimes during a city fair to be sentenced to community service (*St. Louis Post-Dispatch* 2004). In the same year, a state trial judge held that the arrangements for the community court violated the state and federal constitutions, primarily because of its private funding. Citing the Supreme Court decisions involving the Ohio mayor's courts, the judge's opinion concluded that the court's dependence on private money gave the community court judge an inappropriate incentive to rule in ways that the Downtown St. Louis Partnership approved (*State v. Bonner* 2004). The city had just ended the private funding arrangement, perhaps because of a newspaper article that publicized it (Kohler 2004). The court no longer exists.

It appears that business support was much less important in the Red Hook area of Brooklyn (Berman 1998; Fagan and Malkin 2003; Berman and Fox 2005) and in the first community court in Portland (Berman and Feinblatt, with Glazer 2005, 66–76) than it was in Manhattan. In both places, advocates for community courts focused on general community problems rather than on the problems that were of particular concern to businesses.

The Red Hook court was established in 2000 after long planning and intensive consultation with neighborhood residents about their concerns (Berman 1998), and the court was made part of a Community Justice Center that offered residents a wide array of services. One central goal was to deal effectively with crime problems that concerned residents and, in the process, to enhance the credibility of the courts. An unusual feature of the court was that it was given jurisdiction over family and housing cases as well as criminal matters, though it has been primarily a criminal court. In its early years, the large numbers of drug cases turned the court into something of a drug court (Fagan and Malkin 2003, 925–29). The court's initial judge played the kind of activist role that the court's designers had in mind (see M. Wilson 2006). The court's effectiveness in helping to solve community problems is uncertain, but its orientation seems to remain consistent with the mission for which it was created (Meadows 2009).

Domestic Violence Courts

Courts with the label of domestic violence courts take quite different forms, which include creating a special docket for civil protection orders, putting prosecutions for domestic violence in their own division, and integrating domestic violence prosecutions with related cases involving the same people. Unlike some other problem-solving courts, domestic violence courts that decide criminal cases (rather than requests for protection orders) adjudicate guilt.

Domestic violence courts were created with a clear mission (Tsai 2000; Kaye and Knipps 2000; Fritzler and Simon 2000; Keilitz 2000; Shelton 2007). Largely through the efforts of feminist groups, domestic violence increasingly came to be seen as a significant social problem. Specialized courts for domestic violence cases were intended to address that problem. Underlying the drive for domestic violence courts is the belief that courts have been too lenient toward defendants who are accused of domestic violence. One step to overcome this leniency has been modification of court structures in an effort to ensure that complaints of domestic violence are given greater weight.

Domestic violence courts fit the standard problem-solving model to varying degrees. On the whole, however, the fit is quite imperfect (but see Petrucci 2002; Nolan 2009, 14–16). The emphasis of these courts is on victims rather than offenders (Shelton 2007, 10–11), and "these are not 'feel-good' courts" (Berman and Feinblatt, with Glazer 2005, 184).[31] Still, domestic violence courts are generally given the problem-solving label. One reason is that domestic violence is widely thought to be a social problem similar to those addressed by other problem-solving courts. Another reason is that the rhetoric of problem-solving and therapeutic justice is often used to describe the mission of domestic violence courts. Although therapeutic efforts are undertaken primarily to serve victims rather than offenders, some domestic violence courts have a significant element of therapy for offenders (Tsai 2000, 1302–4). Perhaps most important, the problem-solving label

---

31. Ironically, an early (1946) and largely unnoticed domestic violence court, the Home Term Part of the New York City Magistrates' Court, fit the problem-solving model more closely than the current wave of domestic violence courts (Quinn 2008).

has a positive connotation that supporters of domestic violence courts find attractive.

No single domestic violence court stands out as a model for other courts, though the courts in New York City have received considerable attention (Mazur and Aldrich 2003). The number of domestic violence courts is uncertain, in part because of the differing definitions of such courts. But it is clear that the number is large. According to one count, there were 185 domestic violence courts in 2007 (Huddleston, Marlowe, and Casebolt 2008, 19). Domestic violence courts in New York were fostered by the state court system, and funds from the federal Violence Against Women Act have been used to establish some courts.[32]

It appears that domestic violence courts do carry out the mission for which they were created. For instance, a sociologist's study of the court in Salt Lake City found that the court's judges accepted that mission enthusiastically (Mirchandani 2005, 2006). For their part, defense attorneys have complained about what they see as a pro-prosecution orientation in domestic violence courts (Post 2004a, 18; Newmark et al. 2001, 44–45). Of the criminal courts that were intended to change the substance of judicial policy, domestic violence courts are among those that have best lived up to that intent.

Environmental Courts

Scattered across the country, but most common in the South, are perhaps two dozen environmental courts (Keep America Beautiful 2006).[33] Environmental courts vary in characteristics such as the amount of a judge's time that they occupy. What they have in common with each other, and with

---

32. The Violence Against Women Act was part of the Violent Crime Control and Law Enforcement Act of 1994.

33. Some housing courts, such as the one in Cleveland (White 1981), share some of the jurisdiction and mission of environmental courts. These courts should be distinguished from long-standing housing courts that deal primarily or entirely with evictions of tenants. Some of those long-standing courts, such as the Forcible Entry and Detainer Court in Chicago, have been charged with undue favoritism toward landlords, a kind of capture (Lawyers' Committee for Better Housing 2003; see Brill 1987). On the other hand, a set of landlords once sued judges of the New York City Housing Court, which handles evictions and other issues, on the ground that the court was so favorable to tenants that it violated landlords' constitutional rights (*Miller v. Silbermann* 1997). The various types of housing courts are catalogued in F. White (1981, 43–44).

In contrast with the environmental courts discussed in the text, the Vermont Environmental Court hears appeals from administrative decisions involving environmental issues (J. Anderson 1995).

domestic violence courts, is the goal of securing more serious enforcement of the law against certain offenses (Jester 1979; Karr 1997). As a reporter noted about the opening of a Tennessee environmental court, its first session "emphasized the county's commitment to crack down on litterbugs, particularly illegal dumpers and sloppy property owners" (Igo 2006). Their mission parallels that of community courts to a degree, in that they are aimed at improving city life by cleaning up certain visible problems.

The first court labeled as environmental was established in Indianapolis in 1978. The Memphis court, created five years later, seems to have been more influential as a model. It is at least partly responsible for the disproportionate number of environmental courts in the South (Keep America Beautiful 2006). Because environmental courts combine two popular ideas, environmentalism and protection of property values, it is interesting that they have not yet diffused more widely.

The Columbus Environmental Court illustrates the mission underlying environmental courts, and journalistic accounts provide a good sense of its performance (Edwards 1991a, 1991b; Bebbington 1993; Gambini 1995). In 1991, the Ohio legislature created a special judgeship for an environmental court within the Columbus municipal court. The statute gave the environmental court jurisdiction over civil and criminal matters arising under a broad range of local code provisions that included building, housing, air pollution, and health. The goal was to secure more effective enforcement of these provisions by giving them a higher priority and reducing delays. The court's first judge enthusiastically accepted this mission, publicizing his court and taking an active role in enforcing environmental laws. In one instance, he personally monitored compliance with his order that a landlord live in one of his rental properties (Lyttle 2001). Thus, county officials got basically what they wanted when they secured the creation of an environmental court.[34]

Discussion

State courts feature a good deal of judicial specialization in criminal cases as a whole. Many trial courts and a few appellate courts have jurisdiction

---

34. Within a ten-year period, however, the court's first judge also struck down a prohibition on smoking in public buildings, a noise ordinance, and the application of a fire code to flag burning—a rather different form of assertiveness that indicated considerable independence (*Cookie's Diner, Inc. v. Columbus Board of Health* 1994; Mayhood 2001; Ferenchik and Hoholik 2003).

only in criminal law. In trial courts with broad jurisdiction, it is common practice to assign criminal cases to judges who hear only those cases for some period of time.

I have given primary attention to narrower specialization within criminal law. In subsets of criminal cases that are defined by offense or defendant, many trial courts in the states have created high levels of judge concentration, case concentration, or both. With the development of problem-solving courts in the last two decades, the overall level of specialization within criminal law has grown.

There is no single explanation for specialization within criminal law, but an interest in the substance of policy has been the dominant motive. This motive has been made more explicit in criminal law than in most other fields of law, because the goal of attacking crime enjoys something close to consensual support. Put differently, because the norm of judicial neutrality is most strongly contested in criminal law, institutional changes that run counter to this norm have greater legitimacy than in most other fields of law. One manifestation of this reality is the many problem-solving courts in which defense attorneys are asked to depart from their usual advocacy role and defendants are required to plead guilty if they want to stay in the court.

In some instances, the use of specialization to change criminal court outcomes has been quite straightforward. Policy makers who favor heavier sanctions seek and create courts that are given the mission of taking a tough stance. Gun courts and domestic violence courts exemplify this process.

In other instances, the effort to change policy has taken a more complicated form. Both socialized courts of the Progressive Era and problem-solving courts in the current era have garnered support from people with widely divergent political views because they combine goals that appeal to liberals with those that appeal to conservatives. The popularity of drug courts among both conservatives and liberals underlines the effectiveness with which the problem-solving model has been framed. More broadly, the widespread adoption of these courts reflects the wide range of goals that they encompass (McCoy 2003). Thus, they are consistent with the policy stream perspective, which suggests that disparate goals may underlie the consideration and adoption of a particular policy.

The temporal pattern in the adoption of specialized courts in criminal law shows how trends in social thought can shape institutional change. Juvenile courts, women's courts, and domestic relations courts reflected the thinking of Progressives about how to address social problems. The problem-solving courts of the last two decades reflect widely shared unease about how well the criminal justice system addresses the root causes of criminal behavior. In both eras, a therapeutic orientation has shaped prescriptions for change in the courts.

The power of courts to organize themselves has facilitated the growth of judicial specialization within criminal law. Judges can act on their own without securing the enactment of legislation. Further, the decentralization of structural decisions has allowed courts to go their own ways. A court whose judges do not like the idea of drug courts can refuse to adopt it without holding back other courts whose personnel favor the idea.

The ability of courts to create specialized units makes judges' own motivations quite relevant to decisions about specialization. Much of the impetus for the invention and diffusion of problem-solving courts comes from judges' frustration with the standard ways of handling criminal cases. Adoption of the problem-solving model brings with it the promise of a more satisfying work day, one in which judges can feel they are accomplishing something. As a bonus, their power to determine the outcomes of cases is enhanced. Judges may also gain a self-image and recognition from others as innovators.

Interested groups outside the judiciary have played a substantial part in the movement toward specialization within criminal law. In the case of some community courts, businesses have sought specialization to serve their material interests. More often, groups with symbolic rather than material stakes in policy have sought the establishment of specialized courts. Groups that supported Progressive values worked to establish juvenile courts, domestic relations courts, and women's courts. Groups that seek to reduce domestic violence and damage to the environment have lobbied for courts that reflect their orientations. For their part, policy makers in the other branches have established or encouraged the establishment of specialized courts in order to advance their own policy goals. In the case of problem-solving courts, federal funding has been a significant stimulus.

To a degree, specialization in the criminal justice field can be understood as capture of the courts by people within and outside government who seek to influence judicial policy. Yet a theme of capture should not be overstated. For one thing, much of the impetus for specialization has come from the courts themselves. Further, the external advocates of specialization often are people who have no direct stake in the outcomes of cases. To a considerable extent, the movements for socialized courts and problem-solving courts have been driven by ideas rather than interests.

What we know about the operation of these courts underlines the importance of individual judges. When courts set up specialized units, those units are frequently staffed by judges who have a strong commitment to the mission of those units—sometimes, by judges who played key roles in the creation of specialized courts. These judges tend to carry out the court's mission enthusiastically. This zeal can be found in some of the early juvenile courts as well as drug courts, mental health courts, and homeless courts.

Over time, as personnel change, a court's commitment to its mission may atrophy. And when a specialized unit is strongly encouraged by a court system or by the other branches, even the judges who serve initially in such a unit may not share the goals that a court was created to advance. Both tendencies are reflected in the history of juvenile courts. To the extent that problem-solving courts of today depart from the standard ways of doing business in criminal cases, they too may regress to those standard ways.

On the whole, specialized courts in criminal law do not receive much public attention. But because most of these courts reflect widely held values in elite segments of society, they tend to garner support from elites who are aware of them. The most concrete reflection of that support is coverage by the news media, which tends to be laudatory (e.g., Eckholm 2008; *Columbus Dispatch* 2009). To a considerable degree, that favorable coverage reflects the enthusiasm of participants in specialized courts and advocates for them.

In reality, the effectiveness of these courts in achieving their goals is not entirely clear. There is a good deal of evaluation research on some problem-solving courts, but that research is mixed in results and far from definitive. The lack of clear lessons from this research reflects the difficulty of ascertaining effects and, in all likelihood, a complicated reality. The tendency for court missions to weaken over time raises doubts about the long-term effectiveness of specialized courts in addressing the problems that led to their creation. Even while these missions remain strong, it is uncertain how well judges whose training is in the law can adapt to a role that is largely one of a psychologist or social worker.[35]

To a degree, advocates of specialized courts in criminal law have engaged in shallow thinking about the likely consequences of the courts they favor. They have operated largely on the basis of folk theories about the impact of specialization rather than careful analysis. Decision makers who consider the idea of problem-solving courts could seek to glean lessons from the history of juvenile courts and other courts of the Progressive Era, but there is no evidence that they do so.

---

35. I am grateful to Candace McCoy for suggesting that point to me.

This inattention reflects the symbolic element in the creation of specialized criminal courts. The act of creation gives judges and others a feeling that they are helping to solve difficult social problems, the solutions they adopt make intuitive sense, and later adopters perceive that existing courts of the same type have been successful. With some frequency, that has been enough to justify creation of a specialized court.

FIVE

Economic Issues: Government Litigation

The fields of policy that I considered in the last two chapters involve fundamental duties of government. The roles of government in the economic arena—taking in revenue, allocating money, and regulating the economy—can also be regarded as fundamental. But the politics of government economic policy is more complicated than the politics of foreign policy, national security, and criminal justice. In the economic field, the interests of government frequently run counter to the interests of private-sector groups that have significant political influence. Because of that influence, public policy makers do not necessarily favor the government in conflicts between government and private interests. Members of Congress frequently side with taxpayers, people who seek public benefits, and regulated businesses rather than their adversaries in the executive branch.

To the extent that judicial specialization is used to benefit interested groups, then, groups on either side might seek and achieve the adoption of specialized court proposals that they favor. However, most of the specialized federal courts that have dealt with government economic policy were established at the initiative of the executive branch. The reasons for this outcome require investigation, but one likely source is the advantages of the executive branch as advocate in the legislative branch. It can usually win serious consideration of its proposals, and its opposition to proposals from other sources can usually prevent their adoption.

In light of the presumption in favor of generalist courts, one effect of having strong interests on both the government and private sides might be to limit the use of specialization as a means to shape judicial policy. If a proposal for a specialized court is perceived as benefiting one side against the other, the side that might suffer from adoption of that proposal can use suspicions about judicial specialization and the advantage of the status quo to buttress its opposition. This clash of interests helps to explain the continued dominance of generalist courts in government economic policy at both the federal and state levels.

There is an important exception to that dominance. A great deal of adjudication of economic issues occurs in administrative agencies that represent a specialized alternative to trial courts. At both the federal and state levels, administrative tribunals address disputes over government benefit programs (such as social security and veterans' benefits) and regulation of the private sector (such as labor-management relations). With the exception of some bodies that were later transformed into courts, I will not discuss administrative tribunals in this chapter or in chapter 6. But it should be kept in mind that the level of specialization in economic adjudication is considerably higher in the government as a whole than it is in the judiciary alone.

In the field of economic policy, as in criminal justice, judges themselves have played a role in the development of specialized courts. That role, however, has taken a different form. Federal judges have not been important to the creation of specialized courts that deal with economic issues. Once those courts have been created, however, judges who serve on them have a stake in their own status and the status of their courts, a stake that is often shared by lawyers who practice in those courts. The result is to provide an impetus for expanding the jurisdiction of particular courts and moving them along the continuum that goes from administrative tribunals to Article I courts and then to Article III courts. Meanwhile, the existence of a specialized court in a particular field makes it convenient to add to that court's jurisdiction. Both of these forces have helped to increase the role of specialized courts in the adjudication of government economic policy.

As I have noted, there is more judicial specialization on issues of government economic policy at the federal level than there is at the state level. Some states do have specialized courts that adjudicate issues in this area. But overall, specialized state courts occupy much less of this field than do their federal counterparts. Still, the state courts are of interest. Unfortunately, little is known about their origins and performance, so this chapter will deal solely with specialization in the federal courts. The chapter is organized in terms of three major roles of government on economic matters: obtaining revenue, expending money, and regulating the economy.

Revenue

In the nineteenth century, duties on imports were the single largest source of revenue for the federal government. In the twentieth century, the income tax became the dominant source of revenue (S. Carter et al. 2006, vol. 5, 82–84). Thus, it is noteworthy that Congress established specialized courts for disputes involving both sources of revenue and that those courts in modified form continue to exist long after their establishment.

Customs

Today, court cases between the government and private parties over international trade issues are concentrated in the Court of International Trade at the trial level and the Court of Appeals for the Federal Circuit at the intermediate appellate level (see Unah 1998). The current situation represents a culmination of more than a century of history, summarized in table 5.1. At both the trial and appellate levels, that history began with the establishment of a tribunal to deal with customs cases. Over time, that tribunal gained higher status and broader jurisdiction. The two courts in this field today feature high case concentration because they have monopolies over most of the field of international trade; the Court of International Trade also has high judge concentration.[1]

As of 1890, procedures for adjudicating challenges to government decisions about customs duties were quite complicated (Lombardi 1976, 11–19). Federal officials at ports of entry determined the amounts owed through decisions classifying imports (duties varied across types of goods) and appraising their value. An importer could appeal a classification decision to the secretary of the treasury, whose review of cases was "almost perfunctory" (Levett 1923, 94). The importer could then take the case to the appropriate circuit court, with the right to a jury trial.

Appraisals of value (called "appraisement") could be appealed to a two-person body composed of a merchant serving as an appraiser and a government official called a general appraiser. Disagreements between the two were resolved by the collector of customs, another government official. Appeals to the courts were allowed only on grounds of fraud or gross irregularity.

Provisions of the Customs Administrative Act of 1890 changed these procedures (Lombardi 1976, 25–31). The number of general appraisers was increased from four to nine, a group later designated as the Board of General Appraisers, and they were given power over classification of imports as

---

1. This discussion of the Court of International Trade, like later discussions of the Court of Federal Claims and the Court of Appeals for Veterans Claims, has benefited from the overviews of these courts in Sisk (2003b).

Table 5.1 Major events in the history of courts dealing with international trade

Court level and date	Event
Trial level:	
1890	Board of General Appraisers is created
1926	Board is renamed U.S. Customs Court
1956	Court gains Article III status, with jurisdiction and procedures revised
1980	Court is renamed U.S. Court of International Trade, with additional jurisdiction and powers
Appellate level:	
1909	Court of Customs Appeals is created
1929	Court receives patent jurisdiction and is renamed Court of Customs and Patent Appeals
1958	Court gains Article III status
1982	Court is folded into Court of Appeals for the Federal Circuit

well as appraisal. The general appraisers were appointed by the president and confirmed by the Senate; the president could remove them "for inefficiency, neglect of duty, or malfeasance in office" (Customs Administrative Act of 1890, § 12), creating a kind of presumption of permanent tenure. In appraisal, a single general appraiser replaced the existing two-person body. Decisions of that general appraiser could be appealed to a panel of three general appraisers. The more important change was in classification, where appeals from classification decisions now went to three general appraisers rather than to the circuit courts.

The general appraisers' classification decisions could be appealed to the circuit courts in their appellate roles. But it was expected that far fewer cases would be brought to the courts because the Board of General Appraisers was interposed between the original official's decision and the judiciary and because the circuit courts would now be limited to an appellate role. Thus the 1890 Act was intended to substitute a specialized administrative body within the Treasury Department for the federal trial courts in the classification of imported goods.

Those who favored creation of the Board of General Appraisers cited a wide range of defects in the existing system for handling of customs disputes. Among these defects were a conflict of interest in the roles of merchants who helped appraise competitors' goods, the flood of customs cases in the New York circuit court, and lack of uniformity in classifications from port to port. But the dominant motivation for creation of the Board was a desire to protect the government's interest in revenue from customs duties. That motivation was reflected in other provisions of the 1890 legislation as well.

One problem in the status quo cited by proponents of the Board was the perpetration of frauds against the government in appraisal and classification of goods.[2] There seemed to be general agreement that widespread fraud occurred and that the proposed changes in the system would reduce that problem (U.S. Congress 1890a, 826, 830–34). But the bigger problem was that the existing system encouraged litigation about classification of goods by making it profitable. Importers would pass on to consumers the duty they were charged in a port and then challenge that duty in court. If they won a lower rate, they pocketed the difference (U.S. Senate 1882, 2; U.S. Congress 1890b, 4005). Supporters of the legislation also argued that importers had unfair advantages over the government, some of them involving dishonesty, when they challenged the classification of goods in court (U.S. Senate 1882, 11; U.S. Congress 1890a, 834). Substituting the Board for the circuit court as a trial-level tribunal was expected at least to reduce these problems.

There was considerable opposition to the Board proposal in Congress, and some votes on the Board provision and on the legislation as a whole were close. One effect of the proposal would be to eliminate jury trials in classification cases, and opponents argued that this change was undesirable and perhaps unconstitutional. The more fundamental source of their opposition seemed to be a feeling that the legislation was designed to give the government an unfair advantage. One senator charged that the Board was "not a court of law" but "a limited, *ex parte*, revenue tribunal" (U.S. Congress 1890b, 4006).

As it turned out, a provision in the 1890 Act that allowed the introduction of new evidence in the circuit courts undercut the goals of the Board's proponents, because it provided an incentive for importers to withhold evidence

---

2. There was another issue of corruption involving the New York Custom House, which was responsible for about three-quarters of all federal revenue from customs duties (U.S. House of Representatives 1877; Reeves 1975, 61–96, 111–48; Vowell 2005, 126–32, 168–69). For some years after the Civil War, the Custom House was under the control of Senator Roscoe Conkling's Republican machine. Positions were awarded primarily on a patronage basis, and critics questioned both the collective competence of employees and their large numbers. Assessments on employees were a lucrative source of income for Conkling's machine. From 1871 to 1879, the head of the Custom House was Chester Alan Arthur, an ally of Conkling's. Beginning in 1881, President James Garfield and (to nearly everyone's surprise) his successor Arthur took steps to clean up the operation of the Custom House.

from the Board and present it in court. That defect was corrected in a 1908 statute, converting court proceedings into true appeals (Frankfurter and Landis 1928, 149–50). Meanwhile, there were proposals for a specialized court to supplant the remaining roles of the generalist federal courts in customs law, and the 1908 statute did not end interest in those proposals. Indeed, a year later Congress enacted one such proposal as part of the Payne-Aldrich Tariff Act (1909). Under that statute, appeals from decisions of the Board would go to a Court of Customs Appeals, which would be the final arbiter of customs law. Even Supreme Court review of the new court's decisions was disallowed, though that provision was repealed in 1914 (Rich 1980, 7).

Like the legislation that created the Board of General Appraisers, the proposal for a Court of Customs Appeals was approved over considerable opposition in Congress. The Senate vote for the new court was 50–26, with the opposition coming from insurgent Republicans and Democrats (U.S. Congress 1909, 4225). In the Senate debate, senators explicitly discussed general and specific issues about judicial specialization as a structural attribute of courts (U.S. Congress 1909, 4185–220; see Rightmire 1918–19, 28–33; Frankfurter and Landis 1928, 148–52).

Supporters of the Court of Customs Appeals cited the neutral virtues of specialization as benefits to be gained from the new court. Its judges would be more expert in customs law than generalist federal judges, cases would be resolved more quickly, and the law would become more uniform. More broadly, senators cited the value of judicial specialization in Progressive terms: "In creating a special tribunal for this class of cases the committee is in perfect accord with all tendencies of modern times. . . . The tendency is decidedly to specialism" (U.S. Congress 1909, 4219).

Some Senate supporters of the court proposal went beyond the neutral virtues. They argued that the court would serve the government's interest in collecting revenue and limit importers' use of litigation to gain an unfair advantage, in part by reducing delay in the resolution of cases. One senator said that a prime consideration for the committee that approved the court proposal was that the generalist courts tended to rule in favor of importers: "the result was almost always against the Government" (U.S. Congress 1909, 4189).

Opponents of the proposal emphasized this goal of enhancing the government's interests and challenged its legitimacy. Senator William Borah argued that "the object and purpose" of the proposal is "to have a court that will interpret this law for the purpose of getting the revenue for the Government." "That," he said, "has been frankly conceded" (U.S. Congress 1909,

4191). Some senators spoke in broader terms, arguing that specialized courts of this type were inherently subject to capture by the government.

> I am opposed to the establishment of a customs court of appeal for two reasons. The first is that it is a specialized court. It is a court that is to be brought into existence for the purpose of deciding in favor of the Government under all circumstances and no matter what the law or the evidence may be. . . . [The judges] are to be experts, their judicial business is to be confined to the matter of the duties on imports, and they will speedily become, just as all such courts become, the instrumentality of the Government for collecting the revenue; and they can not retain open and impartial minds, for it is impossible that they can escape the environment that will surround them. (U.S. Congress 1909, 4185)

Another senator predicted that "this will be followed by other steps creating other tribunals" with similar purposes (U.S. Congress 1909, 4188).

Most senators were not swayed by the opponents' concerns. The majority view seemed to be that if the government benefited from a new court, that benefit was appropriate. For one thing, the government's interest in customs revenue was important. Moreover, the Court of Customs Appeals would simply redress an unfair advantage for the government's opponents.

Congress enhanced the status of the two customs courts in a series of steps that culminated in the 1950s, when judges on both courts were given Article III status. Strangely, Congress did not specify the terms of judges on the Court of Customs Appeals. Dealing with the ambiguity of the court's status, the Supreme Court held in *Ex parte Bakelite Corporation* (1929) that it was an Article I court.

Along the way, one major step was conversion of the Board from an administrative tribunal into a court. Members of the Board sought that change as early as 1912, and they acted on their own to make the Board more courtlike. Some provisions of the Tariff Act of 1922 moved the Board in that direction. In 1926, Congress provided the title of "court" in routine legislation that aroused little controversy. This action was premised on some practical benefits of the title, such as giving the Board greater credibility with foreign countries from which it sought evidence (U.S. Congress 1926b, 4796–97; U.S. House of Representatives 1925c; Reed 1997, 93–109; Lombardi 1976, 52–60). In 1930 the judges were given life tenure (Lombardi 1976, 60–61).

Another major step was the Customs Courts Act of 1980, under which the Customs Court was renamed the Court of International Trade (CIT) and its powers as a court were augmented (Reed 1997, 170–75). More important, its jurisdiction was expanded. Over time, the portion of international trade litigation that did not involve customs duties had increased. As a result, district courts were handling a good deal of that litigation, and jurisdictional lines between them and the Customs Court were sometimes blurred. The 1980 law clarified the division of jurisdiction between the district courts and the CIT and transferred some jurisdiction from the district courts to the CIT. The CIT was granted exclusive jurisdiction over some trade-related issues in which the district courts had shared its jurisdiction. (The district courts retained jurisdiction over some trade issues.) It also gained jurisdiction over some issues that had been decided by the courts of appeals or that were new to the judiciary. Along with jurisdiction, the legislation gave the CIT the full powers of district courts.

Proponents of the Customs Courts Act, who included the chief judge of the Customs Court, pointed to all the neutral virtues of specialization.[3] One major theme was efficiency. That virtue would be served by moving cases from the overburdened district courts to the underused Customs Court and by eliminating litigation about which court had jurisdiction over a case. Another major theme was that consolidation of jurisdiction in the CIT would produce greater uniformity, which was viewed as sorely lacking under the existing system (Unah 1998, 18–19). Finally, the expertise of the court's judges would be applied more broadly. In his testimony in favor of the bill, a Justice Department official cited all three virtues in the space of two sentences (U.S. House of Representatives 1980a, 53). Although it is possible that supporters of the bill had other ends in mind, the evidence indicates that the neutral virtues were the dominant consideration for them. In any event, the proponents' rationales were convincing: although a few witnesses at hearings expressed opposition to the bill, it was passed by voice vote in both houses.

The conversion of the Court of Customs Appeals into the Court of Customs and Patent Appeals (CCPA) in 1929 and the CCPA's becoming part of the Federal Circuit in 1982 each reduced the concentration of judges on international trade cases at the intermediate appellate level. (Both steps will be discussed in chap. 6.) International trade issues constitute a relatively small portion of Federal Circuit business (see Reed 1997, 179). In fiscal year

---

3. Information on enactment of the Customs Courts Act is taken from U.S. Senate (1978, 1979a, 1979b); U.S. House of Representatives (1980a, 1980b); Stafford (1981–82); and Unah (1998, 17–19).

2009, 3.5 percent of the cases filed and 5.2 percent of the cases decided on the merits fell in this field.[4] However, creation of the CIT kept concentration of judges high at the trial level.[5] Concentration of trade-related cases in a single trial court and a single intermediate appellate court, which had declined somewhat as the district courts heard more noncustoms cases involving international trade, increased with the 1980 legislation.

More than anything else, the Board of General Appraisers and the Court of Customs Appeals were intended to serve the government's interest in maximizing revenue. Their establishment may have achieved that end by deterring importers from appealing customs decisions. More important theoretically is the question of whether the specialized courts in this field have been more favorable to the government's position than the generalist courts would have been. This is a difficult question to probe, and there is little systematic research on the policy positions of the specialized courts in international trade.

Three studies of trade litigation do provide relevant information on those courts in the contemporary period. Scott Hendrickson (2006, 164–77) found that the Customs Court's receipt of Article III status and the security it provided did not increase the likelihood of rulings against the government in classification cases. However, Article III status may have made the court more independent of presidential policy preferences. Isaac Unah (1998, chap. 7) found some evidence that the CIT was less deferential to administrative decisions than were the generalist federal courts. Unah also found that in reviewing administrative decisions, the CIT leaned somewhat in favor of a protectionist stance. Finally, Juscelino Colares (2008) found that the CIT and the Federal Circuit were more deferential to administrative decisions than U.S.-Canadian panels that decided the same kinds of cases under the North American Free Trade Act, a difference that is intriguing but difficult to interpret.[6]

4. Data are from the Federal Circuit Web site (http://www.cafc.uscourts.gov/pdf/Table AppealsFiledTerminated09.pdf).

5. Judge concentration in the CIT has been even higher than the court's jurisdiction suggests, because in at least one period there was some de facto specialization of individual CIT judges in particular types of trade cases (Unah 1998, 20, 94).

6. The American Federation of Labor and Congress of Industrial Organizations (AFL-CIO) suggested another possible effect in hearings on the Customs Courts Act of 1980 when it argued that trade issues affecting local communities should be decided by district courts. Its hypothesis was that courts with direct ties to those communities and with a broader perspective than a trade-oriented court would give more weight to local economic interests (U.S. Senate 1979a, 68–69).

There is also a piece of suggestive evidence from early in the history of the two courts. Testifying before Congress in 1913, a Treasury Department official indicated his satisfaction with the relatively new Court of Customs Appeals, but he expressed dismay with the Board of General Appraisers on several counts (U.S. House of Representatives 1913, 6307, 6134). As one commentator later noted, "it appears the Treasury Department was not entirely pleased with the developing independence of the Board of General Appraisers" (Lombardi 1976, 50).

The backgrounds of judges on the customs courts provide a clue to the intent of appointing officials in the executive branch, and those backgrounds might shape the courts' decisional tendencies.[7] Among the original nine appointees to the Board of General Appraisers, most had relevant experience on the government side (*Harper's Weekly* 1890). But the career backgrounds of members of the Board and its successor courts do not follow a dominant pattern. Many judges have had executive-branch experience in customs and related fields, but many have spent most of their careers in private practice. Service in Congress and other public offices has been common as well.

Of the original five appointees to the Court of Customs Appeals, two had served in government customs positions and a third was elevated from the Board of General Appraisers. Among later appointees to that court and the CCPA, only two had career experience in the customs field. The five appointees in the 1920s were all politicians, four of them current or former members of Congress when they were selected. A 1929 newspaper article was entitled, "Customs Appeals Court Appears as Lame Duck Haven" (Rich 1980, 138). Appointments to the CCPA continued that pattern. Of the ten judges who sat on the court between 1929 and 1955, seven had served in Congress, and one observer referred to the court as a "retirement home" (Baum 1977, 840). Beginning in the 1950s, several judges with specialized experience were appointed to the CCPA, but that expertise was in patent law.

Similarly, it appears that no appointee to the Federal Circuit has had experience in international trade. President Reagan did nominate a lawyer with international trade experience to the Federal Circuit in 1988. Ironically, her record as chair of the International Trade Commission aroused opposition that prevented her confirmation (Unah 1998, 32).

Because there is little evidence on the behavior of the specialized courts in international trade, considerable caution is required in reaching conclu-

---

7. Information on judges' backgrounds was taken primarily from volumes of the *Congressional Directory*, Rich (1980), and Unah (1998, 28–29).

sions about their tendencies. But the lack of substantial opposition to the courts in this field from the private customs bar suggests that if the courts originally leaned toward the government, that leaning did not remain strong.[8] It is noteworthy that customs lawyers and importers supported the expansion of the Customs Court's jurisdiction in 1980 (as did the Treasury and Justice Departments).[9] Since then, the customs bar has advocated expansions in the jurisdiction of the Court of International Trade (Reed 2001).

Income Tax

The history of judicial specialization in review of income tax issues has been quite different from the history for import taxes. For one thing, a long series of proposals for a specialized appellate court in the tax field has failed. Second, the specialized trial court, the Tax Court, stands alongside other trial courts that also hear income tax cases.[10] Finally, the motives for creation of the Tax Court were more complicated than those for the customs courts.

The Tax Court was created in 1924 as the Board of Tax Appeals, an independent agency in the executive branch. A 1926 statute essentially reaffirmed the arrangements created in 1924. In 1942 Congress gave the board the title of Court but retained its status as an executive-branch agency. In 1969 the Tax Court gained the status of an Article I court, and its name was changed to the United States Tax Court.

Taxpayers who are unhappy with assessments by the Internal Revenue Service (IRS) have three options (see R. Howard 2009, 21–27). First, they can take their case to the Tax Court without paying the disputed amount. A Tax Court decision can be appealed to the appropriate court of appeals. Thus, the Tax Court has the unusual feature of being reviewed by twelve different appellate courts. Instead of going to the Tax Court, taxpayers can file a lawsuit in either a district court or the Court of Federal Claims, but to do so they must pay the disputed amount and then sue for its return. The great

---

8. However, familiarity and the advantages of working with fellow specialists on the bench may bias lawyers in favor of an existing court.

9. In one hearing on what became the 1980 legislation, a representative of the American Importers Association expressed some ambivalence about consolidating jurisdiction over international trade matters in the Customs Court (U.S. Senate 1978, 99, 105). However, importers generally supported expanding the reach of the Customs Court in this field (e.g., U.S. Senate 1979a, 73).

10. The Tax Court decides cases involving other taxes collected by the IRS, such as estate and gift taxes, but the income tax dominates its docket.

majority of all tax cases are filed with the Tax Court.[11] The court is based in Washington, D.C., but it holds hearings throughout the country, so that it is not appreciably less convenient than the district courts. Since 1969 the court has had a streamlined small tax case procedure for cases involving claims of $50,000 or less (Davidson 1973).

Creation of the Board of Tax Appeals in 1924 was a case of runaway legislation.[12] The Board was the successor to the Committee on Appeals and Review, a body within the Bureau of Internal Revenue in the Treasury Department. As it had evolved by 1924, the Committee heard appeals from income tax assessments on behalf of the commissioner of internal revenue. A Committee ruling in favor of a taxpayer was final. In part for that reason, the Committee tended to uphold tax assessments. After paying an assessment, a taxpayer could sue in federal court to recover the taxes, but that course was often impractical.

The Treasury Department proposed to make the Board a tribunal within the department. Its rulings could be appealed in court by other side, thus reducing the incentive to rule for the government. From the perspective of department officials, this was a useful improvement that "would protect both the government and the taxpayer." The new structure might also help attack the backlog of appeals to be decided (Holcomb 1925, 271–72; quotation at 272; U.S. House of Representatives 1924b, 7–8).

The provision that emerged from Congress made a bigger change in the status quo. The Board's procedures were formalized. More important, the Board would be outside the Treasury Department and thus beyond the administrative control of the Treasury secretary. The president, rather than the Treasury secretary, would appoint Board members. Treasury Secretary Andrew Mellon disapproved of these changes, and President Coolidge signed the legislation reluctantly (Dubroff 1979, 80). Congressional alterations of the Treasury proposal seem to have reflected sympathy toward taxpayers, and business groups had initially proposed the kind of independent board that Congress ultimately adopted (U.S. House of Representatives 1924a, 459–62).

---

11. In fiscal 2009, about 1,300 tax cases were filed with the district courts and about seventy with the Court of Federal Claims (Administrative Office of the United States Courts 2010, 143, 298). Reports of the Internal Revenue Service indicate that about 30,000 cases a year are filed in the Tax Court (Internal Revenue Service 2009, 61). Between 1994 and 2000, the ratio of filings in the Tax Court to district court filings varied from 11:1 to 19:1 (R. Howard 2007, 113).

12. This discussion of the Tax Court's origins and development is based heavily on Harold Dubroff's (1979) authoritative history of the court.

The Board was to start with twenty-eight members in order to attack the backlog of cases, but the terms of the original members would expire after two years and seven members were to be appointed to serve after that. Some people thought that the income tax would disappear fairly soon and with it the need for the Board (Dubroff 1979, 67–68). In any event, the Board quickly gained support from the administration officials who had initially disliked the 1924 legislation (U.S. House of Representatives 1925b, 9–10). In 1926, when Congress reconsidered the status of the board, there was no serious doubt about its continuation.[13]

When Congress replaced the Committee on Appeals and Review in 1924, it could have established a court rather than an executive-branch board. However, there was no explicit consideration of that alternative. Several possible reasons for this fact have been suggested (Dubroff 1979, 171–72; Ash 1955, 206), and three seem especially important. First, courts are generally thought of as permanent, and the perception that the income tax might disappear made an administrative board seem more appropriate. Second, uncertainty about whether the new body would function well also militated in favor of an administrative board that could be abolished with relative ease. Finally, the administration would have disapproved a court even more than an independent executive agency, and its proposal of an administrative board framed the congressional debate.

Once the Board gained a foothold, there were proposals to convert it into a court. As with the Board of General Appraisers, the primary impetus for these proposals came from the Board of Tax Appeals itself. The campaign to win full court status was long and suffered several defeats before its success in 1969 (see U.S. House of Representatives 1967, 96–100). Beyond a reluctance to create new courts, jurisdictional battles played a part in those defeats. The Treasury Department represented the government in most cases before the Board, the congressional tax committees oversaw the Board, and accountants were allowed to represent clients before the Board.[14] Conflicts between executive-branch departments, between congressional committees, and between lawyers and accountants all slowed movement toward court status (Dubroff 1979, 194–98).

One major question is why the Tax Court has never been given a monopoly over tax litigation at the trial level. The House passed a bill in 1926

---

13. Four decades later, the Justice Department proposed elimination of the Tax Court, but the proposal did not receive serious consideration (Dubroff 1979, 209–10).

14. All these conditions continue to exist, even after conversion of the Board of Tax Appeals to the Tax Court.

that gave the board something close to a monopoly (U.S. House of Representatives 1925a, 13–14), but the Senate did not approve that provision. Removal of the district courts and the Court of Federal Claims from the tax field apparently has not received serious consideration since then. That fact is surprising, since the great majority of tax cases already go to the Tax Court, the existing structure of tax litigation seems anomalous, and the difficulties of tax law for nonspecialist judges are widely acknowledged. Adherence to the existing structure appears to stem from both the inherent advantages of the status quo and attorneys' preference for multiple forums from which to choose. The result is an unusual situation in which a highly specialized court, a moderately specialized court, and a set of generalist courts hear cases in the same field of law.

This situation makes tax law a promising field in which to analyze the impact of specialization on judicial behavior. Indeed, specialists in the tax field have inquired into the decisional tendencies of the Tax Court, both in themselves and in comparison with other courts. In large part, their inquiries have grown out of a debate about whether the Tax Court is unduly favorable to the federal government (Kroll 1996; Maule 1999; An. Smith 2005, 378–85; see Billings, Crumbley, and Smith 1992). The perception of favoritism reflects the government's high winning percentage in the Tax Court and the prior service of many Tax Court judges in the Treasury and Justice Departments, service that some observers think creates a bias in favor of the IRS.

Because of this perception, appointment patterns are a good place to start in probing the court's decisional tendencies. The Tax Court differs from other specialized federal courts in that subject-matter expertise is regarded as a prerequisite for appointment. At least the great majority of Tax Court judges have had experience in tax law, typically as specialists in the field, and that was true of all twenty-seven active and senior judges as of 2010.[15] Many Tax Court judges had achieved distinction in the field before their appointment.

The importance of subject-matter expertise in the appointments of Tax Court judges has not ruled out patronage considerations. The four appointees in 1925 underlined the value of congressional connections: the father of one appointee chaired the House Ways and Means Committee, another

---

15. Biographical information was taken from the Web site of the Tax Court (http://www.ustaxcourt.gov/judges.htm) and from U.S. Senate 1997 (48, 52, 53). A significant share of the court's work is done by special trial judges who are appointed by the court's chief judge; there were five special judges in 2010, all with substantial experience in tax law.

was a former law partner of the ranking Democrat on Ways and Means, a third was a former secretary to the chair of the Senate Finance Committee, and the fourth was recommended by a member of Finance (*New York Times* 1925). Speaking of the board members in 1926, one senator noted that "there is a remarkable number of them related to distinguished gentlemen in the public service" (U.S. Congress 1926a, 3752).

Since that time, political connections have continued to play a role in the selection process. Several of the 2010 judges, for instance, had served as staff members on the congressional tax committees. Even appointments of lawyers serving in the executive branch may reflect patronage considerations rather than an effort to stack the court in favor of government interests.

The numbers of judges with experience on the government side of tax law became a concern early in the court's history, when the Treasury Department had the most influence over appointments (Dubroff 1979, 85–86). But even then, there was some diversity in the sources of judges. A study of judges who served on the Tax Court in a period from the 1970s to the 1990s found considerable diversity. Some judges had spent their full careers in government, others had practiced only in the private sector, and many had split their time between the two. In the aggregate, this group of judges had spent somewhat more time practicing in the private sector than in government (Maule 1999, 407–16). That has also been true of the appointments made since that study was conducted (see R. Howard 2009, 58).

At least in the current era, the locus of judges' professional backgrounds does not appear to have a strong impact. One study did find evidence that judges who came to the Tax Court directly from government service were more likely to rule in favor of the government than were other judges on the court, but the difference was only moderate (about 10 percentage points, and 9 percentage points when controlling for party affiliation) (Altieri et al. 2001, 313). Another study found no significant difference between Tax Court judges with IRS experience and those without this experience (R. Howard 2005).

Ultimately, the question is how the Tax Court compares with the other trial courts in the tax field. Several studies provide data on the relative success of taxpayers in the Tax Court and the district courts (Geier 1991, 998; Caron 1994, 577–81; Caron 1996, 668; R. Howard 2005, 144). The studies agree that taxpayers have substantially higher winning percentages in the district courts. For instance, one study analyzed cases that were decided with opinions and in which one side or the other won a complete victory in twenty-five years from 1968 through 1992. The study found that win rates for taxpayers in the district courts and Court of Federal Claims were about twice as high (31 percent and 33 percent, respectively) as the 16 percent success rate in the Tax Court (Caron 1994, 578). However, the same study found that in all cases disposed of in that period (including those settled out of court), Tax Court litigants won a substantially higher proportion of the total money in dispute—68 percent, compared with 39 percent in the district courts and 41 percent in the Court of Federal Claims (Caron 1994, 579–80; see also Caron 1996, 668). One reason for the dramatic difference between the two measures is that, as noted, they are based on different sets of cases (Caron 1994, 580; Geier 1991, 998).

Even with the complication created by the findings on money won, the data on decisional outcomes provide some evidence that the Tax Court is relatively favorable to the government. However, these data should be interpreted with caution. As in other areas of law, the cases decided at trial are a biased sample of all filings—and, at least in the district courts, a very small sample (Administrative Office of the U.S. Courts 2010, 165). More important, the average characteristics of cases decided in the three sets of courts probably differ considerably. This is in part because taxpayers and lawyers choose courts on the basis of perceived advantages for the specific type of case involved, in part because of differences in jurisdiction and procedure (see Laro 1995, 24–29).

For similar reasons, little can be inferred about the courts' decisional tendencies from litigants' choices about where to file cases. The overwhelming preference of litigants and lawyers for the Tax Court might appear to be strong evidence that the court is more favorable to taxpayers than the Court of Federal Claims and the district courts. But this preference seems to result primarily from procedural considerations—the ability of taxpayers to bring cases in the Tax Court without paying the disputed amount and the availability of the small tax case procedure in that court (U.S. Senate 1968, 118–20). (Those same features may lead to the filing of relatively high proportions of weak cases in the Tax Court, and such a difference would help to explain taxpayers' low rates of victory in the Tax Court.) Articles by practitioners about where to file cases generally emphasize factors other than the courts' overall decisional tendencies (e.g., Bickford 1956, 292–93; Beaman 1957; Gannet 1964; Hamburger 1974).[16]

16. One study did find evidence that the ideological composition of the Tax Court affected the ratio between Tax Court and district court filings, with a more conservative Tax Court producing a higher ratio. This finding suggests that the decisional tendencies of the courts have an impact on choices about where to file cases (R. Howard 2007).

The difficulty of comparing the courts' tendencies in tax law can be reduced through analyses of decisional records that take into account differences in the composition of cases in the various courts or through analyses of the courts' doctrinal positions. A few legal scholars and political scientists have done research on the decisional records of the Tax Court and district courts that incorporates controls for case type (Schneider 2002; R. Howard 2005; Hendrickson 2006, chap. 4; see Schneider 2001). The primary concerns of these studies have been the determinants of the courts' decisions rather than comparison of their relative support for taxpayers and the government. These studies provide some evidence about the impact of judges' own ideological positions and their political environment on their decisions (R. Howard 2005; Hendrickson 2006, chap. 4).[17] One study offered suggestive evidence that when analysis is limited to comparable cases, the decisional tendencies of the Tax Court and district courts are similar (Hendrickson 2006, 136). As yet, however, there is too little evidence to ascertain the effect of specialization in tax law on judges' support for taxpayers and the government.

Because of the technicality of tax law and the expertise of its judges, the Tax Court would seem to have a high potential for insularity. In particular, its judges might resist the guidance of generalist appellate courts. For several decades the court maintained a general policy of following "its own honest beliefs" when they conflicted with a court of appeals rule, on the ground that Tax Court decisions were reviewed by multiple courts of appeals (*Lawrence v. Commissioner* 1957, 716). Arguably, one reason for this policy was a desire to minimize control by generalists. However, the court essentially reversed its position in 1970 (*Golsen v. Commissioner*).

Aside from its effects on insularity, the expertise of Tax Court judges seems likely to produce higher-quality decisions in this technical field. One possible indicator of quality is outcomes on appeal. A study of the 1967–70 period found that the courts of appeals reversed the district courts at a substantially higher rate in tax law than they did the Tax Court: 23 percent versus 13 percent for full reversals, and 38 percent versus 27 percent for other

17. Analyses of the relationship between Tax Court judges' ideological positions and their support for the two sides, in these and other studies, have produced differing results (Altieri et al. 2001; C. King and Lazarus 2003; R. Howard 2005; Hendrickson 2006, 114–18). The relationship between ideology and this decisional behavior may be complicated by differential reactions of judges to different kinds of litigants. For instance, liberals are likely to be more favorable to lower-income individuals than to wealthy individuals and large corporations (R. Howard and Nixon 2003). There are some suggestive findings on this issue in a study by Robert Howard (2009, 68–69).

actions that overturned rulings (Worthy 1971, 253). Even with the limited time period, those findings are striking, especially since the review is by a generalist court. However, factors other than decision quality may come into play in determining the outcomes of appeals.

Expenditures

With some exceptions, legislatures can allow or prohibit lawsuits in which people seek money from government. In two fields, one broad and one narrow, Congress created specialized courts at the same time that it granted a right to sue the federal government. In one of the fields, an interest in protecting the Treasury was important to the congressional choice.

Claims against the Government

Early in the nation's history, monetary claims against the federal government went not to court but to Congress, which paid those claims that its members deemed worthy through special legislation. Congress created the Court of Claims as an advisory body in 1855, and in 1863 it transferred its power over claims to the court. The Court of Claims gradually gained broader jurisdiction and higher status (Cowen, Nichols, and Bennett 1978). The Tucker Act of 1887 was especially important, creating new jurisdiction for the court by yielding the government's sovereign immunity in a wide range of situations. The Tucker Act also gave the generalist trial courts concurrent jurisdiction with the Court of Claims over this new jurisdiction in cases in which the claims were for no more than $10,000. Today, much of the jurisdiction of the Court of Federal Claims is concurrent with either the district courts or administrative bodies.

In 1925 Congress gave commissioners power to conduct hearings in cases. The commissioners' roles increased over the years so that the Court of Claims effectively became a two-level body, with commissioners as decision makers at the trial level and the court's judges at the appellate level. In 1953 the judges gained Article III status, a status that had been in dispute.

In 1982 Congress bifurcated the court. Its judges joined the new Court of Appeals for the Federal Circuit, whose appellate jurisdiction included claims against the government. The commissioners became members of a new Article I trial court, the Claims Court. The name was changed in 1992 to the Court of Federal Claims. For convenience, I sometimes refer to the court in its successive forms and names as a single court, the "claims court."

The Court of Federal Claims occupies an intermediate position on the dimension of case concentration. It has concurrent jurisdiction with the district courts over small monetary claims and tax refund cases, and some kinds of contract disputes can be brought either to the claims court or to agency boards. The court is also intermediate on the dimension of judge specialization, because claims against the government are more diverse in subject matter than fields such as tax and international trade. Because of this diversity, the court has been called a "quasi-specialty court" (Schooner 2003, 720). Leaving aside vaccine cases, to be discussed shortly, 40 percent of all filings in fiscal 2009 involved contracts, 15 percent involved civilian and military pay, 14 percent taxes, and 12 percent Takings claims, with the remainder scattered among other categories (Administrative Office of the U.S. Courts 2010, 298).

There is, however, a narrow specialization within the court (Schooner 2003, 732–36). In the National Childhood Vaccine Injury Act of 1986, Congress established a program of no-fault compensation for injuries and deaths caused by compulsory vaccines for children, with compensation funded by the federal government through a tax on vaccines.[18] The next year Congress set up a group of special masters within the Claims Court to handle these cases, with appeals going to a judge on the court. That provision was part of a budget reconciliation bill, and the reasons for putting these cases in the Claims Court were not made explicit. However, the Claims Court was a logical venue for cases in which litigants sought monetary damages from the government. This "Vaccine Court" has functioned since then, handling contentious issues such as claims that an ingredient in certain vaccines was responsible for cases of autism (A. Allen 1998; M. Levin 2004; see A. Johnson 2009). In 2009, three special masters each rejected one theory linking vaccines to autism in a test case.[19] In fiscal 2009, nearly half the cases filed in the court and three-quarters of the cases pending on the docket at the end of the year involved vaccine compensation (Administrative Office of the U.S. Courts 2019, 298).

The key decisions in the long and complicated history of the claims court came at the outset, when the Court of Claims was created after many years of consideration and then given the power to make final decisions (Wiecek

18. Plaintiffs who are dissatisfied with the Claims Court's action can file a lawsuit in federal district court, but with some restrictions.

19. The decisions were *Cedillo v. Secretary of Health and Human Services* (2009); *Hazlehurst v. Secretary of the Department of Health and Human Services* (2009); and *Snyder v. Secretary of the Department of Health and Human Services* (2009).

1968; Currie 2005, 194–203). The judiciary was allowed to examine claims against the government for a simple reason: this task had become highly burdensome to members of Congress. But that left the question of where the cases should go. Military courts aside, there were no specialized courts in the federal judiciary at that time. But Congress opted to create the Court of Claims as a specialized body rather than to send claims against the government to the federal district courts or circuit courts.

In one sense, that choice was unremarkable. If Congress had chosen to use the generalist courts to review claims in 1855, almost surely it would have been required to give the courts final power over claims because Article III was interpreted to preclude advisory functions for the courts. It was a safer step to begin judicial involvement in claims with an advisory function. The Court of Claims was already operating when Congress did give a court full power of decision over claims, so the easiest path was to maintain this specialized court for the purpose. When President Lincoln argued that a court needed to have the power of decision because Congress did not have sufficient time to attend to these cases, he seemed to assume that this court should be the existing Court of Claims (U.S. Congress 1861–62, 2).

Yet Congress did consider the district courts as an alternative to the Court of Claims, and in 1860 the House Judiciary Committee reported legislation that would have eliminated the Court of Claims and given its jurisdiction to the district courts (U.S. House of Representatives 1860). The decisions to create and maintain the Court of Claims rather than using the generalist courts reflected multiple considerations, including convenience to the government and the advantage of hearing cases in the city where relevant government records were maintained.

One important consideration was the perception that a centralized and specialized court would be more favorable to the government's interests than the decentralized generalist courts. When Congress considered giving jurisdiction over claims to the circuit and district courts in 1824, one member argued that "the courts and juries will always be biased in favor of the individual against the Government," and another concurred that juries "would invariably be biased in favor of the individual claimants, especially as the claimants would be their neighbors" (U.S. Congress 1824, 476–78).

An 1862 House report expressed understandable concern that animosity against the federal government in the South would be reflected in decisions of the courts located in that region. In contrast, the report said, "The records of the Court of Claims prove that the interests of the government may be safely confided to its care. A central tribunal created and sustained by the government is not apt to lean against its interest" (U.S. House of Representatives 1862, 2). The member who presented the Court of Claims bill to the House in that year referred to "the danger of local influences which might be prejudicial to the interests of the Government." He added that the work of the Court of Claims would "be performed under the immediate eye of Congress," which could take corrective action or abolish the court if "any evils shall be found practically to flow from this transfer of jurisdiction from Congress to the court" (U.S. Congress 1861–62, 124). In light of members' nervousness about yielding control over claims to a judicial body, a specialized court in Washington was attractive as a way to protect against the worst possible effects.

From then on, claims against the government were expected to go primarily to the Court of Claims. When legislation in 1887 transferred a large new set of claims from Congress to the courts, it apparently was taken for granted that the Court of Claims would be given jurisdiction over these cases—although the circuit and district courts did receive some concurrent jurisdiction (U.S. House of Representatives 1886).

The proposal to fold the appellate level of the Court of Claims into a new Federal Circuit provided Congress with an opportunity to consider whether the court's trial level should be made a separate court or whether it should be eliminated and its jurisdiction moved to the district courts. Congress did not take that opportunity. Rather, the choice to establish the Claims Court was more or less reflexive, because it was the closest thing to maintaining the status quo (J. Baker 1983, 96). As one commentator put it, the court was created "almost by accident" (Schooner 2003, 715). Committee reports gave little attention to the Claims Court, simply noting the ease of turning the commissioners into judges with the authority to make final decisions (U.S. Senate 1979d, 15; U.S. House of Representatives 1981b, 25–26).

The history of the claims court has hardly been the product of careful design. As one legal scholar pointed out, the Court of Federal Claims "is now a hodgepodge, with an odd assortment of kinds of cases" (Resnik 2003, 802). Further, its overlapping jurisdiction with other bodies does not reflect any systematic consideration of alternative arrangements. The purposes for which the Court of Claims was created have largely lost their relevance since then. Indeed, there have been a few calls to eliminate the Court of Federal Claims. One U.S. senator, Byron Dorgan of North Dakota, cited the "hodgepodge" of cases and a light caseload as reasons to abolish the court (U.S. Congress 2007, S1857; see *Washington Post* 2003a; Margasak 2004b).

The court's judges have shown concern about the court's standing. Among other things, they instigated the 1992 change in the court's name from Claims Court to Court of Federal Claims. According to one scholar,

158 / Chapter Five

"the subtle message here was that this forum was not a *Small Claims* Court but a Court of *Really Big Claims*" (Schooner 2003, 767; emphasis in original). They have also sought to gain greater respect for the court (Billard 1984; T. Carter 1987, 1992).[20]

Whatever the court's standing may be, efforts to abolish it have not gotten very far, and their prospects seem dim. The continued existence of the Court of Federal Claims underlines the staying power of courts that have gained a foothold: barring unusual circumstances, such courts are highly unlikely to be abolished.

The long history of the claims court and the breadth of its jurisdiction would make it difficult to characterize its policy tendencies in general terms. It is noteworthy, however, that the appointees to the court in the 1850s and 1860s came primarily from law practice and judgeships in the states, a pattern suggesting that the federal government did not seek to stack the deck with judges who would be inclined to support the government's interests (Richardson 1882, 793–95). In the court's full history, more of the court's judges have come to the court directly from the executive branch than from any other sector, and several of these judges had represented the federal government on claims and other legal matters. But a substantial proportion came from private practice, and others were in the legislative branch or the judiciary. Through most of the court's history, former members of Congress were well represented.[21]

The willingness of Congress to maintain the claims court and to augment its jurisdiction over time suggests that the court was not blatantly hostile to government interests, but no more than that can be inferred.[22] The overlap in jurisdiction between the claims courts and the district courts provides

20. An addendum to the court's brochure on its history presents data on the court's work in 2006 and, more generally, emphasizes the size and importance of its caseload. The brochure is available at http://www.uscfc.uscourts.gov/sites/default/files/court_info/Court_History_Brochure.pdf.

21. Information on the judges' backgrounds came from Bennett (1978), the *Congressional Directory* for various years, and the Web site of the Court of Federal Claims (http://www.uscfc.uscourts.gov/judges-biographies).

22. Some commentators argue that the absence of a life term gives judges an incentive to curry favor with the government through their decisions (see Zappia 1998). But it should be noted that judges on the Court of Federal Claims, like Tax Court judges, benefit from statutory provisions under which a judge who has served a full term and who seeks reappointment but fails to receive it can retire with the equivalent of a full salary. U.S. Code 28 §178 (Court of Federal Claims); U.S. Code 26 § 7447 (Tax Court). Thus, although judges on the Court of Federal Claims seldom get reappointed, it is not clear that they are worse off as a result (Margasak 2004a). Like football coaches with long-term contracts (Thamel and Evans 2009), judges on the two courts may come out ahead by being fired.

the same opportunity for comparative analysis that the tax field allows. But little use has been made of that opportunity. One study by the General Accounting Office (2000; see L. Smith 2003, 781) analyzed bid protest cases in the claims court and the district courts, cases in which bidders for federal contracts challenged contract procedures or awards. The study found that a majority of cases were brought to the Court of Federal Claims and that bidders did better in that court. However, the report's summary of the reasons that attorneys offered for filing in one venue rather than the other did not indicate any references to differing decisional tendencies. One scholar reported that in contract cases in which litigants have a choice between administrative tribunals and the Court of Federal Claims, most litigants opt for the tribunals. Citing anecdotal evidence, he implied that those tribunals are distinctly more favorable to private litigants (Schooner 2003, 756–57).

In addition to the bid protest study, the work of the Court of Federal Claims in two areas argues against the hypothesis of an inherent pro-government bias in the current era. One area is cases based on the Takings Clause of the Fifth Amendment.[23] The court has exclusive jurisdiction over takings claims for more than $10,000, so large monetary claims against the federal government based on the takings clause are concentrated there.

For several decades, conservatives have sought to expand protections of property from government regulation under the Takings Clause. Given the opportunity to fill many positions on the Court of Federal Claims (the terms of the commissioners who became judges in 1982 ended by 1986), the Reagan and George H. W. Bush administrations staffed the court with conservative judges (W. Moore 1992, 1406). Loren Smith, appointed to the court in 1985 and its chief judge from 1986 to 2000, supported an expansive reading of the Takings Clause and wrote several opinions that reflected his viewpoint (e.g., *Whitney Benefits, Inc. v. United States* 1989; *Loveladies Harbor, Inc. v. United States* 1990). In doing so, he contributed to a shift in the law in which the Federal Circuit and Supreme Court also participated (L. Smith 1996, 1998; Castleton 1992; Kendall and Lord 1998, 535–38).[24] More recently, one of the court's judges issued a ruling that the government

---

23. The clause reads: " . . . nor shall private property be taken for public use, without just compensation."

24. The Court of Federal Claims can provide monetary relief in Takings cases but does not have power to rule that statutes or regulations are unconstitutional. The House passed a bill in 1998 to give the court that power, but the Senate did not act on it. The bill was supported by conservatives who favored a broad reading of the Takings Clause (including Chief Judge Smith) and opposed by liberals. Clearly, the bill's supporters perceived that the Court of Federal Claims was sympathetic to takings claims (Coyle 1997; U.S. House of Representatives 1998).

could be responsible for loss of profits when it regulated businesses in the interest of health and safety; that decision was reversed by the Federal Circuit (*Rose Acre Farms v. United States* 2007, 2009; see Coyle 2008b).

The other area in which the court's record clearly was not pro-government is the cleanup of the savings and loan failures of the 1980s. In a series of rulings, primarily by Chief Judge Smith, the court ruled that Congress had violated the contractual rights of institutions that took over failing savings and loans when it tightened banking regulations in 1989 (e.g., *Winstar v. United States* 1992; *Glendale Federal Bank v. United States* 1999). The decisions were significant because billions of dollars were at stake (Labaton 1998). In that area too, the court received considerable support from the Federal Circuit.[25]

Veterans' Benefits

Until 1988, military veterans were prohibited from going to court to challenge administrative decisions about their benefits.[26] Under the 1933 statute that created the Veterans Administration (VA),[27] its decisions were final, although federal courts allowed judicial review in some limited circumstances (Kramer 1990). Because of another anomalous rule, dating back to a Civil War–era statute, attorneys were limited to fees of ten dollars (raised from five dollars in 1924) for representing a veteran. Veterans' service groups such as the American Legion and Disabled American Veterans filled the void created by that rule, representing veterans for no fees in VA proceedings. This arrangement, which was quite helpful to the groups in recruiting members, was facilitated by the VA's willingness to provide physical space for service group representatives.

That cooperation was part of the clientele relationship between the service groups and the VA. The relationship was reinforced by strong support for veterans' groups in the relevant congressional committees, support that gave the VA an incentive to cooperate with those groups. The relationship

25. The Supreme Court affirmed the Federal Circuit and, indirectly, the Court of Federal Claims on this issue in *United States v. Winstar Corp.* (1996).

26. This discussion of judicial review of veterans' benefits decisions draws from Light (1992) and Helfer (1992).

27. For some reason, the people who name organizations in this field often eschew apostrophes despite grammatical rules to the contrary. Veterans Administration is arguably a non-possessive and thus correct. The same cannot be said of the Department of Veterans Affairs, the Court of Veterans Appeals, or the Court of Appeals for Veterans Claims. It should be noted that the appellate body within Veterans Affairs, the Board of Veterans' Appeals, does have an apostrophe.

among interest groups, administrators, and congressional committees in this field has been called "the tightest of iron triangles" (Shipan 1997, 136; see Light 1992, 5). Yet, veterans (who seek monetary benefits) and administrators (who need to limit expenditures) have some conflicting interests.

It is not difficult to understand why the VA favored a rule that shielded its decisions from judicial review. The motives of the service groups were less obvious but quite strong. Allowing appeals to the courts would threaten the groups' monopoly on representation of veterans. Further, leaders of the veterans' groups believed that the existing arrangements served the interests of veterans. In their view, the amicable relationship between these groups and the VA produced good results for claimants, results that would be jeopardized if judicial review created an adversarial relationship (see U.S. House of Representatives 1986).

The prohibition of judicial review was challenged in Congress as early as 1952. The Senate passed judicial review legislation in four consecutive Congresses beginning in 1979, but those bills were blocked in the House by the adamant opposition of Sonny Montgomery, chair of the House Veterans' Affairs Committee. Montgomery's withdrawal of his opposition and the resulting enactment of judicial review legislation in 1988 reflected several conditions. Three conditions were probably the most important: the linkage between judicial review and creation of a cabinet-level department for veterans; divisions within the veterans' community and the softening of opposition from veterans' service groups; and the option of putting review in a specialized court rather than the generalist courts. Congress chose that option in the Veterans' Judicial Review Act (1988), establishing the Court of Veterans Appeals to hear appeals from administrative decisions about benefits. Appeals from the new court would go to the Federal Circuit.

Congress chose consciously and directly between generalist and specialized courts for veterans' appeals. The Senate had shown a consistent preference for the generalist courts and especially the district courts as the site of judicial review (see U.S. Senate 1979e, 43–45). But the House Committee in 1988 approved a specialized court bill, the House enacted that bill, and a somewhat different specialized court emerged from informal negotiations between the two houses.

The ultimate decision to create the Court of Veterans Appeals was influenced by the position of the Judicial Conference, which had opposed putting these cases in the district courts since 1962 (U.S. House of Representatives 1962, 1853; 1980d, 70–71). The main reason for that position seemed to be the desire of district judges to avoid taking on what might be a large class of new cases, one that did not seem especially interesting or consequential

(U.S. House of Representatives 1988, 24–25). Some federal judges even lobbied against giving these cases to the district courts (Light 1992, 177).

Also important were the positions of participants in the iron triangle, especially the veterans' groups. A court devoted solely to veterans' claims would be less disruptive of existing arrangements than would the entry of generalist courts into the field. Among other things, the veterans' committees in Congress would have jurisdiction over a specialized court. Especially attractive were provisions that favored continued representation of veterans by the veterans' groups.[28] The Court of Veterans Appeals could allow non-lawyers to practice before it, a provision aimed at representatives of the veterans' groups. That privilege would not have been possible in the generalist courts. Further, while the ten-dollar limit on attorneys' fees was eliminated, lawyers were prohibited from charging fees for any services rendered before the first decision of the Board of Veterans' Appeals, and some limits and controls were placed on fees for work in the Court of Veterans Appeals. And because the reviewing courts were in Washington, D.C., it would be easier for a veteran in another part of the country to use a service group representative than to hire an attorney (Helfer 1992, 169–70). These considerations made a specialized court appealing to the House Veterans' Affairs Committee, and a specialized court was probably the only form of judicial review that could be enacted.

Under the 1988 legislation, the Court of Appeals for Veterans Claims (the court's name was changed in 1999) operates essentially as an appellate tribunal, prohibited from subjecting factual findings of the Department of Veterans Affairs to de novo review. Decisions are made by single judges or (much less often) by panels of three judges. The reliance on single-judge decisions reflects the heavy caseloads that the court receives (see Haley 2004). As expected, the court's rules allow representation of veterans by nonattorneys, but only (with one minor exception) if the nonattorney is employed by a veterans' organization that is "recognized by the Secretary of Veterans Affairs for claims representation."[29] A majority of veterans who bring cases to the court file them without representation, though most are represented by the time their case is resolved.[30]

---

28. The Vietnam Veterans of America (VVA), the only veterans' group that did not represent veterans within the VA, strongly favored the district courts over a specialized court (U.S. House of Representatives 1986, 57, 267–72). By one account, the VVA's advocacy was quite important to the adoption of judicial review (Helfer 1992, 161–64).

29. U.S. Court of Appeals for Veterans Claims (2008, Rule 46).

30. Data on representation of litigants are from the court's annual reports (http://www.uscourts.cavc.gov/annual_report/).

In light of the interests arrayed on the two sides of cases that come to the court, it would be plausible for the court to lean strongly toward one side or the other. One clue to the court's policies is its membership, which does not indicate a strong leaning. Several of the court's judges have had experience in veterans' issues, but that experience has not been concentrated on one side: judges have come from veterans' groups, from the executive branch, and from congressional committee staffs.[31] Of course, judges' backgrounds do not necessarily determine the positions they take as judges. In one instance a judge who had served as general counsel to the Veterans Administration and lobbied against allowance of judicial review wrote a series of opinions that pleased a veterans' advocacy group (Wildhaber et al. 1991, 7–23 to 7–24).

There is a body of legal scholarship and other commentary on the court's work (Cragin 1994; Hagel and Horan 1994; Lowenstein and Guggenheim 2006; M. Allen 2007, 2009; see Kornhauser 1991). Some evidence from this work and other sources suggests that the court leans against veterans' claims. One commentator argued that the court effectively had been captured by the executive branch (O'Reilly 2001). On some significant issues, the court has been less favorable to veterans' claims than the Federal Circuit (see M. Allen 2007, 496–512). And when Congress in 2002 modified the standard of review used by the court, to a degree it was suggesting that the court had been too friendly to the administrative decisions it reviewed (see U.S. Congress 2002, 22917; Sisk 2003b, 262–63).[32]

Arguably, the court's practice regarding remands also indicates a pattern of deference to administrative decisions. The court has taken the position that it should reverse the Board of Veterans' Appeals "only in cases in which the only permissible view of the evidence is contrary to the Board's decision" (*Washington v. Nicholson* 2005, 371). As a result, a large minority of its decisions on the merits in the 2005–9 period were simple remands, issued not only when there had been a change in the law but also when the Board applied the law incorrectly or committed a procedural error.[33] These remands add to the pendency of cases and thus increase the waiting time for claimants (O'Reilly 2001, 232–33; M. Allen 2007, 528–29; U.S. Senate 2006a, 93–94).

---

31. Biographical information on current and former judges is posted at the court's Web site (http://www.uscourts.cavc.gov/about/judges/).

32. However, the court argued with some justification that it was following a statutory mandate (*Wensch v. Principi* 2001).

33. Statistics on the court's record for 2000–2009 are in the court's annual report for 2009, at http://www.uscourts.cavc.gov/annual_report/.

Other evidence, however, points in the opposite direction. The court does reverse or vacate Board decisions fully or partially in a substantial proportion of its decisions on the merits—more than one-quarter in the decade from 2000 through 2009. Further, judges on the court have issued strong criticisms of the Department of Veterans Affairs for what they perceived as resistance to the court's decisions (*Jones v. Derwinski* 1991; *Third Annual Judicial Conference* 1994, xxxii–xxxiv; *Ribaudo v. Nicholson* 2007). Although this evidence is far from conclusive, at the least it indicates that the court has not simply rubber-stamped the administrative decisions it reviews.[34]

Regulation

If cases decided within administrative agencies are taken into account, there is considerable specialization in the adjudication of disputes over government economic regulation. Within the courts, however, specialization in this field is limited. In the federal courts, one important source of specialization is the set of rules that give the Court of Appeals for the District of Columbia exclusive jurisdiction or concurrent jurisdiction with other circuits over some kinds of appeals from regulatory decisions. In addition, some courts have been established to review specific types of regulations. The histories of these courts underline the multiplicity of interests that shape decisions about judicial specialization.[35]

The Commerce Court

Congress created the Commerce Court in 1910 and abolished it in 1913. For a body that lasted only three years, the Commerce Court has garnered

---

34. One important facet of the court's work in recent years is a substantial growth in filings that has put considerable pressure on judges (U.S. Senate 2006a). Congress responded by temporarily increasing the court's size to nine members, and the court has begun to make considerable use of the services of retired judges.

35. I do not discuss the Rail Reorganization Court or "Special Court" that adjudicated disputes arising from reorganization of failing freight railroad lines in the northeastern United States. The Special Court, created in 1973 as part of the reorganization legislation, was a special three-judge district court that probably was adopted by analogy with the courts set up to adjudicate price controls (discussed later in this section) and the Judicial Panel for Multidistrict Litigation. Congress gave little attention to the judicial review provision, but some members expressed the need to minimize judicial interference with the reorganization (U.S. Congress 1973a, 36379–81; 1973b, 43091). The reorganization (and to a very limited degree, the Special Court) are discussed in Albright (1974), Hilton (1975), and Harr (1978).

a remarkable volume of scholarly attention.[36] If we leave aside commentaries on legal doctrine, the Commerce Court has been the subject of more research than most specialized courts that have far longer histories and far greater impact. And for many policy makers and commentators, the court's short history has served as a cautionary tale about judicial specialization.

The attention received by the Commerce Court is partly a product of its quick demise. Few government bodies that are designed to be permanent have such short lives. The court is also relevant to scholarly debates about the forces that shaped government regulation of the economy in the late nineteenth and early twentieth centuries.

The Commerce Court was an appellate court with exclusive jurisdiction over several categories of appeals from decisions of the Interstate Commerce Commission (ICC), cases that had been decided by the generalist courts up to that point. Its first judges were new circuit judges appointed by the president. As their terms ended, they would go to the circuit courts and be succeeded by sitting circuit judges, borrowed from their home courts for that purpose and appointed by the chief justice. The use of borrowed judges and the chief justice's power as appointer were invented for the Commerce Court, and these devices were later used for several other courts. Ironically, the Commerce Court did not last long enough for that mechanism to go into operation.

Within five years of the ICC's creation in 1887, there were proposals for one or more specialized courts to review its decisions (Rightmire 1918–19, 97–99; Frankfurter and Landis 1928, 155; Cushman 1941, 85). While shippers of goods made one early proposal, the railroads were the primary interest supporting judicial specialization. Although the railroads were not necessarily unhappy with the ICC's policies, a specialized court might provide a hedge against unfavorable policies (Kolko 1965, 198). But the Commerce Court does not seem to have been a high priority for the railroads.

Rather, the prime mover behind creation of the court was President Taft. His 1910 message to Congress was the starting point for consideration of the court and its establishment later that year (*A Compilation of the Messages and Papers of the Presidents* 1917, 7441–43). Like other supporters of the Commerce Court, Taft cited a series of neutral virtues: reducing delay, securing uniformity in the law, and bringing greater expertise to the field. These

---

36. This scholarship includes Rightmire (1918–19, 97–120); Frankfurter and Landis (1928 153–64); Cushman (1941, 85–105); Dix (1964); Kolko (1965, 183–202); and Skowronek (1982, 251–67).

arguments seem to have been sincere rather than a cover for substantive policy goals in railroad regulation (Skowronek 1982, 262–63). Taft's advocacy of a specialized court in this field was one manifestation of his belief in scientific administration of government (Withers 1956, 86–92, 156–58). Although Taft's case for the Commerce Court differed from the case that Progressives made for socialized courts such as juvenile courts, he acted on similar ideas about expertise and effective administration.

The Commerce Court proposal was one provision of the Mann-Elkins Act of 1910, a broad statute on regulation of commerce, and the court probably would not have been established had it stood alone in a bill (Frankfurter and Landis 1928, 159). In 1913, a House member claimed that creation of the Commerce Court "was caused by the absence of our colleagues at a baseball game," which resulted in a tie vote that sustained the court proposal (U.S. Congress 1913, 4541; cited by Geyh 2006, 81). Indeed, there was no great enthusiasm for the court in Congress, and opposition was voiced more strongly than support.

The opposition came from the same segment of Congress that had opposed the Court of Customs Appeals a year earlier, Democrats and insurgent Republicans, and it had similar themes. Members who argued against creation of the Commerce Court expressed suspicion of specialized courts in general and this court in particular. As they saw it, the power of the railroads and their constant appearances before the court would allow them to persuade the judges toward their point of view. This effect was all the more likely because the legislation shifted defense of ICC rulings from the ICC itself to the Justice Department, whose lawyers had less of a stake in ICC policy (U.S. Senate 1910a, 1–2; U.S. Congress 1910a, 3348; 1910b, 5159, 5162). One senator added another argument: a court "whose only function" was to review ICC orders "and whose only hope of sufficient work to warrant its continued life will depend on welcoming the consideration of suits against the commission's orders" would be inclined to favor such suits (U.S. Senate 1910b, 1).

The similarities between the opposition to the Court of Customs Appeals and Commerce Court are interesting in light of the sides with which the opponents identified. In one instance they charged that the proposed court would be biased in favor of the government, but in the other they charged that the bias would be against government. What the two episodes had in common was a suspicion of specialization as a potential source of bias that would undermine the appropriate functions of courts.

When the Democrats gained seats in both houses in 1910, the fate of the Commerce Court was sealed—or, more accurately, it would have been sealed had President Taft not vetoed two bills to eliminate the court. The court hung on until Taft's defeat in the 1912 election. Although President Wilson's attorney general favored the court,[37] his support was not enough to secure a presidential veto when Congress in 1913 once again enacted legislation to abolish the court.

The performance of the Commerce Court, as perceived by its opponents, strengthened their case. The court appeared to be hostile to ICC regulation, and a series of reversals of its decisions by the Supreme Court reinforced the view that the Commerce Court had gone in the wrong direction. Even the railroads were unhappy with the court, because it was disrupting a system of regulation to which they had become accustomed (Cushman 1941, 94–95, 103; Rightmire 1918–19, 116–18). In its first year, "the Commerce Court succeeded in alienating just about everyone with an interest in its business" (Geyh 2006, 78). It did not help that one judge on the court was impeached and convicted for corruption (Dix 1964, 256; see Bushnell 1992, chap. 10). But none of this had much effect on the court's fate. There probably was nothing that the Commerce Court could have done to overcome the strong doubts that were held by a majority in Congress beginning in 1911.

Commentators have drawn various lessons from the life and death of the Commerce Court (e.g., Dix 1964, 239; Friendly 1973, 153–54; Bruff 1991, 341). It is best not to make too much of a series of events that was at least partly idiosyncratic. The Commerce Court was unusual in the combination of two conditions: it was established despite strong opposition, and the perceived importance of its work ensured that this opposition would not fade away once the court was established. Ordinarily, at least one of those conditions is lacking. Either a new specialized court enjoys something close to consensual support in the body that creates it, or its work lacks the visibility required to sustain opposition after it is created.

Price Controls and Related Regulations

The Emergency Court of Appeals (ECA) was a product of wartime conditions. When the Franklin Roosevelt administration first proposed a system of price controls in 1941, war appeared imminent; when Congress enacted

37. The attorney general was James McReynolds, whom Wilson later appointed to the Supreme Court—according to some accounts, mostly to get rid of him (Abraham 2008, 139). Students of the Supreme Court will recall McReynolds as the bigoted and very unpleasant character who became one of the stalwart opponents of New Deal legislation on the Court (see Hutchinson and Garrow 2002). None of this, of course, should cast any negative light on the Commerce Court.

price controls in 1942, war had begun. A sense of urgency facilitated adoption of price control legislation as well as the system of judicial review that was attached to it.[38]

The administration advocated a system in which any challenge to the validity of a price control adopted by the Office of Price Administration would go to a special appellate court. Based on the Commerce Court model, ECA would be staffed by sitting judges from the district courts and courts of appeals whom the chief justice chose. There were originally three judges; because of increased business, two more were added in 1944 and 1945. When two judges died in 1958, the court continued with three members for the rest of its life.

The purpose behind the ECA proposal was clear: the administration wanted to limit the potential for judicial interference with the price control system (see Hyman and Nathanson 1947, 584–85; W. Wilson 1947, 99–103). Because policy makers perceived that courts had interfered with other types of economic regulation, they thought it important to safeguard price controls against that possibility (Mansfield et al. 1947, 274). The Administration cited the need to resolve cases quickly, to avoid conflicting decisions in different courts, and to develop judicial expertise. It argued that appointments by the chief justice ensured the court's impartiality (U.S. House of Representatives 1941, 334; U.S. Senate 1941, 218, 250–52).

Whether administration officials expected or wanted the court to be impartial is uncertain. Clearly, however, they liked the idea of concentrating challenges to regulations in a single court, thereby reducing the chances that any judge or panel would rule in favor of a challenge. Moreover, the provision for a specialized court was accompanied by other rules that favored the government. ECA was forbidden to issue a stay or a preliminary injunction while an appeal was pending. Its exclusive jurisdiction over challenges to regulations meant that someone who was prosecuted for violation of a regulation could not raise a defense that the regulation was invalid. Nor could such a defendant simultaneously challenge the validity of a regulation in the ECA, because of the short time allowed for challenges after promulgation of a price control regulation.

There was some opposition to the administration proposal in Congress. Indeed, to the consternation of the administration, the House adopted a floor amendment under which cases would go to the courts of appeals under regular procedures rather than to a special court (U.S. Senate 1941, 146–47). But ultimately Congress approved legislation that included the

38. The statute was the Emergency Price Control Act of 1942.

Emergency Court of Appeals and the other attributes of judicial review in the administration proposal.

In *Yakus v. United States* (1944), the Supreme Court addressed the argument that the procedures for judicial review violated the due process clause of the Fifth Amendment. The Court upheld the procedures by a 6-to-3 vote (see Ely 1996). In his dissenting opinion, Justice Owen Roberts complained that "in truth, the court review is a solemn farce" (*Yakus v. United States* 1944, 458). Congress was considering renewal of the price control act when the *Yakus* decision was issued, and the dissents spurred the adoption of procedures that eased the time limit for challenges to regulations and that allowed some challenges by people who were charged with violations of regulations (Hyman and Nathanson 1947, 592–93).[39]

ECA might have been expected to disappear after the emergency of World War II ended. But Congress gave the court additional jurisdiction over rent control after the war was over and then some jurisdiction over price-control issues during the Korean War. The court did not close until it ran out of business in 1961 (*Transcript of Proceedings* 1961). Two of the court's original three judges served throughout its nineteen years, and a third served from 1945 to 1961. All three of the original members and five of the six judges who served on the court were Roosevelt appointees (*Transcript of Proceedings* 1961, 15–16). This pattern suggests the possibility that Chief Justice Harlan Fiske Stone sought to stock the court with judges who would be sympathetic to price controls.

On the whole, ECA judges did seem very reluctant to interfere with administrative policies (Mansfield et al. 1947, 279). But if the court had not been created, generalist judges might have adopted similar policies. Indeed, they did so when the 1944 statute gave them some review power over price regulations. Two scholars who had served in the Office of Price Administration referred gratefully to "the restraint shown by the district courts" (Hyman and Nathanson 1947, 632). At the least, however, concentration of cases in a single court minimized the chances that a court would intervene to put price controls off track.

Nine years after ECA ended its operation, President Nixon and Congress instituted a system of wage and price controls. A year later, in 1971, Congress created judicial review provisions for this system. Accepting an administration proposal, it established the Temporary Emergency Court of Appeals (TECA) to hear cases arising under the wage and price control law. Like ECA, TECA drew its judges from sitting federal judges whom the chief

39. The statute was the Stabilization Extension Act of 1944.

justice selected. Although the Nixon program lasted for only four years, legislation in 1973, 1975, and 1977 established federal controls on allocation and pricing of fuel supplies. That legislation also gave appellate jurisdiction to TECA. In conjunction with the ending of wage and price controls, this legislation converted TECA into an energy court.[40]

The structure of judicial review under the laws of the 1970s differed in some respects from the structure under the laws of the 1940s. Most important, TECA heard appeals from the district courts rather than from administrative decisions. But ECA was an explicit model for TECA, and the two were similar in their purposes and in most attributes (U.S. House of Representatives 1971, 73, 314; U.S. Senate 1971b, 10–12; Nathanson 1972). TECA was substituted for the courts of appeals primarily as a means to streamline judicial review, and its establishment was coupled with other provisions that were intended to limit judicial interference with wage and price controls. The district courts would not have the power to decide constitutional challenges to regulations, and even TECA was generally prohibited from issuing temporary injunctions against the operation of regulations.

There was some disagreement with use of a specialized court and procedure for review of wage and price controls in the Senate hearings (U.S. Senate 1971a, 33, 164). Ralph Nader expressed concern about the chief justice's power to replace a member of TECA (U.S. House of Representative 1971, 512). On the whole, however, substitution of TECA for the courts of appeals received little scrutiny. Two years later, when Congress enacted legislation to give the president power to allocate petroleum supplies, hardly any attention was given to the extension of TECA's jurisdiction to that area. The legislation was enacted with a sense of urgency, and Congress "borrowed heavily" from the wage and price legislation—including its judicial review provisions (Aman 1980, 527–28, 536, 564; quotation from 528). Nor did members of Congress give much attention to their additions of more energy jurisdiction to the court in 1975 and 1977.

TECA's business dwindled over the years, but the court continued to operate and its title appeared increasingly inappropriate. By the early 1990s, it was reported, the court's members were joking that they were the "Permanent Temporary Emergency Court of Appeals" (Sturgess 1991). Congress finally legislated an end to the court in 1992. TECA closed its operations the next year, with the remaining cases in its jurisdiction going to the Federal Circuit.

40. The jurisdictional boundary between TECA and the courts of appeals was somewhat uncertain, and that uncertainty created practical difficulties of the sort that opponents of specialized courts sometimes cite (*Minnesota Law Review* 1980).

The most extensive study of TECA, written in the late 1970s, concluded that the court was highly deferential to administrative decisions. Recognizing the congressional goal of limiting judicial interference with the federal programs that TECA reviewed, the author argued that the court had gone too far in that direction: "Just as agencies may be 'captured' by the industries which they are charged with regulating, a specialized court such as the TECA may become a passive partner with the agencies it reviews" (Elkins 1978, 151). The author's characterization of TECA's leaning seems justified. Whether or not TECA's deference to administrative decisions went further than members of Congress had intended, for the most part that deference was consistent with the explicit and implicit mandate of Congress.[41]

Discussion

In fields of economic policy in which the federal government is a regular litigant, we might expect Congress to create specialized courts to serve the government's interests. Among the specialized courts that were discussed in this chapter, several largely or fully fit that expectation. Congress created the Court of Claims partly because members perceived that a centralized and specialized court would be more sympathetic to the government's interests than the generalist courts. Congress created two courts for customs cases primarily as a means to protect the government's primary revenue source. And the courts that reviewed price controls in the 1940s and 1970s reflected the government's interest in limiting judicial interference with those programs.

For their part, private interests affected by government economic policy might seek to secure an advantage in litigation through court specialization. Those interests have played a part in the creation of some specialized courts in this field, but in each instance something more complicated than a simple effort to gain a litigation advantage was involved. The preferences of railroad companies helped to bring about the Commerce Court, but President Taft's ideas about the desirability of specialized courts were more important. The

---

41. Probably the most visible TECA decision was a 1985 ruling that upheld a district court decision in favor of the federal government. That decision had awarded the government $1.9 billion from the Exxon Corporation on the basis of alleged Exxon overcharges to buyers of oil from one of its fields (*United States v. Exxon Corporation* 1985; see Hershey 1985).

Of the thirty-nine judges whom Chief Justice Warren Burger deputized to TECA, twenty-three had been appointed by Democratic presidents (Ruger 2004, 393). Although TECA reviewed decisions by programs that a Republican president had initiated, Democratic judges as a group might be more favorable than Republicans to wage, price, and energy regulation.

Court of Veterans Appeals served the interests of veterans' groups, but that was because it maintained their advantageous position in veterans' policy rather than because of the court's prospective policies. The independence of the Board of Tax Appeals from the Treasury Department probably owed something to the influence of business groups, but the original proposal for the Board came from the government rather than the private sector.

The claims court, the customs courts, and the Tax Court have been transformed over time, but they (or their successors) all remain in operation after more than three-quarters of a century. Each gained enhanced status and a broadened role over time.[42] The primary reason for broader jurisdiction has been the simple existence of these courts. When new issues arise in the area in which a court works, it is an easy step to add those issues to the court's agenda. The primary reason for enhanced status has been judges' interest in obtaining greater prestige and job security. Congress has not always been receptive to pleas for higher status, but repeated efforts by judges and their allies have brought eventual success in several instances.

Judges on the Emergency Court of Appeals and the Temporary Emergency Court of Appeals had no interest in enhanced status, since they were members of regular Article III courts. But after their creation both courts gained additional jurisdiction, with the result that each lasted considerably longer than anyone would have expected. Here too, the existence of a court working in a particular field encouraged Congress to give the court additional cases that were related to its original work.

The federal government as litigant has the great advantage of appointing judges to freestanding specialized courts. Concern about the use of that power has motivated some opponents of courts in this field. However, the record of appointments indicates that the government has not made maximum use of that advantage. Once a court is created, officials in the executive branch do not necessarily try to select judges who seem favorable to the government's interests. Sometimes, patronage considerations seem to outweigh policy considerations by a considerable margin. The goals that led to creation of a specialized court do not necessarily carry over into appointments for very long, if at all.

Evidence on the actual performance of some specialized courts in this field is scattered or ambiguous. The long-term survival of many of these courts might be taken to indicate that they fulfilled their explicit or implicit missions. But congressional commitment to a court mission often fades as

42. The Tax Court's effective jurisdiction expanded enormously as the income tax was applied to larger and larger numbers of people.

times change. Further, the quick abolition of the Commerce Court is an anomaly; once a court is established as a permanent body, it is difficult to eliminate. Indeed, lawyers for both government and private groups tend to develop a preference for existing courts even if those courts are not especially favorable to their interests. For their part, judges on specialized courts have an interest in maintaining their court and enhancing its power and status.

When Congress creates specialized courts to serve government interests, it often combines judicial specialization with substantive and procedural rules that favor the government. This was true of ECA and TECA in economic regulation and the Board of General Appraisers and Court of Customs Appeals in customs law. To the extent that these courts were favorable to the government—and ECA and TECA appeared to be quite favorable—rules that served government interests may have been more important than specialization in itself. In such instances it is difficult to isolate the impact of judicial specialization in itself on the decisional record of specialized courts.

SIX

Economic Issues: Private Litigation

Government is a litigant in nearly every field of law, but some fields are dominated by lawsuits between private parties. Most of those fields involve economic issues, issues on which interested groups often have a strong stake in the outcomes of cases and the content of legal rules.

Among these interests, the most prominent is the business community. Businesses participate in all fields of private economic litigation. In some fields they are regular participants on one side (as in debt collection and tort law) or on both sides (as in patent and copyright law). Business groups could be expected to advocate judicial specialization when they perceive that it would benefit them, just as the federal government has done in some fields. Because business groups have considerable influence in politics, they might well succeed in some instances, especially because they do not regularly face government as an adversary.

Specialized courts play major roles in three fields of private economic litigation: patents, corporate governance, and bankruptcy. There is also a movement toward specialization in a broad subset of business litigation. Because businesses are prominent litigants in all four fields, one key question is the extent to which their efforts are responsible for these instances of judicial specialization.

Patents

Taxes and patents have been the most common targets for people who advocate increased specialization within the federal courts. Tax law is quite complex, and judges who lack backgrounds in tax law (the overwhelming majority) can find it quite difficult to analyze the issues in cases (see Hand 1947, 169). Patent law is not especially complex, but patent cases often involve complicated facts in technical or scientific fields such as chemistry. Because facts are relatively important at the trial level and the law is relatively important at the appellate level, the current situation is the opposite of what might be expected. Most federal tax cases are heard by a specialized court at the trial level, but appeals go to generalist courts. In contrast, trials in patent cases are in the district courts, but appeals go to the Court of Appeals for the Federal Circuit or, as it is usually called, the Federal Circuit (see Rao 2003, 1123). To a great extent, this outcome reflects historical circumstance.

There are two distinct types of patent cases in the courts. The first is appeals from decisions of the Patent and Trademark Office (until 1975, the Patent Office). Those decisions concern whether to grant a patent to an applicant and which of two competing applicants merits a patent. The second is lawsuits over actual patents, of which the great majority are for infringement of patents.

The most important and most contentious issue in patent law is the standard of patentability, that is, how rigorous the requirements for obtaining a patent should be. The standard is an issue not just in appeals from administrative denials of patents but also in infringement suits. Defendants in those cases frequently challenge the validity of the patents in question, claiming that the Patent and Trademark Office should not have issued them. If the defendant proves invalidity, then the question of whether the patent was infringed is moot.

By and large, patent lawyers favor a lenient standard of patentability (see Rao 2003, 1075). Although they represent both sides in patent infringement cases, those who represent applicants for patents benefit directly from lenient standards of patentability. More fundamentally, patent lawyers believe in the desirability of patents, so they prefer to see more patents issued rather than fewer.[1] This point of view is generally shared by patent examiners in the Patent and Trademark Office. Patent examiners also have practical reasons to adopt lenient standards. Most important, it takes less time to award a patent and thereby dispose of a case than to reject an applicant's patent claims and face further efforts at persuasion by the applicant (Rao 2003, 1075–76; Burk and Lemley 2009, 23–25).

In contrast, many nonspecialists favor more rigorous standards of patentability, in part because they associate patents with monopolies and in

---

1. Lawyers' views of patents, like those of the business community, differ by industry (Coyle 2009). In the information technology field, lawyers and executives have relatively negative views of patents (Burk and Lemley 2009, 4). Overall, however, both lawyers and executives of large corporations tend to favor lenient standards.

part because they perceive that the Patent and Trademark Office has unduly lenient standards. That point of view has been widely held among generalist federal judges since the 1930s. As a result, there has been a long-standing tension between specialists and generalists. That tension is reflected in the contempt expressed by some patent lawyers toward generalist federal judges, including Supreme Court justices (Chisum 1999).

Today, the Court of Appeals for the Federal Circuit hears both types of patent cases at the intermediate appellate level, but the two types were given to specialists more than a half century apart. Appeals from the Patent Office came first.

With a statutory change in 1927, appeals from Patent Office decisions could go to a federal district court or to the District of Columbia court of appeals (see U.S. Senate 1926, 7–8, 31).[2] But at about the same time, the idea of substituting the Court of Customs Appeals (CCA) for the D.C. court of appeals emerged. Congress enacted this idea into law in 1929. The transfer was supported by judges on the two affected courts, Chief Justice William Howard Taft, the Justice Department, the head of the Patent Office, the American Bar Association, and the primary association of patent lawyers (U.S. Senate 1926, 26–27; U.S. House of Representatives 1928a, 4, 6, 14).

The dominant rationale for the change was efficiency: the three judges of the D.C. court of appeals were overworked, with patent cases accounting for a large part of their backlogged docket, while the five judges on the CCA did not have enough cases to fully occupy them. Indeed, some of the CCA judges had been sitting in cases at the D.C. court of appeals to help out (U.S. House of Representatives 1928a, 13; U.S. House of Representatives 1928b, 2; Federico 1940, 946–47). There is no evidence that an interest in the substance of patent policy motivated the jurisdictional change. One congressional report referred to the preference of many patent lawyers for a specialized court (U.S. House of Representatives 1927, 1), but that preference does not seem to have rested on policy considerations. For its part, Congress did not treat the jurisdictional change as a matter of great consequence.

---

2. Some terminology should be clarified. Until 1936, the district court in D.C. was called the Supreme Court of the District of Columbia, but I will refer to it as the district court even prior to that time. The court of appeals was originally called the Court of Appeals for the District of Columbia and underwent two name changes before becoming the Court of Appeals for the D.C. Circuit in 1948; I will refer to it in this early period as the D.C. court of appeals. The current D.C. court of appeals, the equivalent of a state supreme court, was created in 1970. Changes in terminology and structure in the D.C. courts are discussed in Banks (1999, 7–10, 26–32) and summarized in Federal Judicial Center, "Federal Courts of the District of Columbia" (http://www.fjc.gov/public/home.nsf/hisc).

With the passage of the 1929 legislation and a sorting out of venue in the district courts (*Canon v. Robertson* 1929), the renamed Court of Customs and Patent Appeals (CCPA) and the D.C. district court (with appeals to the D.C. court of appeals) became alternative forums for appeals from the Patent Office. In its first quarter century, the CCPA played a fairly passive role in patent law, affirming denials of patents in the great majority of cases.[3] To a degree, this stance reflected the backgrounds of the CCPA's judges. As noted in chapter 5, appointments to the court were based primarily on political patronage. Only one judge, appointed in 1952, had any experience related to patent policy (see Rich 1980, 125–26). Under those circumstances, the easiest course for the court was to affirm the Patent Office at a high rate. Further, despite their specialized role, some CCPA judges probably shared the preference of most generalist judges for a relatively rigorous standard of patentability.

Even so, the court displayed considerable insularity. As suggested in chapter 2, one manifestation of insularity on the part of specialists is skepticism toward higher authorities who are generalists. Compared with the courts of appeals, the CCPA was far less likely to cite or quote from Supreme Court opinions; instead, CCPA opinions mostly cited other CCPA opinions (Baum 1994). Thus, the early CCPA shows that a court's specialization can create a degree of isolation from the judicial mainstream.[4]

During the Eisenhower administration, leaders of the patent bar sought the appointment of patent specialists to the court and succeeded with appointments in 1956 and 1959. The 1956 appointee, Giles Rich, had been active in the politics of patent law (Rich 1963). Both judges shared the dominant point of view in the patent bar. The effect was dramatic. The proportion of patent denials that the court reversed quickly doubled and remained at that higher level. With some resistance from their colleagues, the patent lawyers on the court also secured doctrinal changes that favored a more lenient standard of patentability. This new stance became permanent, in part because additional patent lawyers were appointed to the court. Meanwhile, the courts in the District of Columbia reviewed Patent Office decisions under a more rigorous standard (Dunner 1972).

The patent bar's capture of the CCPA might seem inevitable. But that interpretation is inconsistent with the lengthy period before the capture

3. This discussion of the CCPA is based largely on Baum (1977, 833–46).
4. Not surprisingly, the pattern of citations that existed in the early years of the CCPA continued when new CCPA appointments led to a wide divergence between the court's policy positions and those of the Supreme Court (Baum 1994).

actually occurred. It might not have occurred at all if the Eisenhower administration had not been sympathetic to the claims of patent lawyers. The sharp difference between the court's policies in the first and second halves of its tenure underlines the role that contingency plays in shaping the impact of judicial specialization.

Having now gained what they wanted from the CCPA, patent lawyers and business groups that favored a lenient standard of patentability still faced a generalist and less sympathetic judiciary in patent infringement suits. Indeed, after the patent bar won a change in the key requisite for patentability in the Patent Act of 1952, the Supreme Court interpreted the new criterion of nonobviousness as effectively ratifying the rigorous preexisting judicial standard (*Graham v. John Deere Co.* 1966). Because of the generalist courts' rigorous standard, a high proportion of the patents whose validity was challenged in court were found invalid.

Those who favored a more lenient standard would have been pleased if patent infringement cases were moved into the CCPA or another specialized court. But a long series of efforts to create a specialized court of patent appeals had failed, and those efforts died down by the 1940s (U.S. Senate 1959; Janicke 2001). Then there was a sudden reversal. In the late 1970s, Congress and the executive branch began to consider a proposal to merge the CCPA and the Court of Claims and give the new court jurisdiction over patent appeals from the district courts. Congress adopted that proposal in 1982, creating the Court of Appeals for the Federal Circuit.

The Federal Circuit legislation is consistent with Kingdon's (1984, 2003) process stream perspective on policy making, discussed in chapter 2. Kingdon depicted policy problems and potential solutions as traveling in separate streams, which are joined under favorable conditions through the efforts of entrepreneurs. The Federal Circuit proposal was successfully attached to two sets of perceived problems in somewhat different ways (see Newman 1992, 513–15).

The first set of problems concerned the functioning of the federal appellate courts. In the 1970s, there was growing concern about caseload pressures and intercircuit conflicts in interpretation of the law. Two special federal commissions reflected and publicized this concern. Neither commission favored the use of specialized courts (Study Group on the Case Load of the Supreme Court 1972, 10–17; Commission on Revision of the Federal Court Appellate System 1975, 63–68), but both pointed to the problem of legal conflicts between circuits.

Meanwhile, University of Virginia law professor Daniel Meador was writing about possible solutions to problems in the federal appellate courts. In collaboration with two colleagues, Meador argued for the idea of designating subsets of judges in a circuit to hear all the cases in certain categories for some period of time (Carrington, Meador, and Rosenberg 1976, 167–84). In 1977, new Attorney General Griffin Bell worked with Meador to create the Office for Improvements in the Administration of Justice (OIAJ), and he made Meador head of the office (Meador 1992). Meador and his staff worked to develop a plan for a national court that would hear appeals in fields in which doctrinal uniformity was especially desirable. Because several categories of cases would go to the court, it was thought, the advantages of case concentration would be obtained without the disadvantages of judge concentration.

This idea resulted in a proposal to merge the CCPA with the appellate level of the Court of Claims, with new jurisdiction added to the existing jurisdiction of the two courts. The specific set of fields proposed for inclusion in the new court's jurisdiction changed over time, as some were added and others were dropped because of opposition to their inclusion. A representative of the American Bar Association charged that the OIAJ proposal was "little more than a solution in search of a problem" and that "OIAJ seemed to scurry around rather desperately to find additional categories of appeals to include within the jurisdiction of the new court so that the new court would appear to have an adequate caseload" (U.S. House of Representatives 1980c, 767).

The second set of problems that led to creation of the Federal Circuit concerned the functioning of the economy. Worries about the nation's economic problems impelled President Carter to set up a Domestic Policy Review that gave some emphasis to fostering innovation. That emphasis led to close scrutiny of the patent system, and the Review group proposed creating a single court of patent appeals (Newman 1992, 515–16; Abramson 2007, 6–8).

In part, this proposal reflected the same interest in uniformity that motivated Professor Meador. Uncertainty in the law that resulted from differences in legal standards among federal circuits had long been cited in support of proposals for a court of patent appeals (U.S. House of Representatives 1908, 2; 1909, 2–3). Uncertainty about the validity of patents was now depicted as hampering industrial innovation and thereby damaging the country's economic health. But those who favored a lenient standard of patentability thought that the rigorous standard applied by many federal judges was at least as serious a problem as differential standards. A patent attorney who participated in the Domestic Policy Review as an industry representative linked the two problems directly: "It was clear that patents could never serve as reliable investment incentives when their fate in the courts was so unpredictable, and the judicial attitude in general so hostile" (Newman 2002, 542).

The proposal from the Review group helped to crystallize support for a single court of patent appeals among large corporations. The Justice Department already had a strong inclination to include patent appeals in its Federal Circuit proposal. As other fields dropped in and out of the proposal, patents were the key constant. Corporate support for that part of the Justice proposal gave it additional impetus and played a key part in creation of the Federal Circuit in 1982 (Cihlar 1982).

For people who favored lenient standards of patentability, the idea of giving new patent jurisdiction to a merged CCPA and Court of Claims was especially attractive. The CCPA was the leading judicial proponent of a lenient standard, and its members (especially the patent lawyers on the court) could be expected to have a disproportionate impact on patent decisions in the Federal Circuit. Further, in deciding patent cases brought against the federal government, the Court of Claims generally supported a similar lenient standard (J. Davis and Frei 1982). Thus it was easy to predict that a merger of the two would bring about a more relaxed standard in the adjudication of patent appeals.

Congress began considering legislation to create the Federal Circuit in 1979. The Senate passed one version of the bill in 1979 and the House in 1980, but the two were not reconciled. Both houses passed bills in 1981, and they were reconciled in early 1982 as the Federal Courts Improvement Act of 1982. The basic thrust of the legislation attracted only limited opposition among members of Congress.

The congressional hearings on the Federal Circuit proposal centered on transfer of jurisdiction over patent appeals, generally viewed as the most important feature of the proposed court. The hearings underlined disagreement about the desirability of that provision, even within the patent bar (U.S. House of Representatives 1981a, 71–86). Lawyers who worked for corporations supported the provision, but many litigating attorneys opposed it (Meador 1992, 610; Abramson 2007, 16).

Even with that opposition, the combined support of the Carter and Reagan administrations and the business community was sufficient to secure approval of the Federal Circuit proposal. Supporters were successful in part because they could muster two arguments that minimized the potential negatives of creating the Federal Circuit (U.S. Senate 1979c, 32–34; U.S. House of Representatives 1981b, 18–19, 23). First, they said that the Federal Circuit would not be a specialized court, since it would have jurisdiction over several kinds of cases. Second, the proposal would not add to the size and expense of the federal judiciary, since two existing courts would be merged. At the same time, proponents' emphasis on negative effects of the existing state of patent law created a sense of urgency.

The congressional hearings on the proposal had an air of unreality. The most important effect of creating the Federal Circuit was its near-certain effect on the substance of patent law. But the supporters of the Federal Circuit proposal who welcomed that prospect recognized that it would be controversial. So they left it unspoken and emphasized the uncontroversial problem of conflict in legal standards among the circuits:

> The change was presented in the congressional hearings as a benign one, bringing consistency to the chaotic world of patent litigation, and predictability to the enforcement of valid patent rights. But it was clear from the beginning that advocates of stronger patent protection hoped that the new court would come down squarely on the side of patent holders. (Jaffe and Lerner 2004, 10)

For their part, people in Congress and the executive branch who supported the Federal Circuit proposal as a matter of judicial reform showed almost no awareness of its likely policy impact. That impact was mentioned only by a few opponents of the proposal, and they did not seem to attract much attention (U.S. Senate 1979c, 515–18; U.S. House of Representatives 1980c, 226–27; 1981a, 149, 253).[5] As a result, it appears that few members of Congress who voted to create the Federal Circuit understood the full implications of what they were doing (see Hellman 1980, 355–59; but see U.S. House of Representatives 1980c, 253).

Congress gave the court all the jurisdiction of the CCPA and the appellate level of the Court of Claims. In addition to patent appeals from the district courts, the new court received several other pieces of new jurisdiction, including appeals from decisions in federal employee matters by the Merit Systems Protection Board and appeals from the district courts in cases involving claims against the federal government. It was anticipated that Congress might add to the court's jurisdiction later; a congressional opponent referred to the court as a potential "dumping ground" for new types of cases (U.S. Congress 1981, 27794). Indeed, the court has been given some additional types of cases, including appeals from the Court of Veterans Ap-

5. In a few instances, proponents of giving patent appeals to the Federal Circuit addressed this issue obliquely by arguing that the CCPA's standard of patentability did not differ from that of other federal courts (U.S. Senate 1979c, 114; U.S. House 1981a, 181).

Table 6.1 Cases filed in Court of Appeals for the Federal Circuit, fiscal 2009, by subject matter

Subject	Percentage
Patents	35.9
Federal employees	31.5
Veterans' benefits	11.7
Federal contracts	4.8
International trade	3.5
Trademarks	3.0
Taxes	1.9
Other	7.8

Source: Web site of Court of Appeals for the Federal Circuit,
http://www.cafc.uscourts.gov/pdf/TableAppealsFiledTerminated09.pdf.

peals when that court was created in 1988 and cases formerly heard by the Temporary Emergency Court of Appeals when TECA was abolished in 1992. However, as table 6.1 shows, patent cases remain the single largest source of court business and constitute a substantial share of that business.[6] Thus, the Federal Circuit features a high level of case concentration in patent law and a moderate level of judge concentration.

The Federal Circuit is equal to the courts of appeals in every formal respect, but its judges recognize that some people think of their court differently because of its limited jurisdiction. Some Federal Circuit judges have argued in public settings that their court hears too wide a range of cases to be considered a specialist (Markey 1989, 179–80; Plager 1990, 857–63; Rader 1991, 1004–9). That argument illustrates judges' interest in their status as well as their perception that some people accord specialist judges a lower status than generalists.

When it began operation, the Federal Circuit quickly ruled that it would adopt the body of law established by the CCPA and the Court of Claims, a choice that favored a lenient standard of patentability (*South Corp. v. United States* 1982). In its own decisions it established a series of doctrines that also supported a lenient standard (O'Hearn 1984; Sobel 1988, 1092–105; Federal Trade Commission 2003, chap. 4, 8–19). To take one example, the court has interpreted the statutory presumption that an issued patent is valid as a "strong presumption" that can be overcome only by "clear and convincing

6. In this section I discuss the work of the Federal Circuit only in patent law. Unah (2001; 1998, chap. 8) analyzes its work in international trade, and Abramson (2007) discusses the full range of its work. The court decides "whistleblower" cases under its jurisdiction over federal personnel matters, and critics have charged it with hostility toward whistleblower claims (Coyle 2008a, Eisler 2010).

evidence" (*Al-Site Corporation v. VIS International, Inc.* 1999, 1323; see Burk and Lemley 2009, 133–34).

Patterns in the court's decisions on patent validity present a similar picture. The proportions of challenged patents that the Federal Circuit holds to be valid have been considerably higher than they had been in the courts of appeals (Allison and Lemley 1998, 205–6; Landes and Posner 2003, 337–38). One study showed that in the 1982–94 period, the court affirmed 87 percent of the district court decisions that had held patents to be valid, as against 58 percent of the decisions holding patents invalid (Dunner, Jakes, and Karceski 1995; see also Coolley 1989; Harmon 2009, 1469–87).[7]

Thus, the court acted as expected. The appointments of additional patent lawyers to the court[8] have helped to cement the court's relatively lenient standard of patentability, though the court's patent lawyers have not differed dramatically from their colleagues in their voting records on patent validity (Allison and Lemley 2000; see Jaffe and Lerner 2004, 101–2).[9] Perhaps more important than the backgrounds of judges are their immersion in a field of law in which there is a dominant point of view among lawyers (see Rao 2003, 1114).

For two decades the Supreme Court heard few patent cases and did little to disturb the course of policy in the Federal Circuit, even though the Federal Circuit arguably had diverged from the Supreme Court's doctrinal positions (Desmond 1993). But the Court has intervened more actively since 2002. In this period it has overturned several Federal Circuit decisions, typically with little or no dissent. The most important of the Court's decisions was *KSR International Co. v. Teleflex Inc.* (2007), in which it made clear its collective view that the Federal Circuit had failed to follow the Court's position on nonobviousness as a requisite for patentability.

7. The figures in the text were compiled from tables in the Dunner et al. study (1995) for decisions on three sections of the patent statute, which probably constitute the great majority of all decisions on patent validity.

8. Of the sixteen appointees to the Federal Circuit since its creation, five had extensive experience in patent law prior to appointment. Several other judges had at least some experience in areas of the court's work; several had worked with senators or with presidential administrations. Biographical information on the court's judges is at the court's Web site (http://www.cafc.uscourts.gov/judgbios.html) and the Web site of the Federal Judicial Center (http://www.fjc.gov/public/home.nsf/hisj).

9. One study did find that the relationship between the ideological positions of judges' appointing presidents and their votes on obviousness was stronger for judges who had expertise in patent law prior to their appointments (B. Miller and Curry 2009).

The sources of what one commentator called the Supreme Court's "increasingly disdainful rhetoric directed against the Federal Circuit" (Sween 2008, S4) and the reversals that accompanied it are uncertain. But the consensus in the Court's decisions chastising the Federal Circuit seems to stem in part from a suspicion of specialized courts. Indeed, two justices have alluded in opinions to concerns about the Federal Circuit's specialization.[10] The Court's interventions may also reflect a growing feeling outside the courts that the range of patentable subject matter in fields such as business methods and biotechnology has become too broad (Jaffe and Lerner 2004).

The Federal Circuit has not favored patent owners in all respects. Most important, on some major issues the court has made it more difficult to prove that a patent was infringed. In one instance, the Supreme Court interpreted a significant issue about infringement more favorably to patent owners than had the Federal Circuit (*Festo Corp. v. Shoketsu Kinzoku Kogyo Kabushiki Co.* 2000, 2002; see Abramson 2007, 80). Moreover, the Federal Circuit affirmed findings that a patent had not been infringed nearly as often as it did findings of infringement in the 1982–94 period, and in the last five years of that period the percentages were essentially equal (Dunner, Jakes, and Karceski 1995, 155). Indeed, some scholars have concluded that patent owners do no better at the appellate level than they did before 1982, because a reduction in findings of invalidity has been balanced by an increase in findings of noninfringement (Lunney 2004; Henry and Turner 2006; see Federal Trade Commission 2003, chap. 5, 25–26).

Even on issues of patentability, the Federal Circuit's doctrinal positions do not always favor patent owners and applicants, and that seems to have become increasingly true over time. Especially striking was a 2008 en banc decision that toughened standards for patenting of business methods, a decision with a different tenor from one that the court had issued in 1995.[11] (In *Bilski v. Kappos* [2010], the Supreme Court affirmed the Federal Circuit, but on grounds that seemed more favorable to patent applicants.)

On the whole, however, the Federal Circuit has followed the path in patent law that advocates in the patent bar had sought. The patent bar has no consensus on standards for patent infringement, and for the most part

---

10. *Holmes Group v. Vornado Air Circulation Systems* (2002, 839) (Justice John Paul Stevens); *Laboratory Corporation of America v. Metabolite Laboratories* (2006, 138) (Justice Stephen Breyer).

11. *In re Bilski* (2008). The earlier decision was *State Street Bank & Trust Co. v. Signature Financial Group* (1998). On the significance of *Bilski*, see Kusmer and Shelton (2008).

(especially in its early years) the Federal Circuit supported the lenient standard of patentability that most patent lawyers favor.

The work of the Federal Circuit in patent law demonstrates a high level of assertiveness. This quality is reflected not only in the court's doctrinal innovations but also in its close scrutiny of decisions by district judges and juries (Rooklidge and Weil 2000; see *Control Resources, Inc. v. Delta Electronics, Inc.* 2001). It appears that the familiarity of Federal Circuit judges with patent law has produced an institutional self-confidence that leads to a highly active role in shaping case outcomes and legal rules.

The concentration of patent cases in a single appellate court undoubtedly has increased uniformity in patent law, the primary rationale for creation of the Federal Circuit. However, this uniformity has been far from complete, because of differences among Federal Circuit judges that translate into variation across court panels. In a survey of lawyers who practiced before the federal courts of appeals, the Federal Circuit ranked second highest for the proportions of respondents who thought "the difficulty of discerning circuit law due to conflicting precedents" was significant and that the "unpredictability of results until the panel's identity is known" was a "grave problem" (Tobias 2000, 58, 58n92).

This problem has been evident on the key issue of claim construction, which refers to interpretation of a patent to determine its scope. In a 1995 decision, the Federal Circuit held that claim construction was a matter of law rather than fact, thereby enhancing its power to rule on the scope of patents.[12] Yet uniformity has not developed, because judges on the Federal Circuit differ in their approaches to construction of claims (Wagner and Petherbridge 2004; Bessen and Meurer 2008, 58–61; see K. Moore 2005). In *Phillips v. AWH Corporation* (2005), a dissenting opinion complained eloquently about the court's failure to achieve a coherent approach to claim construction. That matter aside, the thirty-five amicus briefs in that case illustrate the impact of concentrating a field of litigation in a single court.

Corporate Governance: The Delaware Courts

American business operates in a national and international economy, but most public policy on the governance of corporations is state law (Hamilton 2000, 72). Corporations are chartered by states rather than the federal government, and states do the basic regulation of corporations as organiza-

---

12. *Markman v. Westview Instruments, Inc.* (1995). The Supreme Court affirmed the Federal Circuit decision in *Markman v. Westview Instruments, Inc.* (1996).

tions.[13] As a result, state courts play a larger role than federal courts in shaping the law of corporations.

According to the state government of Delaware, more than half of all publicly traded companies in the United States and 63 percent of the Fortune 500 are incorporated in that state.[14] Delaware has been the leading center of incorporation for nearly a century, a status it attained as the result of two pieces of legislation. In 1898, when New Jersey was the primary home of corporations, the Delaware legislature followed New Jersey's lead by adopting similar lenient rules for corporations in order to gain more incorporations. In 1915, the New Jersey legislature enacted more restrictive rules. In response, corporations gravitated to Delaware (D. Sullivan and Conlon 1997, 724). Since that time, the state has maintained its primacy in incorporations. Delaware's attractiveness to corporations serves the state well. Among other things, about 20 percent of state government revenue comes from sources directly connected with incorporations.[15]

Delaware's standing as the leading home for large corporations gives automatic importance to its courts as interpreters of corporation law. At the trial level, the Court of Chancery (often referred to as the Chancery Court) hears all cases in this field. The state has no intermediate appellate court, so the state supreme court hears all appeals from Chancery.

The Chancery Court is an unusual body; only two other states have chancery courts. Delaware's trial courts originally functioned as both law and equity courts. In 1792, a constitutional convention created the position of chancellor, who would hear all equity cases. The Chancery Court over which the chancellor presided has continued, having survived the general movement to eliminate the distinction between law and equity. A second judge was added in 1939, and today there are five judges on the court (Hartnett 1992; Quillen and Hanrahan 1993). Officially, the chief judge has the title of Chancellor, and the other judges are Vice Chancellors.

The court's equity jurisdiction brings it a wide range of cases, including trusts and estates, real estate, an array of commercial and contractual issues, and corporation law. One of its most important decisions was *Belton v. Gebhart* (1952), in which Chancellor Collins Seitz ordered the desegregation of Delaware schools two years before *Brown v. Board of Education*. The court had jurisdiction over some aspects of corporate governance before the

13. The primary exception is the major role of the federal government in securities regulation (see Romano 1993, chap. 1).

14. Web site of the Delaware Division of Corporations (http://corp.delaware.gov/).

15. This information is from the Web site for the Delaware governor's budget (http://budget.delaware.gov/fy2010/operating/10opfinsumcharts.pdf).

state legislature acted in 1898 to garner incorporations, and its jurisdiction in the corporate field has been augmented since then (Quillen and Hanrahan 1993, 834).

The Delaware Supreme Court has existed as a separate body only since 1951 (Dolan n.d.; Horsey and Duffy n.d.). Until that time, an ad hoc supreme court was created for each appeal, drawn from judges who had not heard the case at trial. That system was possible because Delaware was compact and had a small judiciary and few appeals. Demands for a supreme court with its own justices began in the 1930s, in large part because of corporate litigation. "It was an often repeated argument that the old court could not handle adequately the increasing corporate litigation; that a high bench concerned exclusively with the appellate function was vitally necessary if corporations were to continue to use the state as their official home" (Dolan n.d.).

Cases that concern corporate governance make up only a distinct minority of the Chancery Court agenda. For its part, the Delaware Supreme Court received only 7 percent of its cases from the Chancery Court in 2009.[16] But of the work that the two Delaware courts do, corporate governance is regarded as the most important portion by far. The message on the Chancery Court's main Web page focuses on its work in corporate law.[17] In addition, Delaware court decisions have enormous impact on the law in this field. According to a legal scholar, Delaware is "the author of corporate jurisprudence for the country, and in many ways for the world" (Gruson 1986). Based on the perceived importance of cases rather than numbers, there is a high level of case concentration in the Delaware courts at both the trial and appellate levels and a high level of judge concentration in Chancery (see Stempel 1995, 78).

The role of Delaware's courts in corporation law should be put in the context of state policy as a whole. As suggested earlier, Delaware first gained its role as primary home of large corporations by winning what Supreme Court Justice Louis Brandeis called a "race . . . of laxity" (*Louis K. Liggett Co. v. Lee* 1933, 559). But there is considerable disagreement about the character of Delaware policy toward corporations since that time.

Law professor William Cary was the most visible proponent of one point of view. Cary argued that Delaware policy makers maintained the state's enviable position by adopting rules that favor corporate managers over

16. Data on cases in the two courts are from the 2009 annual report of the Delaware Judiciary (http://courts.delaware.gov/AOC/Annual%20Reports/FY09/?index.htm).

17. See http://courts.delaware.gov/courts/court%20of%20chancery/.

stockholders and other constituencies, since officers and directors rather than stockholders effectively control decisions over matters such as incorporation.[18] In Cary's view, Delaware continued to win what he called "the race for the bottom" (Cary 1974, 666).

Some other scholars take the position that, for the most part, Delaware policy makers actually engage in and win a "race to the top" (R. Winter 1977; Easterbrook and Fischel 1991, chap. 8; Romano 1993). Employing economic theory and empirical research, they argue that, if Delaware overly favored management over stockholders, the ultimate effect would be to discourage incorporations in the state. Therefore, the state benefits by making high-quality corporation law that benefits stockholders. Since the 1980s, this conception has been dominant among students of corporation law (Hamilton 2000, 63–68), though some scholars dissent from it to varying degrees (Macey and Miller 1987; M. Eisenberg 1989, 1506–14; Bebchuk and Cohen 2003).

The work of the Delaware courts figures into this debate. Among scholars and observers, there is broad agreement that the decisional law of the Delaware Chancery Court and Supreme Court has reinforced the state's standing as the preeminent home for large corporations. But explanations of that effect vary considerably (Sciulli 2001, 215–21).

Cary (1974) saw judicial policy as part of Delaware's successful race to the bottom. In Cary's view, Delaware's judges establish legal rules that generally appeal to corporate officers and directors. For instance, the Delaware courts favor management on issues involving corporate takeovers. Why do judges take this tack, when they do not benefit directly from it? According to Cary (1974, 688–92), judges want to avoid damaging the state's standing with corporate management, and they know that the legislature would overturn any rulings with potential for damage. Further, judges' sensitivity to the state's interest in incorporations is fostered by their personal ties with the other branches.

Some critics of the Delaware courts took a similar view during the growth in corporate takeover campaigns that began in the 1980s (Monks and Minow 1996, 31–32, 201–4). As they saw it, the state's judges generally sided with the efforts of current management to maintain corporate control, regardless of the interests of stockholders. One business writer pointed out that when the Chancery Court strayed from that position in several decisions, a leading antitakeover lawyer named Martin Lipton "lashed out at the court"

18. Favoring managers over stockholders does not necessarily mean lax regulation; enactment of anti-takeover statutes may benefit managers.

in several memos, including one in which he wrote, "Perhaps it is time to migrate out of Delaware." According to this writer,

> Did Lipton's memos have any effect on the fine, upstanding men (and one woman) who sit on the Delaware courts? *Of course not!* It was pure *coincidence* that within two months the Court of Chancery began producing decisions that were more to Marty Lipton's liking. They've been doing so ever since. (Nocera 1990, 48; emphasis in original)

In a widely noted episode, Delaware Supreme Court Justice Andrew Moore failed to win reappointment in 1994 (Schmitt 1994; Donovan 1994; Henriques 1995). A nominating commission sent only one name to the governor, that of Chancery Judge Carolyn Berger, and the governor chose Berger rather than challenging the one-person list. In one interpretation, Moore was removed because of his strong support for stockholders' rights in some court decisions. That interpretation fits the race for the bottom story. But his removal may have resulted instead from perceived deficiencies in his judicial temperament and the interests of a well-connected law firm.

Scholars who espouse the race to the top conception also incorporate the courts into their story, and some other analysts of the courts have offered support for their position (Winter 1977; Romano 1987; Dreyfuss 1995, 5–23; Sciulli 2001). In this view, Delaware courts support the state's interest in attracting corporations by providing high-quality adjudication, largely a product of the expertise in corporate law that judges develop by hearing many cases in the field. One benefit is to create a degree of certainty and stability in the law that corporations and their representatives find appealing.

Scholars in this camp apply their conception of policy makers' incentives to Delaware's judges, arguing that judges would not serve the state's interests if they took positions that consistently favor managers over stockholders (Winter 1977, 256–57; Dreyfuss 1995, 22–23). They also point to lines of decisions by the Delaware courts that benefit stockholders rather than management (Sciulli 2001, 216; see Meyers 1989).

The evidence that adherents to the competing stories cite shows that the patterns of decisions by the Chancery Court and state supreme court are not fully consistent with either story. For one thing, the overall tenor of those decisions has varied considerably over time (Meyers 1989; D. Sullivan and Conlon 1997). The conception that the courts have been captured by corporate management seems inconsistent with much of the doctrinal output of the Delaware courts. By the same token, the conception that the two courts consistently act on the interests of shareholders rather than corporate management seems unjustified on the basis of the courts' records.

No matter where the truth lies between these competing stories, however, it is clear that case and judge concentration in corporation law affects the development of the law. Delaware judges inevitably develop familiarity with issues in corporation law. Judges also are aware of stakes that the state has in their decisions. One result, it appears, is to foster consistency between legislative and judicial policy in the state.

If the structure of Delaware's courts serves the state's interest in incorporations, to what extent is their structure a product of that interest? As noted earlier, an interest in serving corporations played a part in the creation of a true supreme court in 1951. But it seems inevitable that the state would replace its ad hoc supreme court at some point. The Court of Chancery long predated the incorporation issue. Once the Chancery Court gained jurisdiction over a broad range of issues in corporation law, the general satisfaction of corporate decision makers with its work guaranteed its continued existence.[19] Yet tradition and inertia alone might have produced the same result, so it is uncertain to what extent the current Court of Chancery is a product of explicit efforts to serve the state's interest.

Business Courts

In the past two decades, there has been a movement in the states to create trial courts and court divisions that are devoted to certain kinds of cases in which businesses are parties. These courts, referred to generically as business courts, have now been authorized in more than a dozen states.[20] In Michigan and Oklahoma, these courts were created through legislation. More often, the judicial branch has created business courts itself through administrative orders and rules. But in some of those states, the courts responded to encouragement from the other branches of state government.

A few of these courts, such as the North Carolina Business Court, have jurisdiction throughout a state. Most exist in certain localities, typically one

19. It is also possible that legislation augmenting the court's jurisdiction over issues relating to corporations reflected that satisfaction to some degree.

20. Leaving the Delaware Chancery Court aside, a 2007 article identified business courts in thirteen states and three states with courts for complex litigation that are largely business oriented (Nees 2007, 503; see Drahozal 2009, 494–95). This discussion of business courts is based in part on the exhaustive survey in Bach and Applebaum (2004) and the survey of courts in Nees (2007).

or more large cities. In Illinois, the Circuit Court of Cook County has a Commercial Calendar. In Nevada, there are business courts in Reno and Las Vegas that can hear cases from other places in the state. The commercial division of the Supreme Court in New York (a trial court) has a wider scope, operating in twenty-four counties.

The jurisdiction of business courts varies from state to state, and in some states it is ambiguous. Most often, these courts can hear cases involving issues of corporate governance, defined broadly, and several types of litigation between businesses. Some courts hear only business cases that are defined as complex. Arizona, California, and Connecticut have courts for complex litigation that are not limited to interbusiness cases, and some other courts have jurisdiction over certain types of cases between businesses and nonbusiness parties.

Business courts reflect the interest of state policy makers in attracting businesses to their states. In the absence of fundamental changes in Delaware policies, it is doubtful that any state could make serious inroads on Delaware's position as the primary location for large incorporations. But many state policy makers believe that their states can increase business activity and its attendant economic benefits by creating a favorable "business climate." Indeed, state and local governments use a variety of policies on issues such as taxes and regulation to appeal to businesses.

Interest in the business climate extends to the courts. Most visibly, business groups have argued that pro-plaintiff rules in personal injury law discourage business activity, reinforcing this argument with mechanisms such as rankings of states for "legal climate" relating to tort liability (U.S. Chamber Institute for Legal Reform 2010).[21] That argument affects the thinking of state policy makers as they make decisions about personal injury law. Business courts are another, less visible manifestation of states' interest in the business climate. In contrast with personal injury law, the initiative for this movement has come primarily from state policy makers rather than from the business community.

The creation of business courts and proposals for similar courts in other states are motivated by the belief that these courts will appeal to businesses and thus attract them to a state. Perceptions of Delaware's success support

21. The 2010 rankings, based on a survey of "in-house general counsel, senior litigators or attorneys, and other senior executives" at large companies who "indicated they are knowledgeable about litigation matters" (U.S. Chamber Institute for Legal Reform 2010, 2) put Delaware in first place for the best legal climate, a rank that it has consistently held. It appears that corporate governance is not the only legal field in which Delaware policy makers seek to appeal to the business community.

that belief (Gibson 1990; Wayne 1990; Dreyfuss 1995, 2). Arguing for a Michigan "cyber court" to serve businesses, Governor John Engler referred to Delaware and said, "We think this is a little bit of a case of if we build it, they may come" (Belluck 2001).[22] An Ohio judge who helped to set up a business court program expressed the same idea at greater length: "We believe that once word gets out, other businesses might come to Ohio because they will realize the court system understands their needs. Ohio would be considered a favored state in which to do business" (Cadwallader 2008, C7). A New Jersey business litigator quoted Bruce Springsteen lyrics in support of his hope that a business court would help revive the state's economy (Muccifori 2004).

Business courts, then, reflect competition as a mechanism for the diffusion of innovations (Simmons, Dobbin, and Garrett 2006, 792–95; Shipan and Volden 2008, 842–43). These courts are created to attract business activity that would instead go to other states and to match the efforts of states that already have business courts. But what about these courts is supposed to appeal to businesses? Proponents of business courts have pointed to the neutral virtues of specialization. Providing a separate venue for certain business cases will allow them to be processed more quickly. Uniformity is achieved through specialization; as one proponent argued, "when you have the same judges making decisions repeatedly, it's easier to predict the outcome of a case" (W. Davis 2003, 35). Efficiency and quality of decisions are expected to improve through the selection of able and expert judges for business courts and through the expertise that judges gain by concentrating on one type of case.

People who favor business courts often do not refer to the possibility that these courts will change the substance of judicial policy in ways that please the business community. However, an interest in substantive policy underlies some support for business courts. For instance, a proponent of a New Jersey business court voiced the hope that such a court would alter what he saw as decisional patterns that were unfavorable to business interests (*Metropolitan Corporate Counsel* 2002).

Business court proposals have attracted opponents, who make two kinds of arguments (DeVries 1994; E. Friedman 1996; Junge 1998, 318; Post 2004b). First, some opponents and other commentators believe that business courts might adopt a pro-business bias. Even if a court hears no

---

22. Governor Engler's proposal was enacted in 2001 with the necessary two-thirds majorities in both legislative chambers. But the court never went into operation because it did not receive state funding (Ankeny 2005).

cases with nonbusiness parties, they suggest, a pro-business mission might shape its choices and negatively affect other interests (Rivkin 2001, 41). Legal scholar Rochelle Dreyfuss (1995, 39) has noted that "there is an unsettling quality to a tribunal like Pennsylvania's, which will hear commercial and corporate cases but never see the consumers and employees who are affected by its decisions."

Opponents also cite the neutral virtues, arguing that if special resources are given to business courts, then people engaged in other types of litigation will lose out. Quicker processing of business cases will lead to slower processing of other cases. When proponents talk of getting the best judges into business court, litigators in other fields see that step as working to their detriment.

As yet, there is only limited evidence about the actual operation and impact of business courts (Nees 2007, 524–32; Drahozal 2009, 501–7), so the validity of the arguments for and against them remains quite uncertain. However, these courts probably provide greater efficiency for the cases filed in them. In light of the purposes behind the creation of business courts, development of a pro-business bias is a real possibility. As for hopes that a business court could improve a state's economic situation, it appears that judicial specialization in business cases can have a substantial effect only under unusual circumstances. Even in Delaware, where the circumstances certainly are unusual, the work of the Chancery Court and supreme court is just one part of a broader pattern of state policy that attracts incorporations (Dreyfuss 1995).

Bankruptcy

In both 2008 and 2009, more than one million bankruptcy cases were filed in the federal courts (Administrative Office of the United States Courts 2010, 288). The outcomes of bankruptcy cases filed by individuals have fundamental effects on their lives. Bankruptcies of large businesses affect not only those companies but also their employees, stockholders, and others. That reality is underlined by the wave of corporate bankruptcies that resulted from the national economic problems that began in 2008. Decisions by bankruptcy judges helped determine the fates of companies such as General Motors and thereby shaped national policy and the economy itself (Glater 2009; de la Merced 2009; *Boston Globe* 2009). In turn, it might be consequential that bankruptcy cases go before specialized bankruptcy judges in each judicial district rather than district judges.

The long and circuitous process that produced today's bankruptcy courts is summarized in table 6.2. In that process, issues of substantive policy were important to a key preliminary step, creating federal bankruptcy law. The neutral virtue of efficiency has been important, though mostly implicit, in the evolution of bankruptcy courts. But the primary driving force in that evolution has been the interests of judges.

For the most part, federal district judges want nothing to do with bankruptcy cases. These cases generally seem uninteresting and unimportant to district judges, and in the aggregate they could consume a good deal of judges' time and energy (see U.S. House of Representatives 1983b, 7, 9). For that reason, district judges find it attractive to delegate bankruptcy cases to someone else. At the same time, they do not want their status diluted by sharing that status with the numerous bankruptcy judges, now more than three hundred. For their part, bankruptcy judges have sought enhanced status. Other specialists in the bankruptcy field have supported this goal, because enhancing the status of bankruptcy law improves their own standing (Skeel 2001, 136). The history of bankruptcy adjudication since the 1970s has largely been about conflicts between the two sets of judges over issues that affect their status. Bankruptcy judges have achieved some victories, but their gains have been limited by adamant opposition from generalist federal judges.

During the first century under the Constitution, federal bankruptcy laws were in force for only three periods that totaled eleven years. The last of these laws was repealed in 1878. In the absence of federal laws, the states dealt with bankruptcy-like issues through insolvency laws (C. Warren 1935; U.S. House of Representatives 1890, 1–2; 1896, 2–3).

In the 1890s, Congress considered bankruptcy for several years before enacting the Bankruptcy Act in 1898. Business groups gave strong support to a federal bankruptcy law, so long as it allowed for involuntary bankruptcies alongside voluntary ones.[23] As they saw it, their interests would be

---

23. The House Judiciary Committee in 1894 approved a bill that allowed for only voluntary bankruptcy. A minority report denounced that action in strong terms. In one passage it ascribed "opulent selfishness" and "stupid ignorance" to certain supporters of the bill. It also offered a noteworthy analysis of human motivation: "The great mass of the people are honest and they want honest laws. Even the rogues want everybody else to be honest" (U.S. House of Representatives 1894, 32, 30).

At least in the current era, involuntary bankruptcies are quite uncommon—about six hundred out of one million filings in 2008 (U.S. Census Bureau 2009, table 752). This is because bankruptcy is generally disadvantageous to creditors (Sullivan, Warren, and Westbrook 1994, 812–13).

Table 6.2 Evolution of the system for adjudicating bankruptcy cases

Year	Event
1898	Bankruptcy Act reestablished federal bankruptcy law and created a system in which district courts appointed referees as adjuncts of the court for two-year terms. Referees were paid fees based on the cases they handled rather than salaries. Referees had mostly administrative functions. In matters they handled as judges, their decisions could be reviewed by district judges.
1938	Chandler Act gave many of the referees' administrative duties to trustees or clerks.
1946	Referees' Salary Act of 1946 gave salaries to referees, eliminating the fee system. Their terms were lengthened to six years.
1973	Rules of Bankruptcy Procedure, issued by the Supreme Court, changed the title from referee to bankruptcy judge. Jurisdiction of bankruptcy judges was effectively expanded, and more of their administrative duties were given to other officers. District judges would hear appeals from decisions of bankruptcy judges.
1978	Bankruptcy Act of 1978 created distinct bankruptcy courts as adjuncts of the district courts. Jurisdiction of bankruptcy judges was broadened to include other cases involving the party that files for bankruptcy, and their powers as judges were expanded. Appointment by the district courts was replaced by presidential nomination and Senate confirmation. Terms were increased to fourteen years. A circuit council could establish a panel of bankruptcy judges to hear appeals from bankruptcy courts; otherwise, appeals would generally go to district judges.
1982	Supreme Court's decision in *Northern Pipeline Construction Co. v. Marathon Pipeline Co.* struck down the 1978 statute. The Court ruled that the statute gave bankruptcy judges powers that were appropriate only for Article III judges, so the statute violated Article III. There was no majority opinion, and the two opinions for members of the majority differed in what they depicted as the extent of the constitutional problem.
1984	After some interim measures, the Bankruptcy Amendments and Federal Judgeship Act of 1984 responded to the Supreme Court's decision. Courts of appeals would appoint bankruptcy judges with fourteen-year terms, and they were asked to consider reappointing the sitting bankruptcy judges. Bankruptcy judges were given full power to decide cases under the bankruptcy laws and "core proceedings" that were directly related to the bankruptcy. In cases that were not core proceedings, bankruptcy judges would submit proposed findings of fact and conclusions of law to a district judge, who would make the final decision; with the consent of the parties, the bankruptcy judge could reach a final decision. The procedures for appeals were similar to those in the 1978 law.
1994	Bankruptcy Reform Act of 1994 authorized bankruptcy judges to conduct jury trials with the parties' consent. Each circuit was required to establish an appellate panel of bankruptcy judges unless it met one of two conditions. Appeals from decisions of bankruptcy judges would go to the bankruptcy appellate panel (if it existed) unless a party asked that an appeal go to a district judge instead.

Sources: The history through 1973 is based primarily on U.S. House of Representatives (1977b, 8–9; 1977c, 2–3); the history after 1973 is based on statutes, court decisions, and secondary sources.

better served by federal rather than state adjudication of insolvency (U.S. Senate 1896, iii–xiii, 263–73). Their support was important to the enactment of federal legislation.

Jurisdiction over bankruptcy cases was placed in the district courts. Congress established the position of referee to do most of the work in bankruptcies. There was little attention to this choice, but one committee report noted that this position was "created in order to secure prompt proceedings" (U.S. House of Representatives 1893, 14). The alternatives would have been to give existing district judges considerable new work or to create a set of new judgeships, and both alternatives probably seemed unattractive. District judges may not have been consulted, but almost surely they would have approved the congressional choice.

Under one proposal, referees were to be "assistant judges" selected by the circuit courts to serve as full-time salaried employees. Congress ultimately rejected that proposal. District courts would select the referees, who would be paid from filing fees and commissions drawn from estates rather than through salaries. The House Judiciary Committee explained this change as a means to save the government money (U.S. House of Representatives 1892, 13).

Initially, the referees did primarily administrative work in bankruptcy cases, with judges retaining much of the adjudication that cases required. But once the referee position was created, district judges and the federal judiciary as a whole delegated increasing shares of adjudication to referees. Congress made the referees more like judges in 1938 by giving much of their administrative work to other officials. Thus Congress in 1898 laid the groundwork for a system of adjudication by specialists with little if any consideration of its long-term consequences. But even if Congress had given district judges full responsibility for bankruptcy in 1898, judges' distaste for those cases might well have led to something like the referee system.

According to a 1940 report (Attorney General's Committee 1941), the system established in 1898 did not operate very well in some respects. In choosing referees, district judges emphasized personal acquaintanceship more than relevant experience. Most referees served part-time, and the fee system gave them incentives to attract cases and to increase the size of estates. There was evidence that judges often engaged in little supervision of referees, and the lack of supervision allowed improper practices to develop. Congress acted on these problems in 1946, replacing the fee system with salaries for referees. As a result, the position became full-time for most referees.

A report of the Brookings Institution a quarter century later (Stanley and Girth 1971) identified continuing problems in the bankruptcy system.

Referees were still chosen primarily on the basis of personal ties and political patronage. Administration of cases was inadequate. Interviews with judges indicated that most "left the operation of the bankruptcy courts to the referees, taking action only on complex legal problems or on critical problems of ethics or administration" (Stanley and Girth 1971, 148).[24]

The Brookings report and the report of a federal bankruptcy commission two years later (U.S. House of Representatives 1973) helped to spur congressional consideration of changes in the system in 1977 and 1978. Several proposals were considered, ranging from minor changes in the bankruptcy courts to full Article III status for their judges.

The congressional hearings made clear the gulf between bankruptcy judges and generalist federal judges, each with their allies (U.S. House of Representatives 1977a; U.S. Senate 1978; Seron 1978, 1982; Barnes 1997). The generalist judiciary had enhanced the status of referees in 1973 with rules that gave them the title of judge, expanded their jurisdiction, and reduced their administrative responsibilities. Bankruptcy judges wanted more: Article III status and independence from the district courts (see Cyr 1978). Higher formal status and life tenure had considerable value in themselves, and bankruptcy judges' dependent positions within the district courts rankled them (U.S. House of Representatives 1977c, 10–12). Generalist judges and the Judicial Conference (which included no bankruptcy judges, even on its Bankruptcy Committee) opposed those changes. A representative of a trial lawyers' group expressed the central concern of generalist judges when he argued that creating so many new Article III judgeships "would dilute the significance, and prestige, of district judgeships" (Rifkind 1978, 189).

The Judicial Conference argued against creation of another specialized court. The response from advocates of a separate bankruptcy court was that specialization in bankruptcy already existed (U.S. House of Representatives 1977c, 13–16). One potential change that nobody advocated, least of all generalist judges, was to eliminate the bankruptcy judges and give district judges responsibility for handling bankruptcy cases.

In 1978, the House approved a bill that gave bankruptcy judges Article III status and independence from the district courts (U.S. House of Representatives 1977b), but the Senate-passed bill made more limited changes (*Congressional Quarterly Almanac* 1978a). When the House later passed a

24. Judges most often cited appeals from referees' decisions as a means to evaluate referees' work. But the rate of appeal was low and the standard of review lenient. One reason for the paucity of appeals was that attorneys were reluctant to alienate referees who would approve fees and appoint trustees in the future (Stanley and Girth 1971, 155).

compromise version, Chief Justice Warren Burger felt that it enhanced the bankruptcy judges' status too much, and he undertook last-minute lobbying to prevent its approval in the Senate. His lobbying was aggressive; one senator reported a telephone call to him in which Burger "yelled and screamed" and was "very irate and rude" (Greenhouse 1978). Burger's efforts led to some changes in the final version of the legislation, but he was still unhappy with the outcome. One scholar suggested that the most noteworthy attribute of that outcome was the degree of success that bankruptcy judges had achieved despite their relatively low status. She ascribed that success to their high stakes in the outcome, which made them more persistent than competing groups (Seron 1982, 96).

The 1978 legislation created distinct bankruptcy courts, though they remained adjuncts of the district courts. Bankruptcy judges gained broader jurisdiction and more judicial power. Their terms were lengthened to fourteen years, and they would be selected by the president (with Senate confirmation) rather than by the district courts.

Under the 1978 statute, each circuit council would determine whether to set up a Bankruptcy Appellate Panel (BAP) of bankruptcy judges to hear appeals from rulings of individual bankruptcy judges. If the circuit council did establish a BAP, that body would hear appeals. In other circuits, district judges ordinarily would hear appeals. The option of creating a BAP has remained, with some modification in 1994.[25] Because BAPs exist in some circuits but not in others, their handling of bankruptcy appeals can be compared with that of district judges. Nash and Pardo (2008) concluded that the panels of bankruptcy judges provide higher-quality review of bankruptcy decisions than do district judges, based on rates of citation and affirmance by the courts of appeals (which provide second-level review in bankruptcy cases).

In *Northern Pipeline Construction Co. v. Marathon Pipe Line Co.* (1982), the Supreme Court struck down the 1978 statute as unconstitutional on the ground that it expanded bankruptcy judges' powers to a point that was impermissible without the protection of Article III status. But there was no majority opinion, and the pivotal opinion by Justice William Rehnquist framed the issue narrowly. In Rehnquist's view, it was the bankruptcy courts' power to decide an issue of state common law that created a constitutional problem in this case. Writing in dissent, Chief Justice Burger counseled

---

25. Circuit councils of judges (originally with only court of appeals judges, now also including district judges) are the governing bodies for each judicial circuit. The 1994 modification is described in table 6.2. Berch (1990) discusses the functioning of the panel in the Ninth Circuit.

Congress that no "radical restructuring of the present system of bankruptcy adjudication" would be necessary to meet the Court's mandate (*Northern Pipeline*, 92). Clearly, Burger was worried that Congress would respond to the Court's decision by granting Article III status to bankruptcy judges.

The congressional debate over response to the Supreme Court decision involved the same issues and contending sides as the debate of the late 1970s (see U.S. House of Representatives 1983a; L. King 1983; Taylor 1984a). Congress did not act for two years, and the delay required the Judicial Conference to adopt an interim system for bankruptcy cases.[26] The delay resulted in part from contention over substantive bankruptcy issues.

The debate over alternative proposals was premised on the assumption that the *Northern Pipeline* decision required bankruptcy cases to be decided by Article III judges. In an effort to prevent bankruptcy judges from achieving Article III status, the Judicial Conference proposed instead that Congress create a large number of new district court judgeships and magistrates' positions, as well as bankruptcy administrators, to handle bankruptcy cases (House of Representatives 1983b, 9–10). This proposal failed to win support. The House Judiciary Committee strongly favored converting bankruptcy judges into Article III judges, but opposition from the generalist judiciary once again blocked that option.

Congress ultimately adopted a more complicated response to the Supreme Court decision. Its 1984 legislation gave district courts jurisdiction over bankruptcy cases, but a district court could refer cases to its bankruptcy court. (Not surprisingly, every district court then issued an order that referred all bankruptcy cases to its bankruptcy court.) The legislation allowed bankruptcy judges to make final judgments on nonbankruptcy issues (those not directly related to the bankruptcy) only if the parties consented. In the absence of that consent, district judges would review bankruptcy judges' rulings about nonbankruptcy issues and reach final judgments themselves. Bankruptcy judges were left in their intermediate position between subordination to district judges and Article III status.

Under the legislation, courts of appeals rather than the president would appoint bankruptcy judges. Sitting bankruptcy judges were allowed to serve until October 1986 or, if it came later, until four years after their last

---

26. The interim system may have been inconsistent with *Northern Pipeline*, and lower courts reached conflicting decisions on that matter. The president of the National Conference of Bankruptcy Judges, sitting in the Northern District of Illinois, wrote a long opinion holding that the interim system was unconstitutional (*In the Matter of: Wildman, Debtor* 1983; see Krasno 1984). The opinion expresses strong resentment of generalist judges and their governing bodies, so it provides a good sense of the tensions between bankruptcy judges and the generalist judiciary.

appointment. Because the authority of the sitting judges under interim rules had expired shortly before Congress enacted the legislation, that provision was retroactive.

When President Reagan signed the legislation, he said that it was unconstitutional for Congress to extend the terms of bankruptcy judges. The director of the Administrative Office of the U.S. Courts then announced that this provision was indeed unconstitutional, that he would withhold the salaries of what he called the former bankruptcy judges, and that district judges could appoint them as magistrates or consultants to handle bankruptcy cases until Congress amended the law. The chair of the House Judiciary Committee reacted angrily, and a week later the no-salary order was rescinded (Taylor 1984b, 1984c; Riley 1984). The episode did nothing to heal the conflict between the generalist courts and the bankruptcy judges. Strangely, the Supreme Court never ruled on the reappointments of the bankruptcy judges or on whether the 1984 law complied with its *Northern Pipeline* decision. With relatively minor changes in 1994, the system established in 1984 has continued since that time.

There has been considerable research on the functioning of the current bankruptcy system. One study analyzed the work of the bankruptcy courts in organizational terms, emphasizing the linkages between the courts and their political and social environments (Seron 1978). Some work deals with consumer bankruptcy, which accounts for the great majority of cases (T. Sullivan, Warren, and Westbrook 1989, 1994; Braucher 1993; see E. Warren 2004). One contribution of these studies is to make it clear that judges' practices—such as their steering of debtors' choices between different forms of bankruptcy—vary a good deal. But the most attention has been given to business bankruptcies and specifically to those of large corporations. This body of scholarship relates directly to the impact of specialization, and it raises some interesting issues about concentration of judges.[27]

The debate in this scholarship begins with the fact that rules of venue give large corporations considerable choice about where to file for bankruptcy. In one widely noted case, decision makers in Eastern Airlines wanted to file in the Southern District of New York. Lacking any basis for doing so directly, they had a small subsidiary that was itself solvent file in that district on the basis of connections that established venue in the Southern District. Six minutes later, Eastern Airlines itself filed in the Southern District, based on the filing by its subsidiary (LoPucki 2005, 36–37).

---

27. There also has been scholarship on corporations' use of bankruptcy as a strategic device (Delaney 1992).

With choices over venue, large corporations that file for bankruptcy tend to gravitate toward some federal districts rather than others. At present, the most popular site for these cases is the district of Delaware. The reasons for that preference are a matter of debate. This debate has some similarities with the debate about the role of state courts in maintaining Delaware's advantage as a home for corporations.

In the 1990s, law professor Lynn LoPucki and his collaborators called attention to forum shopping in bankruptcy law (LoPucki and Whitford 1991; T. Eisenberg and LoPucki 1999), and LoPucki (2005) later analyzed this phenomenon at greater length (see LoPucki 2008). In LoPucki's account, many bankruptcy judges want to preside over large corporate bankruptcies, even though they get no tangible benefit from handling these cases and have to do more work. In part, he argues, they do so to gain greater power, status, and celebrity. They also want to please lawyers and other professionals who work in bankruptcy in their districts, people who benefit a good deal from having big corporate cases in their districts (LoPucki 2005, 20–21). To a degree, judges seek the approval of bankruptcy professionals for personal reasons: they work together, and the great majority of bankruptcy judges had been bankruptcy lawyers (Mabey 2005, 123). That approval may also enhance judges' chances of reappointment.

According to LoPucki, bankruptcy judges attract cases to their districts by appealing to corporate managers and lawyers who determine where cases are filed. To appeal to these decision makers, judges are responsive to the practical needs of lawyers and litigants and willing to approve lawyers' fee requests. In addition,

> the courts relaxed conflict of interest standards and granted lawyers and financial advisers unprecedented releases and indemnification from liability for their own wrongdoing. The jobs of executives—including those who led their companies into financial disaster—became more secure, and the courts allowed their companies to pay their executives huge bonuses. . . . Deals made among the case placers were sacrosanct, even if they violated the rights of other parties. Procedures designed to protect small investors and the public were abandoned. (LoPucki 2005, 18)

In other words, judges engaged in a race to the bottom.

Two scholars with a similar perspective have offered an account of how Delaware became the favored location for bankruptcies of large companies (Rasmussen and Thomas 2000, 1371–76). The Southern District of New York (which includes Manhattan) had held that status in the 1980s, based on its convenient location and policies that favored debtor corporations and their attorneys. Then, for idiosyncratic reasons, Continental Airlines took its 1990 bankruptcy case to Delaware.[28] Its executives were happy with the results: the one bankruptcy judge in the district handled the case effectively and treated the corporation and its attorneys well.

Observing these outcomes and knowing that their cases would go to the same judge, other large corporations flocked to Delaware. After a second bankruptcy judge was added, one way that the Delaware court maintained its advantage was by letting potential case filers know which of the two judges would handle their case (Bermant, Hillestad, and Kerry 1997, 40–41). The addition of four more bankruptcy judges in 2006 helped to solidify Delaware's position (LoPucki 2008). Delaware continues to get the biggest share of large corporate bankruptcies by far, with the Southern District of New York second (Marek 2009).

Along with the support it receives from some scholars, LoPucki's argument has been criticized by others. Some of the criticism is based on the strong tone of his 2005 book, one chapter of which is entitled "Corruption" (Dickerson 2006; Jacoby 2006; see LoPucki 2006). And one scholar has explained Delaware's success in attracting large corporate bankruptcies in terms that generally track the race to the top thesis: Delaware bankruptcy judges attract cases because they do their jobs well, and they would draw strong criticism within the state if they unduly favored the interests of corporate managers (Skeel 2001, 230–31).

But there is little doubt about some basic facts. Bankruptcy judges feel pressure from other bankruptcy professionals to take actions that favor the interests of those professionals. In an extreme case, a Philadelphia judge failed to win reappointment in 2000, apparently because of negative comments from local bankruptcy lawyers whom he had displeased with his actions (Groner 2001; LoPucki 2005, 44; *In re United States* 2006). In part because of that pressure and in part because of their own preferences, some (though by no means all) bankruptcy judges want to attract bankruptcies of large corporations. Finally, an interest in attracting those cases affects the choices of some bankruptcy courts. Judges in some districts have adopted procedural changes and approved higher lawyers' fees as means to attract

---

28. This action was set up by two one-sentence proclamations by Delaware's bankruptcy judge that the Delaware court was proper venue for a bankruptcy case in which the debtor is a Delaware corporation (*In the Matter of Ocean Properties of Delaware* 1988; *In the Matter of Delaware & Hudson Railway Company* 1988). Not surprisingly, efforts to change that venue rule through legislation were blocked by Delaware's senators (Rasmussen and Thomas 2000, 1381; LoPucki 2005, 16–17).

lawyers to file there (Rovella 2001). Although there is disagreement on this point, it also appears that some judges have adopted more significant policies that favor corporate management in order to attract cases.

If bankruptcy cases went to district judges rather than to specialized bankruptcy judges, would the same incentives operate? To a degree, they did in a past era: the efforts of bankruptcy judges today to attract big cases have some parallels in the efforts of generalist federal judges to attract railroad reorganization cases in the late nineteenth century (Buckley 1994, 775–78; Skeel 2001, 60–68). On the other hand, the agendas of the federal courts have broadened enormously since then, a change that reduces the interest of district judges in any bankruptcy cases and limits the leverage of bankruptcy lawyers over district judges. With the exception of Delaware, where big bankruptcy cases are important to the state, district judges today would seem unlikely to respond to the considerations that shape the behavior of some bankruptcy judges.[29]

Discussion

At the beginning of the chapter, I raised the question of whether judicial specialization in fields of private economic litigation reflects the interests of the business community. The movement toward special business courts in the states certainly does, and to a considerable degree the creation of the Court of Appeals for the Federal Circuit did so as well. State policy makers have established business courts as means to attract business activity to their states. Several considerations led Congress to establish the Federal Circuit, but one major reason was corporate interest in the outcomes of patent litigation.

In other instances, however, business did not play a major role. The record of the Court of Customs and Patent Appeals during the second half of its tenure was favorable to the same business interests that supported creation of the Federal Circuit, but that outcome was hardly envisioned when Congress gave jurisdiction over patent cases to the Court of Customs Appeals in 1929. The managers of large corporations that go into bankruptcy

---

29. The chief district judge in Delaware ended automatic referral of bankruptcy cases to bankruptcy judges in 1997, and district judges themselves decided some large corporate cases for about a year. The chief judge's order may have been a response to criticisms of the practices of Delaware's bankruptcy judges (LoPucki 2005, 83–96). Almost surely, one reason for the brevity of the period in which district judges heard some cases and for the rescinding of the 1997 order in 2001 was that Delaware district judges, like their colleagues elsewhere, prefer to have someone else hear bankruptcy cases (see Murray 2001).

may benefit from the existence of separate bankruptcy courts, but that benefit was not responsible for the series of steps that ultimately produced the bankruptcy courts.

The Delaware courts are an intermediate case. The Court of Chancery existed long before Delaware's efforts to attract incorporations, but its continued existence was guaranteed and its jurisdiction over corporate governance was expanded once those efforts began. Delaware probably would have created an independent supreme court in any case, but an interest in serving business played a part in that step.

What stands out most about private economic litigation is how little specialization there is in this area. The preponderance of cases still go to generalist state and federal courts, and there is little judicial specialization in the traditional private-law fields of contracts, property, and torts. There might be two reasons for this result.

The first is that other mechanisms to influence the outcomes of litigation seem more likely to pay off. Tort reform is an example. Business and professional groups that seek more favorable outcomes in personal injury cases have achieved considerable success by shaping the attitudes of the public (and thus of jurors), campaigning in judicial elections, and lobbying in courts and legislatures for favorable legal rules (Daniels and Martin 1995, 2004). Thus, they have accomplished a good deal within the existing structure of courts. In contrast, specialized courts offer less certain benefits.

The second reason for the dearth of specialized courts is the difficulty of securing major changes in judicial structure that require legislation. This difficulty is aggravated by the general presumption against judicial specialization. That presumption is not as heavy a barrier when specialization is perceived to serve government interests that legislators support. But when it is private interests that might be served by judicial specialization, the task of enacting legislation is more demanding. This may be especially true in common law fields that have long histories in generalist courts.

State business courts are too new to provide much evidence about the impact of judicial specialization, but the other sets of courts discussed in this chapter indicate some ways in which specialization can affect court policies. The CCPA and the Federal Circuit illustrate how judge and case concentration increase the potential for interested groups to exert influence through the selection of judges. According to one interpretation, the treatment of large corporate bankruptcies in some federal districts shows how judge concentration enhances the direct influence of litigants over judges. The work of the Delaware courts in corporate governance cases occurs in an unusual situation, one in which judges' decisions are perceived as important to the economic interests of their state. In that situation, both dimensions of specialization facilitate the impact of the political environment on judges' perspectives and choices. Taken together, these courts underline the potential for specialization to shape the content of judicial policy.

SEVEN

Putting the Pieces Together

The last four chapters examined the causes and consequences of judicial specialization in four broad fields of legal policy. In this chapter, I pull together the implications of the evidence presented in those chapters to address the issues that were considered in chapter 2. The chapter also addresses two other issues, the desirability of judicial specialization and the future of specialized courts in the United States.

The Causes of Specialization

In chapter 2, I raised four questions concerning the process by which the courts have become more specialized. This section offers evidence on the answers to those questions. I then assess the fit between the study's findings and the alternative theoretical perspectives that might be used to explain the specialization process. Finally, I confront the question of why that process has not gone further than it has.

What Goals?

Of the possible motives for creating specialized courts, the one that has had the greatest impact is an interest in shaping the substance of judicial policy. On occasion, that interest has come from private groups. One example is the proposal for the Court of Appeals for the Federal Circuit, spurred in part by business groups that sought a more lenient standard of patentability. But far more often, it has been government interests that provided the impetus for judicial specialization.

The financial interests of the federal government played a part in creation of the Court of Claims and customs courts at the trial and appellate levels.

Members of Congress anticipated that a court in Washington to adjudicate claims would be more favorable to the government than district courts throughout the country. The Board of General Appraisers and the Court of Customs Appeals were established primarily to safeguard the government's interest in maximizing tariff revenue.

With the Emergency Court of Appeals (ECA) and the Temporary Emergency Court of Appeals (TECA), federal officials sought to maintain effective programs of economic regulation. ECA was designed to minimize judicial interference with price controls in World War II, and TECA was to serve the same purpose for President Nixon's wage and price controls.

Specialized courts in foreign policy and internal security have also been used to further the government's policy goals. In quite different ways, the Court for China and the Court for Berlin were intended to support American foreign policy. Officials in the executive branch have viewed military tribunals as more reliable than civilian courts in securing convictions and punishing malefactors. The Foreign Intelligence Surveillance Court and the Removal Court were created in part to serve the government's interest in dealing effectively with perceived threats to internal security.

In the instances described so far, policy makers in the legislative and executive branches saw specialized courts as more attractive than generalists for review or approval of government actions. In the states, the use of specialization in criminal cases has sometimes come at the initiative of the legislature and executive, as it did in the Providence gun court. Judges and nongovernmental groups have also acted to further their own conceptions of how best to attack crime. This has been true of most of the socialized courts of the Progressive era and problem-solving courts of the current era. The establishment of those courts reflected the initiatives of judges and interest groups as well as supportive legislation and funding from the other branches.

Proposals for specialized courts as means to serve policy goals can arouse opposition from groups that disagree with those goals. Many of the successful proposals benefited from consensual or near-consensual support for the goals they were intended to serve. When officials in the executive branch or the judiciary set up specialized courts on their own, the ability to take unilateral action avoids the need for consensus.

For some courts, interest in substantive policy has been mixed with interest in the neutral virtues of specialization. The uniformity that could be obtained by designating a single court to review price controls reduced the chances that any court would rule against the government. Enhanced efficiency in resolving customs cases was expected to limit importers' incentives to challenge government decisions. And advocates sometimes anticipate that improvements in the quality of decisions that result from judicial expertise will lead to greater success for the set of litigants they support.

In other instances, neutral virtues have played a more independent role. Old-style drug courts were created to handle the flood of drug cases more efficiently, and an interest in efficiency also seems to underlie the designation of special judges to hear death penalty cases. The popularity of business courts reflects a belief that efficiency and high-quality decision making appeal to business leaders and thereby benefit states that create these courts. Across the full set of cases, however, the neutral virtues have been distinctly secondary to concerns about the substance of judicial policy. They certainly have been less important than public debates about judicial specialization would suggest, because advocates of specialized courts often invoke the neutral virtues to support proposals that they make for other reasons.

For legislators and executive-branch officials who act to establish specialized courts, individual self-interest has not played an important role independent of substantive policy and the neutral virtues. Judicial self-interest *has* played an independent role, in two general forms. The first involves job satisfaction in the criminal justice field. For many judges, frustration at assembly-line justice and at the courts' seeming failure to reduce criminal behavior has made the alternative of a therapeutic approach attractive. And those judges have played important roles in the creation and diffusion of socialized courts in the Progressive era and problem-solving courts in the current era. Judges who act to create these courts frequently staff them after their creation, and they regularly attest to the satisfactions they derive from serving in bodies such as drug courts and mental health courts. In the current era, those satisfactions are enhanced by the power that accrues to judges in problem-solving solving courts and the recognition they sometimes gain within and outside the courts.

The other form of self-interest concerns judicial status. Once a specialized body is established, its members want to achieve the highest possible formal status and to maximize their job security. Because of this interest, judges seek to turn administrative tribunals into courts and Article I courts into Article III courts. An interest in status also helps to spur expansions of jurisdiction for specialized courts, expansions that give judges more to do and thus increase their importance (and sometimes their job security). The evolution of bankruptcy courts reflects the self-interest of federal district judges, who preferred to rid themselves of cases that they saw as unworthy of their time but who sought to prevent the bankruptcy judges who decided those cases from achieving a status that diluted the status of district judges.

How Purposive?

The decisions that have enhanced judicial specialization result primarily from concern with the substance of judicial policy. In acting on that concern, how carefully have policy makers chosen between generalist and specialized courts?

The first thing that the historical record tells us is unsurprising. Most of the time, both generalist and specialized courts are left as they were without any consideration of alternatives. Officials in the three branches do not regularly consider whether their goals would be advanced by increasing or decreasing the level of specialization in each field of policy. Although this fact is hardly remarkable, in light of the overall preference for generalist courts it is interesting that many specialized courts remain in existence for long periods without serious inquiry into their continued value.

When specialized courts are created to advance certain policy goals, there is always some consideration of the linkage between ends and means. However, that consideration is often casual. One reason is that the existence of similar specialized courts leads policy makers to assume that a new court would serve the same purposes that the existing courts were intended to serve. This process will be considered shortly, in the discussion of diffusion. Sometimes policy makers' analysis of the relationship between specialization and policy is limited by their focus on other provisions of the legislation that includes judicial specialization. The Emergency Court of Appeals and the Court of Military Appeals are two examples.

To the extent that participants in the policy-making process think explicitly about how specialization might affect court outputs, they tend to act on the basis of folk theories that rest on common-sense notions of causality rather than on extensive and systematic analysis. Most often, these theories involve the idea that a court can be imbued with a mission that will govern its judges' behavior, especially if judges are chosen with that mission in mind. In the field of criminal law, both the courts that were intended to take a tough line on crime and those created to emphasize therapeutic approaches reflect that kind of folk theory.

The absence of careful analysis does not mean that a court will fail to achieve its intended purposes. Military tribunals for civilians are based largely on the casual assumption that military personnel will be more favorable to the prosecution than civilian judges and juries. That casual assumption makes considerable sense, and—with the noteworthy exception of the commissions at Guantánamo—it seems to be borne out by the actual performance of military tribunals.

On the other hand, careful analysis of relevant evidence enhances the chances of success, especially when policy makers are interested in success over the long term. The problem-solving courts of the current era offer a good example. Judges and others who devised and established these courts had available to them a rich body of relevant evidence on the performance of Progressive Era socialized courts. It appears that they ignored that evidence.

If specialized courts often are created without careful analysis of their potential effects, they are hardly unique in that respect. A great deal of government action rests on folk theories about the consequences of prospective policies. The effects of structural attributes of government are especially difficult to analyze, so it is tempting for advocates and policy makers to resort to common-sense notions of causality. Still, it is noteworthy that policy makers who seek to shape judicial policies through specialization often act without thorough consideration of the prospects for success.

Diffusion

Diffusion has played a major part in the growth of judicial specialization, in that the existence of certain specialized courts has encouraged the creation of additional courts. In the states, several courts have diffused geographically. This is true of business courts as well as socialized courts and problem-solving courts in criminal law.

Frequently, a particular type of specialized court has been drawn from one field of judicial policy and applied to another. In the states, juvenile courts provided a general model for other socialized courts, including domestic relations courts and women's courts. The problem-solving model has diffused from drug courts to a variety of other courts that resemble drug courts to varying degrees. This diffusion underlines the flexibility of structural attributes as forms of policy that can be adopted in different contexts once they are initially established.

At the federal level, military tribunals have been applied successively to various situations. In other arenas, the Temporary Emergency Court of Appeals followed the model of the Emergency Court of Appeals, and the

Removal Court was based on the Foreign Intelligence Surveillance Court in some respects.

The key issue about mechanisms of diffusion is the relative importance of learning and emulation.[1] The difference between the two is essentially one of data: how much have decision makers known about the success of an existing specialized court before using it as a model? Any dividing line between learning and emulation is arbitrary, but emulation certainly has been dominant. The simple existence of a model has been more important than clear evidence about the success of that model.

The states provide the best examples. Juvenile courts spread across localities and states on the basis of a general sense that they had been successful in places such as Chicago and Denver, before it could be known how well they actually worked. By and large, the same has been true of problem-solving courts in the current era. The most recent example is the quick adoption of veterans' courts in several localities shortly after the first such court was created in 2008. And the diffusion of the problem-solving model across fields of policy has come with only limited consideration of relevant differences among fields.

Because the federal government is only a single jurisdiction, diffusion of specialized courts ordinarily operates only across fields of law. As a result, the diffusion process is slower, so policy makers have a better chance to assess the success of the models they use. But they typically make only limited use of that chance, in part because there is little systematic information about the consequences of specialization. As a result, they rely more on vague perceptions of the performance of past and current courts than on actual evidence about that performance.[2] In this respect, diffusion has been similar to the broader process by which specialized courts are established.

1. Two other mechanisms can be described as competition and hierarchical influence (see Simmons, Dobbin, and Garrett 2006, 789–801; Shipan and Volden 2008, 841–45). These more specific mechanisms have both operated at the state level. As noted in chapter 6, interstate competition has fostered the development of business courts. Hierarchical influence was manifested in state legislation that encouraged the creation of juvenile courts and funding by the federal government that facilitates problem-solving courts such as drug and mental health courts.

2. One example of vague perceptions is the reference by federal judge Henry Friendly (1973, 154) to the "lack of any serious criticism" of some existing federal specialized courts when he advocated additional specialization in tax and patent law. In the congressional debate over the Court of Veterans Appeals, one member of the House Veterans' Affairs Committee said of the Tax Court and the Court of Military Appeals: "So far as I know, they are both doing a thoroughly competent job" (U.S. Congress 1988, 27789).

Design versus Inadvertence

The final question about the movement toward greater judicial specialization is also the most intriguing: the extent to which that movement reflects support for specialization as such rather than simply being a byproduct of more specific aims. The historical record is mixed in some respects, but the overall pattern is clear: judicial specialization has been a byproduct of other goals rather than an end in itself.

To a degree, the Progressive-era courts reflected an interest in specialization for its own sake. One significant strand of Progressive-era thinking about the courts favored specialized units within courts as a means to provide the same benefits of efficiency and decision quality that specialization was presumed to produce in arenas such as the business world. That strand of thinking played a part in the creation and diffusion of socialized courts. At the federal level, President Taft's own conception of good administration inclined him toward specialization in the fields of customs and railroads, and his initiative and support were keys to creation of the Commerce Court. Yet proposals for judicial specialization in the Progressive Era were limited to specific areas of legal policy in which the case for specialization seemed especially compelling.

In the creation of other specialized courts, people's attention has been focused even more narrowly. By and large, legislators and judges identify problems or opportunities in single areas of law and seek to address those problems through judicial specialization. Advocates of specialized courts sometimes refer to the benefits of specialization in society as a whole. But the impetus for specialized courts comes from people who care about the potential effects of specialization in a specific situation, giving little or no attention to judicial specialization as a general phenomenon.

Thus, the movement toward enhanced specialization has involved nothing that resembles a master plan. Specialized courts are created to serve specific purposes in the areas of legal policy in which they would hold jurisdiction. Some of these courts disappear but others survive, and some of those that survive gain broader jurisdiction over time. The result has been an uneven but substantial growth in the level of specialization along both its dimensions. That growth has been a product of inadvertence rather than design.

Implications for the Theories

In considering the possible sources of judicial specialization in chapter 2, I distinguished among three theoretical perspectives. The first two are the economic and sociological perspectives on institutions. What I have called the process stream perspective is John Kingdon's offshoot of the garbage can model of organizational choice. The discussion so far can be applied to the three perspectives. In somewhat different ways, the findings of this study support each perspective.

The motives for specific decisions about judicial specialization are most consistent with the economic perspective. Most often, proposals for specialized courts have been adopted because advocates and decision makers sought to shape the substance of judicial policy. Policy makers are attracted to specialization proposals because those proposals might benefit the interests of the governments in which they serve or simply because they approve of the policies that a specialized court might adopt.

The emphasis of the sociological perspective on values as a basis for choices about institutions receives less support from the growth of judicial specialization. The perceived virtues of specialization as such have played only a limited part in the adoption of particular proposals. However, the diffusion of specialized courts across states and localities, especially juvenile courts and new-style drug courts, reflects the positive connotations of those specific courts. To a degree, the widespread adoption of those courts resembles the "world culture" strain of the sociological perspective, in which national policy makers reflexively adopt widely approved institutions with only limited consideration of whether those institutions are appropriate for their own countries (Meyer et al. 1997).

Judicial specialization has not been highly purposive. This fact gives some support to the sociological perspective, which leaves more room for off-the-cuff judgments about the relationship between means and ends than does the economic perspective. In contrast, the inadvertence of the broader movement toward specialization supports the economic perspective. Because this perspective emphasizes efforts to seek specific benefits through choices of structural attributes, it implies that trends in the use of these attributes will reflect a series of discrete choices rather than general attitudes toward structural choices. On the whole, that has been the case with judicial specialization.

Useful as these two theoretical perspectives are, the growth of specialization in the courts is probably most consistent with the process stream perspective. A great deal of what has happened can be understood in terms of the availability of judicial specialization as an attribute that can be attached to multiple problems. Specific specialized courts are often established for multiple reasons, and different courts are created to serve quite different purposes. The flexibility of judicial specialization in this respect encourages its use in new situations, and past uses of specialization make it more prominent as an option for reuse. These traits help to explain why specialized courts are frequently adopted with little care and why the diffusion of specialization reflects emulation more than learning. The garbage can model from which Kingdon drew emphasizes the element of chaos in organizational decision making, and the increasing specialization of the judiciary reflects a good deal of chaos. The process that has led to enhanced specialization can be characterized in different ways, but any characterization should account for this chaotic element.

Explaining the Limits on Judicial Specialization

For the most part, American judges remain generalists. The great majority of appellate courts and judges decide a variety of cases. Federal district judges also have very broad jurisdiction. Specialization has gone the furthest in state trial courts, but many and perhaps most judges at that level still hear wide ranges of cases.

In light of the high levels of specialization elsewhere in government and society, the limited specialization of the judiciary is noteworthy. How can the survival of the generalist judge be explained? Insights associated with the sociological perspective on institutions help considerably in sketching out an explanation.

One insight is the power of what Scott Page (2006, 88) called self-reinforcement, one aspect of path dependence. To repeat Page's definition, "self-reinforcement means that making a choice or taking an action puts in place a set of forces or complementary institutions that encourage that choice to be sustained." American courts developed a pattern in which most judges were generalists. The continuation of that pattern over a long period of time has led to the expectation that it will be maintained, and it has also helped put a burden of proof on those who favor judicial specialization.

The dominance of the generalist pattern in early U.S. history may have reflected geography as much as anything else. There was some judicial specialization in state court systems (L. Friedman 2005, 93). However, this specialization was limited. The primary reason may have been a belief that courts should be readily accessible to people, which meant that judicial business was too widely scattered for judges to specialize narrowly without creating a costly proliferation of courts (see Pound 1912–13, 307; Alger 1917, 213; Hurst 1950, 95–96). But even if this pattern was solely a product of geography, it would have weighted the scales in favor of maintaining a nonspecialized court system.

Yet path dependence cannot be a full explanation for the survival of a mostly generalist judiciary. Over time, the courts could have evolved into a highly specialized system just as other sectors of government and society did. The fact that the courts did not evolve in this way is puzzling. After all, a generalist judiciary runs counter to the widely accepted belief that specialization improves efficiency and the quality of outputs, a belief that has powered the movement toward specialization outside the judiciary.

The emphasis in the sociological perspective on values as bases for institutional choices points to what may be the largest part of the explanation. Generalist judges fit the conception of the judge as a neutral third party interposed between disputants. A specialized body seems less neutral, more wedded to a particular way of thinking about the issues that come before it (see Shapiro 1968, 53). For judges themselves, the attribute of being a generalist provides status by distinguishing them from the specialists of the bureaucracy. For many people within and outside the judiciary, the courts are an exception to the general rule that specialization improves the quality of outputs.

The positive value attached to the generalist judge and the long-standing dominance of generalist courts reinforce each other in working against any wholesale departure from the generalist model. Conversion of the federal district courts or courts of appeals into courts that are specialized by subject matter would constitute a major alteration in the structure of government, an alteration that would conflict sharply with many people's conceptions of what the courts should be like. Any attempt to enact such a change would be saddled with a very strong burden of proof. Even the Federal Circuit proposal, involving a far more limited change in the structure of the federal appellate courts, succeeded only because of a favorable conjunction of circumstances.

Unusual as it was in some respects, adoption of the Federal Circuit proposal was typical of successful efforts to establish specialized courts. Supporters of those proposals emphasize their specific purposes. Rather than arguing that it is desirable to move away from the generalist model of American courts, they typically treat their proposals as needed exceptions to the general rule of generalist courts.

Specialization has gone furthest at the level of state trial courts. In part, the relatively high levels of specialization at that level reflect practical considerations. For one thing, trial courts in populous jurisdictions have enough judges to allow a good deal of subject-matter specialization. For another, courts can create specialized units themselves rather than needing to obtain legislative approval, and most specialization at the state trial level is created by courts.

Another reason why specialization has gone furthest at that level relates to characteristics of courts and judges. State trial courts in large cities have greater similarities to bureaucratic agencies than does any other type of court.[3] Judges often feel heavy pressure to keep up with caseloads, and simply processing cases may take precedence over the outcomes of those cases (see Ma. Levin 1975, 90). Courtrooms are often more chaotic than dignified. Judgeships in state trial courts are near the lowest level of prestige in the profession, because of their place in the hierarchy of courts and because lawyers and litigants who appear in those courts tend to be low in status themselves.

Because of those characteristics, apportioning work to state trial judges according to its subject matter may seem as natural as it does in the executive branch. Specialization may be perceived as an obvious way to maximize efficiency and improve the quality of decisions rather than as a sharp break from the generalist ideal. Indeed, certain types of specialization can provide a means for judges to transcend the bureaucratic attributes of their work and to assert their professionalism. This is a large part of the appeal of problem-solving courts to some judges. Business courts have the additional benefit that they put their judges in a milieu of high-prestige litigants and lawyers.

All this being true, urban trial courts in state systems still have gone only a limited distance toward specialization. Even in those courts, permanent assignment of judges to specific types of cases is much less common than it could be. The absence of greater specialization in these courts reflects the forces that have worked against specialization in the judiciary as a whole.

The extent of adherence to the model of generalist judges and courts should not be exaggerated. There is a good deal of specialization in American courts, and it exists in important fields of judicial policy. Moreover, the level of specialization along both its dimensions has undergone uneven but substantial growth. Specialization remains the exception to the rule, but it is an increasingly significant exception.

The Consequences of Specialization

Specialized courts have become more common because advocates and policy makers believe that judicial specialization makes a difference. As

---

3. As noted in chapter 2, Michael Lipsky (1980) characterized urban trial courts as "street-level bureaucracies." I draw here from Lipsky's ideas, but the set of attributes I emphasize differs somewhat from his definition of street-level bureaucracies.

discussed in chapter 2, judicial specialization could have two kinds of effects on court outputs. One kind of effect relates to the neutral virtues: with greater concentration of judges and cases, courts might become more efficient, produce higher-quality outputs, and achieve greater uniformity of legal doctrine. The other kind of effect is on the substance of policy. The question is the extent to which these effects actually occur.

The discussions of particular courts in earlier chapters have indicated the paucity of systematic information about either type of effect. One reason for this paucity is the difficulty of comparing generalist and specialized courts systematically. Even when courts of both types operate in the same field, as they do in federal taxation, they often differ in attributes other than specialization that complicate comparison. Moreover, scholars have made limited use of the opportunities that do exist for systematic comparison. For instance, there are few studies of changes that occur when some form of jurisdiction is transferred from a generalist court to a specialized body.

All this being true, enough information is available to allow some tentative judgments about those effects. The clearest finding is perhaps the most predictable: the effects of judicial specialization are not uniform. Rather, they are contingent both on the form that specialization takes and on other attributes of specialized courts and the situations in which they operate.

The Neutral Virtues

In the world at large, efficiency is the virtue most closely associated with specialization. Because of that association, advocates and policy makers have expected that judge concentration would allow more efficient processing of cases. That expectation surely has some accuracy, but there is little evidence on this issue.

Specialization can enhance efficiency simply by bringing additional resources to the courts. When a court with its own judges is created to hear cases in a particular field, its creation generally increases the number of available judges. When jurisdiction over benefits claims by military veterans was given to a Court of Veterans Appeals, these cases were decided by a new set of judges rather than adding to the caseloads of district judges. Similarly, the existence of separate bankruptcy courts has resulted in a large corps of judges who decide bankruptcy cases. If those cases were decided by district judges, it is unlikely that the number of district judges would have increased enough to compensate for the growing bankruptcy workload.

Judicial specialization may actually reduce efficiency by design when it is aimed at securing more careful consideration of certain cases. One premise underlying most socialized and problem-solving courts is that judges and other court personnel should take more time to deal with some types of criminal cases. For this reason, true problem-solving courts are almost inevitably boutiques, to use the term that some commentators employ. If these courts heard large numbers of cases and functioned as intended, they would quickly run up against limitations in needed resources. Of course, if the premises behind problem-solving courts are valid, these courts are a reminder that efficiency in itself is not always a virtue.

I have defined quality as judges' effectiveness in accomplishing what they seek to accomplish with their decisions. Advocates of specialized courts argue that concentration of judges enhances expertise and thus the quality of decisions. That argument is made with the greatest force in fields in which the law or case facts are unusually complex, such as patents and taxes. Given the complaints of some generalist judges about the complexities in those two fields, the argument almost surely has some validity. But here too, we have little meaningful evidence of differences in the quality of decision making between generalist and specialized courts.

In large part, this lack of evidence reflects the difficulty of measuring the quality of judges' work, a difficulty with which legal scholars have wrestled (e.g., Choi and Gulati 2004; Choi, Gulati, and Posner 2009; Symposium 2005). One potentially useful measure is reversal rates. One study provided summary evidence on reversal rates of Tax Court judges and district judges in tax cases (Worthy 1971, 253); another study looked more closely at reversal rates for district courts and panels of bankruptcy judges in bankruptcy cases (Nash and Pardo 2008). Both studies found that judges on specialized courts were affirmed by the courts of appeals at higher rates than district judges in the same legal fields, even though the reviewers were themselves generalists. In contrast, another study found that the Federal Circuit reversed district courts at somewhat lower rates than the overall rate for the specialized trial courts that it reviews (Morley 2008, 383–84). Even within a single field, the cases decided by generalist and specialized judges might differ enough to skew comparisons, and comparisons across fields present even greater difficulties. Still, reversal rates merit consideration as indicators of decision quality.

Where litigants have a choice between generalist and specialized courts, their choices might provide a clue to the comparative quality of decisions in the two courts. For instance, business lawyers' preference for the Delaware courts could reflect the perceived expertise of those courts in corporate organization. But litigators' preferences among alternative venues can result from perceptions of courts' policy positions as well as the quality of decisions. When the Court of Customs and Patent Appeals (CCPA) and the federal district court in District of Columbia both had jurisdiction over appeals of patent denials, the near-monopoly of business that the CCPA eventually gained was a result of the relative frequency with which it overturned Patent Office decisions rather than any advantage in expertise (Baum 1977, 839). Similarly, criminal defendants who opt for problem-solving courts rather than regular trial courts are attracted by the prospect that they will get more favorable outcomes in problem-solving courts. The overwhelming preference of litigants for the Tax Court over the district courts seems to reflect quite different considerations, the need to pay the disputed tax before going to a district court and the availability of special procedures for small tax cases in the Tax Court.

Commentators typically think of enhanced uniformity of decisions as an automatic result of case concentration, and they are surely right to a degree. Yet the enhancement should not be exaggerated. As one scholar has pointed out, uniformity is more directly a function of the number of "decisional units" that decide cases in a field than the number of courts (Legomsky 2007, 428–31). So long as cases in a specialized court are decided by multiple judges or panels, there remains the potential for disparities and conflicts in legal interpretations. Patent lawyers' unhappiness with conflicting legal standards and decisional tendencies in the Court of Appeals for the Federal Circuit underlines this reality, because uniformity was the key virtue cited by advocates of concentrating patent appeals in a single court.

The Substance of Policy

The neutral virtues certainly are important. However, the impact of specialization on the substance of judicial policy is of greater theoretical interest, and it is more consequential as well.

As summarized in table 2.1, high levels of judicial specialization along its two dimensions can affect the substance of court policies by immersing judges in the subject matter that their court considers and enhancing the influence of interested groups. Those mechanisms operate through the selection of judges and through their experiences on the bench. Both immersion in a field and the enhanced influence of interests potentially make courts more like administrative agencies, and specialized courts sometimes can develop missions similar to those often found in the administrative arena.

Among the specialized courts that were created to advance certain judicial policies, some have carried out this mission. Other courts have adopted distinctive approaches to policy that their creators did not intend. Several conditions foster the impact of judicial specialization on the substance of policy.[4]

The first and perhaps most powerful condition is selection of judges whose own attitudes give them a commitment to a particular policy orientation. Most judges possess considerable autonomy in their work, and this is especially true of judges who hold lengthy terms. For that reason, ex ante influence over judicial policies through the selection of judges is usually far more effective than ex post influence on judges who already sit on a court. Selection can take the form of appointment or election to a full-time and permanent position on a specialized court or assignment to a specialized unit for part-time or temporary service, but in either case it is a key process in shaping court policies.

The importance of judicial selection is illustrated by problem-solving courts. Many judges who serve on drug courts or mental health courts, to take two examples, strongly support the model of judging they are asked to follow. As a result, they work enthusiastically to handle their criminal cases in the nontraditional ways that the problem-solving model entails. The same was true of some early juvenile courts, which reflected the commitment of the judges who staffed them.

Like socialized courts and problem-solving courts, those that are set up to promote severity in criminal justice are most likely to follow their mandated path if their judges have a personal commitment to their missions. The Chicago Weed Court was staffed by a judge who suffered from hay fever; the Providence Gun Court was staffed by a judge who had once sentenced a defendant to death despite the absence of capital punishment in Rhode Island. It appears that the Providence judge followed through on expectations.

---

4. Judges' adherence to certain policies should be distinguished from success in achieving the broader goals that underlay the creation of their court. Even when judges are fully devoted to the mission of their courts, they cannot necessarily guarantee success for that mission. Drug courts, mental health courts, and homeless courts have only limited capacities to ameliorate the social problems they address. Judges on a state business court might do exactly what the architects of that court hoped, but this does not necessarily mean that businesses will be attracted to their state.

No evidence is available on the Chicago judge, but it is a safe bet that he meted out tough justice on people who contributed to his affliction.

The Federal Circuit illustrates another route to the same result. The Court of Customs and Patent Appeals and the Court of Claims favored a lenient standard of patentability because of the collective views of their judges. Those who supported that lenient standard could be confident that these judges would adhere to their positions when the two courts were merged into the Federal Circuit. Indeed, the Federal Circuit fulfilled the hopes of those advocates in that respect.

Judges are sometimes selected to shape a court's policies in ways that do not accord with the court's initial mission. The Reagan administration appointed strong conservatives to the Claims Court, and one result (perhaps intended) was that the court became favorable to Takings claims against the federal government. That stance contrasted with the efforts of nineteenth-century members of Congress to create a court that would protect the government's financial interests. If Chief Justice Rehnquist used his appointment power to create a pro-Republican leaning in the Special Division that selected special prosecutors, he was imposing an orientation on a court that was created with no policy mission at all.

Officials who choose judges do not necessarily emphasize policy considerations of any type. Even when a federal court has been created to protect the interests of the federal government, patronage opportunities often outweigh policy considerations in the selection of judges for that court (Chase 1972, 45–47). In some courts, patronage plays a substantial part in judicial selection from the start. Later on, when any policy mission for a specialized court has become less salient, appointing officials tend to perceive courts with narrow jurisdiction as relatively unimportant, so they give considerable weight to political reward as a consideration in appointments. In effect, the executive branch voluntarily gives up much of its opportunity to shape legal policy through the appointment power.

A similar process may occur for different reasons in the staffing of state criminal courts. Juvenile courts moved away from the policy orientation that their inventors wanted to foster. One reason was that the wide diffusion of juvenile courts and their continuation over many years meant that they were often staffed by judges who did not share that orientation.

If problem-solving courts gain the same foothold that juvenile courts achieved, they may suffer a similar fate. Judges who perceive drug court or mental health court as a duty rather than an opportunity may well deviate from the original mandate of those courts. Even in the early years of problem-solving courts, judges have sometimes been pressed into service on those courts despite a lack of enthusiasm for that assignment (Durkin et al. 2009, 10–11). That situation probably will become more common over time. As a result, the distinctiveness of these courts may wear away.[5]

Concentration of judges sometimes leads to the selection of lawyers who are already specialists in the court's work, especially in fields in which specialized knowledge seems important. In the Tax Court, for instance, tax expertise is effectively a prerequisite for appointment. Even when judges are selected without concern for their policy positions, selection of specialists may give a court a distinctive policy orientation if specialists tend to favor one of the competing interests in a field. Perhaps the best example is the broad (though not uniform) support of the patent bar for a lenient standard of patentability.

Concentration of judges and of cases each facilitates the use of judicial selection to shape court policies, but in practice case concentration has a more powerful effect. If one court has a monopoly over a particular type of case, officials can choose judges with that field in mind as an efficient means to influence judicial policy in the field. If all gun cases or all domestic violence cases in a populous county are to be heard by a single judge, that judge can be chosen to bring a particular orientation to those cases regardless of whether duty in a specialized courtroom constitutes all of the judge's work or only a small portion of that work. Similarly, it makes considerable difference that a dozen judges hear all patent appeals rather than the many dozens who sit on the various circuits of the federal courts of appeals, even if the agenda of the Federal Circuit allows its judges to think of themselves as generalists.

A second condition that facilitates the impact of specialization on judicial policy is the existence of strong incentives for judges to lean in favor of one side in a field rather than its competitor. Specialization enhances the capacity of interested groups to create such incentives, which are of two broad types.

The first is direct personal incentives, whether concrete or symbolic. If Lynn LoPucki (2005) is accurate in his reading of the bankruptcy courts, those courts provide an excellent example of this kind of incentive. Bankruptcy professionals benefit from having large corporate bankruptcies in their districts, and judges feel a degree of pressure from the professionals

---

5. Because the problem-solving model requires close cooperation among participants in the court, a fading of commitment by participants other than judges can also undercut that model. Pressure to dispose of criminal cases efficiently can also weaken missions that require courts to spend more time on each case, as is true of problem-solving courts.

with whom they interact to help attract those cases. Responsiveness to that pressure reflects an interest in respect and good relations with fellow workers and, to a degree, an interest in reappointment. Judges in some problem-solving courts feel a milder pressure from other participants in those courts who are strongly committed to therapeutic justice, just as judges in ordinary criminal courts feel pressure to accept plea bargaining and other practices that prosecutors and defense attorneys favor.

The other type of incentive is based on a feeling of responsibility for the success of a government program. The judges who served on the Emergency Court of Appeals undoubtedly recognized that their decisions would shape the functioning of the price control program during World War II, and that recognition militated against decisions that might weaken a seemingly vital program. Similarly, judges on the Delaware Court of Chancery perceive that their decisions affect the state's standing as the leading center for business incorporations. The judges' audiences in the state share that perception. As a result, judges have good reasons to support what they perceive as the state's interests.

The two types of incentives combine for members of military tribunals. They typically serve during times of perceived peril to national interests, so they want to avoid interfering with efforts to protect those interests. Further, they are usually part of a military hierarchy, and that position creates direct pressure on them to support military policy.

Even under considerable pressure, judges may diverge from the mission they have been given. Judge Herbert Stern refused to play his assigned role in the U.S. Court for Berlin despite the considerable efforts of the State Department to control him and its power to remove him from that position. For their part, some judges on the military commissions at Guantánamo have taken a more evenhanded and independent approach than the Defense Department preferred, even though they were subject to hierarchical control within the military. The self-image of these judges may have insulated them from pressure. And in Judge Stern's case, he could be fired by the State Department (as he was), but he still had his lifetime appointment as a federal district judge.

To the extent that specialization strengthens the incentives for judges to favor one interest in litigation, both dimensions of specialization play a part. Judge concentration makes a particular field of policy more important to judges, so that they are more susceptible to certain kinds of pressures. Bankruptcy is a good example, because judges who heard a wide range of cases would have less reason to follow the path favored by bankruptcy professionals. Case concentration may be even more important, because any pressure that operates in a field of policy is focused more heavily on a limited number of judges. If corporate governance cases in Delaware went to many trial courts rather than a single court, judges who decided occasional cases in that field would feel less responsibility for Delaware's effort to attract and maintain incorporations in the state.

A third condition that strengthens the linkage between specialization and the substance of judicial policy operates on a quite different level. Success in imposing a policy-oriented mission on a specialized court is facilitated by bundling of specialization with other provisions that favor the desired policies. The Emergency Court of Appeals was part of a package of provisions for judicial review that were designed to limit judicial interference with wartime price controls. When Congress and the executive branch created the Foreign Intelligence Surveillance Court, lenient requirements for issuance of warrants were established. In these and other instances, any effects of specialization in itself were reinforced by other provisions that favored the government.

In chapter 2, I emphasized the potential effects of concentration of judges that operate through judges' immersion in the subject matter of their court. Some courts provide hints of these effects, but the evidence is ambiguous. The Court of Customs and Patent Appeals was highly insular in its approach to patent cases. But that insularity did not lead to consistent effects on patent decisions, because the court's membership shaped its policies more than anything else. The specialization of the Court of Military Appeals may have led to assertiveness in its oversight of the military justice system, but even generalist civilian judges might have acted in a similar way.

Among the things that we know about the effects of judicial specialization, perhaps the most important is that case concentration is consequential. In debates and discussions about judicial specialization, people almost always have concentration of judges in mind. Judges on the bankruptcy courts and those on the Court of International Trade are generally perceived as similar in their degrees of specialization, even though cases involving international trade are decided by nine judges and bankruptcy cases are dispersed among more than three hundred judges. The standard conception of judicial specialization is reflected in the insistence of judges on the Federal Circuit that they are not specialists because they hear cases in several areas of policy.

Whether or not case concentration is treated as a dimension of specialization, however, it is clear that the concentration of a specific type of case in a single court can make considerable difference. Case concentration facilitates the use of judicial selection to shape court policies, and it can affect policy in other ways as well.

One implication is that action to increase case concentration should be treated as significant, even if that action has only marginal effects on concentration of judges. Establishment of federal borrowed-judge courts and state problem-solving courts in which judges serve only part-time constitutes a substantial change in one structural attribute of the judiciary. Of course, the two dimensions of specialization correlate with each other; typically, action that produces high concentration of judges also produces high case concentration. When such a step is contemplated, the potential effects of both dimensions should be taken into account.

Evaluating Judicial Specialization

Discussion of the effects of judge and case concentration leads to a broad normative question, the merits of judicial specialization. I have not addressed that question explicitly so far. In that respect the analysis in this book diverges from the strong normative theme in scholarship on judicial specialization.

Judicial specialization can be evaluated from many perspectives. One way to approach evaluation is by thinking about the debates over specialized courts as a clash of two ideals. One ideal is based on the perceived benefits of specialization in any sector of government or society. The other ideal is based on the perceived benefits of avoiding specialization specifically in the judiciary.

It is difficult to weigh these ideals against each other in the abstract. We also lack much empirical evidence with which to assess the relative importance of the two sets of perceived benefits. But even if we had considerably more evidence than we do, the multiple dimensions and forms of judicial specialization and the complexity and contingency of its effects would make it difficult to reach firm conclusions.

For those reasons, I am reluctant to take a firm position on the desirability of judicial specialization—and especially specialization as a general phenomenon. If we could agree on clear criteria for evaluation of judicial specialization, and if we had sufficient evidence of its effects, it is likely that we would find it desirable in some situations and undesirable in others. As I have emphasized, we are a long way from that point.

Still, legislators and judges have to make choices about specialization when proposals come before them. How should they approach those choices? One obvious recommendation is that they need to gather as much information as they can. Decisions whether to create specialized courts are typically made on the basis of limited information, and predictions about the effects of specialization frequently rest on folk theories whose validity is questionable. Limited as our understanding of specialization is, it can inform choices more than it has. As noted earlier, proponents of problem-solving courts in the states have given little if any attention to the very relevant histories of juvenile courts and other courts of the Progressive Era. Seldom has the effect of a proposed structural change on the substance of judicial policy been as certain as it was when Congress considered transferring patent infringement suits to a new Federal Circuit. Yet members of Congress and even the executive-branch officials who championed that transfer seemed more or less oblivious to that effect.

Proponents of specialized courts are often assigned a burden of proof. That burden seems appropriate. Specialization can have major consequences. Most important, it facilitates the development of policy-oriented missions for courts. The existence of such missions is troubling, especially when they arise from a reduction in courts' independence from external influence and control. In this respect more than any other, if courts become more like administrative agencies, then the justification for giving courts a place in the making of law and policy is weakened (Shapiro 1968, 53; but see Unah 1998, 9).

Thus, the continued (if reduced) dominance of generalist courts in the United States almost surely is a good thing. At the same time, a general preference for generalists in the judiciary may well be compatible with the selective use of specialized courts to serve particular functions. That, of course, is the current situation.

This does not mean, however, that the balance between generalist and specialized courts in the United States today is close to ideal. It seems highly unlikely that the haphazard process by which specialized courts are established has resulted in their being in the right places. Like the movement toward judicial specialization as a whole, the choices of fields in which to use specialized courts has been a matter of inadvertence rather than design. That is one more reason for caution in moving toward higher levels of specialization in the courts.

The Future of Judicial Specialization

The specialized courts that exist in the state and federal judicial systems represent only a portion of those that have been proposed. At the federal level, legal scholars and commentators regularly suggest new courts. For instance, there has been a long-standing interest in creating a court of tax appeals to hear appeals that currently go to the courts of appeals (H. Miller 1975; Cords 2005, 1051),[6] and there have also been recurrent proposals to shift appeals in social security cases from the district courts to a new specialized court (Rains 1987; Arzt 2006). Among the various proposals in recent years have been two types of copyright courts (Landau and Biederman 1999; Mac-Lean 2006b), a court to deal with executive privilege claims (Fein 2007), and a court to hear disputes over elections (Foley 2008).

Many of these proposals represent only the ideas of a few advocates, but some receive serious consideration. In addition to the courts that Congress actually has created, the idea of a court of tax appeals has attracted considerable support at some points, and it was initially included in the Justice Department proposal for the Federal Circuit (Meador 1992, 592). A number of scholars and commentators have expressed support for the idea of a National Security Court to handle prosecutions of suspected terrorists, a court that would be something of a compromise between military courts and the generalist federal courts (Goldsmith and Katyal 2007; Lunday and Rishikof 2008; Sulmasy 2009). Interest in several possible types of specialized courts to adjudicate immigration cases has extended to Congress (Roberts 1980; Legomsky 2007, 464–68; U.S. Senate 2006b).[7] In the last three Congresses, the House has passed bills for a pilot program to channel patent cases to a self-selected subset of district judges; the Senate has not yet acted on any of these bills (Gitter 2009).

At the state level, the several forms of business courts and the array of problem-solving courts are available for wider adoption. The invention of the veterans' treatment court in 2008 and its quick adoption in several cities are reminders of how easily state trial courts can develop new types of specialized courts. The idea of health courts to hear medical malpractice cases has received considerable discussion, with support coming primarily from supporters of tort reform (Fortado 2004; Post 2006; P. Howard 2009). Some participants in the congressional debate over changes in the health

6. There also has been interest in giving the Tax Court exclusive jurisdiction over tax cases at the trial level (Geier 1991).

7. In 2006, the Senate passed a bill that asked the General Accountability Office to study three proposals that would move immigration appeals from the federal courts of appeals to other bodies. (The bill was S. 2611, 109th Congress; the GAO provision was section 707.) The House did not act on the bill.

care system advocated that the federal government encourage states to establish health courts (Alonso-Zaldivar and Werner 2009).

The historical record underlines the difficulty of predicting what will happen to these proposals and possibilities. Where legislation is needed to establish specialized courts, its fate depends on the conjunction of circumstances that Kingdon (1984, 2003) has described. After decades of proposals for a court of patent appeals had failed, several favorable circumstances had to come together to produce the Federal Circuit in 1982. Nor was it preordained that patent appeals now go to a single court but tax appeals still go to the federal courts of appeals. Because of the difficulty of enacting legislation and the presumption in favor of generalist courts, it will always be the case that most ideas for specialized courts that require legislative action come to nothing.

By the same token, courts that are established as permanent bodies through legislation tend to become permanent. Government organizations are not necessarily immortal (see Kaufman 1976; D. Lewis 2003), as the quick demise of the Commerce Court makes clear. However, once a specialized court becomes established, it is considerably more likely that its jurisdiction will be expanded than that it will be abolished.

In the federal court system, this means that a kind of ratcheting effect leads to a slow and uneven growth in the degree of judicial specialization. Military tribunals and other courts created by the executive branch come and go, and courts that Congress establishes as temporary bodies eventually end their work. But as more specialized courts are created through legislation and new increments are added to their work, the portion of federal jurisdiction that is entrusted to specialized courts increases.

The situation is considerably more fluid in the states, because so much specialization comes in the form of units that courts create themselves. As a result, particular forms of specialized courts ebb and flow. Of the socialized courts that were created in the Progressive Era, only the juvenile courts survived. The problem-solving courts of the current era have burgeoned. But no type of problem-solving court has become nearly as widespread as juvenile courts, and none have received the degree of statutory support that juvenile courts gained. Should funding decline or judges become disillusioned with the problem-solving approach, these courts will cease to grow and might even disappear.

Still, the more likely long-term prospect in the states is an increase in the extent of judicial specialization. The relative weakness of the generalist ideal at the state trial level reduces resistance to the creation of specialized courts.

Future growth in the numbers of cases and judges will make specialization more attractive and more feasible. State court systems today feature greater specialization by subject matter and litigant than they did a century ago, and that trend is likely to continue—albeit in fits and starts.

Whatever the trends of the future may be, court systems in the United States will continue to feature a good deal of specialization. That specialization sometimes has powerful effects on the work of the courts. Those realities merit greater attention from students of the courts and from policy makers who shape the structure of the judiciary.

REFERENCES

The main reference section, with books, reports, and articles, is followed by sections with legislative, statutory, and regulatory materials and with court decisions and documents.

BOOKS, REPORTS, AND ARTICLES

Abraham, Henry J. 1998. *The Judicial Process*, 7th ed. New York: Oxford University Press.

———. 2008. *Justices, Presidents, and Senators: A History of U.S. Supreme Court Appointments from Washington to Bush II*, 5th ed. Lanham: Rowman & Littlefield.

Abramson, Bruce D. 2007. *The Secret Circuit: The Little-Known Court Where the Rules of the Information Age Unfold*. Lanham: Rowman & Littlefield.

Administrative Office of the U.S. Courts. 2010. *2009 Annual Report of the Director: Judicial Business of the United States Courts*. Washington, DC: U.S. Government Printing Office.

Albright, Joseph. 1974. "A Hell of a Way to Run a Government." *New York Times Magazine*, November 3, 16–17, 94–99, 102–5, 110.

Alger, George W. 1917. "The Organization of the Courts." *Annals of the American Academy of Political and Social Science* 73:211–18.

Allen, Arthur. 1998. "Shot in the Dark: Did the DPT Vaccine Make Some Children Catastrophically Sick?" *Washington Post*, August 30, W10–15, 21–23.

Allen, Michael P. 2007. "Significant Developments in Veterans Law (2004–2006) and What They Reveal About the U.S. Court of Appeals for Veterans Claims and the U.S. Court of Appeals for the Federal Circuit." *University of Michigan Journal of Law Reform* 40:483–568.

———. "The United States Court of Appeals for Veterans Claims at Twenty: A Proposal for a Legislative Commission to Consider Its Future." *Catholic University Law Review* 58:361–410.

Allison, John R., and Mark A. Lemley. 1998. "Empirical Evidence on the Validity of Litigated Patents." *AIPLA Quarterly Journal* 26:185–275.

———. 2000. "How Federal Circuit Judges Vote in Patent Validity Cases." *Florida State University Law Review* 27:745–66.

Alonso-Zaldivar, Ricardo, and Erica Werner. 2009. "Health Negotiators Look at Malpractice Changes." Associated Press, September 11.

Alt, James E., and Alberto Alesina. 1996. "Political Economy: An Overview." In *A New Handbook of Political Science*, ed. Robert E. Goodin and Hans-Dieter Klingemann, 645–74. New York: Oxford University Press.

Altieri, Mark P., Jerome E. Apple, Penny Marquette, and Charles K. Moore. 2001. "Political Affiliation of Appointing President and the Outcome of Tax Court Cases." *Judicature* 84:310–13.

Aman, Alfred C., Jr. 1980. "Institutionalizing the Energy Crisis: Some Structural and Procedural Lessons." *Cornell Law Review* 65:491–598.

American Journal of International Law. 1907. "An Act Creating a United States Court for China and Prescribing the Jurisdiction Thereof, 1906." 1:234–38.

Anderson, Gary M., William F. Shughart II, and Robert D. Tollison. 1989. "On the Incentives of Judges to Enforce Legislative Wealth Transfers." *Journal of Law and Economics* 32:215–28.

Anderson, Jon. 1995. "Environmental Enforcements." *Vermont Bar Journal and Law Digest* 21(5): 14–15.

Ankeny, Robert. 2005. "A Conversation with Diane Akers, Bodman L.L.P." *Crain's Detroit Business*, March 14, 11.

Anthony, J. Garner. 1955. *Hawaii Under Military Rule.* Stanford: Stanford University Press.

Ariens, Michael. 1994. "Know the Law: A History of Legal Specialization." *South Carolina Law Review* 45:1003–61.

Arzt, Robin J. 2006. "Proposal for a United States Social Security Court." In American Bar Association, *A Social Security Court: Does the Structure of Such a Court Enhance its Justifications or its Criticisms?* http://www.abanet.org/adminlaw/conference/2006/handouts/socsec.pdf.

Ash, Robert. 1955. "Procedures Effective Under 1954 Code Which Affect Tax Settlement or Litigation." *Journal of Taxation* 3:204–9.

Atkins, Burton M. 1974. "Opinion Assignments on the United States Court of Appeals: The Question of Issue Specialization." *Western Political Quarterly* 27:409–28.

Atkins, Burton M., and William Zavoina. 1974. "Judicial Leadership on the Court of Appeals: A Probability Analysis of Panel Assignment in Race Relations Cases on the Fifth Circuit." *American Journal of Political Science* 18:701–11.

Attorney General's Committee on Bankruptcy Administration. 1941. *Administration of the Bankruptcy Act.* Washington, DC: Government Printing Office.

Baar, Carl. 2003. "Trial Court Unification in Practice." *Judicature* 76:179–84.

Babb, Barbara A. 1998. "Where We Stand: An Analysis of America's Family Law Adjudicatory Systems and the Mandate to Establish Unified Family Courts." *Family Law Quarterly* 32:31–65.

Bach, Mitchell L., and Lee Applebaum. 2004. "A History of the Creation and Jurisdiction of Business Courts in the Last Decade." *The Business Lawyer* 60:147–275.

Baker, Donald P. 1997. "If Under 21, the Bar Scene May Be a Bust." *Washington Post*, March 11, A3.

Baker, Joan E. 1983. "Is the United States Claims Court Constitutional?" *Cleveland State Law Review* 32:55–101.

Baker, Nancy V. 2006. *General Ashcroft: Attorney at War.* Lawrence: University Press of Kansas.

Baker, Peter. 2007. "Bush Retreats on Use of Executive Power." *Washington Post*, January 18, A4.

Baker, Thomas E. 1994. *Rationing Justice on Appeal: The Problems of the U.S. Courts of Appeals.* St. Paul: West Publishing.

Baldwin, William H. 1912. "The Court of Domestic Relations of Chicago." *Journal of the American Institute of Criminal Law and Criminology* 3:400–406.

Ball, Howard. 2007. *Bush, the Detainees, and the Constitution: The Battle Over Presidential Power in the War on Terror*. Lawrence: University Press of Kansas.

Balla, Steven J. 2001. "Interstate Professional Associations and the Diffusion of Policy Innovations." *American Politics Research* 29:221–45.

Bamford, James. 1982. *The Puzzle Palace: A Report on America's Most Secret Agency*. Boston: Houghton Mifflin.

———. 2006. "Big Brother is Listening." *Atlantic Monthly*, April, 65–70.

———. 2008. *The Shadow Factory: The Ultra-Secret NSA From 9/11 to the Eavesdropping on America*. New York: Doubleday.

Banks, Christopher. 1999. *Judicial Politics in the D.C. Circuit Court*. Baltimore: Johns Hopkins University Press.

Barker, Kim. 1999. "New Court Tries Prevention." *Seattle Times*, February 21, B1, B5.

Barnes, Jeb. 1997. "Bankrupt Bargain? Bankruptcy Reform and the Politics of Adversarial Legalism." *Journal of Law & Politics* 13:893–935.

Barrett, John Q. 2000. "Special Division Agonistes." *Widener Law Symposium Journal* 5:17–48.

Barrow, Deborah J., and Thomas G. Walker. 1988. *A Court Divided: The Fifth Circuit Court of Appeals and the Politics of Judicial Reform*. New Haven: Yale University Press.

Bass, Jack. 1981. *Unlikely Heroes*. New York: Simon and Schuster.

Baum, Lawrence. 1977. "Judicial Specialization, Litigant Influence, and Substantive Policy: The Court of Customs and Patent Appeals." *Law & Society Review* 11:823–50.

———. 1994. "Specialization and Authority Acceptance: The Supreme Court and Lower Federal Courts." *Political Research Quarterly* 47:693–703.

———. 2003. "Judicial Elections and Judicial Independence: The Voter's Perspective." *Ohio State Law Journal* 64:15–41.

———. 2010. "Judicial Specialization and the Adjudication of Immigration Cases." *Duke Law Journal* 59:1501–61.

Bawn, Kathleen. 1995. "Political Control Versus Expertise: Congressional Choices About Administrative Procedures." *American Political Science Review* 89:62–73.

Beaman, Walter H. 1957. "When Not to Go to the Tax Court: Advantages and Procedures in Going to the District Court." *Journal of Taxation* 7:356–58.

Bean, Philip. 2002. "Drug Courts, the Judge, and the Rehabilitative Ideal." In *Drug Courts in Theory and in Practice*, ed. James L. Nolan, Jr., 235–54. New York: Aldine de Gruyter.

Bebbington, Jim. 1993. "A Day in the Life of Environmental Court." *Columbus Monthly*, July, 97–100.

Bebchuk, Lucian Arye, and Alman Cohen. 2003. "Firms' Decisions Where to Incorporate." *Journal of Law & Economics* 46:383–422.

Becker, Bernie. 2008. "Military Appeal Process is Challenged." *New York Times*, November 28, A24.

Bederman, David J. 1988. "Extraterritorial Domicile and the Constitution." *Virginia Journal of International Law* 28:451–94.

Belden, Evelina. 1920. *Courts in the United States Hearing Children's Cases*. Washington, DC: Government Printing Office.

Belenko, Steven, Jeffrey A. Fagan, and Tamar Dumanovsky. 1994. "The Effects of Legal Sanctions on Recidivism in Special Drug Courts." *Justice System Journal* 17:53–81.

Belknap, Michal R. 1992. *To Improve the Administration of Justice: A History of the American Judicature Society*. Chicago: American Judicature Society.

Bell, Griffin, with Ronald J. Ostrow. 1982. *Taking Care of the Law*. New York: William Morrow.

Bell, John. 1988. "Principles and Methods of Judicial Selection in France." *Southern California Law Review* 61:1757–94.

Bell, Lauren Cohen. 2002. *Warring Factions: Interest Groups, Money, and the New Politics of Senate Confirmation*. Columbus: Ohio State University Press.

Bell, Lauren C., and Kevin M. Scott. 2006. "Policy Statements or Symbolic Politics? Explaining Congressional Court-Limiting Attempts." *Judicature* 89:196–201.

Belluck, Pam. 2001. "Michigan Plans a High-Tech Lure." *New York Times*, February 22, A10.

Bendor, Jonathan B. 1985. *Parallel Systems: Redundancy in Government*. Berkeley and Los Angeles: University of California Press.

Bendor, Jonathan, Terry M. Moe, and Kenenth W. Shotts. 2001. "Recycling the Garbage Can: An Assessment of the Research Program." *American Political Science Review* 95:169–90.

Bennett, Marion T. 1978. *The United States Court of Claims: A History, Part I*. Washington, DC: Committee on the Bicentennial of Independence and the Constitution of the Judicial Conference of the United States.

Berch, Michael A. 1990. "The Bankruptcy Appellate Panel and Its Implications for Adoption of Specialist Panels in the Courts of Appeals." In *Restructuring Justice: The Innovations of the Ninth Circuit and the Future of the Federal Courts*, ed. Arthur D. Hellman, 165–91. Ithaca: Cornell University Press.

Berens, Michael J. 1996. "Holding the Purse Strings." *Columbus Dispatch*, November 19, 1A, 2A.

Berkson, Larry, and Susan Carbon. 1978. *Court Unification: History, Politics and Implementation*. Washington, DC: National Institute of Law Enforcement and Criminal Justice.

Berman, Greg. 1998. *Red Hook Diary: Planning a Community Court*. New York: Center for Court Innovation.

Berman, Greg, ed. 2000. "'What is a Traditional Judge Anyway? Problem Solving in State Courts." *Judicature* 84:78–85.

Berman, Greg, and John Feinblatt, with Sarah Glazer. 2005. *Good Courts: The Case for Problem-Solving Justice*. New York: The New Press.

Berman, Greg, and Aubrey Fox. 2005. "Justice in Red Hook." *Justice System Journal* 26:77–90.

Bermant, Gordon, Arlene Jorgensen Hillestad, and Aaron Kerry. 1997. *Chapter 11 Venue Choice by Large Public Companies*. Washington, DC: Federal Judicial Center.

Bernstein, Robert, and Tammy Seltzer. 2003. "Criminalization of People with Mental Illnesses: The Role of Mental Health Courts in System Reform." *University of the District of Columbia Law Review* 7:143–62.

Berry, Frances Stokes, and William D. Berry. 1990. "State Lottery Adoptions and Policy Innovations: An Event History Analysis." *American Political Science Review* 84:395–415.

Bessen, James, and Michael J. Meurer. 2008. *Patent Failure: How Judges, Bureaucrats, and Lawyers Put Innovators at Risk*. Princeton: Princeton University Press.

Bhati, Avinash Singh, John K. Roman, and Aaron Chalfin. 2008. *To Treat or Not to Treat: Evidence on the Prospects of Expanding Treatment to Drug-Involved Offenders*. Washington, DC: Urban Institute.

Bickford, Hugh C. 1956. *Successful Tax Practice*, 3rd ed. Englewood Cliffs: Prentice-Hall.

Billard, Mary. 1984. "Revitalizing a Judicial Backwater." *American Lawyer*, January, 60–61.

Billings, B. Anthony, D. Larry Crumbley, and L. Murphy Smith. 1992. "Are Tax Court Decisions Subject to the Bias of the Judge?" *Tax Notes* 55:1259–67.

Binder, Stephen R. 2003. "The Homeless Court Program: Taking the Court to the Streets." Paper presented at annual conference of National Legal Aid and Defender Association, Seattle.

Blankenburg, Erhard. 1996. "Changes in Political Regimes and Continuity of the Rule of Law in Germany." In *Courts, Law, and Politics in Comparative Perspective*, by Herbert Jacob et al., 257–314. New Haven: Yale University Press.

Blankenburg, Erhard, and Ralf Rogowski. 1984. "West German Labor Courts and the British Tribunal System: A Socio-Legal Comparison." Working Paper 1984–88, Disputes Processing Research Program, University of Wisconsin.

Blum, Vanessa. 2005. "Troubled Tribunals Soldier On." *Legal Times*, October 10, 1, 18.

Bogira, Steve. 2005. *Courtroom 302: A Year Behind the Scenes in an American Criminal Courthouse*. New York: Alfred A. Knopf.

Bollens, John. 1957. *Special District Governments in the United States*. Berkeley and Los Angeles: University of California Press.

Boston Globe. 2009. "Old GM, Unions in Retiree Health Deal." November 13, 6.

Bozzomo, James W., and Gregory Scolieri. 2004. "A Survey of Unified Family Courts: An Assessment of Different Jurisdictional Models." *Family Court Review* 42:12–37.

Bradfute, Richard Wells. 1975. *The Court of Private Land Claims: The Adjudication of Spanish and Mexican Land Grant Titles, 1891–1904*. Albuquerque: University of New Mexico Press.

Braucher, Jean. 1993. "Lawyers and Consumer Bankruptcy: One Code, Many Cultures." *American Bankruptcy Law Journal* 67:501–83.

Bravin, Jess. 2007. "Membership of New Guantánamo Review Panel May be Challenged." *Wall Street Journal*, July 9, A3.

Brenner, Saul. 1984. "Issue Specialization as a Variable in Opinion Assignment on the U.S. Supreme Court." *Journal of Politics* 46:1217–25.

Brenner, Saul, and Harold J. Spaeth. 1986. "Issue Specialization in Majority Opinion Assignment on the Burger Court." *Western Political Quarterly* 39:520–27.

Brigham, John 1987. *The Cult of the Court*. Philadelphia: Temple University Press.

Brill, Steven. 1987. "The Stench of Room 202." *The American Lawyer*, April, 1, 15–18.

Brudney, James J., and Corey Ditslear. 2009. "The Warp and Woof of Statutory Interpretation: Comparing Supreme Court Approaches in Tax Law and Workplace Law." *Duke Law Journal* 58:1231–311.

Bruff, Harold H. 1991. "Specialized Courts in Administrative Law." *Administrative Law Review* 43:329–66.

Buckley, F. H. 1994. "The American Stay." *Southern California Interdisciplinary Law Journal* 3:733–79.

Bureau of Justice Assistance, U.S. Department of Justice. 1993a. *Assessment of the Feasibility of Drug Night Courts*. Washington, DC: U.S. Government Printing Office.

———. 1993b. *Special Drug Courts*. Washington, DC: Bureau of Justice Assistance.

Burk, Dan L., and Mark A. Lemley. 2009. *The Patent Crisis and How the Courts Can Solve It*. Chicago: University of Chicago Press.

Burns, Nancy. 1994. *The Formation of American Local Governments: Private Values in Public Institutions*. New York: Oxford University Press.

Bushnell, Eleanore. 1992. *Crimes, Follies, and Misdemeanors: The Federal Impeachment Trials*. Urbana: University of Illinois Press.

Butts, Jeffrey A., and John Roman, eds. 2004a. *Juvenile Drug Courts and Teen Substance Abuse*. Washington, DC: Urban Institute Press.

———. 2004b. "Drug Courts in the Juvenile Justice System." In *Juvenile Drug Courts and Teen Substance Abuse*, ed. Jeffrey A. Butts and John Roman, 1–25. Washington, DC: Urban Institute Press.

Cadwallader, Bruce. 2008. "New Court Will Focus on Complex Business Cases." *Columbus Dispatch*, September 3, C7.

Canon, Bradley C., and Kenneth Kolson. 1971. "Rural Compliance with Gault: Kentucky, a Case Study." *Journal of Family Law* 10:300–26.

Carns, Teresa W., Michael G. Hotchkin, and Elaine M. Andrews. 2002. "Therapeutic Justice in Alaska's Courts." *Alaska Law Review* 19:1–55.

Caron, Paul L. 1994. "Tax Myopia, or Mamas Don't Let Your Babies Grow Up to be Tax Lawyers." *Virginia Tax Review* 13:517–90.

———. 1996. "Tax Myopia Meets Tax Hyperopia: The Unproven Case of Increased Judicial Deference to Revenue Rulings." *Ohio State Law Journal* 57:637–70.

Carpenter, Daniel P. 1998. "The Corporate Metaphor and Executive Department Centralization in the United States, 1888–1928." *Studies in American Political Development* 12:162–203.

Carrington, Paul D., Daniel J. Meador, and Maurice Rosenberg. 1976. *Justice on Appeal*. St. Paul: West Publishing.

Carter, Susan B., et al. 2006. *Historical Statistics of the United States*. New York: Cambridge University Press.

Carter, Terry. 1987. "No Respect." *National Law Journal*, November 23, 1, 23.

———. 1992. "U.S. Claims Court Anxious to Secure Further Respect." *Los Angeles Daily Journal*, January 3, 1, 5.

Caruso, David B. 2002. "Crackdown Will Target Illegal Drivers." *Columbus Dispatch*, April 14, A10.

Cary, William L. 1974. "Federalism and Corporate Law: Reflections Upon Delaware." *Yale Law Journal* 83:663–705.

Casey, Pamela M., and David B. Rottman. 2005. "Problem-Solving Courts: Models and Trends." *Justice System Journal* 26:35–56.

Casey, Pamela M., David B. Rottman, and Chantal G. Bromage. 2007. *Problem-Solving Justice Toolkit*. Williamsburg: National Center for State Courts.

Casper, Jonathan D. 1972. *The Politics of Civil Liberties*. New York: Harper & Row.

Castleton, Tom. 1992. "Claims Court Crusader: Chief Judge Smith Puts Property Rights Up Front." *Legal Times*, August 17, 1, 16–17.

Chase, Deborah J., and Peggy Fulton Hora. 2000. "The Implications of Therapeutic Jurisprudence for Judicial Satisfaction." *Court Review* 37:12–20.

Chase, Harold W. 1972. *Federal Judges: The Appointing Process*. Minneapolis: University of Minnesota Press.

Cheng, Edward K. 2008. "The Myth of the Generalist Judge." *Stanford Law Review* 61:519–72.

Chiang, Harriet. 1998. "Stanley P. Golde—East Bay Judge." *San Francisco Chronicle*, October 7, C2.

Chicago Daily Tribune. 1911a. "Bachelor to Fix Family Woe." January 15, 2.

———. 1911b. "Mothers-in-Law Lesson Ignored?" May 6, 16.

———. 1911c. "Court Decides All Wives are Entitled to Salaries." May 12, 1.

———. 1911d. "Judge Goodcook; Proud of It." June 19, 3.

———. 1912. "Domestic Court Racks Judge." September 17, 7.

———. 1928. "Special Court Created to Try Racket Cases." December 30, 7.

———. 1930. "Judge Gets Hay Fever, Delaying the Weed Court." August 22, 2.

———. 1932. "Drive on Auto Theft Promised by Prystalski." September 4, 9.

Chicago Tribune. 1982. "Judges 'Soft' on Guns Hit." October 12, A11.

Chisum, Donald S. 1999. "The Supreme Court and Patent Law: Does Shallow Reasoning Lead to Thin Law?" *Marquette Intellectual Property Law Review* 3:1–24.

Choi, Stephen J., and G. Mitu Gulati. 2004. "Choosing the Next Supreme Court Justice: An Empirical Ranking of Judge Performance." *Southern California Law Review* 78:23–118.

Choi, Stephen J., Mitu Gulati, and Eric A. Posner. 2009. "Judicial Evaluations and Information Forcing: Ranking State High Courts and Their Judges." *Duke Law Journal* 58:1313–81.

Chong, Dennis. 2000. *Rational Lives: Norms and Values in Politics and Society.* Chicago: University of Chicago Press.

Christenson, Dino, Brett Curry, and Banks Miller. 2009. "Experts in Crime: The Effect of an Exclusively Criminal Docket on Judicial Behavior." Paper presented at the annual meeting of the Southern Political Science Association, New Orleans.

Chutkow, Dawn M. 2008. "Jurisdiction Stripping: Litigation, Ideology, and Congressional Control of the Courts." *Journal of Politics* 70:1053–64.

Cihlar, Frank P. 1982. *The Court American Business Wanted and Got: The United States Court of Appeals for the Federal Circuit.* Washington, DC: National Chamber Foundation.

Cinquegrana, Americo R. 1989. "The Walls (and Wires) Have Ears: The Background and First Ten Years of the Foreign Intelligence Surveillance Act of 1978." *University of Pennsylvania Law Review* 137:793–828.

Clark, David S. 1988. "The Selection and Accountability of Judges in West Germany: Implementation of a *Rechtsstaat.*" *Southern California Law Review* 61:1795–847.

Clines, Francis X. 1999. "Tradition of Local Justice Ends in Ohio." *New York Times,* August 10, A8.

Coan, George R. 1975. "Operational Aspects of a Central Hearing Examiners Pool: California's Experiences." *Florida State University Law Review* 3:86–92.

Cockburn, Andrew. 2000. "The Radicalization of James Woolsey." *New York Times Magazine,* July 23, 26.

Cohen, Gary. 2002. "The Keystone Kommandos." *The Atlantic,* February, 46–59.

Cohen, Michael D., James G. March, and Johan P. Olsen. 1972. "A Garbage Can Model of Organizational Choice." *Administrative Science Quarterly* 17:1–25.

Colares, Juscelino F. 2008. "Alternative Methods of Appellate Review in Trade Remedy Cases: Examining Results of U.S. Judicial and NAFTA Binational Review of U.S. Agency Decisions from 1989 to 2005." *Journal of Empirical Legal Studies* 5:171–96.

Coleman, Chrisena. 2006. "Crime's Shot Down." *New York Daily News,* May 7, 45.

Columbus Dispatch. 2009. "DUI-Only Courts Seem to Reduce Repeat Offenders." June 7, B3.

Committee on Federal Courts, Association of the Bar of the City of New York. 2005. "The Surge in Immigration Appeals and Its Impact on the Second Circuit Court of Appeals." *The Record of the Association of the Bar of the City of New York* 60:243–57.

Committee on Immigration and Nationality Law and Committee on Communications and Media Law. 2004. "Dangerous Doctrine: The Attorney General's Unfounded Claim of Unlimited Authority to Arrest and Deport Aliens in Secret." *The Record of the Association of the Bar of the City of New York* 59:5–38.

Commission on Revision of the Federal Court Appellate System. 1975. *Structure and Internal Procedures: Recommendations for Change.* Washington, DC: Commission on Revision of the Federal Court Appellate System.

A Compilation of the Messages and Papers of the Presidents. 1917. New York: Bureau of National Literature.

Congressional Quarterly Almanac. 1978a. "Congress Approves New Bankruptcy System." 34:179–82.

———. 1978b. "Controls Tightened on Use of Wiretaps." 34:186–93.

Cook, Beverly Blair. 1993. "Moral Authority and Gender Difference: Georgia Bullock and the Los Angeles Women's Court." *Judicature* 77:144–55.

Coolley, Ronald B. 1989. "What the Federal Circuit Has Done and How Often: Statistical

Study of the CAFC Patent Decisions—1982 to 1988." *Journal of the Patent and Trademark Office Society* 71:385–93.

Cooper, Caroline S. 2007. "Drug Courts." In *Future Trends in State Courts 2007*, ed. Carol R. Flango, Chuck Campbell, and Neal Kauder, 50–53. Williamsburg: National Center for State Courts.

Cooper, Claire. 2003. "Homeless Court Offers Gentle Justice." *Sacramento Bee*, February 15, A1.

Cooper, Joseph. 1970. "The Origins of the Standing Committees and the Development of the Modern House." *Rice University Studies* 56 (Summer):1–167.

Cords, Danshera. 2005. "Collection Due Process: The Scope and Nature of Judicial Review." *University of Cincinnati Law Review* 73:1021–57.

Corkery, Michael. 2009. "A Florida Court's 'Rocket Docket' Blasts Through Foreclosure Cases." *Wall Street Journal*, February 18, A1.

Council of State Governments Justice Center. 2008. *Mental Health Courts: A Primer for Policymakers and Practitioners*.

Cowen, Wilson, Philip Nichols, and Marion T. Bennett. 1978. *The United States Court of Claims: A History, Part II*. Washington, DC: Committee on the Bicentennial of Independence and the Constitution of the Judicial Conference of the U.S.

Coyle, Marcia. 1997. "Fight Over Plan to Widen Claims Court Jurisdiction." *National Law Journal*, September 29, A10.

———. 2008a. "Federal Circuit a 'Hostile' Forum? *National Law Journal*, January 14, 1, 7.

———. 2008b. "Uneasy Over Eggs." *National Law Journal*, December 15, 1, 17.

———. 2009. "Damages a Hurdle to Patent Reform." *National Law Journal*, March 23, 1, 18.

Cragin, Charles L. 1994. "The Impact of Judicial Review on the Department of Veterans Affairs' Claims Adjudication Process: The Changing Role of the Board of Veterans' Appeals." *Maine Law Review* 46:23–41.

Craig, David W. 1995. "The Court for Appeals—and Trials—of Public Issues: The First 25 Years of Pennsylvania's Commonwealth Court." *Widener Journal of Public Law* 4:321–72.

Crawford, James, and Brian Opeskin. 2004. *Australian Courts of Law*. South Melbourne, Australia: Oxford University Press.

Currie, David P. 2005. *The Constitution in Congress: Democrats and Whigs 1829–1861*. Chicago: University of Chicago Press.

Currie, David P., and Frank I. Goodman. 1975. "Judicial Review of Federal Administrative Action: Quest for the Optimum Forum." *Columbia Law Review* 75:1–88.

Curry, Brett W. 2005. "The Courts, Congress, and the Politics of Federal Jurisdiction." PhD diss., Ohio State University.

Cushman, Robert E. 1941. *The Independent Regulatory Commissions*. New York: Oxford University Press.

Cyr, Conrad K. 1978. "Structuring a New Bankruptcy Court: A Comparative Analysis." *American Bankruptcy Law Journal* 52:141–85.

Dal Bó, Ernesto. 2006. "Regulatory Capture: A Review." *Oxford Review of Economic Policy* 22:203–25.

Daly, Christopher B. 1995. "Justice Draws a Powerful Weapon." *Washington Post*, February 24, A3.

Damle, Sarang Vijay. 2005. "Specialize the Judge, Not the Court: A Lesson from the German Constitutional Court." *Virginia Law Review* 91:1267–311.

Daneman, Matthew. 2008. "N.Y. Court Gives Veterans Chance to Straighten Out." *USA Today*, June 2, 3A.

Daniels, Stephen, and Joanne Martin. 1995. *Civil Juries and the Politics of Reform*. Evanston: Northwestern University Press.

———. 2004. "The Strange Success of Tort Reform." *Emory Law Journal* 53:1225–62.

Daughen, Joseph P. 1995. "Public Enemy No. 1 to Death Penalty Foes." *Philadelphia Daily News*, July 14, 3.

Davenport, Christian. 1999. "Nuisance Crimes May Get Own Court." *Austin American-Statesman*, July 27, B1.

Davidson, Ann S. 1973. "Litigation in the Small Tax Case Division of the United States Tax Court—The Taxpayer's Dream?" *George Washington Law Review* 41:538–59.

Davis, James F., and Frederick S. Frei. 1982. "The New Court of Appeals for the Federal Circuit: Its Patent Law Legacy From the Court of Claims." *APLA Quarterly Journal* 10:243–69.

Davis, Morris. 2009. "Justice and Guantánamo Bay." *Wall Street Journal*, November 11, A21.

Davis, Wendy N. 2003. "Special Problems for Specialty Courts." *American Bar Association Journal* 89 (February): 32–37.

Day, L. B. 1928. "The Development of the Family Court." *Annals of the American Academy of Political and Social Science* 136:105–11.

de la Merced, Michael J. 2009. "Judges Approves U.S. Financing for G.M." *New York Times*, June 26, B3.

Delaney, Kevin J. 1992. *Strategic Bankruptcy: How Corporations and Creditors Use Chapter 11 to Their Advantage*. Berkeley and Los Angeles: University of California Press.

Denbeaux, Mark, et al. 2006. *No-Hearing Hearings. CSRT: The Modern Habeas Corpus?* Seton Hall University School of Law. http://law.shu.edu/news/final_no_hearing_hearings_report.pdf.

Derthick, Martha. 1979. *Policymaking for Social Security*. Washington, DC: Brookings Institution.

Desmond, Robert. 1993. "Nothing Seems 'Obvious' to the Court of Appeals for the Federal Circuit: The Federal Circuit, Unchecked by the Supreme Court, Transforms the Standard of Obviousness Under the Patent Law." *Loyola of Los Angeles Law Review* 26:455–90.

DeVries, Douglas K. 1994. "Establishing Business Courts Would Create a Special Class of Litigants and Deny Access to Others." *California Bar Journal*, July, 12.

Dickerson, A. Mechele. 2006. "Words That Wound: Defining, Discussing, and Defeating Bankrupty 'Corruption.'" *Buffalo Law Review* 54:365–400.

Dickerson, Mark A. 1999. "The Georgia Office of State Administrative Hearings." *Journal of the National Association of Administrative Law Judges* 19 (Fall): 121–24.

Di Lello, Edward V. 1993. "Fighting Fire with Firefighters: A Proposal for Expert Judges at the Trial Level." *Columbia Law Review* 93:473–507.

Distaso, John. 2001. "Deporting Terror Suspects: Smith Bill to Allow Secret Evidence Still Has Chance." *Manchester Union Leader*, November 9, A2.

Dix, George E. 1964. "The Death of the Commerce Court: A Study in Institutional Weakness." *American Journal of Legal History* 8:238–60.

Dobbs, Michael. 2004. *Saboteurs: The Nazi Raid on America*. New York: Knopf.

Dolan, Paul. n.d. "The Supreme Court of Delaware 1900–1950." http://courts.delaware.gov/Courts/Supreme%20Court/?history.htm.

Donovan, Karen. 1994. "Shareholders' Advocates Protest Justice's Removal." *National Law Journal*, June 6, B1, B2.

Dorf, Michael C., and Jeffrey A. Fagan. 2003. "Problem-Solving Courts: From Innovation to Institutionalization." *American Criminal Law Review* 40:1501–11.

Douglass, Paul F. 1933. *The Mayors' Courts of Hamilton County, Ohio*. Baltimore: Johns Hopkins Press.

Downs, Anthony. 1967. *Inside Bureaucracy*. Boston: Little, Brown.

Drahozal, Christopher R. 2009. "Business Courts and the Future of Arbitration." *Cardozo Journal of Conflict Resolution* 10:491–507.

Dreyfuss, Rochelle C. 1995. "Forums of the Future: The Role of Specialized Courts in Resolving Business Disputes." *Brooklyn Law Review* 61:1–44.

Dreyfuss, Rochelle Cooper. 1990. "Specialized Adjudication." *Brigham Young University Law Review* 1990:377–441.

Drug Court Clearinghouse, Bureau of Justice Assistance. 2007. *Drug Court Activity Update: April 12, 2007*. Washington, DC: American University.

Dubroff, Harold. 1979. *The United States Tax Court: An Historical Analysis*. Chicago: Commerce Clearing House.

Dunner, Donald R. 1972. "Court Review of Patent Office Decisions—Comparative Analysis of CCPA and District Court Actions." In *1972 Patent Law Annual*, ed. Virginia Shook Cameron, 109–50. New York: Matthew Bender.

Dunner, Donald R., J. Michael Jakes, and Jeffrey D. Karceski. 1995. "A Statistical Look at the Federal Circuit's Patent Decisions: 1982–1994." *Federal Circuit Bar Journal* 5:151–80.

Durkheim, Emile. 1893/1933. *The Division of Labor in Society*. Glencoe: Free Press.

Durkin, Mary, Fred Cheesman, Scott Maggard, David Rottman, Tracy Sohoni, and Dawn Rubio. 2009. *Process Evaluation of the Philadelphia Community Court*. Williamsburg: National Center for State Courts.

Dwyer, Jim. 2008. "A Sister and Social Worker, and the Last of Her Kind." *New York Times*, August 27, B1.

Easterbrook, Frank H., and Daniel R. Fischel. 1991. *The Economic Structure of Corporate Law*. Cambridge: Harvard University Press.

Eckholm, Erik. 2008. "Innovative Courts Give Some Addicts Chance to Straighten Out." *New York Times*, October 15, A1, A18.

Eckley, Timothy S. 2008. "Veterans Court in Session in Buffalo." *Judicature* 92:43–44.

Economos, James P., and David C. Steelman. 1983. *Traffic Court Procedure and Administration*, 2nd ed. Chicago: American Bar Association.

Edwards, Randall. 1991a. "Health, Safety Officials Eager for Gavel to Fall." *Columbus Dispatch*, October 21, F1.

———. 1991b. "Here Comes the Environmental Judge." *Columbus Dispatch*, October 21, F1.

Eggen, Dan. 2007. "NSA Spying Part of Broader Effort." *Washington Post*, August 1, A1, A4.

Eisenberg, Melvin Aron. 1989. "The Structure of Corporation Law." *Columbia Law Review* 89:1461–525.

Eisenberg, Theodore, and Lynn M. LoPucki. 1999. "Shopping for Judges: An Empirical Analysis of Venue Choice in Large Chapter 11 Reorganizations." *Cornell Law Review* 84:967–1003.

Eisenstein, James, and Herbert Jacob. 1977. *Felony Justice: An Organizational Analysis of Criminal Courts*. Boston: Little, Brown.

Eisler, Peter. 2010. "Whistle-Blowers' Rights Get Second Look." *USA Today*, March 15, 6A.

Eligon, John. 2008. "New York Court Offers Home Foreclosure Help." *New York Times*, June 19, A25.

Elkins, James R. 1978. "The Temporary Emergency Court of Appeals: A Study in the Abdication of Judicial Responsibility." *Duke Law Journal* 1978:113–53.

Ely, James W., Jr. 1996. "Property Rights and the Supreme Court in World War II." *Journal of Supreme Court History* 1:19–34.

Fagan, Jeffrey, and Victoria Malkin. 2003. "Theorizing Community Justice Through Community Courts." *Fordham Urban Law Journal* 30:897–953.

Fallon, Richard H., Jr. 1988. "Of Legislative Courts, Administrative Agencies, and Article III." *Harvard Law Review* 101:915–92.

Federal Trade Commission. 2003. *To Promote Innovation: The Proper Balance of Competition and Patent Law and Policy.* http://www.ftc.gov/os/2003/10/innovationrpt.pdf.

Federico, P. J. 1940. "Evolution of Patent Office Appeals." *Journal of the Patent Office Society* 22:838–64, 920–49.

Fein, Bruce. 2007. "Get Strong, Congress." *Slate Magazine*, July 18. http://www.slate.com/toolbar.aspx?action=print&id=2170479.

Feld, Barry C. 1991. "Justice by Geography: Urban, Suburban, and Rural Variations in Juvenile Justice Administration." *Journal of Criminal Law and Criminology* 82:156–210.

———. 1999. *Bad Kids: Race and the Transformation of the Juvenile Court.* New York: Oxford University Press.

Ferenchik, Mark, and Suzanne Hoholik. 2003. "Noise Ordinance Ruled Unconstitutional." *Columbus Dispatch*, January 3, C1–2.

Fidell, Eugene R. 1997. "Going on Fifty: Evolution and Devolution in Military Justice." *Wake Forest Law Review* 32:1213–31.

Finn, Peter, and Andrea K. Newlyn. 1993. *Miami's "Drug Court": A Different Approach.* Washington, DC: National Institute of Justice, U.S. Department of Justice.

Finnemore, Martha. 1996. "Norms, Culture, and World Politics: Insight from Sociology's Institutionalism." *International Organization* 50:325–47.

Finnemore, Martha, and Kathryn Sikkink. 1998. "International Norm Dynamics and Political Change." *International Organization* 52:887–917.

Fisher, Louis. 2003. *Nazi Saboteurs on Trial: A Military Tribunal and American Law.* Lawrence: University Press of Kansas.

———. 2005. *Military Tribunals and Presidential Power: American Revolution to the War on Terrorism.* Lawrence: University Press of Kansas.

Fisher, Margaret. 2002. *Youth Courts: Young People Delivering Justice.* Chicago: American Bar Association.

Flango, Victor E. 2005. "DWI Courts: The Newest Problem-Solving Courts." *Court Review* 42:22–24.

Flango, Victor E., and Carol R. Flango. 2006. "What's Happening with DWI Courts?" In *Future Trends in State Courts 2006.* http://www.ncsconline.org/WC/Publications/Trends/2006/DWICourtsTrends2006.pdf.

Flemming, Roy B. 1998. "Contested Terrains and Regime Politics: Thinking About America's Trial Courts and Institutional Change." *Law & Social Inquiry* 23:941–65.

Flexner, Bernard, Reuben Oppenheimer, and Katharine F. Lenroot. 1929. *The Child, the Family, and the Court: A Study of the Administration of Justice in the Field of Domestic Relations.* Washington, DC: U.S. Government Printing Office.

Foley, Edward B. 2008. "Let's Not Repeat 2000." *Legal Times*, April 21, 62–63.

Fortado, Lindsay. 2004. "States Weigh Med-Mal Courts." *National Law Journal*, December 13.

Fox, Aubrey, and Robert V. Wolf. 2004. *The Future of Drug Courts.* New York: Center for Court Innovation.

Fox, Sanford J. 1970. "Juvenile Justice Reform: An Historical Perspective." *Stanford Law Review* 22:1187–239.

Francis, Wayne L., and James W. Riddlesperger. 1982. "U.S. State Legislative Committees: Structure, Procedural Efficiency, and Party Control." *Legislative Studies Quarterly* 7:453–71.

Franck, Thomas M. 1992. *Political Questions/Judicial Answers: Does the Rule of Law Apply to Foreign Affairs?* Princeton: Princeton University Press.

Frankfurter, Felix, and James M. Landis. 1928. *The Business of the Supreme Court: A Study in the Federal Judicial System.* New York: Macmillan.

French, Robert. 2000. "Federal Courts Created by Parliament." In *The Australian Federal Judicial System*, ed. Brian Opeskin and Fiona Wheeler, 123–59. Melbourne, Australia: Melbourne University Press.

Fried, Joseph P. 1988. "Queens Gets Court to Speed Drug Cases." *New York Times*, March 28, B1, B4.

Friedman, Elaine R. 1996. "New Business Courts Gain Acceptance." *National Law Journal*, December 30, B1, B2.

Friedman, Lawrence M. 2005. *A History of American Law*, 3rd ed. New York: Touchstone.

Friendly, Henry J. 1973. *Federal Jurisdiction: A General View.* New York: Columbia University Press.

Fritzler, Randal B., and Leonore M.J. Simon. 2000. "The Development of a Specialized Domestic Violence Court in Vancouver, Washington Utilizing Innovative Judicial Paradigms." *UKMC Law Review* 69:139–77.

Fujitani, Jay M. 1984. "Controlling the Market Power of Performing Rights Societies: An Administrative Substitute for Antitrust Regulation." *California Law Review* 72:103–37.

Fuller, Jack. 1974. "Gun Court: 72 Charged, 1 Goes to Jail." *Chicago Tribune*, November 19, 3.

Galanter, Marc. 1974. "Why the 'Haves' Come Out Ahead: Speculations on the Limits of Legal Change." *Law & Society Review* 9:95–160.

Gambini, Steve. 1995. "Dealing with Those Dirty Little Jobs." *The Booster* (Columbus), September 13, 25.

Gamboa, Suzanne. 2001. "5-Year-Old Terrorist Court Still Waiting for First Case." *Associated Press State & Local Wire*, October 10.

Gamm, Gerald, and Kenneth Shepsle. 1989. "Emergence of Legislative Institutions: Standing Committees in the House and Senate, 1810–1825." *Legislative Studies Quarterly* 14:39–66.

Gannet, Herbert M. 1964. "Choice of Forum: A Checklist of Points to Consider." In *Proceedings of the New York University Twenty-second Annual Institute on Federal Taxation*, ed. Henry Sellin, 75–93. Albany: Matthew Bender.

Garcia, Patricia A. 2003. *Problem Solving Courts.* Chicago: American Bar Association.

Garrett, Geoffrey, and Peter Lange. 1995. "Internationalization, Institutions, and Political Change." *International Organization* 49:627–55.

Geary, David. 2005. "Folk Knowledge and Academic Learning." In *Origins of the Social Mind: Evolutionary Psychology and Child Development*, ed. Bruce J. Ellis and David F. Bjorkland, 493–519. New York: Guilford Press.

Geier, Deborah A. 1991. "The Tax Court, Article III, and the Proposal Advanced by the Federal Courts Study Committee: A Study in Applied Constitutional Theory." *Cornell Law Review* 76:985–1035.

Gellman, Barton. 2008. *Angler: The Cheney Vice Presidency.* New York: Penguin Press.

Gemmill, William N. 1914. "Chicago Court of Domestic Relations." *Annals of the American Academy of Political and Social Science* 52:115–23.

General Accounting Office, U.S. 2000. *Bid Protests: Characteristics of Cases Filed in Federal Courts*, Report GAO/GGD/OGC-00-72.

Georgakopoulos, Nicholas L. 2000. "Discretion in the Career and Recognition Judiciary." *University of Chicago Law School Roundtable* 7:205–25.

Getis, Victoria. 2000. *The Juvenile Court and the Progressives*. Urbana: University of Illinois Press.

Geyh, Charles Gardner. 2006. *When Courts and Congress Collide: The Struggle for Control of America's Judicial System*. Ann Arbor: University of Michigan Press.

Gibson, Howard. 1990. "State Has Designs on Delaware." *National Law Journal*, October 29, 3, 36.

Gillman, Howard. 2006. "Party Politics and Constitutional Change: The Political Origins of Liberal Judicial Activism." In *The Supreme Court and American Political Development*, ed. Ronald Kahn and Ken I. Kersch, 138–68. Lawrence: University Press of Kansas.

Gitter, Donna M. 2009. "Should the United States Designate Specialist Patent Trial Judges? An Empirical Analysis of H.R. 34 in Light of the English Experience and the Work of Professor Moore." *Columbia Science and Technology Law Review* 10:169–99.

Glaberson, William. 2007a. "Military Judges Dismiss Charges for 2 Detainees." *New York Times*, June 5, A1, A21.

———. 2007b. "Court Advances War Crime Trials." *New York Times*, September 25, A1, A26.

———. 2008. "Detainee Convicted on Terrorism Charges." *New York Times*, November 4, A19.

Glater, Jonathan D. 2009. "Judge in Case is Known for His Brisk Approach." *New York Times*, June 2, B7.

Glazier, David. 2005. "Precedents Lost: The Neglected History of the Military Commission." *Virginia Journal of International Law* 46:5–81.

Glendon, Mary Ann, Michael Wallace Gordon, and Paolo G. Carozza. 1999. *Comparative Legal Traditions in a Nutshell*, 2nd edition. St. Paul: West Group.

Glennon, Michael J. 1990. *Constitutional Diplomacy*. Princeton: Princeton University Press.

Glick, Henry R., and Scott P. Hays. 1991. "Innovation and Reinvention in State Policy-making: Theory and the Evolution of Living Will Laws." *Journal of Politics* 53:835–50.

Goerdt, John A. 1992. *Small Claims and Traffic Courts: Case Management Procedures, Case Characteristics, and Outcomes in 12 Urban Jurisdictions*. Williamsburg: National Center for State Courts.

Goldberg, Deborah, Sarah Samis, Edwin Bender, and Rachel Weiss. 2005. *The New Politics of Judicial Elections 2004*. Washington, DC: Justice at Stake Campaign.

Golden, Tim. 2004a. "After Terror, a Secret Rewriting of Military Law." *New York Times*, October 24, 1, 12, 13.

———. 2004b. "Administration Officials Split Over Stalled Military Tribunals." *New York Times*, October 25, A1, A8, A9.

———. 2006. "For Guantánamo Review Boards, Limits Abound." *New York Times*, December 31, 1, 20.

Goldkamp, John S. 2003. "The Impact of Drug Courts." *Criminology and Public Policy* 2:197–206.

Goldkamp, John S., and Cheryl Irons-Guynn. 2000. *Emerging Judicial Strategies for the Mentally Ill in the Criminal Caseload: Mental Health Courts in Fort Lauderdale, Seattle, San Bernardino, and Anchorage*. Washington, DC: Bureau of Justice Assistance, U.S. Department of Justice.

Goldman, T. R. 2006. "Pushing Back on Military Justice." *Legal Times*, July 17, 1, 10.

Goldsmith, Jack. 2007. *The Terror Presidency: Law and Judgment Inside the Bush Administration*. New York: W. W. Norton.

Goldsmith, Jack L., and Neal Katyal. 2007. "The Terrorists' Court." *New York Times*, July 11, A23.

Goldstein, Judith. 1993. *Ideas, Interests, and American Trade Policy*. Ithaca: Cornell University Press.

Gonzales, Alberto R. 2001. "Martial Justice, Full and Fair." *New York Times*, November 30, A25.

Goodin, Robert E. 1996. "Institutions and Their Design." In *The Theory of Institutional Design*, ed. Robert E. Goodin, 1–53. New York: Cambridge University Press.

Gordon, Meryl. 1994. "Street Justice." *New York Magazine*, December 5, 46–57.

Gormley, Ken. 2010. *The Death of American Virtue: Clinton v. Starr*. New York: Crown Publishers.

Gormley, William T., Jr., and Steven J. Balla. 2004. *Bureaucracy and Democracy: Accountability and Performance*. Washington, DC: CQ Press.

Graham, Erin, Charles R. Shipan, and Craig Volden. 2008. "The Diffusion of Policy Diffusion Research." Paper presented at the annual meeting of the American Political Science Association, Boston.

Greenhouse, Linda. 1978. "Lobbying by Burger Provokes Criticism." *New York Times*, November 19, 39.

———. 2003. "Opponents Lose Challenge to Government's Broader Use of Wiretaps to Fight Terrorism." *New York Times*, March 25, A12.

Griffin, Patricia A., Henry J. Steadman, and John Petrila. 2002. "The Use of Criminal Charges and Sanctions in Mental Health Courts." *Psychiatric Services* 53:1285–89.

Groner, Jonathan. 2001. "Bankruptcy Judge Sues to Keep Post." *Legal Times*, November 5, 6.

———. 2004. "Court's Mantra: Request Denied." *Legal Times*, January 19, 1, 8.

Gruson, Lindsey. 1986. "Tiny Delaware's Corporate Clout." *New York Times*, June 1, § 3, 6.

Guthrie, Chris, Jeffrey Rachlinski, and Andrew J. Wistrich. 2009. "The 'Hidden Judiciary': An Empirical Examination of Executive Branch Justice." *Duke Law Journal* 58:1477–530.

Hagel, Lawrence B., and Michael P. Horan. 1994. "Five Years Under the Veterans' Judicial Review Act: The VA is Brought Kicking and Screaming Into the World of Meaningful Due Process." *Maine Law Review* 46:43–66.

Haines, Charles Grove. 1933. "The General Structure of Court Organization." *Annals of the American Academy of Political and Social Science* 167:1–11.

Haley, Sarah M. 2004. "Single-Judge Adjudication in the Court of Appeals for Veterans Claims and the Devaluation of Stare Decisis." *Administrative Law Review* 56:535–74.

Hall, Michael. 2004. "And Justice for Some." *Texas Monthly*, November, 154–57, 259–63.

Hall, Peter A., and Rosemary C. R. Taylor. 1996. "Political Science and the Three New Institutionalisms." *Political Studies* 44:936–57.

Hamburger, Max J. 1974. "Choice of Forum for Litigation: The United States Tax Court." In *Proceedings of the New York University 32nd Annual Institute on Federal Taxation*, ed. S. Theodore Reiner, 1315–39. New York: Matthew Bender.

Hamilton, Robert W. 2000. *The Law of Corporations in a Nutshell*. St. Paul: West, 2000.

Hamm, Keith E., and Ronald D. Hedlund. 1994. "Committees in State Legislatures," in *Encyclopedia of the American Legislative System*, ed. Joel H. Silbey, vol. II, 669–99. New York: Charles Scribner's Sons.

Hand, Learned. 1947. "Thomas Walter Swan." *Yale Law Journal* 57:167–72.

Hansen, Wendy L., Renée J. Johnson, and Isaac Unah. 1995. "Specialized Courts, Bureaucratic Agencies, and the Politics of U.S. Trade Policy." *American Journal of Political Science* 39:529–57.

Harley, Herbert. 1917. "Business Management for the Courts." *Virginia Law Review* 5:1–26.

Harmon, Robert L. 2009. *Patents and the Federal Circuit*, 9th ed. Arlington: BNA Books.

Harper's Weekly. 1890. "The New Board of General Appraisers Appointed Under the Customs Administration Act." August 9, 625–26.

Harr, John E., ed. 1978. *The Great Railway Crisis: An Administrative History of the United States Railway Association*. Washington, DC: Nat'l Academy of Public Administration.

Harrington, Christine B. 1982. "Delegalization Reform Movements: A Historical Analysis." In *The Politics of Informal Justice*, vol. 1, ed. Richard L. Abel, 35–71. New York: Academic Press.

Harris, Shane. 2010. *The Watchers: The Rise of America's Surveillance State*. New York: Penguin Press.

Hartley, Roger E. 2003. "Review of *Reinventing Justice: The American Drug Court Movement*, by James L. Nolan, Jr." *Justice System Journal* 24:230–36.

Hartnett, Maurice A., III. 1992. "The History of the Delaware Court of Chancery." *The Business Lawyer* 48:367–72.

Hausegger, Lori, Matthew Hennigar, and Troy Riddell. 2009. *Canadian Courts: Law, Politics, and Process*. Don Mills, Ontario: Oxford University Press.

Hawes, Joseph M. 1971. *Children in Urban Society: Juvenile Delinquency in Nineteenth-Century America*. New York: Oxford University Press.

Hay, Colin. 2006. "Constructivist Institutionalism." In *The Oxford Handbook of Political Institutions*, ed. R. A. W. Rhodes, Sarah A. Binder, and Bert A Rockman, 56–74. New York: Oxford University Press.

Heinz, John P., Robert L. Nelson, Rebecca L. Sandefur, and Edward O. Laumann. 2005. *Urban Lawyers: The New Social Structure of the Bar*. Chicago: University of Chicago Press.

Helfer, Lawrence R. 1992. "The Politics of Judicial Structure: Creating the United States Court of Veterans Appeals." *Connecticut Law Review* 25:155–71.

Hellman, Arthur D. 1990. "Deciding Who Decides: Understanding the Realities of Judicial Reform." *Law and Social Inquiry* 15:343–61.

Henderson, Thomas A., Jr., et al. 1984. *The Significance of Judicial Structure: The Effect of Unification on Trial Court Operations*. Washington, DC: National Institute of Justice, U.S. Department of Justice.

Hendrickson, Scott. 2003. "Institutional Structure and its Effect on Judicial Decision Making: The Case of the Court of International Trade." Paper presented at the annual meeting of the Midwest Political Science Association, Chicago.

———. 2006. "Examining Judicial Independence: Article I v. Article III Courts." PhD diss., Washington University.

Henriques, Diana B. 1995. "Top Business Court Under Fire." *New York Times*, May 23, C1, C6.

Henry, Matthew D., and John L. Turner. 2006. "The Court of Appeals for the Federal Circuit's Impact on Patent Litigation." *Journal of Legal Studies* 35:85–115.

Hentoff, Nat. 2004. "Tribunals Are Defying a U.S. Supreme Court Decision that These Prisoners Must Get Due Process—Basic Fairness." *Chicago Sun-Times*, December 5, 38.

Hershey, Robert D., Jr. 1985. "Court Bids Exxon Pay $1.9 Billion." *New York Times*, July 2, 31, 34.

Heumann, Milton. 1978. *Plea Bargaining: The Experiences of Prosecutors, Judges, and Defense Attorneys*. Chicago: University of Chicago Press.

Higginbotham, Patrick E. 1980. "Bureaucracy—The Carcinoma of the Federal Judiciary." *Alabama Law Review* 31:261–72.

Hilton, George W. 1975. *The Northeast Railroad Problem*. Washington, DC: American Enterprise Institute.

Hinckley, Frank E. 1906. *American Consular Jurisdiction in the Orient*. Washington, DC: W. H. Lowdermilk.

Hines, Cragg. 2004. "Supremes to Texas Appeals Court: You Still Don't Get It." *Houston Chronicle*, November 21, 3.

Hoffman, Charles W. 1919–20. "Social Aspects of the Family Court." *Journal of the American Institute of Criminal Law and Criminology* 10:409–22.

Hoffman, Morris B. 2000. "The Drug Court Scandal." *North Carolina Law Review* 78: 1437–534.

———. 2002. "The Denver Drug Court and Its Unintended Consequences." In *Drug Courts in Theory and in Practice*, ed. James L. Nolan, Jr., 67–87. New York: Walter deGruyter.

Holcomb, Alfred E., ed. 1925. *Proceedings of the Seventeenth Annual Conference on Taxation*. New York: National Tax Association.

Hora, Peggy Fulton. 2009. "Through a Glass Gavel: Predicting the Future of Drug Treatment Courts." In *Future Trends in State Courts 2009*, ed. Carol R. Flango, Amy M. McDowell, Charles F. Campbell, and Neal B. Kauder, 134–39. Williamsburg: National Center for State Courts.

Horowitz, Donald L. 1977. *The Courts and Social Policy*. Washington: Brookings Institution.

Horsey, Henry R., and William Duffy. N.d. "The Supreme Court of Delaware Until 1951: The 'Leftover Judge' System." http://courts.delaware.gov/Courts/Supreme%20Court/?history.htm.

Howard, J. Woodford, Jr. 1981. *Courts of Appeals in the Federal Judicial System: A Study of the Second, Fifth, and District of Columbia Circuits*. Princeton: Princeton University Press.

Howard, Philip K. 2009. "Just Medicine." *New York Times*, April 2, A27.

Howard, Robert M. 2004. "Specialized Federal Courts Versus General Courts: Ideology and Expertise in Tax Decisions." Paper presented at the annual conference of the American Political Science Association, Chicago.

———. 2005. "Comparing the Decision Making of Specialized Courts and General Courts: An Exploration of Tax Decisions." *Justice System Journal* 26:135–48.

———. 2007. "Controlling Forum Choice and Controlling Policy: Congress, Courts and the IRS." *Policy Studies Journal* 35:109–23.

———. 2009. *Getting a Poor Return: Justice and Taxes*. Albany: State University of New York Press.

Howard, Robert M., and David C. Nixon. 2003. "Local Control of the Bureaucracy: Federal Appeals Courts, Ideology, and the Internal Revenue Service." *Washington University Journal of Law and Policy* 13:233–56.

Huddleston, C. West, III, Douglas B. Marlowe, and Rachel Casebolt. 2008. *Painting the Current Picture: A National Report Card on Drug Courts and Other Problem-Solving Court Programs in the United States*. Alexandria: National Drug Court Institute.

Hurst, James Willard. 1950. *The Growth of American Law: The Law Makers*. Boston: Little, Brown.

Hurst, Willard. 1953. "Changing Popular Views About Law and Lawyers." *Annals of the American Academy of Political and Social Science* 287:1–7.

Hutchinson, Dennis J., and David J. Garrow, eds., 2002. *The Forgotten Memoir of John Knox: A Year in the Life of a Supreme Court Clerk in FDR's Washington*. Chicago: University of Chicago Press.

Hutto, Daniel D. 2008. *Folk Psychological Narratives: The Sociocultural Basis of Understanding Reasons*. Cambridge: MIT Press.

Hyman, Jacob D., and Nathaniel L. Nathanson. 1947. "Judicial Review of Price Control: The Battle of the Meat Regulations." *Illinois Law Review* 42:584–634.

Hynes, Charles J. 2005. "Brooklyn's Specialized Gun Court." *Brooklyn Daily Eagle*, July 5.

Igo, Stephen. 2006. "Trash the Topic During First Environmental Court in Wise." *Kingsport Times-News*, October 29, A3.

Igra, Anna R. 2007. *Wives Without Husbands: Marriage, Desertion, and Welfare in New York, 1900–1935*. Chapel Hill: University of North Carolina Press.

Ikenberry, G. John. 1988. "Conclusion: An Institutional Approach to American Foreign Economic Policy." *International Organization* 42:219–43.

———. 1998–99. "Institutions, Strategic Restraint, and the Persistence of American Postwar Order." *International Security* 23:43–78.

Inciardi, James A., Duane C. McBride, and James E. Rivers. 1996. *Drug Control and the Courts*. Thousand Oaks: Sage Publications.

Internal Revenue Service, U.S. 2009. *Data Book, 2008*. http://www.irs.gov/pub/irs-soi/08databk.pdf.

Isikoff, Michael, and William Booth. 1993. "Miami 'Drug Court' Demonstrates Reno's Unorthodox Approach." *Washington Post*, February 20, A1, A8.

Jacob, Herbert. 1997. "The Governance of Trial Judges." *Law & Society Review* 31:3–30.

Jacoby, Melissa B. 2006. "Fast, Cheap, and Creditor-Controlled: Is Corporate Reorganization Failing?" *Buffalo Law Review* 54:401–38.

Jaffe, Adam B., and Josh Lerner. 2004. *Innovation and Its Discontents: How Our Broken Patent System is Endangering Innovation and Progress, and What to Do About It*. Princeton: Princeton University Press.

Jameson, J. Franklin. 1894. "The Origin of the Standing-Committee System in American Legislative Bodies." *Political Science Quarterly* 9:246–67.

Janicke, Paul M. 2001. "To Be or Not to Be: The Long Gestation of the U.S. Court of Appeals for the Federal Circuit (1887–1982)." *Antitrust Law Journal* 69:645–67.

Jester, David A. 1979. "The Indianapolis Environmental Court." *Urban Law Annual* 17: 209–14.

Johnson, Avery. 2009. "Vaccine Makers Enjoy Immunity." *Wall Street Journal*, February 24, 6.

Johnson, Carrie, and Amy Goldstein. 2009. "Choice of Drug Czar Indicates Focus on Treatment, Not Jail." *Washington Post*, March 12, A4.

Johnson, Fred R. 1930. *Domestic Relations Division of the Municipal Court of Philadelphia*. Philadelphia: Thomas Skelton Harrison Foundation.

Johnston, David, and William Rashbaum. 2008. "New York Police Fight with U.S. on Surveillance." *New York Times*, November 20, A1, A26.

Johnston, James H. 2001. "Swift and Terrible: A Military Tribunal Rushed to Convict After Lincoln's Murder." *Washington Post*, December 9, F1.

Jordan, Ellen R. 1981. "Specialized Courts: A Choice?" *Northwestern University Law Review* 76:745–85.

Journal of the American Judicature Society. 1918. "Success of Organized Courts." 1 (February): 133–51.

Judicature. 2006. "A Conversation About Judicial Independence and Impartiality." 89:339–43.

Junge, Ember Reichgott. 1998. "Business Courts: Efficient Justice or Two-Tiered Elitism?" *William Mitchell Law Review* 24:315–21.

Karr, Paul. 1997. "New Environmental Courts Single Out Polluters, Developers for Swifter Compliance." *Alaska Bar Rag* 21 (July–August): 19.

Kaufman, Herbert. 1960. *The Forest Ranger: A Study in Administrative Behavior*. Baltimore: Johns Hopkins Press.

————. 1976. *Are Government Organizations Immortal?* Washington, DC: Brookings Institution.

Kaye, Judith S. 2004. Delivering Justice Today: A Problem-Solving Approach." *Yale Law & Policy Review* 22:125–51.

Kaye, Judith S., and Susan K. Knipps. 2000. "Judicial Responses to Domestic Violence: The Case for a Problem-Solving Approach." *Western State University Law Review* 27:1–13.

Keaton, Diane. 1991. "Death Penalty Experts." *California Lawyer*, April, 28.

Keep America Beautiful. 2006. "A Brief History of Environmental Courts." http://www.kabtoolbox.org/toolbox.asp?id=189&rid=190.

Keilitz, Susan. 2000. *Specialization of Domestic Violence Case Management in the Courts: A National Survey.* Williamsburg: National Center for State Courts.

Kendall, Douglas T., and Charles P. Lord. 1998. "The Takings Project: A Critical Analysis and Assessment of the Project So Far." *Boston College Environmental Affairs Law Review* 25:509–87.

Keohane, Robert O. 1988. "International Institutions: Two Approaches." *International Studies Quarterly* 32:379–96.

————. 1997. "International Relations and International Law: Two Optics." *Harvard International Law Journal* 38:487–502.

Kerry, Nancy, and Susan Pennell. 2001. *San Diego Homeless Court Program: A Process and Impact Evaluation.* San Diego: San Diego Association of Governments.

King, Chad M., and Ellen Lazarus. 2003. "Decision Making on the United States Tax Court." Paper presented at annual meeting of the Midwest Political Science Association, Chicago.

King, Kimi Lynn, and James Meernik. 1999. "The Supreme Court and the Powers of the Executive: The Adjudication of Foreign Policy." *Political Research Quarterly* 52:801–24.

King, Lawrence P. 1983. "The Unmaking of a Bankruptcy Court: Aftermath of *Northern Pipeline v. Marathon.*" *Washington and Lee Law Review* 40:99–120.

King, Ryan S., and Jill Pasquarella. 2009. *Drug Courts: A Review of the Evidence.* Washington, DC: The Sentencing Project.

Kingdon, John W. 1984. *Agendas, Alternatives, and Public Policies.* Boston: Little, Brown.

————. 2003. *Agendas, Alternatives, and Public Policies,* 2nd ed. New York: Longman.

Kittrell, Marvin F. 1996. "ALJs in South Carolina." *South Carolina Lawyer* 7 (May/June): 42–44.

Klaidman, Daniel. 2008. "Now We Know What the Battle was About." *Newsweek*, December 22, 46.

Koh, Harold Hongju. 1990. *The National Security Constitution: Sharing Power After the Iran-Contra Affair.* New Haven: Yale University Press.

Kohler, Jeremy. 2004. "Nuisance-Violation Court is Struck Down." *St. Louis Post-Dispatch,* September 25, 22.

Kolko, Gabriel. 1965. *Railroads and Regulation 1877–1916.* Princeton: Princeton University Press.

Komesar, Neil K. 1994. *Imperfect Alternatives: Choosing Institutions in Law, Economics, and Public Policy.* Chicago: University of Chicago Press.

Kondo, LeRoy L. 2002. "Untangling the Tangled Web: Federal Court Reform Through Specialization for Internet Law and Other High Technology Cases." *UCLA Journal of Law and Technology* 2002 (Spring): 1–106. http://www.lawtechjournal.com/articles/2002/01_020309_kondo.pdf.

Koremenos, Barbara, Charles Lipson, and Duncan Snidal. 2001. "The Rational Design of International Institutions." *International Organization* 55:761–99.

Kornblum, Stephanie. 2003. "Winning the Battle While Losing the War: Ramifications of the Foreign Intelligence Surveillance Court of Review's First Decision." *Seattle University Law Review* 27:623–57.

Kornhauser, Anne. 1991. "Today's Veterans Have More Rights, Advocates." *Legal Times,* February 18, 1991, 1, 20, 21.

Kramer, Kenneth B. 1990. "Judicial Review of the Theoretically Non-Reviewable: An Overview of Pre-COVA Court Action on Claims for Veteran Benefits." *Ohio Northern University Law Review* 17:99–120.

Krasner, Stephen D. 1976. "State Power and the Structure of International Trade." *World Politics* 28:317–47.

Krasno, Miriam R. 1984. "The Bankruptcy Courts—Caught in Limbo?" *Judicature* 67:307–9.

Krehbiel, Keith. 1991. *Information and Legislative Organization.* Ann Arbor: University of Michigan Press.

Kritzer, Herbert M. 1996. "The Data Puzzle: The Nature of Interpretation in Quantitative Research." *American Journal of Political Science* 40:1–32.

———, ed. 2002. *Legal Systems of the World: A Political, Social, and Cultural Encyclopedia.* Santa Barbara: ABC-CLIO.

———. 2003. "The Government Gorilla: Why Does Government Come Out Ahead in Appellate Courts?" In *In Litigation: Do the "Haves" Still Come Out Ahead?,* ed. Herbert M. Kritzer and Susan Silbey, 342–70. Stanford: Stanford University Press.

Kroll, Glenn. 1996. "Are Tax Court Judges Partial to the Government?" *Oil and Gas Tax Quarterly* 45:135–75.

Kross, Anna M., and Harold M. Grossman. 1937. "Magistrates' Courts of the City of New York: History and Organization." *Brooklyn Law Review* 7:133–79.

Kundu, Sudip. 2005. "Privately Funded Courts and the Homeless: A Critical Look at Community Courts." *Journal of Affordable Housing and Community Development Law* 14:170–94.

Kurkjian, Stephen. 1986. "The Sanctum Sanctorum of Bugs and Wiretaps." *Washington Post,* July 24, A21.

Kusmer, Toby H., and Eric M. Shelton. 2008. "Assailing Key Patents." *National Law Journal,* November 10, 27.

Labaton, Stephen. 1998. "The Debacle That Buried Washington." *New York Times,* November 22, C1, C12.

Landau, Michael, and Donald E. Biederman. 1999. "The Case for a Specialized Copyright Court: Eliminating the Jurisdictional Advantage." *Hastings Communications and Entertainment Law Journal* 21:717–84.

Landes, William M., and Richard A. Posner. 1975. "The Independent Judiciary in an Interest-Group Perspective." *Journal of Law and Economics* 18:875–901.

———. 2003. *The Economic Structure of Intellectual Property Law.* Cambridge: Harvard University Press.

Langer, Lilly M., George J. Warheit, and Stuart Alan. 2000. *Teen Tobacco Court Evaluation Study of Courts Held in Broward County, Florida.* Miami: Center for Youth Development, Florida International University.

Lanni, Adriaan. 2005. "The Future of Community Justice." *Harvard Civil Rights-Civil Liberties Law Review* 40:359–405.

Laro, David. 1995. "The Evolution of the Tax Court as an Independent Tribunal." *University of Illinois Law Review* 1995:17–29.

Larrabee, John. 1994. "'You're Going to Jail Fast' in Nation's First Gun Court." *USA Today,* December 19, 3A.

Lasry, Lex. 2007. *David Hicks v. the United States: Summary of the Report of the Independent Observer for the Law Council of Australia*. Canberra: Law Council of Australia.

Lawyers' Committee for Better Housing. 2003. *No Time for Justice: A Study of Chicago's Eviction Court*. Chicago: Lawyers' Committee for Better Housing.

LeDuff, Charlie. 2004. "Lifting Hurdles as the Homeless Rebound." *New York Times*, December 29, A15.

Lee, Tahirih V. 2004. "The United States Court for China: A Triumph of Local Law." *Buffalo Law Review* 52:923–1075.

Legal Times. 1997. "Intelligence on the FISA Court." April 14, 18–20.

Legomsky, Stephen H. 1986. "Forum Choices for the Review of Agency Adjudication: A Study of the Immigration Process." *Iowa Law Review* 71:1297–403.

———. 1990. *Specialized Justice: Courts, Administrative Tribunals, and a Cross-National Theory of Specialization*. Oxford: Clarendon Press.

———. 2006. "Deportation and the War on Independence." *Cornell Law Review* 91: 369–409.

———. 2007. "Learning to Live with Unequal Justice: Asylum and the Limits to Consistency." *Stanford Law Review* 60:413–74.

Lemert, Edwin M. 1967. "The Juvenile Court—Quest and Realities." In *Task Force Report: Juvenile Delinquency and Youth Crime*, by President's Commission on Law Enforcement and Administration of Justice, 91–106. Washington, DC: U.S. Government Printing Office.

Leonnig, Carol D., and Dafna Linzer. 2005a. "Spy Court Judge Quits in Protest." *Washington Post*, December 21, A1, A6.

———. 2005b. "Judges on Surveillance Court to be Briefed on Spy Program." *Washington Post*, December 22, A1, A12.

Lepawsky, Albert. 1932. *The Judicial System of Metropolitan Chicago*. Chicago: University of Chicago Press.

Lerner-Wren, Ginger. 2000. *Broward's Mental Health Court: An Innovative Approach to the Mentally Disabled in the Criminal Justice System*. Williamsburg: National Center for State Courts.

Levett, Benjamin Arthur. 1923. *Through the Customs Maze: A Popular Exposition and Analysis of the United States Customs Tariff Administrative Laws*. New York: Customs Maze Publishing Co.

Levin, Aaron. 2008. "Special Veterans' Court Focuses on MH Recovery." *Psychiatric News* 43 (September 19): 16.

Levin, Martin A. 1975. "Delay in Five Criminal Courts." *Journal of Legal Studies* 4:83–131.

Levin, Myron. 2004. "Taking It to Vaccine Court." *Los Angeles Times*, August 7, A1, A24.

Lewis, David E. 2002. "The Politics of Agency Termination: Confronting the Myth of Agency Immortality." *Journal of Politics* 64:89–107.

———. 2003. *Presidents and the Politics of Agency Design: Political Insulation in the United States Government Bureaucracy, 1946–1997*. Stanford: Stanford University Press.

Lewis, Neil A. 2005. "2 Prosecutors Faulted Trials for Detainees." *New York Times*, August 1, A1, A12.

Lewis, Neil A., and David E. Sanger. 2004. "Administration Changing Review at Guantánamo Bay." *New York Times*, July 1, A9.

Lichtblau, Eric. 2008. *Bush's Law: The Remaking of American Justice*. New York: Pantheon.

Lichtblau, Eric, and David Johnston. 2007. "Court to Oversee U.S. Wiretapping in Terror Cases." *New York Times*, January 18, A1, A16.

Light, Paul Charles. 1982. *The President's Agenda*. Baltimore: Johns Hopkins Press.

———. 1992. *Forging Legislation*. New York: W. W. Norton.

Lindesmith, Alfred P. 1965. *The Addict and the Law*. Bloomington: Indiana University Press.

Lipetz, Marcia J. 1984. *Routine Justice: Processing Cases in Women's Court*. New Brunswick: Transaction Books.

Lipsky, Michael. 1980. *Street-Level Bureaucracy: Dilemmas of the Individual in Public Services*. New York: Russell Sage Foundation.

Liptak, Adam. 2005. "Courts Criticize Judges' Handling of Asylum Cases." *New York Times*, December 26, A1, A26.

Lobingier, Charles Sumner. 1932. "A Quarter Century of Our Extraterritorial Court." *Georgetown Law Journal* 20:427–55.

Locy, Toni. 2004. "Tribunal Struggles with First Hearings." *USA Today*, August 30, 12A.

Lombardi, Joseph E. 1976. *The United States Customs Court: A History of Its Origin and Evolution*. New York: United States Customs Court.

LoPucki, Lynn M. 2005. *Courting Failure: How Competition for Big Cases is Corrupting the Bankruptcy Courts*. Ann Arbor: University of Michigan Press.

———. 2006. "Where Do You Get Off? A Reply to *Courting Failure*'s Critics." *Buffalo Law Review* 54:511–48.

———. 2008. "The Delaware Court Wins." *National Law Journal*, February 11, 26.

LoPucki, Lynn M., and William C. Whitford. 1991. "Venue Choice and Forum Shopping in the Bankruptcy Reorganization of Large, Publicly Held Companies." *Wisconsin Law Review* 1991:11–63.

Los Angeles Times. 2009. "Not a Vindication" (editorial). February 2, A14.

Lou, Herbert H. 1927. *Juvenile Courts in the United States*. Chapel Hill: University of North Carolina Press.

Lounsberry, Emilie. 2007. "Plugging Tirelessly Toward High Court." *Philadelphia Inquirer*, October 30, B1.

Lovejoy, Clarence E. 1956. "Jersey Justice Prevails Afloat, Too." *New York Times*, September 6, 33.

Lowenfeld, Andreas F. 1985. "Hijacking, Freedom, and the 'American Way.'" *Michigan Law Review* 83:1000–1015.

Lowenstein, David J., and Jack Achiezer Guggenheim. 2006. "Vetting the Appellate Standard of Review: What Was, What Is, and What Should Be the Standard of Review Employed by the United States Court of Appeals for Veterans Claims." *Whittier Law Review* 27:755–86.

Lunday, Kevin E., and Harvey Rishikof. 2008. "Due Process is a Strategic Choice: Legitimacy and the Establishment of an Article III National Security Court." *California Western International Law Review* 39:87–133.

Lunney, Glynn S., Jr. 2004. "Patent Law, the Federal Circuit, and the Supreme Court: A Quiet Revolution." *Supreme Court Economic Review* 1:1–79.

Lurie, Jonathan. 1992. *Arming Military Justice: The Origins of the United States Court of Military Appeals, 1775–1950*. Princeton: Princeton University Press.

———. 1998. *Pursuing Military Justice: The History of the United States Court of Appeals for the Armed Forces, 1951–1980*. Princeton: Princeton University Press.

Lurigio, Arthur J., and Jessica Snowden. 2009. "Putting Therapeutic Jurisprudence Into Practice: The Growth, Operations, and Effectiveness of Mental Health Court." *Justice System Journal* 30:196–218.

Lyttle, Eric. 2001. "The Judge and the Slumlord." *Columbus Monthly*, December, 94–101.

Mabey, Ralph R. 2005. "The Evolving Bankruptcy Bench: How Are the 'Units' Faring?" *Boston College Law Review* 47:105–27.

Macey, Jonathan R. 1992. "Organizational Design and Political Control of Administrative Agencies." *Journal of Law, Economics & Organization* 8:93–110.

Macey, Jonathan R., and Geoffrey P. Miller. 1987. "Toward an Interest-Group Theory of Delaware Corporate Law." *Texas Law Review* 65:469–523.

MacLean, Pamela A. 2006a. "Immigration Bench Plagued by Flaws." *National Law Journal*, February 6, A18.

———. 2006b. "Mixed Reaction to Copyright Court for 'Little Guy.'" *National Law Journal*, April 24, 2006, 9.

Macris, Gina. 2002. "Truancy Court in R.I. Is Judged as Top Model." *Providence Journal*, May 7, C1, C3.

Magalhães, Pedro C., Carlo Guarnieri, and Yorgos Kaminis. 2006. "Democratic Consolidation, Judicial Reform, and the Judicialization of Politics in Southern Europe." In *Democracy and the State in the New Southern Europe*, ed. Richard Gunther, P. Nikiforos Diamandouros, and Dimitri A. Sotiropoulos, 138–96. New York: Oxford University Press.

Maitland, Leslie. 1982. "A Closed Court's One-Issue Caseload." *New York Times*, October 14, B16.

Mansfield, Harvey C., and Associates. 1947. *A Short History of OPA*. Washington, DC: U.S. Office of Price Administration.

March, James G., and Johan P. Olsen. 1976. *Ambiguity and Choice in Organizations*. Bergen, Norway: Universitetsforlaget.

———. 1984. "The New Institutionalism: Organizational Factors in Political Life." *American Political Science Review* 78:734–49.

———. 1989. *Rediscovering Institutions: The Organizational Basis of Politics*. New York: Free Press.

Marek, Lynne. 2008. "Courts for Veterans Spreading Across U.S." *National Law Journal*, December 22, 1, 7.

———. 2009. "Delaware, New York Courts Retain Popularity." *National Law Journal*, April 27, 6.

Margasak, Larry. 2004a. "Judges on Little-Known Court Paid for Life." *Seattle Post-Intelligencer*, April 18 (Web edition).

———. 2004b. "Light Load of Claims Judges is Examined." *Seattle Post-Intelligencer*, April 19, A3.

Markey, Howard T. 1989. "The First Two Thousand Days: Report of the U.S. Court of Appeals for the Federal Circuit." *BNA's Patent, Trademark and Copyright Journal* 38:179–92.

Maron, Dana Fine. 2009. "Courting Drug-Policy Reform." *Newsweek* (Web edition), October 7. http://www.newsweek.com/id/216886.

Mather, Lynn M. 1979. *Plea Bargaining or Trial? The Process of Criminal-Case Disposition*. Lexington: Lexington Books.

Mattingly, Elizabeth. 2004. "What I Have Learned as a Mental Health Court Judge: And It Wasn't What I Expected." http://www.sconet.state.oh.us/Boards/acmic/resources/learned.pdf.

Matza, Michael. 1995. "Firing a Shot at Crime in R.I. 'Gun Court.'" *Philadelphia Inquirer*, February 3, A1.

Maule, James Edward. 1999. "Instant Replay, Weak Teams, and Disputed Calls: An Empirical Study of Alleged Tax Court Judge Bias." *Tennessee Law Review* 66: 351–426.

Mayer, Jane. 2008. *The Dark Side: The Inside Story of How the War on Terror Turned into a War on American Ideals*. New York: Doubleday.

Mayhood, Kevin. 2001. "Fire Code Cannot Restrict Flag Burning, Judge Rules." *Columbus Dispatch*, November 29, C2.

Mays, G. Larry, Stephen G. Ryan, and Cindy Bejarano. 1997. "New Mexico Creates a DWI Drug Court." *Judicature* 81:122–25.

Mazur, Robyn, and Liberty Aldrich. 2003. "What Makes a Domestic Violence Court Work? Lessons from New York." *Judges' Journal* 42 (Spring): 5–10.

McColloch, Claude. 1949. "Now It Can be Told: Judge Metzger and the Military." *American Bar Association Journal* 35:365–68, 444–48.

McCoy, Candace. 2003. "The Politics of Problem-Solving: An Overview of the Origins and Development of Therapeutic Courts." *American Criminal Law Review* 40:1513–39.

———. 2006. Review of *Good Courts: The Case for Problem-Solving Justice*, by Greg Berman and John Feinblatt. *Law and Politics Book Review* 16:964–69.

McCubbins, Mathew D. 1985. "The Legislative Design of Regulatory Structure." *American Journal of Political Science* 29:721–48.

McCubbins, Mathew D., Roger G. Noll, and Barry R. Weingast. 1987. "Administrative Procedures as Instruments of Political Control." *Journal of Law, Economics, and Organization* 3:243–77.

———. 1989. "Structure and Process, Politics and Policy: Administrative Arrangements and the Political Control of Agencies." *Virginia Law Review* 75:431–82.

McFarland, Mary C. 2004. "The Role of Quasi-Judicial Officers in Today's Changing Courts." *The Court Manager* 19 (2): 18–24.

McGrory, Brian. 1994. "Wanted: Maximum's Impact." *Boston Globe*, September 27, 1.

McIntosh, Wayne V., and Cynthia L. Cates. 1997. *Judicial Entrepreneurship: The Role of the Judge in the Marketplace of Ideas*. Westport: Greenwood Press.

McQuillan, Laurence. 1982. "America's Super-Secret Spy Court." *San Francisco Examiner*, October 24, A1, A28.

Meador, Daniel J. 1983. "An Appellate Court Dilemma and a Solution Through Subject Matter Organization." *University of Michigan Journal of Law Reform* 16:471–92.

———. 1989. "A Challenge to Judicial Architecture: Modifying the Regional Design of the U.S. Courts of Appeals." *University of Chicago Law Review* 56:603–42.

———. 1992. "Origin of the Federal Circuit: A Personal Account." *American University Law Review* 41:581–620.

———. 2002. "Retrospective on the Federal Circuit: The First 20 Years—A Historical View." *Federal Circuit Bar Journal* 11:557–61.

Meadows, Kieran K. 2009. "Justice Center a Success, But Budget Cuts Loom." *The Brooklyn Rail*, March. http://brooklynrail.org/2009/03/.

Meason, James E. 1990. "The Foreign Intelligence Surveillance Act: Time for Reappraisal." *The International Lawyer* 24:1043–58.

Meekins, Tamar M. 2006. "'Specialized Justice': The Over-Emergence of Specialty Courts and the Threat of a New Criminal Defense Paradigm." *Suffolk University Law Review* 40:1–55.

Mennel, Robert M. 1973. *Thorns and Thistles: Juvenile Delinquents in the United States 1825–1940*. Hanover: University Press of New England.

Merryman, John Henry. 1969. *The Civil Law Tradition*. Stanford: Stanford University Press.

Metropolitan Corporate Counsel. 2002. "Civil Justice Reform." November, 53.

Meyer, John W., John Boli, George M. Thomas, and Francisco O. Ramirez. 1997. "World Society and the Nation-State." *American Journal of Sociology* 103:144–81.

Meyers, William. 1989. "Showdown in Delaware: The Battle to Shape Takeover Law." *Institutional Investor* 23:64–77.

Michel, Lou. 2008a. "Giving Vets in Trouble Help, Not Jail." *Buffalo News*, January 12, A1, A2.

———. 2008b. "'Today' to Showcase Local Court for Veterans." *Buffalo News*, September 22, B1, B2.

Middleton, Martha. 1992. "Do Drug Courts Work?" *National Law Journal*, November 2, 1, 45.

Miles, Rufus E., Jr. 1978. "The Origin and Meaning of Miles' Law." *Public Administration Review* 38:399–403.

Miller, Banks, and Brett Curry. 2009. "Expertise, Experience, and Ideology on Specialized Courts: The Case of the Court of Appeals for the Federal Circuit." *Law & Society Review* 43:839–64.

Miller, Chuck, Keith H. Cole, Jr., and Sandra Minderhout Griffin. 1995. "Criminal Law." *SMU Law Review* 48:1077–112.

Miller, Gary. 2000. "Rational Choice and Dysfunctional Institutions." *Governance* 13: 535–47.

Miller, Greg. 2007. "New Limits Put on Overseas Surveillance." *Los Angeles Times*, August 2, A16.

Miller, H. Todd. 1975. "A Court of Tax Appeals Revisited." *Yale Law Journal* 85:228–52.

Minnesota Law Review. 1980. "The Appellate Jurisdiction of the Temporary Emergency Court of Appeals." 64:1247–73.

Mintrom, Michael. 1997. "Policy Entrepreneurs and the Diffusion of Innovation." *American Journal of Political Science* 41:738–70.

Mirchandani, Rekha. 2005. "What's So Special about Specialized Courts? The State and Social Change in Salt Lake City's Domestic Violence Court." *Law & Society Review* 39:379–417.

———. 2006. "'Hitting Is Not Manly': Domestic Violence Court and the Re-Imagination of the Patriarchal State." *Gender & Society* 20:781–804.

Moe, Terry M. 1989. "The Politics of Bureaucratic Structure." In *Can the Government Govern?*, ed. John E. Chubb and Paul E. Peterson, 267–329. Washington, DC: Brookings Institution.

———. 2005. "Power and Political Institutions." *Perspectives on Politics* 3:215–33.

Moe, Terry M., and Scott A. Wilson. 1994. "Presidents and the Politics of Structure," *Law and Contemporary Problems* 57 (Spring): 1–44.

Moley, Raymond. 1929. "The Municipal Court of Chicago." In *The Illinois Crime Survey*, ed. John H. Wigmore, 393–419. Chicago: Illinois Association for Criminal Justice.

———. 1932. *Tribunes of the People: The Past and Future of the New York Magistrates' Courts*. New Haven: Yale University Press.

Monks, Robert A.G., and Nell Minow. 1996. *Watching the Watchers: Corporate Governance for the 21st Century*. Cambridge: Blackwell.

Moore, Geoffrey Michael. 1994. "The Phoenix in China: The Evolution of American Extraterritorial Jurisdiction in China, 1844–1917." MA thesis, California State University, Fullerton.

Moore, Kimberly A. 2002. "Are District Court Judges Equipped to Resolve Patent Cases?" *Federal Circuit Bar Journal* 12:1–33.

———. 2005. "*Markman* Eight Years Later: Is Claim Construction More Predictable?" *Lewis and Clark Law Review* 9:231–47.

Moore, W. John. 1992. "Just Compensation." *National Journal*. June 13, 1404–7.

Morley, Michael. 2008. "The Case Against a Specialized Court for Federal Benefits Appeals." *Federal Circuit Bar Journal* 17:379–400.

Morrow, James D. 1994. *Game Theory for Political Scientists*. Princeton: Princeton University Press.

Moulton, Beatrice A. 1969. "The Persecution and Intimidation of the Low-Income Litigant as Performed by the Small Claims Court in California." *Stanford Law Review* 21:1657–84.

Mucciaroni, Gary. 1992. "The Garbage Can Model and the Study of Policy Making: A Critique." *Polity* 24:459–82.

Muccifori, Thomas A. 2004. "Odd Man Out: New Jersey is Surrounded by States that Have Seen the Benefits of Business Courts." *New Jersey Law Journal*, August 2, 379.

Mullen, William. 1973. "New Court to Handle Shoplifters Opened." *Chicago Tribune*, April 18, 9.

Mullin, Megan. 2008. "The Conditional Effect of Specialized Governance on Public Policy." *American Journal of Political Science* 52:125–41.

Murphy, Walter F. 1962. *Congress and the Court*. Chicago: University of Chicago Press.

Murray, Shannon D. 2001. "About-Face on Judges." *National Law Journal*, October 8, A17.

Nard, Craig Allen, and John F. Duffy. 2007. "Rethinking Patent Law's Uniformity Principle." *Northwestern University Law Review* 101:1619–75.

Nardulli, Peter F., James Eisenstein, and Roy B. Flemming. 1988. *The Tenor of Justice: Criminal Courts and the Guilty Plea Process*. Urbana: University of Illinois Press.

Nash, Jonathan Remy, and Rafael I. Pardo. 2008. "An Empirical Investigation into Appellate Structure and the Perceived Quality of Appellate Review." *Vanderbilt Law Review* 61:1745–822.

Nathanson, Nathaniel L. 1971. "The Administrative Court Proposal." *Virginia Law Review* 57:996–1015.

———. 1972. "Price-Control Standards and Judicial Review: An Historical Perspective." *The Practical Lawyer* 18 (February): 59–71.

National Center for State Courts. 1976. *Parajudges: Their Role in Today's Court Systems*. Denver: National Center for State Courts.

National Council of Juvenile Court Judges. 1965. *Judges Look at Themselves: Profile of the Nation's Juvenile Court Judges*. Chicago: National Council of Juvenile Court Judges.

National Drug Court Institute. N.d. *DWI Courts and DWI/Drug Courts: Reducing Recidivism and Saving Lives*. http://www.ndci.org/dwi_drug_court.htm.

National Institute of Justice. 2006. *Drug Courts: The Second Decade*. Washington, DC: U.S. Department of Justice.

National Law Journal. 1997. "Stadium Drunks Have It Good, Says Philly Council President." December 15, A27.

Navarro, Mireya. 1998. "Florida Gives Teen-Age Smokers a Day in Court." *New York Times*, July 20, A1, A14.

Nees, Anne Tucker. 2007. "Making a Case for Business Courts: A Survey of and Proposed Framework to Evaluate Business Courts." *Georgia State University Law Review* 24:477–532.

New York Times. 1909a. "Wants Marital Courts." January 24, 16.

———. 1909b. "Want Special Court for Domestic Woes." January 29, 4.

———. 1910. "Suffragettes Start Fight on New Court." September 2, 18.

———. 1925. "Coolidge Enlarges Tax Appeals Board." March 19, 4.

Newman, Pauline. 1992. "The Federal Circuit—A Reminiscence." *George Mason University Law Review* 14:513–28.

————. 2002. "Origins of the Federal Circuit: The Role of Industry." *Federal Circuit Bar Journal* 11:541–64.

Newmark, Lisa, Mike Rempel, Kelly Diffily, and Kamala Mallik Kane. 2001. *Specialized Felony Domestic Violence Courts: Lessons on Implementation and Impacts from the Kings County Experience*. Washington, DC: Urban Institute.

Nii, Jenifer K. 1998. "Utah Kids Who Light Up May Land in Tobacco Court." *Deseret News* (Salt Lake City), August 5, A1.

Nisbett, Richard, and Lee Ross. 1980. *Human Inference: Strategies and Shortcomings of Social Judgment*. Englewood, Cliffs: Prentice-Hall.

Nocera, Joseph. 1990. "Delaware Puts Out." *Esquire*, February, 47–48.

Nolan, James L., Jr. 2001. *Reinventing Justice: The American Drug Court Movement*. Princeton: Princeton University Press.

————. 2009. *Legal Accents, Legal Borrowing: The International Problem-Solving Court Movement*. Princeton: Princeton University Press.

Offe, Claus. 2006. "Political Institutions and Social Power: Conceptual Explorations." In *Rethinking Political Institutions: The Art of the State*, ed. Ian Shapiro, Stephen Skowronek, and Daniel Galvin, 9–31. New York: New York University Press.

Offices of Inspectors General. 2009. *Unclassified Report on the President's Surveillance Program*. http://www.fas.org/irp/eprint/psp.pdf.

O'Hearn, Timothy J. 1984. "Patent Law Reform Via the Federal Courts Improvement Act of 1982: The Transformation of Patentability Jurisprudence." *Akron Law Review* 17:453–72.

O'Reilly, James T. 2001. "Burying Caesar: Replacement of the Veterans Appeals Process Is Needed to Provide Fairness to Claimants." *Administrative Law Review* 53:223–55.

Page, Scott E. 2006. "Path Dependence." *Quarterly Journal of Political Science* 1:87–115.

Paik, Leslie. 2009. "Maybe He's Depressed: Mental Illness as a Mitigating Factor for Drug Offender Accountability." *Law & Social Inquiry* 34:569–602.

Palazzolo, Joe. 2009. "Spy Court Up and Running in Its New Home." *The BLT: The Blog of Legal Times* (http://legaltimes.typepad.com/), March 12.

Pastore, Ann L., and Kathleen Maguire, eds. N.d. *Sourcebook of Criminal Justice Statistics*. http://www.albany.edu/sourcebook/.

Pear, Robert. 1986. "New Court Sought for Benefit Cases." *New York Times*, March 9, 1, 29.

Pegram, John B. 2000. "Should There Be a U.S. Trial Court With a Specialization in Patent Litigation?" *Journal of the Patent and Trademark Office Society* 82:765–96.

Perry, Tony. 2000. "Homeless Court Offers New Hope for the Down and Out." *Los Angeles Times*, May 1, A3.

Peters, Philip G. 2007. "Doctors and Juries." *Michigan Law Review* 105:1453–95.

Petersen, William, and David Matza, eds. 1963. *Social Controversy*. Belmont: Wadsworth.

Petrucci, Carrie J. 2002. "Respect as a Component in the Judge-Defendant Interaction in a Specialized Domestic Violence Court that Utilizes Therapeutic Jurisprudence." *Criminal Law Bulletin* 38:263–95.

Philadelphia Inquirer. 1995. "L'Affaire Mumia in Court" (editorial). August 13, E4.

Pierce, David E. 1992. *Evaluating the Institutional Impact of the Special Oil and Gas Panel of the U.S. Court of Appeals for the Fifth Circuit*. Washington, DC: Federal Judicial Center.

Pierson, Paul. 2000. "The Limits of Design: Explaining Institutional Origins and Change." *Governance* 13:475–99.

Pierson, Paul, and Theca Skocpol. 2002. "Historical Institutionalism in Contemporary Political Science." In *Political Science: The State of the Discipline*, ed. Ira Katznelson and Helen V. Milner, 693–721. New York: W. W. Norton.

Plager, S. Jay. 1990. "The United States Courts of Appeals, the Federal Circuit, and the Non-Regional Subject Matter Concept: Reflections on the Search for a Model." *American University Law Review* 39:853–67.

Platt, Anthony M. 1969. *The Child Savers: The Invention of Delinquency.* Chicago: University of Chicago Press.

Polsky, Andrew J. 1989. "The Odyssey of the Juvenile Court: Policy Failure and Institutional Persistence in the Therapeutic State." *Studies in American Political Development* 3:157–98.

Posner, Richard A. 1983. "Will the Federal Courts of Appeals Survive Until 1984? An Essay on Delegation and Specialization of the Judicial Function." *Southern California Law Review* 56:761–91.

———. 1995. *Overcoming Law.* Cambridge: Harvard University Press.

———. 1996. *The Federal Courts: Challenge and Reform.* Cambridge: Harvard University Press.

———. 2006. *Not a Suicide Pact: The Constitution in a Time of National Emergency.* New York: Oxford University Press.

———. 2008. *How Judges Think.* Cambridge: Harvard University Press.

Possley, Maurice. 1986. "Greylord Defendant's Court Called Real Zoo." *Chicago Tribune,* November 14, 1, 2.

Post, Leonard. 2004a. "A Big Step for Specialty Courts." *National Law Journal,* May 10, 1, 18.

———. 2004b. "Some Courts are All Business." *National Law Journal,* May 17, 1, 18.

———. 2006. "ABA Rejection of Special Health Courts Sparks Clash." *National Law Journal,* February 27, 6.

Pound, Roscoe. 1912–13. "The Administration of Justice in the Modern City." *Harvard Law Review* 26:302–28.

———. 1940. *Organization of Courts.* Boston: Little, Brown.

Powell, Ronald W. 2004. "Court Program Helps Homeless." *San Diego Union-Tribune,* August 19, B1.

Pritchett, C. Herman. 1961. *Congress Versus the Supreme Court, 1957–1960.* Minneapolis: University of Minnesota Press.

Provine, Doris Marie. 1996. "Courts in the Political Process in France." In Herbert Jacob, Erhard Blankenburg, Herbert M. Kritzer, Doris Marie Provine, and Joseph Sanders, *Courts, Law, and Politics in Comparative Perspective,* 177–248. New Haven: Yale University Press.

Prugh, R. Mitchell. 2007. "Title Procedure Before General Magistrates and Child Support Enforcement Hearing Officers." *Florida Bar Journal* 81 (July–August): 77–80.

Quillen, William T., and Michael Hanrahan. 1993. "A Short History of the Delaware Court of Chancery—1792–1992." *Delaware Journal of Corporate Law* 18:819–66.

Quin, Leah. 2001. "Jury's Still Out on Community Court." *Austin American-Statesman,* February 5, A1.

Quinn, Mae C. 2000. "Whose Team am I on Anyway? Musings of a Public Defender About Drug Treatment Court Practice." *New York University Review of Law and Social Change* 26:37–75.

———. 2006. "Revisiting Anna Moscowitz Kross's Critique of New York City's Women's Court: The Continued Problem of Solving the 'Problem' of Prostitution with Specialized Criminal Courts." *Fordham Urban Law Journal* 33:665–726.

———. 2008. "Anna Moscowitz Kross and the Home Term Part: A Second Look at the Nation's First Criminal Domestic Violence Court." *Akron Law Review* 41:733–62.

Rader, Randall R. 1991. "Specialized Courts: The Legislative Response." *American University Law Review* 40:1003–14.

Rains, Robert E. 1987. "A Specialized Court for Social Security? A Critique of Recent Proposals." *Florida State University Law Review* 15:1–30.

Rao, Arti K. 2003. "Engaging Facts and Policy: A Multi-Institutional Approach to Patent System Reform." *Columbia Law Review* 103:1035–135.

Rasmussen, Robert K., and Randall S. Thomas. 2000. "Timing Matters: Promoting Forum Shopping by Insolvent Corporations." *Northwestern University Law Review* 94: 1357–408.

Raustiala, Kal. 2006. "The Evolution of Territoriality: International Relations and American Law." In *Territoriality and Conflict in an Era of Globalization*, ed. Miles Kahler and Barbara F. Winter, 219–49. New York: Cambridge University Press.

Redlich, Allison D., et al. 2005. "The Second Generation of Mental Health Courts." *Psychology, Public Policy, and Law* 11:527–38.

Reed, Patrick C. 1997. *The Role of Federal Courts in U.S. Customs and International Trade Law*. Dobbs Ferry: Oceana Publications.

———. 2001. "Expanding the Jurisdiction of the U.S. Court of International Trade: Proposals by the Customs and International Trade Bar Association." *Brooklyn Journal of International Law* 26:819–42.

Reeves, Thomas C. 1975. *Gentleman Boss: The Life of Chester Alan Arthur*. New York: Alfred A. Knopf.

Resnik, Judith. 2003. "Of Courts, Agencies, and the Court of Federal Claims: Fortunately Outliving One's Anomalous Character." *George Washington Law Review* 71:798–817.

Revesz, Richard L. 1990. "Specialized Courts and the Administrative Lawmaking System." *University of Pennsylvania Law Review* 138:1111–74.

Reynolds, Maura. 2006. "Plan to Reroute Immigration Appeals Hits Some Red Lights." *Los Angeles Times*, April 2, A23.

Rich, Giles S. 1963. "Congressional Intent—Or, Who Wrote the Patent Act of 1952." In *Patent Procurement and Exploitation: Protecting Intellectual Rights*, ed. Institute on Patent Law, 61–78. Washington, DC: Bureau of National Affairs.

———. 1980. *A Brief History of the United States Court of Customs and Patent Appeals*. Washington, DC: U.S. Government Printing Office.

Richards, Peter Judson. 2007. *Extraordinary Justice: Military Tribunals in Historical and International Context*. New York: New York University Press.

Richardson, William A. 1882. "History, Jurisdiction, and Practice of the Court of Claims of the United States." *Southern Law Review* 7:781–811.

Rifkind, Simon. 1951. "A Special Court for Patent Litigation? The Danger of a Specialized Judiciary." *American Bar Association Journal* 37:425–26.

Rifkind, Simon H. 1978. "Bankruptcy Code—Specialized Court Opposed." *American Bankruptcy Law Journal* 52:187–91.

———. 1985. "Music Copyrights and Antitrust: A Turbulent Courtship." *Cardozo Arts and Entertainment Law Journal* 4:1–18.

Rightmire, George W. 1918–19. "Special Federal Courts." *Illinois Law Review* 13:15–33, 97–120.

Riley, John. 1984. "Bankruptcy Crisis Eases; Judges to Press Suit." *National Law Journal*, August 6, 10, 60.

Risen, James, and Eric Lichtblau. 2005. "Bush Lets U.S. Spy on Callers Without Courts." *New York Times*, December 16, A1, A6.

Rivkin, Victoria. 2001. "Courting Tech Business." *ABA Journal* 87 (July): 39–41.

Roberts, Maurice A. 1980. "Proposed: A Specialized Statutory Immigration Court." *San Diego Law Review* 18:1–24.

Rodgers, Daniel T. 1982. "In Search of Progressivism." *Reviews in American History* 10 (December): 113–32.

Rogers, Everett M. 2003. *Diffusion of Innovations*, 5th ed. New York: Free Press.

Roman, John, Jeffrey A. Butts, and Alison S. Rebeck. 2004. "American Drug Policy and the Evolution of Drug Treatment Courts." In *Juvenile Drug Courts and Teen Substance Abuse*, ed. Jeffrey A. Butts and John Roman, 27–54. Washington, DC: Urban Institute Press.

Romano, Roberta. 1987. "The State Competition Debate in Corporate Law." *Cardozo Law Review* 8:709–25.

———. 1993. *The Genius of American Corporate Law*. Washington, DC: AEI Press.

Rooklidge, William C., and Matthew F. Weil. 2001. "Judicial Hyperactivity: The Federal Circuit's Discomfort with Its Appellate Role." *Berkeley Technology Law Journal* 15:725–52.

Rosenberg, Carol. 2007. "Aussie Captive's Deal: Freedom by Year-End." *Miami Herald*, March 31, A1, A6.

———. 2008a. "Marine Colonel Defends Dismissal of Guantánamo Judge." *Miami Herald*, June 2.

———. 2008b. "Judge Bans General From Guantánamo Trial Role." *Miami Herald*, August 14.

Rosenberg, Tina. 1995. "Deadliest D.A." *New York Times Magazine*, July 16, 20–25, 34, 42.

Rothman, David J. 1978. "The State as Parent: Social Policy in the Progressive Era." In *Doing Good: The Limits of Benevolence*, by Willard Gaylin, Ira Glasser, Steven Marcus, and David J. Rothman, 67–96. New York: Pantheon.

Rottman, David B. 2002. *Community Courts: Prospects and Limits*. Williamsburg: National Center for State Courts.

Rovella, David E. 2001. "Leading a Charge to Dethrone Delaware." *National Law Journal*, August 13, A1, A10, A12.

Ruger, Theodore W. 2004. "The Judicial Appointment Power of the Chief Justice." *University of Pennsylvania Journal of Constitutional Law* 7:341–402.

———. 2006. "Chief Justice Rehnquist's Appointments to the FISA Court: An Empirical Perspective." *Northwestern University Law Review* 101:239–58.

Russell, Robert T. 2009. "Veterans Treatment Courts Developing Throughout the Nation." In *Future Trends in State Courts 2009*, ed. Carol R. Flango, Amy M. McDowell, Charles F. Campbell, and Neal B. Kauder, 130–33. Williamsburg: National Center for State Courts.

Ryan, John Paul, Allan Ashman, Bruce D. Sales, and Sandra Shane-DuBow. 1980. *American Trial Judges: Their Work Styles and Performance*. New York: Free Press.

Ryerson, Ellen. 1978. *The Best-Laid Plans: America's Juvenile Court Experiment*. New York: Hill and Wang.

Sample, James, Lauren Jones, and Rachel Weiss. 2007. *The New Politics of Judicial Elections 2006*. Washington, DC: Justice at Stake Campaign.

Sanders, Elizabeth. 2006. "Historical Institutionalism," In *The Oxford Handbook of Political Institutions*, ed. R. A. W. Rhodes, Sarah A. Binder, and Bert A. Rockman, 39–55. New York: Oxford University Press.

Sarasota Herald-Tribune. 1998. "Arresting Beachwear." March 16, A14.

Satel, Sally L. 1998. "Observational Study of Courtroom Dynamics in Selected Drug Courts." *National Drug Court Institute Review* 1:43–72.

Savage, Charlie. 2009a. "Holder Defends Decision to Use U.S. Court for 9/11 Trial." *New York Times*, November 19, A18.

———. 2009b. "Trial Without Major Witness Will Test Tribunal System." *New York Times*, December 1, A18, A23.

Scalia, Antonin. 1987. "To Preserve Elite Federal Courts." *Los Angeles Daily Journal*, February 20, 4.

Scheiber, Harry N., and Jane L. Scheiber. 1997. "Bayonets in Paradise: A Half-Century Retrospect on Martial Law in Hawai'i." *University of Hawaii Law Review* 19:477–648.

Scherer, Nancy. 2005. *Scoring Points: Politicians, Activists, and the Lower Federal Court Appointment Process*. Stanford: Stanford University Press.

Schickler, Eric. 2001. *Disjointed Pluralism: Institutional Innovation and the Development of the U.S. Congress*. Princeton: Princeton University Press.

Schmitt, Richard B. 1994. "Delaware Governor Picks Trial Judge to Succeed Moore on Supreme Court." *Wall Street Journal*, May 26, B7.

Schneider, Daniel M. 2001. "Empirical Research on Judicial Reasoning: Statutory Interpretation in Federal Tax Cases." *New Mexico Law Review* 31:325–58.

———. 2002. "Assessing and Predicting Who Wins Federal Tax Trial Decisions." *Wake Forest Law Review* 37:473–538.

Schneider, Jeffrey M. 2008. *Youth Courts: An Empirical Update and Analysis of Future Organizational and Research Needs*. Washington, DC: Hamilton Fish Institute.

Schneider, Thomas P., and Robert C. Davis. 1995. "Speedy-Trial Homicide Courts." *Criminal Justice* 9 (Winter): 24–29.

Schlossman, Steven L. 1977. *Love and the American Delinquent: The Theory and Practice of "Progressive" Juvenile Justice, 1825–1920*. Chicago: University of Chicago Press.

Schmitt, Rick, and Mary Curtius. 2005. "Bush Defends Eavesdropping as Defense Against Terrorism." *Los Angeles Times*, December 18, A1, A27.

Schooner, Steven. 2003. "The Future: Scrutinizing the Empirical Case for the Court of Federal Claims." *George Washington Law Review* 71:714–72.

Schulte, Fred, and James Drew. 2008. "Their Day in Court." *Baltimore Sun*, December 22, 1A.

Schwartz, David L. 2008. "Practice Makes Perfect? An Empirical Study of Claim Construction Reversal Rates in Patent Cases." *Michigan Law Review* 107:223–84.

Schwartz, Edward P., Pablo T. Spiller, and Santiago Urbiztondo. 1994. "A Positive Theory of Legislative Intent." *Law and Contemporary Problems* 57 (Winter–Spring): 51–74.

Schwartz, Emma. 2006. "A Simmering Border Dispute." *Legal Times*, April 3, 1, 16.

———. 2008. "A Court of Compassion: How Special Courts Can Serve Justice and Help Mentally Ill Offenders." *U.S. News & World Report*, February 18, 39.

Schwartz, Helene E. 1981. "Oversight of Minimization Compliance Under the Foreign Intelligence Surveillance Act: How the Watchdogs Are Doing Their Jobs." *Rutgers Law Journal* 12:405–89.

Sciulli, David. 2001. *Corporate Power in Civil Society: An Application of Societal Constitutionalism*. New York: New York University Press.

Scully, Eileen P. 2001. *Bargaining with the State from Afar: American Citizenship in Treaty Port China 1844–1942*. New York: Columbia University Press.

Seabury, Samuel. 1932. *In the Matter of the Investigation of the Magistrates' Courts in the First Judicial Department and the Magistrates Thereof, and of Attorneys-at-Law Practicing in Said Courts*. New York: Supreme Court Appellate Division—First Judicial Department.

Segal, Jeffrey A. 1997. "Separation-of-Powers Games in the Positive Theory of Law and Courts." *American Political Science Review* 91:28–44.

Seron, Carroll. 1978. *Judicial Reorganization: The Politics of Reform in the Federal Bankruptcy Court*. Lexington: Lexington Books.

———. 1982. "Court Reorganization and the Politics of Reform: The Case of the Bankruptcy Court." In *The Politics of Judicial Reform*, ed. Philip L. Dubois, 87–98. Lexington: Lexington Books.

Shane, Scott, and William Glaberson. 2008. "Rulings Clear Military Trial of a Detainee." *New York Times*, July 18, A1, A14.

Shapiro, Martin. 1968. *The Supreme Court and Administrative Agencies*. New York: Free Press.

———. 1981. *Courts: A Comparative and Political Analysis*. Chicago: University of Chicago Press.

Shelton, Donald E. 2007. *The Current State of Domestic Violence Courts in the United States, 2007*. Williamsburg: National Center for State Courts.

Shesgreen, Deirdre. 2001. "Security, Civil Liberty Concerns Collide in Debate Over Secret Court Proposals." *St. Louis Post-Dispatch*, September 30, B1, B7.

Shipan, Charles R. 1997. *Designing Judicial Review: Interest Groups, Congress, and Communications Policy*. Ann Arbor: University of Michigan Press.

Shipan, Charles R., and Craig Volden. 2006. "Bottom-Up Federalism: The Diffusion of Antismoking Policies from U.S. Cities to States." *American Journal of Political Science* 50:825–43.

———. 2008. "The Mechanisms of Policy Diffusion." *American Journal of Political Science* 52:840–57.

Siegel, Robert. 1999. "Broward County, Florida's, Mental Health Court. . ." Reported on "All Things Considered," National Public Radio, March 12.

Silverstein, Gordon. 1997. *Imbalance of Powers: Constitutional Interpretation and the Making of American Foreign Policy*. New York: Oxford University Press.

Simmons, Beth A., Frank Dobbin, and Geoffrey Garrett. 2006. "Introduction: The International Diffusion of Liberalism." *International Organization* 60:781–810.

Simon, Herbert A. 1947. *Administrative Behavior: A Study of Decision-Making Processes in Administrative Organization*. New York: Macmillan.

Sisk, Gregory C. 2003a. "The Tapestry Unravels: Statutory Waivers of Sovereign Immunity and Money Claims Against the United States." *George Washington Law Review* 71:602–707.

———. 2003b. "The Trial Courts of the Federal Circuit: Diversity by Design." *Federal Circuit Bar Journal* 13:241–66.

Skeel, David A., Jr. 2001. *Debt's Dominion: A History of Bankruptcy Law in America*. Princeton: Princeton University Press.

Skoler, Daniel L., and Cynthia E. Weixel. 1981. "Social Security Adjudication in Five Nations: Some International Perspectives and Comparisons." *Administrative Law Review* 33:269–84.

Skowronek, Stephen. 1982. *Building a New American State: The Expansion of National Administrative Capacities 1877–1920*. New York: Cambridge University Press.

Slapper, Gary, and David Kelly. 2001. *The English Legal System*, 5th ed. London: Cavendish.

Smith, Adam. 1776/1963. *An Inquiry Into the Nature and Causes of the Wealth of Nations*. Homewood: Richard D. Irwin.

Smith, Andre L. 2005. "Deferential Review of Tax Court Decisions of Law: Promoting Expertise, Uniformity, and Impartiality." *Tax Lawyer* 58:361–404.

Smith, Barbara E., Arthur J. Lurigio, Robert C. Davis, Sharon Goretsky Elstein, and Susan J. Popkin. 1994. "Burning the Midnight Oil: An Examination of Cook County's Night Drug Court." *Justice System Journal* 17:41–52.

Smith, Claire. 1997. "In Philadelphia, Fans Are Penalized, Too." *New York Times*, November 24, A1, A14.

Smith, Loren A. 1996. "Life, Liberty and Whose Property?: An Essay on Property Rights." *University of Richmond Law Review* 30:1055–69.

262 / References

———. 1998. "The Morality of Regulation." *William and Mary Environmental Law and Policy Review* 22:507–19.

———. 2003. "Why a Court of Federal Claims?" *George Washington Law Review* 71:773–90.

Smith, Reginald Heber. 1919. *Justice and the Poor*. New York: Scribner's Sons.

Smith, Steven S. 1994. "The Congressional Committee System." in *Encyclopedia of the American Legislative System*, ed. Joel H. Silbey, vol. II, 641–67. New York: Charles Scribner's Sons.

Sobel, Gerald. 1988. "The Court of Appeals for the Federal Circuit: A Fifth Anniversary Look at Its Impact on Patent Law and Litigation." *American University Law Review* 37:1087–139.

Solomon, Andrew T. 2006. "A Simple Prescription for Texas's Ailing Court System: Stronger Stare Decisis." *St. Mary's Law Journal* 37:417–76.

Solomon, Freda F. 1987. "Progressive Era Justice: The New York City Women's Court." Paper presented at Berkshire Conference on the History of Women, Wellesley.

———. 2005. *New York City's Gun Court Initiative: The Brooklyn Pilot Program*. New York: New York City Criminal Justice Agency.

Spence, David B. 1999. "Managing Delegation Ex Ante: Using Law to Steer Administrative Agencies." *Journal of Legal Studies* 28:413–59.

Spencer, J. R., ed. 1989. *Jackson's Machinery of Justice*. Cambridge: Cambridge University Press.

Spiller, Pablo T., and Rafael Gely. 1992. "Congressional Control or Judicial Independence: The Determinants of U.S. Supreme Court Labor-Relations Decisions, 1949–1988." *RAND Journal of Economics* 23:463–92.

Stafford, Jane Lynn. 1981–82. "Customs Court Reform." *International Trade Law Journal* 7:119–49.

Stanley, David T., and Marjorie Girth. 1971. *Bankruptcy: Problem, Process, Reform*. Washington, DC: Brookings Institution.

St. Louis Post-Dispatch. 2004. "Sentence First, Verdict After" (editorial). September 30, C10.

Steadman, Henry J., Susan Davidson, and Collie Brown. 2001. "Mental Health Courts: Their Promise and Unanswered Questions." *Psychiatric Services* 52:457–58.

Stein, Harry H. 2006. *Gus J. Solomon: Liberal Politics, Jews, and the Federal Courts*. Portland: Oregon Historical Society Press.

Steinbock, Daniel J. 2005. "Data Matching, Data Mining, and Due Process." *Georgia Law Review* 40:1–84.

Stempel, Jeffrey W. 1995. "Two Cheers for Specialization." *Brooklyn Law Review* 61:67–128.

Stern, Herbert J. 1984. *Judgment in Berlin*. New York: Universe Books.

Strasser, Fred. 1990. "Corporate Sentences Draw Fire." *National Law Journal*, March 12, 3, 9.

Strickland, Shauna M., Chantal G. Bromage, Sarah A. Gibson, and William E. Raftery. 2008. *State Court Caseload Statistics, 2007*. Williamsburg: National Center for State Courts.

Study Group on the Case Load of the Supreme Court. 1972. *Report of the Study Group on the Caseload of the Supreme Court*. Washington, DC: Federal Judicial Center.

Sturgess, Garry. 1991. "Permanent Temporary Court." *Legal Times*, January 14, 7.

Sullivan, Daniel P., and Donald E. Conlon. 1997. "Crisis and Transition in Corporate Governance Paradigms: The Role of the Chancery Court of Delaware." *Law & Society Review* 31:713–62.

Sullivan, Teresa A., Elizabeth Warren, and Jay Lawrence Westbrook. 1989. *As We Forgive our Debtors: Bankruptcy and Consumer Credit in America*. New York: Oxford University Press.

———. 1994. "The Persistence of Local Legal Culture: Twenty Years of Evidence from the Federal Bankruptcy Courts." *Harvard Journal of Law & Public Policy* 17:801–65.

Sulmasy, Glenn. 2009. *The National Security Court System: A Natural Evolution of Justice in an Age of Terror*. New York: Oxford University Press.

Summerford, William A. 1973. "The United States Court of Military Appeals: A Study in Judicial Process and Administration." PhD diss., University of Tennessee.

Sutton, John R. 1985. "The Juvenile Court and Social Welfare: Dynamics of Progressive Reform." *Law & Society Review* 19:107–45.

———. 1988. *Stubborn Children: Controlling Delinquency in the United States, 1640–1981*. Berkeley and Los Angeles: University of California Press.

Sviridoff, Michele, David B. Rottman, Brian Ostrom, and Richard Curtis. 2000. *Dispensing Justice Locally: The Implementation and Effects of the Midtown Community Court*. Amsterdam: Harwood Academic Publishers.

Swanson, James L., and Daniel R. Weinberg. 2001. *Lincoln's Assassins: Their Trial and Execution*. Santa Fe: Arena Editions.

Sween, Gretchen S. 2008. "Surveying High Court's Recent Patent Jurisprudence." *National Law Journal*, December 1, S4, S5, S8.

Swift, Charles. 2007. "The American Way of Justice." *Esquire*, March, 192–99, 213.

Swindler, William F. 1983. "Toward 1987: A 'Pre-Constitutional' Law Case." *Supreme Court Historical Society 1983 Yearbook*. http://www.supremecourthistory.org/04_library/subs_volumes/04_c20_f.html.

Symposium. 2002. "Problem Solving Courts: From Adversarial Litigation to Innovative Jurisprudence." *Fordham Urban Law Journal*. 29:1751–2132.

Symposium. 2005. "Empirical Measures of Judicial Performance." *Florida State University Law Review* 32:1001–415.

Tan, Shannon. 2000. "In Providence, Truancy Put to Judgment," *Boston Globe*, October 15, 2000, B6, B7.

Tanenhaus, David S. 2004. *Juvenile Justice in the Making*. New York: Oxford University Press.

Taylor, Stuart, Jr. 1984a. "The Free-for-All on the Bankruptcy Express." *New York Times*, March 2, 10.

———. 1984b. "U.S. Official Won't Pay Bankruptcy Judges." *New York Times*, July 13, D1, D4.

———. 1984c. "Burger Said to Support Ban on Bankruptcy Pay." *New York Times*, July 14, A35, A39.

———. 1987. "Scalia Proposes Major Overhaul of U.S. Courts." *New York Times*, February 16, 1, 12.

Terry, W. Clinton, III, ed. 1999. *The Early Drug Courts: Case Studies in Judicial Innovation*. Thousand Oaks: Sage Publications.

Thamel, Pete, and Thayer Evans. 2009. "Notre Dame Fires Weis and Starts Its Search." *New York Times*, December 1, B13.

Thelen, Kathleen. 2004. *How Institutions Evolve: The Political Economy of Skills in Germany, Britain, the United States, and Japan*. New York: Cambridge University Press.

Thelen, Kathleen, and Sven Steinmo. 1992. "Historical Institutionalism in Comparative Politics." In *Structuring Politics: Historical Institutionalism in Comparative Analysis*, ed. Sven Steinmo, Kathleen Thelen, and Frank Longstreth, 1–32. New York: Cambridge University Press.

Thompson, Anthony C. 2002. "Courting Disorder: Some Thoughts on Community Courts." *Washington University Journal of Law and Policy* 10:63–99.

Thompson, Michael, Fred Osher, and Denise Tomasini-Joshi. 2007. *Improving Responses to People with Mental Illnesses: The Essential Elements of a Mental Health Court.* New York: Council of State Governments Justice Center.

Tobias, Carl. 2000. "The White Commission and the Federal Circuit." *Cornell Journal of Law and Public Policy* 10:45–62.

Toobin, Jeffrey. 1999. *A Vast Conspiracy: The Real Story of the Sex Scandal that Nearly Brought Down a President.* New York: Random House.

———. 2008. "Camp Justice." *The New Yorker*, April 14, 32–38.

Transcript of Proceedings. 1961. (See entry in Court Decisions and Documents below.)

Tsai, Betsy. 2000. "The Trend Toward Specialized Domestic Violence Courts: Improvements on an Effective Innovation." *Fordham Law Review* 68:1285–327.

Tucker, Eric. 2008. "Terror Appeals Judge Waits for Cases." Associated Press, March 18.

Tyler, Tom R. 1988. "What is Procedural Justice?: Criteria Used by Citizens to Assess the Fairness of Legal Procedures." *Law & Society Review* 22:137–61.

Unah, Issac. 1997. "Specialized Courts of Appeals' Review of Bureaucratic Actions and the Politics of Protectionism." *Political Research Quarterly* 50:851–78.

———. 1998. *The Courts of International Trade: Judicial Specialization, Expertise, and Bureaucratic Policy-Making.* Ann Arbor: University of Michigan Press.

———. 2001. "The Incidence and Structure of Conflict on the U.S. Court of Appeals for the Federal Circuit." *Law & Policy* 23:69–93.

Urry, Mark. 2006. "San Diego Stand Down Court: Homeless Veteran Outreach Court." In *Taking the Court to Stand Down*, ed. American Bar Association Commission on Homelessness and Poverty and National Coalition for Homeless Veterans, 9–15. Chicago: American Bar Association.

U.S. Census Bureau. 2009. *The 2010 Statistical Abstract.* http://www.census.gov/compendia/statab/.

U.S. Chamber Institute for Legal Reform. 2010. *Lawsuit Climate 2010: State Liability Systems Survey.* http://www.instituteforlegalreform.com/images/stories/documents/pdf/lawsuitclimate2010/2010LawsuitClimateReport.pdf.

U.S. Court of Appeals for Veterans Claims. 2008. *Rules of Practice and Procedure.* http://www.uscourts.cavc.gov/court_procedures/RulesonorafterApril12008.cfm.

Valentine, Steven R. 2002. "Flaws Undermine Use of Alien Terrorist Removal Court." *Legal Backgrounder* (Washington Legal Foundation), 17, no. 12.

Vinter, Robert D. 1967. "The Juvenile Court as an Institution." In *Task Force Report: Juvenile Delinquency and Youth Crime*, by President's Commission on Law Enforcement and Administration of Justice, 84–90. Washington, DC: U.S. Government Printing Office.

Volden, Craig. 2006. "States as Policy Laboratories: Emulating Success in the Children's Health Insurance Program." *American Journal of Political Science* 50:294–312.

Vowell, Sarah. 2005. *Assassination Vacation.* New York: Simon & Schuster.

Wagner, R. Polk, and Lee Petherbridge. 2004. "Is the Federal Circuit Succeeding? An Empirical Assessment of Judicial Performance." *University of Pennsylvania Law Review* 152:1105–80.

Waite, Edward F. 1921. "Courts of Domestic Relations." *Minnesota Law Review* 5:161–71.

Wald, Patricia A. 2009. "Foreword." 1 Mil. Comm'n Rptr. xv. (Report of decisions of the Military Commissions at Guantánamo)

Walker, Daniel, and C. George Niebank. 1953. "The Court of Military Appeals—Its History, Organization, and Operation." *Vanderbilt Law Review* 6:228–40.

Walker, Jack L. 1969. "The Diffusion of Innovations Among the American States." *American Political Science Review* 63:880–99.

Walker, Sam. 1994. "Rhode Island Takes Aim at Criminals Using Guns, Setting up a Special Court." *Christian Science Monitor*, October 25, § 1, 4, 6.

Walter, Donna. 2002. "Community Court Proposed for Downtown St. Louis." *St. Louis Daily Record*, January 10.

Ward, Richard, and Amanda Akhtar. 2008. *Walker and Walker's English Legal System*, 10th ed. Oxford: Oxford University Press.

Warren, Charles. 1935. *Bankruptcy in United States History*. Cambridge: Harvard University Press.

Warren, Elizabeth. 2004. "Vanishing Trials: The Bankruptcy Experience." *Journal of Empirical Legal Studies* 1:913–42.

Warren, George. 1942. *Traffic Courts*. Boston: Little, Brown.

Washington Post. 1985. "Mayor Koch Seeks to Put Courts Into Subway Stations." February 5, A9.

———. 2003a. "Court of Extravagance." March 26, A16.

———. 2003b. "Court Dismissed From Eagles' Nest." December 8, D10.

Waters, Nicole L., Shauna M. Strickland, and Sarah A. Gibson. 2009. *Mental Health Court Culture: Leaving Your Hat at the Door*. Williamsburg: National Center for State Courts.

Watson, Amy, Patricia Hanrahan, Daniel Luchins, and Arthur Lurigio. 2001. "Mental Health Courts and the Complex Issue of Mentally Ill Offenders." *Psychiatric Services* 52:477–81.

Wayne, Leslie. 1990. "Pennsylvania Proposes Plan for Business Court." *New York Times*, September 12, C2.

Weidner, Robert R. 2001. *"I Won't Do Manhattan": Causes and Consequences of a Decline in Street Prostitution*. New York: LFB Scholarly Publishing.

Weiner, Jennifer. 1998. "Special Courts Will Hit Truancy Where It Starts: In Schools." *Philadelphia Inquirer*, February 11, R1.

Weinstein, Jack B. 2009. "Preliminary Reflections on Administration of Complex Litigations." *Cardozo Law Review De Novo* 1:1–19.

Weir, Tom. 1993. "Many Bear Philadelphia Boo Burden." *USA Today*, October 19, 1C.

Wendt, Alexander. 1999. *Social Theory of International Politics*. New York: Cambridge University Press.

———. 2001. "Driving With the Rearview Mirror: On the Rational Science of Institutional Design." *International Organization* 55:1019–49.

Weyland, Kurt. 2006. *Bounded Rationality and Policy Diffusion: Social Sector Reform in Latin America*. Princeton: Princeton University Press.

White, Frederic P. 1981. "The Cleveland Housing Court Act: New Answer to an Old Problem." *Cleveland State Law Review* 30:41–56.

White, Josh. 2007. "Australian's Plea Deal Was Negotiated Without Prosecutors." *Washington Post*, April 1, A7.

Whitin, Frederick H. 1914. "The Women's Night Court in New York City." *Annals of the American Academy of Political and Social Science* 52:181–87.

Wiecek, William M. 1968. "The Origin of the United States Court of Claims." *Administrative Law Review* 20:386–406.

Wilber, Del Quentin. 2009. "Surveillance Court Quietly Moving." *Washington Post*, March 2, A2.

Wilber, Del Quentin, and R. Jeffrey Smith. 2009. "Intelligence Court Releases Ruling in Favor of Warrantless Wiretapping." *Washington Post*, January 16, A10.

Wildhaber, Michael E., Ronald B. Abrams, Barton F. Stichman, and David F. Addlestone. 1991. *Veterans Benefits Manual: An Advocate's Guide to Representing Veterans and Their Dependents*. Washington, DC: National Veterans Legal Services Project.

Williams, Frank J., Nicole J. Dulude, and Kimberley A. Tracey. 2007. "Still a Frightening Unknown: Achieving a Constitutional Balance between Civil Liberties and National Security during the War on Terror." *Roger Williams University Law Review* 12: 675–749.

Williams, Victor. 1996. "A Constitutional Charge and a Comparative Vision to Substantially Expand and Subject Matter Specialize the Federal Judiciary." *William and Mary Law Review* 37:535–671.

Willis, John T. 1972. "The United States Court of Military Appeals: Its Origin, Operation and Future." *Military Law Review* 55:39–93.

Willrich, Michael. 2003. *City of Courts: Socializing Justice in Progressive Era Chicago.* New York: Cambridge University Press.

Wilson, James Q. 1989. *Bureaucracy: What Government Agencies Do and Why They Do It.* New York: Basic Books.

Wilson, Michael. 2006. "Justice, Sentence and Civics Lesson, Under One Roof." *New York Times,* August 22, C15.

Wilson, Peter. 2004. "Clinton's Outburst: Racism at the Top." *The Australian,* September 11, 15.

Wilson, Tracy. 2001. "Delivering Justice Where It's Needed." *Los Angeles Times,* September 4, § 2, 1.

Wilson, William Jerome. 1947. "The Price Control Act of 1942." In *The Beginnings of OPA,* by William Jerome Wilson, John A. Hart, and George R. Taylor, 1–128. Washington, DC: U.S. Office of Price Administration.

Winchell, Cora M. 1921. "A Study of the Court of Domestic Relations of the City of Chicago as an Agency in the Stabilization of the Home." MA diss., University of Chicago.

Winick, Bruce J., and David B. Wexler, eds. 2003. *Judging in a Therapeutic Key: Therapeutic Jurisprudence and the Courts.* Durham: Carolina Academic Press.

Winter, Christine. 1975. "Unwary Chicagoans Find Smokers Court is No Joke." *Chicago Tribune,* December 1, C18.

Winter, Ralph K., Jr. 1977. "State Law, Shareholder Protection, and the Theory of the Corporation." *Journal of Legal Studies* 6:251–92.

Wiseman, Jacqueline P. 1979. *Stations of the Lost: The Treatment of Skid Row Alcoholics.* Chicago: University of Chicago Press.

Withers, John Lovelle. 1956. "The Administrative Theories and Practices of William Howard Taft." PhD diss., University of Chicago.

Wittenauer, Cheryl. 2003. "New Court Aimed at Eradicating Pesky Behaviors Downtown." *Association Press State & Local Wire,* January 31.

Wittes, Benjamin. 1996a. "Inside America's Most Secretive Court." *Legal Times,* February 19, 1996, 1.

———. 1996b. "Will 'Removal Court' Remove Due Process?" *Legal Times,* April 23, 1, 16–17.

———. 1997. "Anti-Terrorism Act: Rhetoric vs. Reality." *Legal Times,* June 2, 1, 18, 20.

Wold, John T. 1978. "Going Through the Motions: The Monotony of Appellate Court Decisionmaking." *Judicature* 62:58–65.

Wolf, Robert Victor. 2001. "New Strategies for an Old Profession: A Court and a Community Combat a Streetwalking Epidemic." *Justice System Journal* 22:347–59.

Wolf, Robert V. 2005. *California's Collaborative Justice Courts: Building a Problem-Solving Judiciary.* San Francisco: Judicial Council of California.

Wood, Diane P. 1997. "Generalist Judges in a Specialized World." *SMU Law Review* 50:1755–68.

Woods, Jim. 2006. "Mayor of Brice Reopens Court with Ticketing Twist." *Columbus Dispatch,* July 27, D4.

Worthington, George E., and Ruth Topping. 1925. *Specialized Courts Dealing with Sex Delinquency: A Study of the Procedure in Chicago, Boston, Philadelphia and New York.* New York: Frederick H. Hitchcock.

Worthy, K. Martin. 1971. "The Tax Litigation Structure." *Georgia Law Review* 5:248–68.

Wright, George Cable. 1956. "Novel Court Sits in Boating Cases." *New York Times,* February 12, 80.

Yan, Holly. 2009. "Picking Up the Pieces." *Dallas Morning News,* April 8, 1B, 7B.

Yngvesson, Barbara, and Patricia Hennessey. 1975. "Small Claims, Complex Disputes: A Review of the Small Claims Literature." *Law & Society Review* 9:219–74.

Zappia, Andrew P. 1998. "Court of Federal Claims: A Case Against Reform." *National Law Journal,* March 2, A25.

Zegart, Amy B. 1999. *Flawed by Design: The Evolution of the CIA, JCS, and NSC.* Stanford: Stanford University Press.

LEGISLATIVE, STATUTORY, AND REGULATORY MATERIALS

America's Law Enforcement and Mental Health Project. 2000. Public Law 106-515, 106th Congress, 2nd Session.

Antiterrorism and Effective Death Penalty Act of 1996. Public Law 104-132, 104th Congress, 2nd Session.

Bankruptcy Act. 1896. 30 Stat. 544, 54th Congress, 2nd Session.

Bankruptcy Act of 1978. Public Law 95-598, 95th Congress, 2nd Session.

Bankruptcy Amendments and Federal Judgeship Act of 1984. Public Law 98-353, 98th Congress, 2nd Session.

Bankruptcy Reform Act of 1994, Public Law 103-394, 103rd Congress, 2nd Session.

Chandler Act. 1938. Public Law 75-696, 75th Congress, 2nd Session.

Customs Administrative Act of 1890. 26 Stat. 131, 51st Congress, 1st Session.

Customs Courts Act of 1980. Public Law 96-417, 96th Congress, 2nd Session.

Detainee Treatment Act of 2005. (Part of the Department of Defense Appropriations Act of 2006.) Public Law 109-148, 109th Congress, 1st Session.

Emergency Price Control Act of 1942. Public Law 77-421, 77th Congress, 2nd Session.

Ethics in Government Act. 1978. Public Law 95-521, 95th Congress, 2nd Session.

Federal Courts Improvement Act of 1982. Public Law 97-164, 97th Congress, 2nd Session.

Federal Register. 2001. "Detention, Treatment, and Trial of Certain Non-Citizens in the War Against Terrorism." 66:57833–36.

———. 2009. "Executive Order 13492: Review and Disposition of Individuals Detained at the Guantánamo Bay Naval Base and Closure of Detention Facilities." 74:4897–900.

Foreign Intelligence Surveillance Act of 1978. Public Law 95-511, 95th Congress, 2nd Session.

Foreign Intelligence Surveillance Act of 1978 Amendments Act. 2008. Public Law 110-261, 110th Congress, 2nd Session.

Intelligence Authorization Act for Fiscal Year 2002. 2001. Public Law 107-108, 107th Congress, 1st Session.

Mann-Elkins Act of 1910. Public Law 61-218, 61st Congress, 2nd Session.

Military Commissions Act of 2006. Public Law 109-366, 109th Congress, 2nd Session.

National Childhood Vaccine Act of 1986. Public Law 99-660, 99th Congress, 2nd Session.

Patent Act of 1952. Public Law 82-593, 82nd Congress, 2nd Session.

Payne-Aldrich Tariff Act. 1909. Public Law 61-5, 61st Congress, 1st Session.

Referees' Salary Act of 1946. Public Law 79-464, 79th Congress, 2nd Session.

Stabilization Extension Act of 1944. Public Law 78-383, 78th Congress, 2nd Session.

Tariff Act of 1922. Public Law 67-318. 67th Congress, 2nd Session.

U.S. Congress. 1824. *Annals of the Congress of the United States*, Vol. 41, 18th Congress, 1st Session.

———. 1861-62. *Congressional Globe*, Vol. 32, Appendix. 37th Congress, 2nd Session.

———. 1890a. *Congressional Record*, Vol. 21, pt. 1. 55th Congress, 1st Session.

———. 1890b. *Congressional Record*, Vol. 21, pt. 4. 55th Congress, 1st Session.

———. 1909. *Congressional Record*, Vol. 44, pt. 4. 61st Congress, 1st Session.

———. 1910a. *Congressional Record*, Vol. 45, pt. 3. 61st Congress, 2nd Session.

———. 1910b. *Congressional Record*, Vol. 45, pt. 5. 61st Congress, 2nd Session.

———. 1913. *Congressional Record*, Vol. 50, pt. 5. 63rd Congress, 1st Session.

———. 1926a. *Congressional Record*, Vol. 67, pt. 4. 69th Congress, 1st Session.

———. 1926b. *Congressional Record*, Vol. 67, pt. 5. 69th Congress, 1st Session.

———. 1973a. *Congressional Record*, Vol. 119, pt. 28. 93rd Congress, 1st Session.

———. 1973b. *Congressional Record*, Vol. 119, pt. 33. 93rd Congress, 1st Session.

———. 1978a. *Congressional Record*, Vol. 124, pt. 7. 95th Congress, 2nd Session.

———. 1978b. *Congressional Record*, Vol. 124, pt. 21. 95th Congress, 2nd Session.

———. 1981. *Congressional Record*, Vol. 127, pt. 21, 97th Congress, 1st Session.

———. 1988. *Congressional Record*, Vol. 134, pt. 19, 100th Congress, 2nd Session.

———. 2002. *Congressional Record*, Vol. 148, pt. 17. 107th Congress, 2nd Session.

———. 2007. *Congressional Record* (Daily Edition), Vol. 153, no. 26. 110th Congress, 1st Session.

U.S. House of Representatives. 1860. *Court of Claims*. House Report No. 513, 36th Congress, 1st Session.

———. 1862. *To Establish a Court for the Investigation of Claims*. House Report No. 34, 37th Congress, 2nd Session.

———. 1877. *Commissions to Examine Certain Custom-Houses of the United States*. Ex. Doc. No. 8, 45th Congress, 1st Session.

———. 1886. *Bringing Suits Against the Government of the United States*. House Report No. 1077, 49th Congress, 1st Session.

———. 1890. *Uniform System of Bankruptcy*. House Report No. 1380, 51st Congress, 1st Session.

———. 1892. *A Uniform System of Bankruptcy*. House Report No. 1674, 52nd Congress, 1st Session.

———. 1893. *A Uniform System of Bankruptcy*. House Report No. 67, 53rd Congress, 1st Session.

———. 1894. *A Uniform System of Bankruptcy: Views of the Minority*. House Report No. 206, Part 3, 53rd Congress, 2nd Session.

———. 1896. *Uniform Law on the Subject of Bankruptcies*. House Report No. 1228, 54th Congress, 1st Session.

———. 1906. *United States District Court for China*. House Report No. 4332, 59th Congress, 1st Session.

———. 1908. *To Establish a United States Court of Patent Appeals, and for Other Purposes*. House Report No. 1415, 60th Congress, 1st Session.

———. 1909. *Court of Patent Appeals*. House Report No. 2145, 60th Congress, 2nd Session.

———. 1913. *Tariff Schedules*. Hearings before the Committee on Ways and Means, 62nd Congress, 3rd Session.

———. 1924a. *Revenue Revision*. Hearings before the Committee on Ways and Means, 68th Congress, 1st Session.

———. 1924b. *The Revenue Bill of 1924*. House Report No. 179, 68th Congress, 1st Session.

———. 1925a. *The Revenue Bill of 1926*. House Report No. 1, 69th Congress. 1st Session.

———. 1925b. *Revenue Revision, 1925*. Hearings before the Committee on Ways and Means, 67th Congress, 1st Session.

———. 1925c. *To Amend Tariff Act of 1922 to Change Title of Board of General Appraisers to United States Customs Court*. House Report No. 1201, 68th Congress, 2nd Session.

———. 1926. *To Amend Section 52 of Judicial Code and Other Statutes Affecting Procedure in Patent Office*. Hearings before the Committee on Patents, 69th Congress, 1st Session.

———. 1927. *Change in Title of the United States Court of Customs Appeals*. House Report No. 1803, 69th Congress, 2nd Session.

———. 1928a. *Change in Title of the United States Court of Customs Appeals*. Hearings before the Committee on the Judiciary, 70th Congress, 1st Session.

———. 1928b. *Change the Title of the United States Court of Customs Appeals*. House Report No. 874, 70th Congress, 1st Session.

———. 1941. *Price-Control Bill*. Hearings before the Committee on Banks and Currency, 77th Congress, 1st Session.

———. 1949. *Uniform Code of Military Justice*. Hearings before a Subcommittee of the Committee on Armed Services, 81st Congress, 1st Session.

———. 1962. *Judicial Review of Veterans' Claims*. Hearings before a Subcommittee of the Committee on Veterans' Affairs, 87th Congress, 2nd Session.

———. 1967. *U.S. Tax Court*. Hearings before a Subcommittee of the Committee on the Judiciary, 90th Congress, 1st Session.

———. 1971. *Economic Stabilization*. Hearings before the House Committee on Banking and Currency, 92nd Congress, 1st Session.

———. 1973. *Report of the Commission on the Bankruptcy Laws of the United States*. House Document 93-137, 93rd Congress, 1st Session.

———. 1977a. *Bankruptcy Court Revision*. Hearings before a Subcommittee of the House Judiciary Committee, 95th Congress, 1st Session.

———. 1977b. *Bankruptcy Law Revision*. House Report 95-595, 95th Congress, 1st Session.

———. 1977c. *Constitutional Bankruptcy Courts*. Report by the Staff of the Subcommittee on Civil and Constitutional Rights, Committee on the Judiciary. Committee Print No. 3, 95th Congress, 1st Session.

———. 1978. *Foreign Intelligence Electronic Surveillance*. Hearings before a Subcommittee of the Permanent Select Committee on Intelligence, 95th Congress, 2nd Session.

———. 1980a. *Customs Courts Act of 1980*. Hearings before a Subcommittee of the Committee on the Judiciary, 96th Congress, 2nd Session.

———. 1980b. *Customs Courts Act of 1980*. House Report 96-1235, 96th Congress, 2nd Session.

———. 1980c. *Industrial Innovation and Patent and Copyright Law Amendments*. Hearings before a Subcommittee of the Committee on the Judiciary, 96th Congress, 2nd Session.

———. 1980d. *Judicial Review of Veterans' Claims*. Hearings before a Subcommittee of the Committee on Veterans' Affairs, 96th Congress, 2nd Session.

———. 1981a. *Court of Appeals for the Federal Circuit—1981*. Hearings before a Subcommittee of the Committee on the Judiciary, 97th Congress, 1st Session.

———. 1981b. *Court of Appeals for the Federal Circuit Act of 1981*. House Report 97-312, 97th Congress, 1st Session.

———. 1983a. *Bankruptcy Court Act of 1983*. Hearings before a Subcommittee of the Committee on the Judiciary, 98th Congress, 1st Session.

———. 1983b. *Bankruptcy Court Act of 1983*. House Report 98-9, 98th Congress, 1st Session.

———. 1986. *H.R. 585 and Other Bills Relating to Judicial Review of Veterans' Claims*. Hearings before the Committee on Veterans' Affairs, 99th Congress, 2nd Session.

———. 1988. *Veterans' Judicial Review Act*. House Report 100-963, 100th Congress, 2nd Session.

———. 1996. *Terrorism Prevention Act*. House Report 104-518, 104th Congress, 2nd Session.

———. 1998. *Tucker Act Shuffle Relief Act of 1997*. House Report 105-424, 105th Congress, 2nd Session.

———. 2007. *Habeas Corpus for Detainees*. Hearings before the Committee on Armed Services, 110th Congress, 1st Session. A copy of the Abraham statement, from which the quotation in the text is taken, is available at http://armedservices.house.gov/pdfs/FC072607/Abraham_Testimony072607.pdf.

U.S. Senate. 1882. *Letter from the Secretary of the Treasury*. Executive Document No. 48, 47th Congress, 1st Session.

———. 1896. *The Torrey Bankrupt Bill*. Senate Document No. 237, 54th Congress, 1st Session.

———. 1905. *District Court of the United States for China and Korea*. Senate Document No. 95, 58th Congress, 3rd Session.

———. 1910a. *Court of Commerce*. Senate Report No. 355, Part 2, 61st Congress, 2nd Session.

———. 1910b. *Commerce Court, Etc.* Senate Document No. 623, Part 2, 61st Congress, 2nd Session.

———. 1926. *Procedure in the Patent Office*. Hearings before the Committee on Patents, 69th Congress, 2nd Session.

———. 1941. *Emergency Price Control Act*. Hearings before the Committee on Banking and Currency, 77th Congress, 1st Session.

———. 1949. *Uniform Code of Military Justice*. Hearings before a Subcommittee of the Committee on Armed Services, 81st Congress, 1st Session.

———. 1959. *Single Court of Patent Appeals—A Legislative History*. Study No. 20, Subcommittee on Patents, Trademarks, and Copyrights of the Committee on the Judiciary, 85th Congress, 2nd Session.

———. 1967. *Establishing the Court of Military Appeals as the U.S. Court of Military Appeals*. Senate Report 90-806, 90th Congress, 1st Session.

———. 1968. *United States Tax Court*. Hearings before a Subcommittee of the Committee on the Judiciary, 90th Congress, 2nd Session.

———. 1971a. *Economic Stabilization Legislation*. Hearings before the Committee on Banking, Housing and Urban Affairs. 92nd Congress, 1st Session.

———. 1971b. *Economic Stabilization Act of 1971*. Senate Report 92-507, 92nd Congress, 1st Session.

———. 1976. *Electronic Surveillance Within the United States for Foreign Intelligence Purposes*. Hearings before a Subcommittee of the Committee on the Judiciary, 94th Congress, 2nd Session.

———. 1977. *Foreign Intelligence Surveillance Act of 1977*. Hearings before a Subcommittee of the Committee on the Judiciary, 95th Congress, 1st Session.

———. 1978. *Customs Courts Act*. Hearings before a Subcommittee of the Committee on the Judiciary, 95th Congress, 2nd Session.

————. 1979a. *Customs Courts Act of 1979, S. 1654.* Hearings before a Subcommittee of the Committee on the Judiciary, 96th Congress, 1st Session.

————. 1979b. *Customs Courts Act of 1979.* Senate Report 96-466, 96th Congress, 1st Session.

————. 1979c. *Federal Courts Improvement Act of 1979.* Hearings before a Subcommittee of the Committee on the Judiciary, 96th Congress, 1st Session.

————. 1979d. *Federal Courts Improvement Act of 1979.* Senate Report 96-304, 96th Congress, 1st Session.

————. 1979e. *Veterans' Administration Adjudication Procedure and Judicial Review Act.* Senate Report 96-178, 96th Congress, 1st Session.

————. 1995. *Counterterrorism Legislation.* Hearings before a Subcommittee of the Committee on the Judiciary, 104th Congress, 1st Session.

————. 1997. *Nominations of David L. Aaron, Mary Ann Cohen, Margaret Ann Hamburg, M.D., Stanford G. Ross, Ph.D., and David W. Wilcox, Ph.D.* Hearings before the Committee on Finance, 105th Congress, 1st Session.

————. 2006a. *Battling the Backlog, Part II: Challenges Facing the U.S. Court of Appeals for Veterans Claims.* Hearings before the Committee on Veterans' Affairs, 109th Congress, 2nd Session.

————. 2006b. *Immigration Litigation Reduction.* Hearings before the Committee on the Judiciary, 109th Congress, 2nd Session.

USA Patriot Act of 2001. Public Law 107-56, 107th Congress, 1st Session.

Veterans' Judicial Review Act. 1988. Public Law 100-687, 100th Congress, 2nd Session.

Violent Crime Control and Law Enforcement Act of 1994, Public Law 103-322. 103rd Congress, 2nd Session.

COURT DECISIONS AND DOCUMENTS

Citations to court decisions are in the standard formats: volume of reporter, abbreviated name of reporter, first page of decision, and (except for Supreme Court decisions) abbreviated name of court in parentheses.

Al Odah v. United States. 2007. Reply to Opposition to Petition for Rehearing (U.S. Supreme Ct., 06-1196).

Al-Site Corporation v. VSI International, Inc. 1999. 174 F.3d 1308 (Fed. Cir.).

Armstrong v. Board of Education. 1963. 323 F.2d 333 (5th Cir.).

Belton v. Gebhart. 1952. 87 A.2d 862 (Del. Ct. of Chancery).

Bilski v. Kappos. 2010. 2010 U.S. LEXIS 5521.

Bismullah v. Gates. 2007. 510 F.3d 178 (D.C. Cir.).

————. 2008. 514 F.3d 1291 (D.C. Cir.).

————. 2009. 551 F.3d 1068 (D.C. Cir.).

Boumediene v. Bush. 2007. 476 F.3d 981 (D.C. Cir.).

————. 2008. 553 U.S. 723.

Canon v. Robertson. 1929. 32 F.2d 295 (D. Md.).

Cedillo v. Secretary of Health and Human Services. 2009. 2009 U.S. Claims LEXIS 146 (Ct. of Fed. Claims).

Control Resources, Inc. v. Delta Electronics, Inc. 2001. 133 F. Supp. 2d 121 (D. Mass.).

Cookie's Dinner, Inc. v. Columbus Board of Health. 1994. 640 N.E.2d 1231 (Franklin County Municipal Ct., Ohio).

Depiero v. City of Macedonia. 1999. 180 F.3d 770 (6th Cir.).

Duncan v. Kahanamoku. 1946. 327 U.S. 304.

Dynes v. Hoover. 1858. 61 U.S. 65.

Ex parte Bakelite Corporation. 1929. 279 U.S. 438.

Ex parte Milligan. 1866. 71 U.S. 2.

Ex parte Quirin. 1942. 317 U.S. 1.

Ex parte Quirin. 1942. Brief for Respondent (Under the Title *In the Matters of the Application of Burger et al.*).

Festo Corp. v. Shoketsu Kinzoku Kogyo Kabushiki Co. 2000. 234 F.3d 558 (Fed. Cir.).

———. 2002. 535 U.S. 722.

Floroiu v. Gonzales. 2007 481 F.3d 970 (7th Cir.).

Glendale Federal Bank v. United States. 1999. 43 Fed. Cl. 390 (Ct. of Federal Claims).

Golsen v. Commissioner. 1970. 54 T.C. 742 (Tax Ct.).

Graham v. John Deere Co. 1966. 383 U.S. 1.

Hall v. Federal Energy Regulatory Commission. 1983. 700 F.2d 218 (5th Cir.).

Hamdi v. Rumsfeld. 2004. 542 U.S. 507.

Hamdan v. Rumsfeld. 2006. 548 U.S. 557.

Hazlehurst v. Secretary of the Department of Health and Human Services. 2009. 2009 U.S. Claims LEXIS 183 (Ct. of Fed. Claims).

Holmes Group v. Vornado Air Circulation Systems. 2002. 535 U.S. 826.

In re All Matters Submitted to the Foreign Intelligence Surveillance Court. 2002. 218 F. Supp. 2d 611 (Foreign Intelligence Surveillance Ct.).

In re: Atamian. 2007. 247 Fed. Appx. 373 (3d Cir.).

In re: Babbitt. 2002. 290 F.3d 386 (D.C. Cir.).

In re Bilski. 2008. 545 F.3d 943 (Fed. Cir.).

In re: Directives [Redacted Text] Pursuant to Section 105B of the Foreign Intelligence Surveillance Act. 2008 (Foreign Intelligence Surveillance Ct. of Review). Available at http://www.fas.org/irp/agency/doj/fisa/fiscr082208.pdf.

In re Gault. 1967. 387 U.S. 1.

In re Guantánamo Detainee Cases. 2005. 355 F. Supp. 2d 443 (D.D.C.).

In re Motion for Release of Court Records. 2007. 526 F. Supp. 2d 484 (Foreign Intelligence Surveillance Ct.).

In re: North. 1993. 10 F.3d 831 (D.C. Cir.).

In re: Sealed Case No. 02-001. 2002. 310 F.3d 717 (Foreign Intelligence Surveillance Ct. of Review).

In re United States. 2006. 463 F.3d 1328 (Fed. Cir.).

In the Matter of a Charge of Judicial Misconduct or Disability. 1994. 39 F.3d 374 (D.C. Cir.).

In the Matter of Delaware & Hudson Railway Company. 1988. 96 B.R. 467 (Bankruptcy Ct., D. Del.).

In the Matter of Ocean Properties of Delaware. 1988. 95 B.R. 304 (Bankruptcy Ct., D. Del.).

In the Matter of: Wildman, Debtor. 1983. 30 B.R. 133 (Bankruptcy Ct., N.D. Ill.).

Jones v. Derwinski. 1991. 1 Vet. App. 596 (Ct. of Veterans Appeals).

Katz v. United States. 1967. 389 U.S. 347.

Kent v. United States. 1966. 383 U.S. 541.

Kinsella v. Singleton. 1960. 361 U.S. 234.

KSR International Co. v. Teleflex Inc. 2007. 550 U.S. 398.

Laboratory Corporation of America v. Metabolite Laboratories. 2006. 548 U.S. 124.

Lawrence v. Commissioner. 1957. 27 T.C. 713 (Tax Ct.).

Louis K. Liggett Co. v. Lee. 1933. 288 U.S. 517.

Loveladies Harbor, Inc. v. United States. 1990. 21 Cl. Ct. 153 (Claims Ct.).

Markman v. Westview Instruments, Inc. 1995. 52 F.3d 967 (Fed. Cir.).

———. 1996. 517 U.S. 370.

Massachusetts v. Laird. 1970. 400 U.S. 886.

Miller v. Silbermann. 1997. 951 F. Supp. 485 (S.D.N.Y.).

Northern Pipeline Construction Co. v. Marathon Pipe Line Co. 1982. 458 U.S. 50.

Parhat v. Gates. 2008. 532 F.3d 834 (D.C. Cir.).

Phillips v. AWH Corporation. 2005. 415 F.3d 1303 (Fed. Cir.).

Rasul v. Bush. 2004. 542 U.S. 466.

Reid v. Covert. 1957. 354 U.S. 1.

Ribaudo v. Nicholson. 2007. 20 Vet. App. 552 (Ct. of Appeals for Veterans Claims).

Rose Acre Farms v. United States. 2007. 75 Fed. Cl. 527 (Ct. of Fed. Claims).

———. 2009. 559 F.3d 1260 (Fed. Cir.).

Sarnoff v. Shultz. 1972. 409 U.S. 929.

Schenck v. United States. 1919. 247 U.S. 47.

Shahinaj v. Gonzales. 2007. 481 F.3d 1027 (8th Cir.).

Snyder v. Secretary of Health and Human Services. 2009. 88 Fed. Cl. 706 (Ct. of Fed. Claims.)

South Corp. v. United States. 1982. 690 F.2d 1368 (Fed. Cir.).

State v. Bonner. 2004. Cause No. 044-250 (unpublished) (Mo. Circuit Ct., 22nd Circuit).

State v. Osborn. 1960. 160 A.2d 42 (N.J.).

State Street Bank & Trust Co. v. Signature Financial Group. 1998. 149 F.3d 1368 (Fed. Cir.).

Third Annual Judicial Conference of the United States Court of Veterans Appeals. 1994. 8 Vet. App. xxxv.

Transcript of Proceedings of the Final Session of the Court. 1961. 299 F.2d 1 (Emergency Ct. of Appeals).

Tumey v. Ohio. 1927. 273 U.S. 510.

United States v. Exxon Corporation. 1985. 773 F.2d 1240 (Temporary Emergency Ct. of Appeals).

United States v. Hamdan. 2007. 1 Mil. Comm'n Rptr. 6 (U.S. Military Comm'n).

United States v. Jawad. 2008a. 1 Mil. Comm'n Rptr. 322 (U.S. Military Comm'n).

———. 2008b. 1 Mil. Comm'n Rptr. 329 (U.S. Military Comm'n).

———. 2008c. 1 Mil. Comm'n Rptr. 345 (U.S. Military Comm'n).

———. 2008d. 1 Mil. Comm'n Rptr. 349 (U.S. Military Comm'n).

United States v. Khadr. 2007a. 1 Mil. Comm'n Rptr. 152 (U.S. Military Comm'n).

———. 2007b. 1 Mil. Comm'n Rptr. 443 (U.S. Ct. of Military Comm'n Review).

United States v. Pearson. 2000. 203 F.3d 1243 (10th Cir.)

United States v. Ponds. 1952. 3 C.M.R. 119 (Ct. of Military Appeals).

United States v. Tiede, 1979. 86 F.R.D. 227 (U.S. Ct. for Berlin).

United States v. United States District Court. 1972. 407 U.S. 297.

United States v. Winstar Corp. 1996. 518 U.S. 839.

United States ex rel. Toth v. Quarles. 1955. 350 U.S. 11.

Ward v. Village of Monroeville. 1972. 409 U.S. 57.

Washington v. Nicholson. 2005. 19 Vet. App. 362 (Ct. of Appeals for Veterans Claims).

Weinar v. Rollform Inc. 1984. 744 F.2d 797 (Fed. Cir.).

Wensch v. Principi. 2001. 15 Vet. App. 362 (Ct. of Veterans Appeals).

Whitney Benefits, Inc. v. United States. 1989. 18 Cl. Ct. 394 (Claims Ct.).

Winstar v. United States. 1992. 25 Cl. Ct. 541 (Claims Ct.).

Yakus v. United States. 1944. 321 U.S. 414.

Youngstown Sheet & Tube Co. v. Sawyer. 1952. 343 U.S. 579.

Yates v. United States. 1957. 354 U.S. 298.

Zweibon v. Mitchell. 1975. 516 F.2d 594 (D.C. Cir.).

INDEX

Courts that have changed names over time are listed under their current or most recent names. Specific state courts are listed under the name of their state or city.

Gun Courts: behavior, performance, and
policies, 30–31, 103–4, 221–22; creation, 29–30, 103–4, 132, 208; generally,
95, 97, 118; selection and backgrounds
of judges, 30, 103, 221. *See also* Providence courts

Hamdan, Salim, 78–81
Hamza al Bahlul, Ali, 80
Harley, Herbert, 105
Hawaii Provost Courts, 71–73
Health Courts, proposed, 228–29
Hendrickson, Scott, 145
Henley, Stephen, 81
Hentoff, Nat, 75
Hicks, David, 79
Homeland Security Department, U.S., 89
Homeless Courts: behavior, performance, and
policies, 125–26; creation, 118, 124–25;
generally, 97
Hoover, J. Edgar, 73
Housing Courts, 19, 130n33
Howard, Robert, 26, 153n
Hurst, Willard, 105

Igra, Anna R., 111
Illinois courts, 3, 192
Immigration and Naturalization Service,
U.S., 89, 91n
immigration courts, proposed, 228
*In re All Matters Submitted to the Foreign In-
telligence Surveillance Court*, 86
In re: Sealed Case No. 02-001, 86–87
institutionalist theories, 43–50, 214–16
interest groups: potential and actual influ-
ence over specialized courts, 34–35,
37–39; roles in creation of specialized
courts, 133, 171–72. *See also* Business
Courts; *specific courts*
Internal Revenue Service, 165–67
Interstate Commerce Commissions, 16

Jackson, Andrew, 71, 73n
Jaffe, Adam B., 182
Judicial Conference, U.S., 161, 298
Judicial Panel on Multidistrict Litigation, 12
Justice Department, U.S.: in backgrounds
of Tax Court judges, 150; in creation of,
and changes in, specialized courts, 117,
124, 147, 149n13, 177, 180–81, 228;
home for Foreign Intelligence Surveil-

lance Court, 83;as litigant, 74n, 85n28,
89–91
judges: attitudes toward judicial specialization, 2, 52, 54; roles in creation of and
change in specialized courts, 53–55,
133–35, 138, 209–10; selection for
specialized courts, 35–38, 40, 92–93,
221–23. *See also specific courts*
judicial specialization, defined, 6–7
Juvenile Courts: behavior, performance,
and policies, 29, 31, 56, 107–9, 134,
222, 227; creation and structural change,
29, 42, 48, 50, 106–7, 109, 132–33,
166, 212, 214, 229; generally, 18–20,
27, 95, 97, 119, 121, 211; selection
and backgrounds of judges, 40, 108–9,
221–22

Kansas City courts, 110
Khadr, Omar, 79
Kingdon, John, 45–46, 179, 214–15, 229
Koch, Edward, 102n
Kollar-Kotelly, Colleen, 87, 88n32

Lamberth, Royce, 85, 87, 89
Land Court, 19
Legomsky, Stephen, 26
Lepawsky, Albert, 101
Lerner, Josh, 182
Light, Paul, 57
Lincoln, Abraham, 71–72, 156
Lindsey, Ben, 107
Lipsky, Michael, 31, 217n
Lipton, Martin, 189–90
"Liquor Court," 104–5
Lobingier, Charles, 65
Lombardi, Joseph E., 146
LoPucki, Lynn, 26, 202–3, 223
Los Angeles courts, 112
Lurie, Jonathan, 26, 56, 70

Malkin, Victoria, 126
Marine Navigation Court, 97, 103
Matza, David, 105
Mayors' Courts, 104
McCaffery, Seamus, 102
McCoy, Candace, 115, 134n
McReynolds, James, 167n
Meador, Daniel, 179–80
Meason, James E., 86
Mellon, Andrew, 148

Water Courts, 18–19
Weed Court, 95, 97, 101, 221–22
Weinstein, Jack, 12
Weyland, Kurt, 48n
Wilfley, Lebbius, 65
Williams, Frank, 79n18
Williams, Victor, 23
Willrich, Michael, 27, 95
Wilson, Woodrow, 167

Women's Courts: behavior, performance, and policies, 113–14; creation, 112–13, 132–33, 211; generally, 27, 97, 106; selection and backgrounds of judges, 113
Wood, Diane, 2–3
Workers' Compensation Courts, 18–19

Yakus v. United States, 169
Youth Courts, 118n

THE CHICAGO SERIES IN LAW AND SOCIETY
Edited by John M. Conley and Lynn Mather

Series titles, continued from frontmatter:

RIGHTS OF INCLUSION: LAW AND IDENTITY IN THE LIFE STORIES OF
AMERICANS WITH DISABILITIES *by David M. Engel and Frank W. Munger*

THE INTERNATIONALIZATION OF PALACE WARS: LAWYERS, ECONOMISTS,
AND THE CONTEST TO TRANSFORM LATIN AMERICAN
STATES *by Yves Dezalay and Bryant G. Garth*

FREE TO DIE FOR THEIR COUNTRY: THE STORY OF THE JAPANESE
AMERICAN DRAFT RESISTERS IN WORLD WAR II *by Eric L. Muller*

OVERSEERS OF THE POOR: SURVEILLANCE, RESISTANCE,
AND THE LIMITS OF PRIVACY *by John Gilliom*

PRONOUNCING AND PERSEVERING: GENDER AND THE DISCOURSES
OF DISPUTING IN AN AFRICAN ISLAMIC COURT *by Susan F. Hirsch*

THE COMMON PLACE OF LAW: STORIES FROM
EVERYDAY LIFE *by Patricia Ewick and Susan S. Silbey*

THE STRUGGLE FOR WATER: POLITICS, RATIONALITY, AND IDENTITY
IN THE AMERICAN SOUTHWEST *by Wendy Nelson Espeland*

DEALING IN VIRTUE: INTERNATIONAL COMMERCIAL ARBITRATION
AND THE CONSTRUCTION OF A TRANSNATIONAL
LEGAL ORDER *by Yves Dezalay and Bryant G. Garth*

RIGHTS AT WORK: PAY EQUITY REFORM AND THE POLITICS
OF LEGAL MOBILIZATION *by Michael W. McCann*

THE LANGUAGE OF JUDGES *by Lawrence M. Solan*

REPRODUCING RAPE: DOMINATION THROUGH TALK
IN THE COURTROOM *by Gregory M. Matoesian*

GETTING JUSTICE AND GETTING EVEN: LEGAL CONSCIOUSNESS
AMONG WORKING-CLASS AMERICANS *by Sally Engle Merry*

RULES VERSUS RELATIONSHIPS: THE ETHNOGRAPHY OF
LEGAL DISCOURSE *by John M. Conley and William M. O'Barr*